NEO-NOIR

NEO-NOIR

EDITED BY
MARK BOULD,
KATHRINA GLITRE
AND GREG TUCK

WALLFLOWER PRESS
LONDON & NEW YORK

First published in Great Britain in 2009 by
Wallflower Press
6 Market Place, London W1W 8AF
www.wallflowerpress.co.uk

A catalogue record for this book is available from the British Library.

ISBN 978-1-906660-17-8 (pbk)
ISBN 978-1-906660-18-5 (hbk)

Book design by Elsa Mathern

Printed by Imprint Digital, India

Contents

Notes on Contributors

Mark Bould is a Reader in Film and Literature at the University of the West of England and co-editor of *Science Fiction Film and Television*. His books include *Film Noir: From Berlin to Sin City* (2005), *The Cinema of John Sayles: Lone Star* (2009) and, as co-editor, *Parietal Games: Critical Writings By and On M. John Harrison* (2005) and *Red Planets: Marxism and Science Fiction* (2009).

Rebecca Feasey is a Senior Lecturer in Film and Media Communications at Bath Spa University. She has previously published in the areas of cult film, celebrity culture, contemporary Hollywood stardom, and the representation of gender in popular television.

Carl Freedman is Professor of English and Director of English Graduate Studies at Louisiana State University. The author or editor of half a dozen books and the author of many dozens of essays and reviews, his most recent edited collection is *Conversations with Samuel R. Delany* (2009).

Edward Gallafent teaches in the Department of Film and Television Studies at the University of Warwick. He is the author of *Clint Eastwood: Actor and Director* (1994), *Astaire and Rogers* (2000) and *Quentin Tarantino* (2006).

Kathrina Glitre is a Senior Lecturer in Film Studies at the University of the West of England. She is the author of *Hollywood Romantic Comedy: States of the Union, 1934–65* (2006) and is currently completing a project entitled *Starring Cary Grant* on film acting and casting in the classical Hollywood studio system.

Suzy Gordon has taught Film Studies at the universities of Sussex, Glasgow and the West of England, and published widely on women, film and psychoanalysis, with a particular focus on Melanie Klein.

Helen Hanson is a Senior Lecturer in Film in the Department of English at the University of Exeter. She is the author of *Hollywood Heroines: Women in Film Noir and the Female Gothic Film* (2007) and the co-editor of *The Femme Fatale: Images, Histories, Contexts* (forthcoming).

Mike Hodges is primarily known as a filmmaker (*Get Carter, Pulp, The Terminal Man* and, latterly, *Black Rainbow, Croupier, I'll Sleep When I'm Dead*) but has also written and directed plays for BBC radio (*Shooting Stars and Other Heavenly Pursuits, King Trash*) and the theatre (*Soft Shoe Shuffle*). His first novel, *Watching The Wheels Come Off*, will be published in 2010. The theme of all these works is a bleak, blackly humorous take on the world as he sees it.

Hyangjin Lee is a professor of sociology in the College of Intercultural Communication at Rikkyo University and an honorary researcher in East Asian Culture at the University of Sheffield. She is the author of *Contemporary Korean Cinema: Identity, Culture and Politics* (2000) and *Sociology of Korean Wave: Women, Family and Fandom* (2008), and has worked as the director of the UK Korean Film Festival since 2001.

Robert Miklitsch is a Professor in the Department of English at Ohio University. His books include *From Hegel to Madonna: Towards a General Economy of Commodity Fetishism* (1998) and *Roll Over Adorno: Critical Theory, Popular Culture, Audiovisual Media* (2006). His essay, 'Real Fantasies: Connie Stevens, *Silencio*, and Other Sonic Phenomena in *Mulholland Drive*' appeared in *Lowering the Boom: Critical Studies in Film Sound* (2008) and a book on sound and source music in 1940s noir, *Audio Noir: Audiovisuality in Classic American Noir*, is forthcoming.

Greg Singh is the author of *Film After Jung: Post-Jungian Approaches to Film Theory* (2009). He is currently completing his PhD at the University of Reading on the experience of narrative closure in popular film cultures and its effects across media forms, and a second book on film and affect.

Deborah Thomas is the author of numerous essays and books on film, including *Beyond Genre: Melodrama, Comedy and Romance in Hollywood Films* (2000) and *Reading Hollywood: Spaces and Meanings in Hollywood Films* (2001), as well as a monograph on *Buffy the Vampire Slayer* (2005). Until her retirement in 2007, she was Professor of Film Studies at the University of Sunderland.

Greg Tuck is a Senior Lecturer in Film Studies at the University of the West of England. He is on the editorial board of *Film-Philosophy*, and is currently writing *Philosophy, Cinema and Sex* and co-editing a collection on film and philosophy.

Ginette Vincendeau is Professor of Film Studies at King's College, London. Among her publications are *Stars and Stardom in French Cinema* (2000), *Jean-Pierre Melville, 'An American in Paris'* (2003) and *La Haine* (2005), and the co-edited collection, *Journeys of Desire: European Actors in Hollywood* (2006).

Sherryl Vint is an Associate Professor at Brock University, Ontario, and an editor of *Extrapolation*, *Humanimalia* and *Science Fiction Film and Television*. She is the author of *Bodies of Tomorrow: Technology, Subjectivity, Science Fiction* (2007) and *Animal Alterity: Science Fiction and the Question of the Animal* (forthcoming).

Mike Wayne teaches film studies at Brunel University, where he convenes an MA in Documentary Practice. He is co-director of a feature-length documentary, *Listen To Venezuela*. Among other works, he is the author of *Marxism and Media Studies: Key Concepts and Contemporary Changes* (2003).

Linda Ruth Williams is Professor of Film at Southampton University. She writes and researches on contemporary cinema, sexuality and censorship. Her books include *The Erotic Thriller in Contemporary Cinema* (2005) and the co-edited volume, *Contemporary American Cinema* (2006). She is currently writing a biography of Ken Russell and a monograph about Steven Spielberg and children.

'If Only My Leg Didn't Itch'

A FOREWORD BY MIKE HODGES

When I came to make *Get Carter* at the fag end of the 1960s, the term film noir wasn't in common usage outside France. Even so, this film fitted the category perfectly, stemming as it did from the same form and source (anger and revenge against social injustice wrapped up as a thriller) as many in that 1940s genre which emerged so soon after the Wall Street Crash.

With sugar sweet being more addictive and profitable, one could argue it's surprising that any bitter noir films were made at all. Each being an artefact of the capitalist system. Forget the art, stupid; face the fact. All films are made in the pursuit of money, mazuma, gelt, shekels, which has always been (and especially nowadays) synonymous with the *pursuit of happiness*. No wonder the term was included in the American Constitution, the very country where capitalism reigns supreme (despite the odd glitch) and film noir took root. Although the social compost in which these dark films grow has constantly changed (as this collection of essays illuminates) they still keeping coming. *Get Carter* being one.

The 1960s for many of us was a hopeful and exciting decade when radical ideological dreams seemed realisable. Those dreams, however, soon faded, overtaken like many human endeavours by greed and corruption. With a fault line of class and privilege fracturing British society from the monarchy at the top (by divine right, no less) down to the un-elected House of Lords (sustained by a skewed system of bestowing knighthoods and other honours) to the nursery slopes of the exclusive public schools (private schools enjoying charitable status) and ending up with (in those days) a trusting and gullible populace, those dreams quickly evaporated.

For my own part the true condition of Great Britain was only revealed during my National Service (a compulsory two years) in the Royal Navy. In the mid-

1950s I was posted as an *ordinary* seaman to a minesweeper with duties that took us into every fishing port around our coast. The poverty and deprivation I witnessed in those hell holes blew the scales off my bourgeois eyes for ever. Soon after leaving the navy (now, significantly, an *able* seaman) I somehow got a menial job in television. Here, under cosy, warm studio lights I was now able to observe at first hand the other end of the social spectrum (the potbelly as opposed to the underbelly): the politicians and civil servants, the bishops and cardinals, the journalists and actors, indeed anyone who thought themselves worthy enough to be seen and heard. If my first revelatory experience brought William Hogarth to mind, the second brought with it Swift and Juvenal (he of the *Sixteen Satires*).

When I gravitated in the late 1960s from current affairs programmes (including a two-year stint on the tough investigative weekly *World in Action*) to filmed fiction (a place where one has distinctly more opportunities to tell the truth) needless to say I followed in the footsteps of those subversive forties American filmmakers who also had a social axe to grind. Hence *Get Carter*, *Rumour*, *The Manipulators*, *Pulp*, *The Terminal Man*, *Black Rainbow*, *Croupier* and *I'll Sleep When I'm Dead*.

Making these films was one thing but, as I was to discover, getting proper exhibition (especially in the UK) was another. In the 1940s and 1950s, the Hollywood studio system, for sound commercial reasons, guaranteed distribution of all its films. For the directors (in particular, Douglas Sirk, the bleakest and most talented in my opinion) this meant their films were not just made – but seen. The circle of subversion was complete.

Not so in my case.

At the end of *Pulp*, my second feature, it was prescient of me to have Michael Caine (as Mickey King, his leg in plaster from a bullet wound and incarcerated in a corrupt fascist politician's palace) look straight at the camera and say: 'I'll get the bastards yet.'

Fat chance, Mickey!

No wonder he adds wistfully, 'If only my leg didn't itch.'

Dorset, August 2009

Parallax Views: An Introduction

MARK BOULD, KATHRINA GLITRE AND GREG TUCK

In *The Lookout* (2007), former champion high-school hockey player Chris Pratt (Joseph Gordon-Levitt) is left brain-damaged by a car crash. Now a lowly janitor/ nightwatchman, he suffers from forms of aphasia, synaesthesia and Tourette's, as well as short-term memory dysfunction and severe difficulties with sequencing memories and planning future actions. Robbers, playing on his loneliness, his sense of anger, injustice and loss, and on his desire for a normal life, lure him into their plot to hold up the bank where he works. He has no idea he is just the fall guy and, when he tries to back out of the deal, the gang turn on him and the heist goes sour. He makes off with the money and the robbers abduct his friend, Lewis (Jeff Daniels). Chris must find a way to save him without getting them both killed. The only problem is that he will have to sequence the plan and remember all its elements in the right order.

The extent of the problem facing Chris is well-established. After the opening crash sequence, the story – like many noir stories – resumes with a male voice-over. With a few exceptions, Chris's words are matched by the images: a montage of him performing familiar actions.

I wake up. I turn off the alarm. I look outside so that I know what to wear. I take a shower. And I shave. Sometimes I cry for no reason. [Cut to a close-up of an exercise book in which this sentence, written in pencil, is being erased.] But I'm getting a handle on it. I wake up. I get dressed. I take my meds. When Lewis is gone, I make the coffee, which can be tricky. I eat breakfast but I don't read the paper. It confuses me, which makes me mad. [Cut to the notepad, with the words 'I get mad easily' being erased.] I wake up. I put on my coat and go to class. [The key rack by the door has two notes stuck to it: 'Take key when leaving' and 'Lock the door from outside'.] I wake up.

Although the temporal relationship between performing the actions, speaking the words, and writing and erasing the words is initially unclear, it does establish a pattern of repetition. Cut to a shot that tracks down the exercise book, on alternate lines of which are written:

> I wake up
> I turn off the alarm
> I take a shower
> I wake up [over the erased 'Sometimes I cry for no reason']
> I get dressed
> I make coffee
> I eat breakfast
> I wake up [over the erased 'I get mad easily']
> I go to class

Linear progression keeps hitting a brick wall. *Our* temporal confusion is retrospectively resolved by the discovery that this recitation is part of the class. Chris's therapy group have each been trying to list a 'typical day', but as he later tells Lewis, 'I kept getting stuck on "I wake up".'

Just a few days later, both of their lives depend on Chris being able to formulate and follow a not-uncomplicated sequence of events. Their only hope lies in the advice Lewis gave the dejected Chris: 'Don't think of it as a list, think of it as a story instead. Everything's a story ... Stories are what help us make sense of the world ... Start at the end. Can't tell a story if you don't know where it's going ... You just gotta start at the end and work backwards.'

Chris's plight – and method – resonates very strongly with those of the genre theorist, critic and historian. The construction of genre is always a retrospective activity, predicated on recognising similarities to and differences from what has gone before (and come since). Just as Chris must settle upon one of the countless narratives available to him that will enable him to achieve certain goals, so the theorist, critic and historian of genre must choose – selecting, emphasising and making central certain texts, figures, cycles, tendencies, critical methodologies, and so on, while discarding, downplaying and marginalising others.

Too often, theorists, critics and historians have tried to impose neat linear trajectories upon individual genres, treating them as discrete entities that 'spring full-blown from the head of Zeus' (Altman 1987: 93), evolve and then die out (see Neale 2000: 211–14). This collection seeks a more complex understanding. Genre is messy; genres mutate. They are not rigidly-defined pigeonholes into which examples can be neatly placed, but baggy and broad, errant and loose. They are governed by 'contamination' and 'impurity' (Derrida 1980: 59). Is *White Heat* (1949) a gangster movie or a film noir? *The Reckless*

Moment (1949), a film noir or a melodrama? *Blade Runner* (1982), science fiction or neo-noir? To ask such questions is to miss the point. The either/or construction seeks definitive answers as if a film – or a genre – exists in a cultural vacuum. It mistakes the industrial purpose of generic filmmaking, which lies in familiarity *and* novelty, repetition *and* difference. In the context of Hollywood production, as Janet Staiger argues, the notion that genres were once 'pure' is an illusion which typically results from mapping 'a subjective order visible in the present … onto the past' and then mistaking it for 'the order visible in the past' (2003: 186). The same criticism can be levelled against attempts to reign in textual excess by invoking a generic dominant to which all the other material in the text is subordinated. There is no available position from which to objectively make such a judgement (and even if there were, one would still have to explore and explicate the sheer variety of potential relationships between the dominant and other textual elements, as well as the precise relationships within any individual text). Individual films are polysemic, contradictory and incoherent, spilling over with material that cannot be easily reduced or in good conscience ignored in order to cut them to some pre-existing pattern. Consequently, there will always be exceptions to – and disagreements over – generic definitions. Instead, the conceptual usefulness of genre depends on identifying, exploring and analysing relationships, the complex patterns and networks of intertextual and intercultural exchange.

Film noir is a particularly notorious case, in this respect. When it comes to debating definitions or identifying first (and last) examples, its peculiar history makes it seem unique:[1] the people making sexy, violent crime thrillers and melodramas in the US in the 1940s and 1950s did not know they were making 'film noir' until Anglophone critics in the 1960s and 1970s discovered that was how the French had been identifying them since the 1940s. Certainly, few genres have attracted such intense and recurring debates around such fundamentally irresolvable questions (see Neale 2000: 151–4), with critics never quite agreeing upon whether it is a genre or a style or a theme or a mood or a form or a texture or a cycle; whether it was produced in the US (or in various national cinemas, including the US, France, Germany, the UK and Japan) from the early 1940s (or possibly the 1920s or the 1930s) until the mid-1950s (or late 1950s, or continually without break until the present). And when theorists, critics and historians seem to agree that it is a genre, they still disagree about how they know this: is it by narrative structure or character types or iconography or visual style? When it was made? Where it was made? Or by whom? Different critics privilege different films and lay different emphases on the mutually articulating themes (sex, crime, corruption, murder, betrayal), characters (the gumshoe, the femme fatale, the criminal, the fall-guy) and locations (the city, night time).

And yet somehow, film noir still seems instantly recognisable. You don't have to read the critics or know the term 'film noir' to have generic understanding of a film like *The Killers* (1946) – or how such a film is different to either version of *Ocean's Eleven* (1960, 2001) or *The Italian Job* (1969, 2003). Not all heists go wrong in the way that noir imagines they will; in noir (and neo-noir), the heist will usually fail because the gang are greedy, selfish and back-stabbing, or because the material world seems to conspire against their success – not because someone was only supposed to blow the bloody doors off. Genre is about *more* than the mere presence of a narrative event, character type or stylistic tic. Genre operates across the whole of the narrative: we might say that genre is a particular way of imagining a fictional world. Thus, low-key lighting, expressionist framing, hard-boiled dialogue or a pervading sense of anxiety are not, in themselves, enough to put you in the world of noir. But in the right combination, one which seems to fuse rather than simply combine such elements, film noir emerges. Even if we never can agree quite where or when or how often.

If such problems attend film noir, imagine those posed by neo-noir. What is neo-noir? What is the nature of its 'newness' and its 'noirness'? How are they related? Is the term even useful or necessary?

The simplest explanation of (or retrospective story about) neo-noir requires film noir to be a US phenomenon. Neo-noir can then be seen to emerge in the late 1960s and early 1970s when Hollywood, in financial crisis, turned to the possibilities of a genre that appeared to have died out a decade earlier (before it was even identified in the US *as* a genre) but which was gaining attention in popular and academic critical writing about classical Hollywood. While films such as *Harper* (1966), *Tony Rome* (1967), *Madigan* (1968) and *Marlowe* (1969) did little more than update the setting of the detective story, a number of film-makers (many of them film school graduates, former television directors or European *émigrés*) took inspiration from the French New Wave's revisioning of Hollywood crime films and sought to revitalise the American crime film, often also incorporating modernist film techniques derived from European arthouse cinema. In this version of the story, the first cycle of neo-noir production can be found somewhere among such films as *Seconds* (1966), *Bonnie and Clyde* (1967), *Point Blank* (1967), *Targets* (1968), *The Anderson Tapes* (1971), *Klute* (1971), *Sweet Sweetback's Baadasssss Song* (1971), *The Offence* (1972), *Charley Varrick* (1973), *The Friends of Eddie Coyle* (1973), *The Long Goodbye* (1973), *Serpico* (1973), *Thieves Like Us* (1973), *Badlands* (1973), *Chinatown* (1974), *The Conversation* (1974), *The Parallax View* (1974), *The Taking of Pelham One Two Three* (1974), *Dog Day Afternoon* (1975) and *Taxi Driver* (1976). A second cycle was inaugurated in the early 1980s by the success of *The Postman Always Rings Twice* (1981) and *Body Heat* (1981), both of which rendered more explicit the sexual tensions underpinning their sources in James M. Cain's novels and earlier adaptations. In some sense, despite subsequent peaks and troughs of production, this second cycle has never really ended, with the makers of crime thrillers and erotic thrillers continually drawn to – at the very least – the visual style of noir.

Although useful, this thumbnail history of neo-noir is far too simple and unilinear. Crucially, it overlooks the global circulation of Hollywood crime thrillers (both classical and post-classical) and of the term 'film noir' and the images and ideas associated with it. Film noir is often conceptualised as a coalescence of German Expressionism, French poetic realism and American hard-boiled fiction, but there is absolutely no reason to suppose that the cultural exchanges stopped when these elements met and combined in Los Angeles in the early 1940s. For example, is there any reason beyond US-centricity to consider *Tirez sous le pianiste/Shoot the Pianist* (1960), *Bande à part* (1964) or *Le Samouraï* (1967) as bridges between, rather than simply examples of, film noir or neo-noir? As Andrew Spicer argues, film noir needs to be understood 'as a transnational cultural phenomenon' (2007: 1). David Desser likewise contends that 'film noir has always been a global genre or mode' (2003: 520) and discusses two types of neo-noir narrative, which can be traced through global cinema – identifying *Lung fu fong wan/City on Fire* (1987) as the source of the recent 'heist going bad' cycle (more often attributed to the influence of *Reservoir Dogs* (1992)) and finding 'couples on the run' in *Fuyajo/Sleepless Town* (1998), *Adorenarin doraibu/Adrenaline Drive* (1999), *Hy ry -gai/City of Lost Souls* (2000) and *Hysteric* (2000).

A transnational global approach suggests a more continuous mode of production than that experienced in the US context alone. This might seem to negate the need for a separate term 'neo-noir'. However, there is one other significant difference between film noir and neo-noir. While many of the makers of film noir would have been conscious of the work of their contemporaries and predecessors, none of them set out to make something called 'film noir'. Similarly, an audience might well have been aware of an array of crime thrillers and melodramas like the one they were watching, but none of them knew they were watching a film noir. The concept and the category simply did not exist for them. Neo-noir is made and watched by people familiar with the concept of film noir. The conventions have entered the idiom of popular culture (as demonstrated by pastiches such as *Dead Men Don't Wear Plaid* (1982) and the 'Charmed noir' (2004) episode of *Charmed* (1998–2006); see also Naremore 1998: 254–9). Neo-noir knows its past. It knows the rules of the game.

The degree to which this awareness is acknowledged varies greatly. Few films go as far as *Femme Fatale* (2002), in which Laure (Rebecca Romijn-Stamos) watches *Double Indemnity* (1944) on television, but many refer indirectly to the 'classics' through costuming, *mise-en-scène*, lighting, framing, dialogue and so on: think of the Woman in the Blonde Wig (Ching-hsia Lin) in *Chung Hing sam lam/Chungking Express* (1994), for example. The polar extremes of such awareness can be explored through *Get Carter* (1971) and

Noir in noir: *Get Carter*

Pulp (1972) – both British, both directed by Mike Hodges before any broad Anglophone consensus about film noir as a genre had emerged, but demonstrating quite different 'takes' on neo-noir, reflecting different national and transnational influences.

Get Carter shares many traits with the kinds of US crime movies listed earlier as generating the first cycle of neo-noir. It proffers a particularly bleak view of the world, emphasised by location shooting (which also links it to semi-documentary noirs, such as *The House on 92nd Street* (1945)) and the alienating effects of zoom lenses; its stylistic experimentation and sexual frankness are influenced by European arthouse cinema. At the same time, it is undoubtedly a 'British' film, carefully located in national and regional contexts. London-based gangland heavy Jack Carter (Michael Caine) returns to Newcastle for his brother's funeral. His investigation reveals that his brother was murdered. After uncovering a web of vice and corruption, Carter revenges himself upon those who have harmed his family. Although the narrative and its desolate conclusion are distinctly noirish, the film eschews the expressionist style of film noir – it more closely resembles the tradition of 1960s social realism, taken at moments to an almost anthropological extreme – so as better to capture the decay and dereliction of the declining northern city in which it is set. Indeed, the only hint the film gives us that it *knows* it is working in this narrative tradition – beyond, of course, the consummate skill with which it does so – are two shots of Carter, northbound on a train, reading Raymond Chandler's *Farewell, My Lovely* (1940), not only alluding to the hard-boiled literary roots of film noir but also demonstrating a self-consciousness about American narrative traditions in a British context. This is emphasised in the first of the two shots: Carter is sitting next to a young boy reading a comic. The comparison reeks of the postwar dismay at the Americanisation of British culture and moral panics about literacy, crime fiction and comics, while also establishing the gulf between fiction and 'reality'. Complex as it is, this is the only such moment in the film, and it might be best described as minimally foregrounded self-consciousness.

Its minimalism becomes particularly evident when contrasted with *Pulp*, which deflates noir in a radically different manner. It revels in reflexive game-playing, metaleptic shenanigans and a sense of needing to renew noir so as to forestall it becoming merely a self-enclosed, glamorous and nostalgic aesthetic. Protagonist Chester Thomas King (Michael Caine), known as Mickey, is a hack writer of pulp crime fiction, churning out novels such as *My Gun is Long* and *The Knee Trembler*, under an array of pseudonyms: Guy Strange, Gary Rough, Dan Wild, Les Behan, Susan Eager, Paul S. Cumming, Dr O. R. Gann and S. Odomy. The film opens in a dictation service's typing pool, with a middle-aged woman transcribing Mickey's description of a sex scene. As he reaches the words, 'I put my hand on her...', there is a cut to a long shot of the room and his voice is drowned out by the sound of typewriters. This gag is repeated as another woman, transcribing a fight scene, reaches 'I smashed my knee into his...', and twice more as a fight scene, in which the hero whips another man, becomes a description of queer, S&M arousal. These interruptions open up a critical gap between the material being described and the film itself, which is further emphasised by Michael Caine's narration. His flat southeast London accent is profoundly at odds with Mickey's narrative voice, which sounds like a pastiche of Mickey Spillane, and his bored, almost perfunctory, delivery is equally at odds with the lurid subject matter it describes. This series of disjunctions is elaborated yet further when the film cuts to Mickey King stepping out of a building and hailing a cab, actions which initially match the ongoing narration, as if it has seamlessly switched from his recorded dictation to his own voice-over. Quickly, however, his experience of the world falls short of the effortless occupation of it he describes.

Mickey is hired to ghost-write the memoirs of Preston Gilbert (Mickey Rooney), a self-obsessed former star of Hollywood gangster movies who, in exile on a Mediterranean island, has become involved with local fascist politicians and criminals. Like many a noir protagonist, Mickey is soon caught up in an elaborate series of events – at one point he describes it as being 'like some pornographic photograph: difficult to work out who was doing what and to whom' – over which he has no control and which might result in his death. However, this is not some grim story of inescapable fate, but an absurd comedy that opens up a rift between noir romanticisation, pulp melodrama and the ridiculous, relentless comedy of everyday life. Its absurdity marks it as quite different from *Get Carter*, but its self-reflexivity links it more directly to the modernist tradition of films such as *À bout de souffle/Breathless* (1960), *Bande à part* and *Point Blank*.

Neo-noir, unlike so many of its protagonists, is hardly lacking in self-knowledge, and between the poles of minimal and excessive self-consciousness exemplified by Hodges' two films, it reworks, works up, works over, works with and works against classical noir. It knows how to be noir. It knows that people are rarely as good as, and often far worse than, we might wish. It knows that even the simplest plans go wrong. It knows that trust is in short supply and that our desires far exceed our talents. And it knows that it knows these things. But this does not necessarily make neo-noir any more knowable than film noir.

Therefore, in bringing together the following essays, we have not sought to impose some orthodoxy on what constitutes neo-noir but rather, as the title of this essay suggests, to bring to bear multiple perspectives on a subject whose nature changes depending upon the position from which one is viewing it. For example, analysis can start from the corpus, looking at patterns of representation across a range of films, such as typical narrative structures, character types or stylistic conventions. Alternatively, it can focus on one or two 'touchstone' texts, examined as being, in some sense, typical or paradigmatic. In this collection, we have sought to achieve a balance between the two, beginning with the general – Kathrina Glitre's discussion of the implications of the shift from black-and-white noir to colour neo-noir – and ending with the specific – Deborah Thomas's analysis of *Memento* (2000), a film which, like *The Lookout*, requires its protagonist to make sense of the world by telling stories.

However, as with the narratives of so many of these films, the journey from the general to the specific does not proceed in a simple and linear fashion, but combines elements of both methods. The views taken are also affected by theoretical perspectives: Marxist, feminist, psychoanalytic. Most essays retain a US-centric approach (including US co-productions), but others eschew such bias entirely. Thus, the femme fatale – for many, the icon of noir – is discussed in very different ways by Linda Ruth Williams, Rebecca Feasey and Suzy Gordon. Williams positions the femme fatale as 'revenger' within three modes of US neo-noir: family noir, corporate noir and teen noir. Feasey focuses on the extratextual circulation of Sharon Stone's star image as inextricably bound up with *Basic Instinct*'s (1992) Catherine Tramell, neo-noir femme fatale *par excellence*. Gordon moves beyond the US horizon, to analyse two films made by women from New Zealand, *Crush* (1992) and *In the Cut* (2003), focusing on the ways in which these films and *The Last Seduction* (1994) require us to rethink established feminist-psychoanalytic accounts of anxiety in noir. Anxiety is also an issue in Sherryl Vint and Mark Bould's essay, figured through the damaged bodies of the male protagonists in *Fight Club* (1999) and *The Machinist* (2004); they take a Marxist perspective, linking the 'anorexic subjectivity' of these protagonists to alienation under consumer capitalism.

Comparative frameworks are used by Carl Freedman, Edward Gallafent and Helen Hanson, to articulate the differences between the old and new – not simply between film noir and neo-noir, but also between 1970s 'modernist' noir and 1980s 'postmodernist' noir. Freedman considers the way in which *Body Heat*'s revisioning of *Double Indemnity* displaces labour with leisure (particularly sex), bringing a Marxist perspective to bear, as well as a sensitivity to specific historical contexts. Gallafent considers a particular moment in time, to explore how *Jagged Edge* (1985) and *To Live and Die in L.A.* (1985) rearticulate genre, arguing that the films invoke signs of noir, only 'to proclaim their distance from classical noir'. Hanson focuses on sound in US neo-noir, but particularly the ways in which 1970s conspiracy films, such as *Klute* and *The Conversation*, experimented with sound to create complex sound styles that evoke the theme of paranoia; this is compared to the use of old-fashioned standards in 1980s thrillers, such as *Body Heat* and *Someone to Watch Over Me* (1987) to evoke a more reassuring mood of nostalgia. Robert Miklitsch also considers music and sound in US neo-noir, but focuses on the 'neo-modernist' period of the late 1960s and 1970s, analysing a number of films in close detail.

To begin to flesh out the transnational aspects of neo-noir – and this is only a start – Ginette Vincendeau, Mike Wayne and Hyangjin Lee explore non-US films. Vincendeau's exploration of the changing representation of the Parisian 'lower depths' draws on a wide range of French *policiers* and crime films, from the populist poetic realist films of the 1930s, to Jean-Pierre Melville's stylised 'black-and-white-in-colour' films of the 1960s and 1970s, focusing in detail on the last 15 years. Her essay also has the advantage of paying the most concerted attention to the ultimate noir milieu – the city. Wayne's focus on reification considers both text and context, specifically the industrial context of British film distribution and the ways in which we might think of gambling as a central metaphor in both neo-noir and late capitalism. Lee's essay maps out cross-cultural exchanges in the gangster neo-noirs of Japan, Hong Kong and South Korea as they articulate Western and transnational narrative forms with local Confucian traditions.

Another facet of generic production and circulation is illuminated by Greg Singh's essay on ways in which film noir is prefigured in the *Max Payne* videogame franchise. Specifically, Singh is interested in the affective responses of the single player game. Greg Tuck is also concerned with affective responses – namely, the affect of black comedy within neo-noir. Providing a valuable way of thinking about different types of humour, Tuck connects David Lynch and the Coen brothers, key neo-noir filmmakers, to surrealist black comedy, while distinguishing Quentin Tarantino's brand of humour as more 'sentimental'.

At the end of *The Lookout*, Chris does indeed save his friend and himself, but there are nonetheless unexpected outcomes – he was not narrating backwards from a fixed universal point but from the localised, contingent ending upon which he had settled. Likewise, we have not aspired to produce the final word on neo-noir, but have attempted to offer multiple ways in. Despite our best efforts, there are neglected areas, notably Latin American neo-noir, queer sexuality and neo-noir, and neo-noir television. There will undoubtedly be films discussed that some will dispute are neo-noir – and others omitted that will seem to some like glaringly obvious oversights. But that's genre for you: there are any number of ways in, but there may very well be no way out.

NOTE

1   However, many if not all genres are named retrospectively once a pattern of production and/or consumption is established. For example, few would dispute that Jules Verne and H. G. Wells were writing science fiction decades before the term was coined by Hugo Gernsback in the late 1920s; or that the term 'slasher' could only come into use after *Halloween* (1978), *Friday the 13th* (1980) and their imitators were in circulation.

REFERENCES

Altman, Rick (1987) *The American Film Musical*. Bloomington: Indiana University Press.
Derrida, Jacques (1980) 'The Law of Genre', *Critical Inquiry*, 7, 1, 55–81.
Desser, David (2003) 'Global Noir: Genre Film in the Age of Transnationalism', in Barry Keith Grant (ed.) *Film Genre Reader III*. Austin: University of Texas Press, 516–36.
Naremore, James (1998) *More than Night: Film Noir in Its Contexts*. London: University of California Press.
Neale, Steve (2000) *Genre and Hollywood*. London: Routledge.
Spicer, Andrew (2007) 'Introduction', in Andrew Spicer (ed.) *European Film Noir*. Manchester: Manchester University Press, 1–22.
Staiger, Janet (2003 [1997]) 'Hybrid or Inbred: The Purity Hypothesis and Hollywood Genre History', in Barry Keith Grant (ed.) *Film Genre Reader III*. Austin: University of Texas Press, 185–99.

1

Under the Neon Rainbow: Colour and Neo-Noir

KATHRINA GLITRE

The difficulties of writing about colour in film are manifold. Consider *Red Rock West* (1992). In 1994, I described the film in my diary as 'film noir – or rather film orange – that golden light that pervades such heated, tense films', after seeing it in a run-down cinema on Times Square. Re-watching it on DVD, 13 years later, I am disappointed: the film seems too bright, too white, more blue than I remembered. And not orange at all. This is not just my memory playing tricks on me, although memory is undoubtedly part of how we understand colour (and neo-noir). It is not just physiological, although this too plays its part (colour is a trick of the light, the eye and the brain). Nor is it simply technological, reducing the resolution from celluloid to DVD, averaging the analogue resonance to suit a digital spectrum. Indeed, the film's original colour may just have faded with time (as DeLuxe film stock is prone to do).

Colour is objective *and* subjective. It is relative, cultural and specific: what I call red will appear to be the same as green to someone who is colour blind; what I call magenta, you may call pink; what I call shocking pink may not 'shock' you at all. Amidst these complexities, it is still necessary to write about colour in neo-noir. Colour plays an important part.

Flashback

In the gap between the classic and modernist cycles of film noir, the switch to colour television (mid-1960s) meant that colour film stock became 'virtually universal' (Neale 1985: 143) throughout the Hollywood film industry. In a sense, then, this changing technological expectation required neo-noir to 'remediate' classic noir. Before considering what kind of strategies neo-noir uses to represent the noir world in colour and, in turn, how this affects the neo-noir world, we need to reflect on the centrality of black-and-whiteness to critical arguments about film noir.

It is a critical commonplace to note that an 'expressionist' style is fundamental to film noir. Whatever else film noir may be – a genre, a cycle, a critical construction – it is most immediately recognised through its stylistic motifs, as catalogued in moody prose by any number of scholars. The use of chiaroscuro lighting is frequently commented on, but it is less often noted that such lighting is particularly suited to black-and-white film. Black-and-white is usually described as monochromatic ('one colour'), but it is also achromatic ('without colour'). Monochromatic images have one tonal scale, in this case from white to black, through shades of grey; this scale is about brightness – precisely about degrees of light (*chiaro*) and dark (*scuro*). Consequently, as Rudolf Arnheim notes, 'in black-and-white film there is but one way to achieve extreme contrast: through the difference between black and white' (2006: 54). Chiaroscuro lighting relies on such contrasts: sources of bright light and pools of darkness; ominous shadows thrown on plain, pale walls. These low-key effects are crucial to the expression of the classic noir world's moral ambivalence and paranoia, revealing as it obscures: what lurks in the shadows? The noir world is a treacherous place, where internal anxieties bleed out, disrupting realism in favour of expressionist stylisation. At the same time, however, the hard contrast created by such low-key lighting also connotes a sense of 'toughness', well-suited to the hard-boiled narratives.

This starts to explain why film noir was in black-and-white. Other common explanations of noir style include budgetary constraints, war-time rationing of electricity and film stock, and the influence of *émigré* directors such as Fritz Lang, Robert Siodmak and Otto Preminger. It is worth taking a moment to reflect further: even a high-budget A-picture like *The Big Sleep* (1946), directed by an American director, Howard Hawks, was in black-and-white. Why? The Technicolor three-strip process had been around since the early 1930s, producing films such as *The Wizard of Oz* (1939), *Gone with the Wind* (1939) and Disney's colour animations. But these films were associated with fantasy and spectacle, not realism. Paradoxically, the conventions of realism continued to privilege black-and-white film well into the 1950s and beyond, especially for 'serious' dramas and social problem films (see Naremore 1998: 169–72). Colour – like spectacle more generally – was associated with femininity, escapism and the 'exotic' Other (see Neale 1985: 152–5).

Unsurprisingly, then, the few colour films from the period that have been described as film noir are often centrally concerned with women: *Leave Her to Heaven* (1945), *Niagara* (1953), *Slightly Scarlet* (1956), *A Kiss Before Dying* (1956) and *Party Girl* (1958).[1] Most film noir critics treat these films as marginal examples – not, I suspect, just because they are in colour, or because they are about women, or because they emphasise psychological melodrama (rather than hard-boiled crime), but because of the ways in which these three aspects mutually reinforce each other's Otherness. Indeed, those critics who discuss the films in any detail (for example, Naremore 1998: 186–90 and Christopher 2006: 223–9) do so in discrete sections on colour noir. In the process, the films' 'difference' becomes exaggerated.

For the most part, colour noirs employ quite conventional Technicolor techniques. Until the 1950s, Technicolor operated a virtual monopoly on colour film in Hollywood, including having their own consultant, Natalie M. Kalmus, and cameramen working on every Technicolor film. In 'Color Consciousness', Kalmus outlined the principles of harmony and psychological affect underpinning Technicolor aesthetics, emphasising the need for restraint and suggesting that colour 'amplifies the picture in a similar manner' to the musical score (2006: 28). In other words, colour was understood to complement narrative in a conventionally classical way: it was carefully planned and controlled to support narrative by enhancing characterisation and emotional registers. In this respect, Technicolor logic *required* red to signal 'danger', 'anger', 'passion' and so on (2006: 26).

The main signifier of noir style in these films remains the use of chiaroscuro lighting. Indeed, according to James Naremore, *Slightly Scarlet* used conventional black-and-white lighting set-ups to achieve these effects (1998: 189). However, it is harder to achieve chiaroscuro in colour, because brightness is not the only attribute to consider: the tonal contrast between light and dark, white and black, may be weakened by competing factors of hue (the actual colours) and saturation (the strength of the colours). For example, red and green are complementary colours: they stand out most strongly in relation to each other, creating high colour contrast.[2] In terms of brightness, however, red and green have *the same* tonal contrast, so in black-and-white photography there will be no noticeable difference between the two. So, while the presence of red and green will

Classic chiaroscuro: tonal contrast in *Niagara*

make little difference to chiaroscuro in a black-and-white film, in a colour film they may detract attention from the light/dark contrast. Hues can also be divided into cool and warm colours: cool colours (shades of purple, through blue to green and greenish yellow) tend to recede visually; warm colours (shades of yellow through orange to red to reddish-purple) tend to advance visually. Generally speaking, then, red will stand out more than blue – unless the area of blue is significantly larger than the area of red, or the red is desaturated (washed out), but the blue is saturated (deep). High saturation creates visual 'energy', as do brightness, warmth and area. However, saturation levels do not affect a colour's brightness, so in black-and-white a desaturated red would be exactly the same shade of grey as a saturated red.

Consequently, colour noirs often enhance the tonal contrast of chiaroscuro by adding colour contrast. *Leave Her to Heaven* is a good example: Ellen Berent (Gene Tierney) and Richard Harland (Cornel Wilde) return from riding to find the house shrouded in blue shadows intermittently relieved by amber source lights: the contrast between light and dark is thus reinforced by the complementary contrast between cool blue and warm yellowy-orange. This lighting retains verisimilitude, since the colours are motivated by the *mise-en-scène*; the symbolic and stylistic effect is *in addition* to the primary drive of narrative realism.

Niagara provides one exception to this general rule, when George Loomis (Joseph Cotten) murders his wife, Rose (Marilyn Monroe), in the Niagara Falls Bell Tower. The scene combines chiaroscuro lighting, noir *mise-en-scène* and matte paintings with live action in a way that enables a highly stylised representation of the murder, including an unusual 'aerial' composite shot looking directly down at the floor from above the bells. The shot I am interested in, though, is of Rose, standing centre frame, dressed in a black suit and white blouse: on the left, blue-green sky is seen through the louvres of a shutter, gradually obliterated by George's grey-blue suit as he moves forward; on the right, a red light has turned the entire wall red and casts its glow on to her hair. According to Kalmus, 'the law of emphasis states ... that nothing of relative unimportance in a picture shall be emphasized. If, for example, a bright red ornament were shown behind an actor's head, the bright color would detract from the character and action. Errors of this nature must be carefully avoided' (2006: 28–9). Here, such an 'error' is actively embraced. The presence of the red light breaks the rules of verisimilitude: it seems unrealistic that such a light should be there. But in terms of noir composition, its presence is extremely effective, creating a balanced contrast between cool blue-grey and warm red to express emotional crisis and the danger of the situation.

This more expressionist use of red light echoes the alternating red, white and green neon lighting at the climax of *Rope* (1948), when Rupert Cadell (James Stewart) realises the full horror of what his students, Brandon Shaw (John Dall) and Phillip Morgan (Farley Granger), have done (see Naremore 1998: 188). What is a minor note in *Rope* becomes a major motif in *Vertigo* (1958): red and green are repeatedly contrasted. The first time we see Madeleine Elster (Kim Novak), the jade-green satin stole she is wearing draws our attention because it stands out against the baroque scarlet wallpaper. The first time we see Judy Barton (Kim Novak) she is wearing a similar shade of green, but when she and Scottie Ferguson (James Stewart) revisit the baroque restaurant, she wears a lilac dress that clashes horribly with the red. When Judy is finally 'transformed' (back) into 'Madeleine', the scene is overwhelmed by jade light that filters through the net curtains from the neon sign outside (a sign that appears red during the day). The film also uses colour to signal psychological obsession – notably during Scottie's psychedelic nightmare – in a way that has influenced neo-noir.

To summarise: in classic noir, colour tends to reinforce established patterns of noir representation. Thus, the films' most overt, attention-grabbing uses of colour do one or more of the following: enhance the femme fatale's charac- terisation (for example, Rose's fuchsia dress in *Niagara*); emphasise a morally dangerous location through garish *mise-en-scène* (for example, the gangster's beach house in *Slightly Scarlet*); or accentuate chiaroscuro lighting by using contrasting colours. For the most part, these uses of colour have a plausible diegetic source, complying with classical realist aesthetics. These scenes also tend to be quite isolated, with large stretches of the films using entirely con- ventional high-key lighting and realist *mise-en-scène*.

The new black

How does the use of colour in neo-noir compare?[3] By the time of the modern- ist phase of neo-noir, colour film was the norm and connoted social 'realism' in a way it had not often done during the classic period. Technicolor's monopoly had collapsed in the 1950s, following the Supreme Court's 1950 anti-trust rul- ing and the advent of single-strip brands such as Eastman Color, DeLuxe and Metrocolor. The quality of this new film stock varied, however, and single-strip techniques produced a brighter, less saturated range of colours than the three- strip Technicolor process. Colour film stock also had difficulty dealing with low lighting levels. Consequently, a number of neo-noirs made in the 1960s and 1970s lack chiaroscuro and tend towards naturalist colour. Naremore, for exam- ple, criticises *Harper* (1966) and *Marlowe* (1969):

> Whatever their incidental virtues, neither of these films was able to provide a visual cor- relative for the shadowy, decadent romanticism of the 1940s. Even in the 1970s, color films dealing with noir subjects were sometimes flatly and brightly lit' (1998: 190).

Similarly, Mark Bould notes that the 1964 remake of *The Killers* (1946) 'is brightly- and uniformly-lit, conventionally shot and in colour ... Arguably, the noir world has become ubiquitous and normalised, rendering a stylistically distinct representation superfluous or impossible' (2005: 11).

Point Blank (1967), however, suggested more evocative possibilities for col- our and neo-noir style. Strongly influenced by European art cinema, the film made extensive use of modernist techniques, narratively and stylistically. Indi- vidual scenes exhibit distinct colour preferences. Lynne Walker's (Sharon Acker) apartment is almost devoid of colour, with silvery whites and greys dominating the furnishings, costumes and make-up. Lynne's sister, Chris (Angie Dickinson), is associated with warmer colours: the walls of her apartment, the sheets on her bed, the robe she puts on, the dress she wears the next day, are all shades of yellow; she later wears red and tomato; even Walker (Lee Marvin) wears mustard and ochre when he is with her. Frederick Carter (Lloyd Bochner) and his employees all wear muddy brown and moss green suits, to match his office. Broadly speaking, the film's colour 'warms up' as the narrative progresses, moving from whites, greys and blues to yellows, browns and oranges, but the final scene returns to cool colours, using diffuse blue, green and magenta lighting to highlight the grey stone. The film's hallucinatory qualities – summed up by Walker's line, 'Did it happen? A dream? A dream' – are also expressed through colour, most notably during the fight at the Movie House. The club mixes purple and crimson décor with red and magenta spotlights and coloured projections, with gels rotating through blue, green, yellow, magenta and cyan. The glut of colours is matched by a cacophony – the screeches of the singer and audience members finally echoed by the screams of a dancer finding the unconscious bodies, and extreme close-ups of their gaping mouths matching the scene's opening shot of the singer standing behind a projected image, as if in the mouth of a screaming woman. The scene ends with Walker blinking into the projector's red light, which casts molten patterns on his face. We recognise this shot from the very beginning of the film, when the entirely red screen came into focus to reveal Walker's face. Colour is not used in isolation, then, but as part of a complex system of stylistic choices that iterate and reiterate the trauma and violence of betrayal in such a way as to leave us uncertain as to whether this is, indeed, a dead man's dream.

The 1970s saw a number of cinematographers using colour film stock in innovative ways, although not always for conventional 'noir' effects. Vilmos Zsigmond, for example, 'flashed' the film stock on *The Long Goodbye* (1973) to 'degrade contrasts', producing 'a rather diffused, pastel-colored photography' (Naremore 1998: 203–4). Consequently, the film lacks brightness, colour is relatively muted throughout and chiaroscuro effects are similarly understated. Others achieved a more ominous, noir style: Gordon Willis combined colour with low-level light to produce distinctively dark films such as *Klute* (1971) and *The Parallax View* (1974); and, for *Taxi Driver* (1976), Michael Chapman underexposed the film stock, then overexposed the bright points of source lighting during printing to ensure dense blacks and high contrast (see Naremore 1998: 192). Modern high-speed colour film deals more easily with low light levels, but many neo-noir cinematographers continue to use pre- and post-production effects to enhance the look of the film. For example, on *Se7en* (1995), Darius Khondji flashed the negative by illuminating it with 'certain colour tones according to the atmosphere … colouring … the darkest shadows' (Khondji quoted in Darke 1996: 20); a few hundred prints also used silver retention to restore luminosity and density to whites and blacks, enhancing contrast.

While filmmakers will each have their own techniques, there are also recurring strategies and conventions around the use of colour in American neo-noir. (These are tendencies, rather than rules: an individual neo-noir may use one or some of these strategies, in varying combinations and degrees.)

1. Neo-noir predominantly relies on co-ordinated use of neutral colours (whites, blacks, greys, browns) off-set by areas of saturated primary colours, which become more prevalent during scenes of dramatic conflict.

2. Specifically, neo-noir favours the primaries of *light*: red, green, blue. These colours are used in all aspects of *mise-en-scène*. Blue filters are commonly used to tint scenes, as in *Red Rock West*, when Sheriff Wayne Brown (J. T. Walsh) chases Michael Williams (Nicolas Cage) through misty woods. Blue and green can dominate entire films: blue in *Heat* (1995), *Payback* (1999) and *The Deep End* (2001); green and blue in *Underneath* (1995); green in *Fight Club* (1999). The shades of green found in neo-noir are quite distinct, tending towards acidic, medicinal jade greens, rather than 'natural', 'healthy' shades of grass green (which are all but absent). Red is usually reserved for key scenes and *mise-en-scène* motifs (for example, John Doe's (Kevin Spacey) apartment in *Se7en*). In particular, red is often combined with black and white to maximise dramatic impact – especially when blood is involved – as in *The Grifters* (1990), *Reservoir Dogs* (1992) and *Sin City* (2005).

3. Cyan and magenta are quite common in lighting, especially in postmodern 1980s neo-noirs such as *Blood Simple* (1984), *Manhunter* (1986) and *Black Widow* (1987), but are rarely used for sets, props and costumes. Yellow is uncommon in neo-noir, presumably because it is too 'happy' and optimistic for the noir world view. When yellow does appear, it is the faded colour of the past (see 6 below) or the jaundiced hue of corruption: think of Yellow Bastard (Nick Stahl) in *Sin City* or Loren Visser's (M. Emmet Walsh) pale yellow suit in *Blood Simple*. Even yellow neon is comparatively scarce.

4. Secondary and tertiary pigments are usually kept to a minimum, as are pale and pastel colours: shades of purple, pink, peach – even orange – are rarely seen in neo-noir, perhaps because they seem too feminine. The association of orange with neo-noir is much more about the quality of light and atmosphere than other aspects of *mise-en-scène*: it is the dusty, desert sunlight, the flame of the fire, the aura of body heat.

5. Colours tend to be spatially controlled. Large areas of neutrals will be off-set by smaller blocks of primary hues. Fabrics are usually plain; when present, patterns are geometric or, occasionally, baroque (nothing flowery). Seedy motels may have (suitably grubby) patterned décor to signal run-down conditions. Short depth of field (an all but inevitable by-product of low light levels and zoom

lenses) often aids these effects, blurring background objects to create a more uniform shade and diffusing the light cast by neons and source lights. For example, in *Black Widow* when Alex Barnes (Debra Winger) watches Catherine Petersen (Theresa Russell) from her car, the background is split between red and green; later shots reveal the red is cast by a neon light, while a change in focus reveals that the green area was actually a dumpster.

6. The *range* of colours in particular settings may also be limited, creating an overall colour tendency for individual scenes, as in *Point Blank*. This tendency involves what Arnheim describes as colour's 'qualitative' tone-scale (2006: 53): the scale of difference from, for example, blue to sea green to green, or from yellow to ochre to brown. The hue changes, but remains closely related to the other colours. This is quite different from the 'quantitative' tonal contrast between degrees of lightness (Arnheim 2006: 53). For example, sepia photography is monochrome: brown is the only colour; the shades are quantities of brightness. A film such as *Chinatown* (1974), however, creates a sense of the 'sepia-tinted' dust-bowl Depression era by limiting the colour palette to qualitative shades of creams, yellows and browns, with splashes of other colours thrown in. This qualitative sepia tendency was a common strategy in post-classical Hollywood revisionist genre films: *Bonnie and Clyde* (1967), *McCabe & Mrs Miller* (1971) and *The Godfather* (1972) use these kinds of techniques to revisit the mythology of gangster movies and westerns. It is a convention that has become particularly associated with representations of a *generic* past and remains a common strategy for period neo-noirs, such as *Devil in a Blue Dress* (1995), *L.A. Confidential* (1997) and *The Black Dahlia* (2006). The saturated, brownish colour palette suggests 'the past' without resorting to black-and-white (although *The Man Who Wasn't There* (2001) does go this far), but it also lends the films a nostalgic glamour that often feels quite oppressive. The end of *The Black Dahlia* seems to recognise this, offering a momentary reprieve: when Kay Lake (Scarlett Johansson) opens the door to Dwight 'Bucky' Bleichhert (Josh Hartnett), pure light bounces off her white angora sweater and the white flowers and wall behind her. Redemption is cut short, however, as Bucky hallucinates the Black Dahlia's mutilated corpse lying on the lawn; rubbing his eyes he turns away, and the sepia tones fade back in for the final shots.

7. A few films, including *D.O.A.* (1988), *Dead Again* (1991) and *Memento* (2000), combine colour with black-and-white sequences. *Dead Again* simply uses black-and-white for flashbacks: the past is black-and-white, the present colour. *Memento* is more complex, since the black-and-white sequences (although in the past) provide more coherent, chronological narration than the colour scenes (which begin in the present and work their way backwards). In both cases, switching between colour and black-and-white footage facilitates the organisation of plot time, but also works thematically to suggest the rupture of past and present as a traumatic event. *D.O.A.* works differently: the present is

in black-and-white, while the flashback is in colour. However, the sequences in the 'present' most closely remake the original 1950 film (the past), while the flashback tells a completely new, 'modern' story about a college professor, Dexter Cornell (Dennis Quaid). In this respect, the relationship between black-and-white and colour plays with our extratextual, generic understanding of past/present in a typically postmodern way. The shift to colour is very knowing: the camera tracks right revealing, letter by letter, a hand writing in white chalk on a blackboard, C-O-L-O-R. As the final letter is revealed, the black-and-white image becomes colour: Dex is teaching an English class about colour as metaphor.

8. One of the most common strategies is the combination of colour *with* lighting. Neon signs, brake lights, shaded lamps all help colour the neo-noir environment. This is not just about the colour of the lamplight, but also about how the light cast seeps through, staining the diegetic world unnatural shades. This kind of coloured lighting goes much further than the blue-yellow contrast used to accentuate chiaroscuro in *Leave Her to Heaven*, although the colours can still fulfil this function. For example, in *The Long Goodbye*, the scene where Marlowe (Elliott Gould) first telephones Mrs Wade (Nina van Pallandt) proves an exception to the film's otherwise low contrast visuals: reddish light suffuses the bar, off-set by small green lights on the wall; the camera zooms in slowly to focus on Marlowe's face, backlit, almost obliterated, by the bright, bluish-white light flooding through an open doorway behind him, while reddish fill light illuminates his face. The scene's use of coloured light proves typical of neo-noir bar-rooms – for example, the red exit sign and wall lights at the Pinehaven Tavern in *Body Heat* (1981) and the magenta neons that shine through to Julian Marty's (Dan Hedaya) office behind the bar in *Blood Simple*. Like many postmodern neo-noirs, *Blood Simple* is overloaded with coloured light to create visual interest. These lighting effects are not always convincingly motivated by *mise-en-scène*: as Marty sits out back, the foreground is awash with blue light apparently coming from a fly-zapper on the wall, while the interior, visible through an open door behind him, provides yellow-orange contrast. Some films abandon motivated source lighting altogether (as with the lighting at the end of *Point Blank*), but most follow *Blood Simple*'s lead and contrive some kind of *mise-en-scène* explanation. Even so, the effect usually exceeds the cause. Such lighting is especially prevalent in low-budget, cable and direct-to-video productions, such as *The Last Seduction* (1994) and *The Set Up* (1995), providing relatively cheap visuals in the same way that chiaroscuro did for classic noir and demonstrating the impossibility of separating economic and aesthetic considerations.

In some respects, these uses of colour offer a continuation of classic noir: excessive colour is still associated with morally dangerous locations, especially those spaces where seductions, conspiracies and crimes take place, such as bars, clubs and alleyways. However, a stylised colour system is usually present

Flat white: tonal uniformity in *The Last Seduction*

across the whole film, not just in isolated scenes, and although these colours are still (generally) motivated by *mise-en-scène*, their effects often exceed the motivation. The neo-femme fatale's relationship to colour is also slightly different. She is usually dressed, head-to-toe, in one colour: in *Body Heat*, Matty Walker (Kathleen Turner) is wearing white when Ned Racine (William Hurt) spills a cherry-red snow-cone down her front; in *The Grifters*, Lilly Dillon (Anjelica Huston) is also first seen in white, but wears red when she accidentally kills her son, Roy (John Cusack); Catherine Tramell (Sharon Stone) wears shades of beige, cream and white in *Basic Instinct* (1992); and in *The Last Seduction*, Bridget Gregory (Linda Fiorentino) wears black or grey suits with white shirts, until the final scene when she wears dark, mossy green. As the prevalence of white suggests, the symbolic meanings attached to colours under the Technicolor regime do not necessarily apply in neo-noir. Instead, the femme fatale is most often associated with a 'monochrome' look, signalling her emotional control and single-mindedness. Conversely, when Bridget attempts to tell Mike Swale (Peter Berg) the *truth*, colour floods the shot, the green pool table light behind them contrasting strongly with red fill light washing over their faces and bodies in the foreground.

This wash of coloured light across a large space is typical of neo-noir and needs to be considered as quite distinct from conventional chiaroscuro lighting. The presence of complementary coloured light certainly provides visual contrast, but – as in this scene – it does not always involve a *tonal* contrast between light and dark (i.e., if you turn down the colour in this scene, the image is quite evenly grey). Side-lighting, back-lighting and Venetian blinds are used in almost every neo-noir mentioned here, but the kind of complex, layered chiaroscuro effects found in classic noir are relatively rare. Indeed, light breaking through blinds is often diffused to create a soft haze that is very different from the crisp, high contrast of classic noir, although bars of shadow are still likely to fall on walls and faces. In combination with the use of coloured filters and the blurring effect of short depth of field, these washes of colour and hazy light often seem to flatten space, whereas classic noir more commonly emphasised spatial depth. Chiaroscuro lighting helped express the ambivalence of the classic noir world; in neo-noir, colour shapes a different moral universe.

The world through jade-tinted glasses

The first few shots of *Underneath* are monochrome, jade green. It is not immediately apparent *why*. In the context of a narrative film, the colour seems excessive, even beyond meaning, because it does not conform to conventional codes of realism, colour symbolism or psychological motivation. Naremore suggests that the film, like 'a great many retro or "neo-noir" films use[s] colored light ... to evoke the monochromatic tradition of high contrast, black-and-white thrillers' (1998: 192). Implicitly, colour is assumed to achieve an equivalent effect to black-and-white chiaroscuro. But colour, by definition, is *not* black-and-white. Colour – even monochrome colour – exceeds the binary ambivalence of black-and-white: there is light, dark and *green*.

Colour proliferates, escapes and exceeds meaning. As David Batchelor notes, 'the idea that colour is beyond, beneath or in some other way at the limit of language has been expressed in a number of ways by a number of writers' (2000: 81). He summarises Julia Kristeva's semiotic-psychoanalytic argument concisely:

> Colour, for Kristeva, is linked to 'subject/object indeterminacy', to a state before the self is formed in language, before the world is fully differentiated from the subject. And colour always exists as a disruption in the symbolic order ... Consequently, 'the chromatic experience constitutes a menace to the "self"'. Or, as Kristeva then puts it: 'Colour is the shattering of unity.' It is as if colour begins not just to interrupt the process of self-formation, but to throw it into reverse; it is as if colour serves to de-differentiate the self and de-form the world. (2000: 82, quoting Kristeva 1980: 220–1)

The shattering of unity. The phrase might describe neo-noir as much as the power of colour.

In neo-noir, the world is not what it seems. Corruption is no longer confined to Los Angeles: the city, the small town, the desert, the past, the present, even the future – all duplicitous, corrupt and degenerate. People's motives are hidden, sometimes even from themselves (*Fight Club, Memento, The Machinist* (2004)). In *The Conversation* (1974), Harry Caul (Gene Hackman) obsessively attempts to piece together fragments of sound to discover the 'truth', only to realise he has been manipulated; still unsure who by and why, he ends up tearing apart his home searching for surveillance equipment. Paranoia and conspiracy dominate neo-noir, short-circuiting epistemological and moral certainty. (Science fiction noirs like *Blade Runner* (1982) and *Dark City* (1998) take such conspiracies to the logical extreme.) A world peopled with anti-heroes, conspirators, femme fatales and psychopaths is inherently a world in which the very concept of the unified 'self' is under threat. Colour provides a particularly affective way of representing this threat.

Naremore notes that *Underneath* includes 'whole sequences [shot] through red, blue, or green filters' (1998: 193), but he does not connect this choice of colours to the spectrum: these are the primaries of light. At a basic level, then, the filmmakers have foregrounded the 'splitting' of white light into the colours of the spectrum. This fragmentation is carried through at all levels: spatially, temporally, visually, aurally, experientially. The opening jade-tinted shots show a man (Peter Gallagher) driving a truck, overtaking a van on a highway; an older man (Paul Dooley) sits next to him. In one shot, an out-of-focus bar of muted red appears along the bottom of the otherwise green frame. Neither man speaks, but they exchange looks, and we might infer from the way the driver watches the van's reflection in the wing mirror that *something is going on here*. Before we can find out what, the scene cuts to the same man (Gallagher) in the back of a yellow taxi – in 'natural' colour. He stares out the window, which reflects a suburban street in its highly polished surface. The scene cuts to him driving the truck, then back to him in the cab. A disembodied woman's voice asks, 'Are you gettin' off at Austin?' A male voice (that we might recognise as Gallagher's) grunts a reply. Their conversation continues, but all we see is the man staring out the window: we *might* assume that he is remembering this conversation. The sequence cuts to a bus, where the owner of the voice is revealed and we see her talking to the man 'in person'. They introduce themselves as Susan (Elisabeth Shue) and Michael (Gallagher). Aurally, the short conversation continues without interruption, as visually the scene cuts back to the taxi, then to the bus, then to the bus station and finally to the cab arriving at its destination: his mother's house. In less than two-and-a-half minutes, we have seen Michael in four different locations at four different times, but remain very uncertain as to what is past, present or future.

At a pragmatic level, the monochromatic green alerts us to pay attention, enabling us to follow the fact of spatial-temporal disjunction; indeed, we might say that the experience of fragmentation *is the point* of this sequence. The abstract colour is also part of the film's system of *mise-en-scène* and narrative structure. Inside Michael's mother's house, the living room is partitioned by wooden frames that hold rectangles of blue, green or yellow glass. The glass is used at various points to cast coloured light on to people's faces and even to 'split' the screen into distinct boxes: for example, Michael is seen through a blue glass rectangle, isolated from his mother (Anjanette Comer) on the other side of the partition. The film often draws attention to transparent and reflective surfaces, such as the wing mirror and taxi window. The monochrome green is retrospectively 'explained' in this way – the red armoured truck has green-tinted windows – but (as with *Blood Simple*) the effect exceeds diegetic motivation: even shots within the truck appear green, not just those through the windscreen. And, why *green*? For the same reason that the truck is red and the framed glass is blue: the film exploits colour not as a 'natural' phenomenon, but as an abstract mode of expression.

Batchelor's discussion of colour provides another way of conceptualising this artificial, coloured surface. Focusing on Pop Art and Minimalism, he argues, 'something important happened to colour in art in the 1960s' (2000: 98): the use of light industrial materials – paint, plastics, metals, lights – led to what he terms the 'digitalisation of colour' (2000: 105). Traditionally, artists blended their own colours from small tubes of oil paint (an analogue continuum of colour); contemporary artists were able to pick a can of paint in the exact shade they wanted, using a colour chart.[4] In this respect, 'digital colour is individuated; it comes in discrete units; there is no mergence or modulation' (ibid.). Batchelor's description resonates with the kind of delimited, 'flat' colours found in neo-noir; metaphorically, this sense of individuated digital colours can be linked to fragmentation and neo-noir's mood of alienation. In *Underneath*, for example, the 'discrete units' of coloured glass which isolate Michael from the world around him reiterate the opening sequence's fragmentation of space, just as a split-focus diopter lens visualises his alienation from his family. Strikingly, Batchelor links digitalised colours to 'works of art that refer, directly or indirectly, to the experience of modernity. These colours are more ... urban colours than the colours of nature. Artificial colours, city colours, industrial colours' (2000: 106). We are undoubtedly in neo-noir territory here, from the corrupt neon cities of *Taxi Driver* and *Se7en*, to the sickly, fluorescent green of the 'toxic waste part of town' where Tyler Durden (Brad Pitt) lives in *Fight Club*, and the literally digital colours of *Dark City* and *Sin City*.

Individuated, artificial colour often occurs alongside excessive colour as loss of control. In Western culture, vivid colours have repeatedly been associated with intoxication, hallucination, irrationality and chaos. In most cases, this has been constructed as a dangerous loss of control, as something 'apocalyptic ... Colour requires, or results in, or perhaps just is, a loss of focus, of identity, of self. A loss of mind, a kind of delirium, a kind of madness perhaps' (Batchelor 2000: 51). Scottie's hallucinations in *Vertigo* are a good example of this 'kind of madness', as are the patients' psychotic breaks in *Shock Corridor*.[5] It also explains why morally and physically dangerous locations in neo-noir are swamped with coloured neon light. The metaphoric use of colour as loss of control usually occurs in individual scenes: the Movie House brawl in *Point Blank*, for example, or the Lust murder scene in *Se7en*. In other films, colour – often specifically red – accumulates and intensifies through the narrative, indicating the protagonist's gradual loss of control. Thus, the muted qualitative shades of *Slam Dance* (1987) initially seem almost 'black-and-white', but increasing amounts of red begin to appear, finally overwhelming the frame in the violently red and magenta hotel room where Smiley (Harry Dean Stanton) is killed.

As these examples suggest, colour as 'madness' or loss of control frequently becomes attached to the threat to self. The most basic way that identity is threatened in neo-noir is through the device of the nemesis. In films such as *Blade Runner*, *Black Widow*, *Basic Instinct* and *Se7en*, the moral distinctions between investigator and criminal disintegrate: an investigator tracking a criminal, becomes obsessed and 'corrupted', losing sense of him/her 'self'. The extent to which colour expresses this relationship varies, but *Manhunter* is a good example. Will Graham (William Petersen) is hunting for a serial killer nicknamed the Tooth Fairy (Tom Noonan); Will previously suffered a breakdown after identifying too closely with another serial killer, Dr Hannibal Lecktor (Brian Cox). To 'recover the mindset' (his words), Will visits Lecktor in prison. The cell is white and pale grey (including Lecktor's uniform) while Will is dressed in dark colours, including a jade green shirt (a colour that links Will, Lecktor *and* the Tooth Fairy). While Lecktor reads the Tooth Fairy file, Will abstractedly stares to the left: a dissolve shows Lecktor's sink, seen through the bars of the cell, illuminated from within by an unmotivated magenta glow. The camera pans right to Lecktor's bookcase: purple light enhances lilac book covers and complements the jade spines of others. Panning past the shelf to the white brick wall, the image loses focus and the scene cuts back to Will staring at that space (offscreen). He jumps when Lecktor's voice calls him back to reality. Previously, the conversation used conventional shot/reverse-shot cutting; now, as they discuss the Tooth Fairy, straight-on shots of Will and Lecktor from the middle of the line of axis are intercut, as if they are reflections of each other. Lecktor is not fooled – 'You came here to look at me, to get the old scent back again' – and asks if Will knows how he caught him. Agitated, Will bangs on the door to leave, escaping as Lecktor explains, 'Because we're just alike. You want the scent? Smell yourself.' Will flees the building and leans over a railing, panting. A point-of-view shot fills the frame with out of focus green grass. Colour here is 'a loss of focus, of identity, of self' (Batchelor 2000: 51). Unsurprisingly, the Tooth Fairy is associated with a riot of greens, orange-reds, blues and patterns and it should not be forgotten that his preferred name, the driving force of his psychotic fantasy, is *Red* Dragon.

The nemesis trope is taken further in *Fight Club*, *Lost Highway* (1997), *Mulholland Dr.* (2001), *Fear X* (2003) and *The Machinist*, shattering the barriers between self/other, reality/fantasy, memory/dream, and maintaining a 'psychotic' uncertainty for both the characters and the spectator. As Fred Madison (Bill Pullman) says in *Lost Highway*, 'I like to remember things my own way … How I remembered them, not necessarily the way they happened.' This might also serve as a way of grasping the film's plot: there is no 'true' meaning. It does not matter whether Fred literally becomes Pete Dayton (Balthazar Getty) or whether Renee Madison and Alice Wakefield (Patricia Arquette) are literally the same woman. What matters is the discontinuous, dream-like uncertainty of experiencing the film.

The tense abstraction of the first section of the film, focusing on Fred and Renee's marriage, is enhanced by the muted, limited palette of colours. Frequently shot against neutral-coloured walls and with shallow depth of field, without back-lighting, Fred (and later Pete) seems to merge with the background. This lends resonance to the uncanny moment when Fred disappears into the darkness, the night Renee is (apparently) murdered: the shadowy corridor engulfs him. We next see him, still in darkness, in front of a mirror (a similar shot of Pete occurs later in the film). It is not clear where this mirror is, since there is no mirror in the living room and he does not reply when Renee calls his name. *Two* shadows are seen moving across the living room walls towards the hallway: Fred alone emerges from the darkness. This deceptive, flat-deep darkness contrasts with the flashing blue lightning motif, which appears at those moments when the two stories/worlds collide, most notably when Pete replaces Fred in the jail cell. Colour, *mise-en-scène* and music repeatedly link Pete and Fred: each of these 'flashes' of connection makes Pete's head hurt (as Fred's did prior to the changeover). For example, seeing a photograph of Mr Eddy (Robert Loggia), Renee, Alice and Andy (Michael Massee), Pete asks Alice, 'Is that you? Are both of them you?' Her answer ('That's me,' pointing to the blonde) seems to cause his nosebleed. He goes upstairs in search of the bathroom: thudding music begins (a track called 'Rammstein', by Rammstein); a long corridor leads to a red curtain that reminds us of Fred and Renee's bedroom; bizarrely, the doors have numbers on them. Blue lightning flashes behind Pete as he approaches and opens door 26. Inside, orange light seems to make the image waver, like volcanic heat. Renee/Alice (or someone else?) is reflected in a mirror, wearing an orange wig. The intense colour, sound and image end abruptly as Pete shuts the door and leans against the wall. The sequence is reiterated at the Lost Highway Hotel: Fred watches Renee leave Mr Eddy/Dick Laurent, then approaches room 26 himself, blue lightning flashing behind him; 'Rammstein' returns, as he cracks Mr Eddy/Dick Laurent on the head and abducts him. Helped by the Mystery Man (Robert Blake), Fred kills Dick Laurent and returns home. 'Making sense' of *Lost Highway* requires radically reconceptualising time and space, so that Fred's final utterance of 'Dick Laurent is dead' can be understood as initiating the events of the past. Such discontinuity ensures a coherent 'self' cannot exist. Fred's head 'explodes'. Unity is shattered.

Conclusion: (no) exit

Few neo-noirs shatter unity as extremely as *Lost Highway*, but even *Basic Instinct* shows signs of this kind of epistemological uncertainty, refusing to resolve, once and for all, the question, 'Did she, or didn't she?' As the mention of the monochrome, self-controlled femme fatale reveals, however, the threat to the 'self' remains primarily a threat to *male* identity (with one or two exceptions, such as *Mulholland Dr.*). In this respect, neo-noir's use of colour, although breaking with classic realism and Technicolor aesthetics, remains quite conventional: colour is associated with danger and the Other, as something to be feared. *Sin City*, for example, uses colour almost exclusively for women, villains and blood. As Batchelor argues, such 'chromophobia' is typical of Western culture: colour is routinely regarded as dangerous, trivial, or both: 'either way, colour is ... other to the higher values of Western culture. Or perhaps culture is other to the higher values of colour. Or colour is the corruption of culture' (2000: 23). Neo-noir continues this tradition, associating vivid, excessive and artificial colour with degeneration, destruction and death.

It is impossible to do justice to every ramification of colour within each neo-noir film, but I have endeavoured to indicate some of the commonest patterns within US neo-noir, at least. One particular motif appears in almost every neo-noir mentioned here: at some point, we see a red or green exit sign, but the protagonist fails to take its advice. Focusing on shattered unity and identity enabled an exploration of colour's affect on the neo-noir world, but it also indicates the ways in which neo-noir involves an intensification and development of classic noir themes. Noir characters remain trapped in patterns of behaviour that are beyond their control: there is no exit.

NOTES

1   Most of the others – *Second Chance* (1953), *I Died a Thousand Times* (1955), *House of Bamboo* (1955), *The Trap* (1959) – justify colour through the spectacle of location shooting: respectively, Mexico, the desert, Japan, the desert again. *Shock Corridor* (1963) uses colour to signal mental patients' psychotic breaks, using footage from *House of Bamboo* and stock footage of tribal dancing and waterfalls.

2   In painting, the primary colours are red, blue and yellow; in photography, the primary colours are red, blue and *green* (for additive methods) or cyan, yellow and magenta (for subtractive methods). In any case, a primary colour's complementary colour is created by mixing the *other* two primaries (for example, blue paint + yellow paint = green paint, which is the complementary of red paint; blue light + green light =

cyan light, which is the complementary of red light). Both models prove useful, here, since the composition of *mise-en-scène* often relies on the visual codes of pigment colours, but also includes lighting as part of the *mise-en-scène*.

3   This essay focuses on US cinema. Other, culturally-specific, conventions are possible: as Ginette Vincendeau argues in this collection, the subdued, neutral colour schemes of Jean-Pierre Melville's *policiers* influenced French neo-noir.

4   Comparing Caravaggio's careful gradations of chiaroscuro to Andy Warhol's uniform, delimited colours effectively illustrates Batchelor's distinction. Let me stress, Batchelor's argument is about the *conceptualisation* of colour. His use of the term 'digital colour' is metaphorical rather than literal: 'digital colour' does not necessarily have to be produced by digital technology. However, digital technology *does* necessarily produce 'digital colour'; the digital image is incapable of analogue colour since it is based on pixels.

5   This intensification of colour can also be represented positively as 'liberation from constraint' rather than 'loss of control' – as 'bliss, *jouissance*, ecstasy' (Batchelor 2000: 32). This use of colour is rare in neo-noir. *Wild at Heart* (1990) is a notable exception: Lula Fortune's (Laura Dern) orgasms are accompanied by rainbow hues (part of the film's *Wizard of Oz* motif).

REFERENCES

Arnheim, Rudolf (2006 [1935]) 'Remarks on color film', in Angela Dalle Vacche and Brian Price (eds) *Color: The Film Reader*. London: Routledge, 53–6.

Batchelor, David (2000) *Chromophobia*. London: Reaktion Books.

Bould, Mark (2005) *Film Noir: From Berlin to Sin City*. London: Wallflower Press.

Christopher, Nicholas (2006) *Somewhere in the Night: Film Noir and the American City*. New and Expanded Edition. Emeryville: Shoemaker & Hoard.

Darke, Chris (1996) 'Inside the light', *Sight & Sound*, April, 18–20.

Kalmus, Natalie M. (2006 [1935]) 'Color Consciousness', in Angela Dalle Vacche and Brian Price (eds) *Color: The Film Reader*. London: Routledge, 24–9.

Kristeva, Julia (1980) *Desire in Language: A Semiotic Approach to Literature and Art*, trans. Thomas Gora, Alice Jardine and Leon S. Roudiez. Oxford: Basil Blackwell.

Naremore, James (1998) *More than Night: Film Noir in its Contexts*. Berkeley: University of California Press.

Neale, Steve (1985) *Cinema and Technology: Image, Sound, Colour*. London: British Film Institute/Macmillan Education.

2

Audio-Noir: Audiovisuality in Neo-Modernist Noir

ROBERT MIKLITSCH

Film noir for most people is associated with certain indelible images: neon signs and nightmare alleys, rain-glistening streets and Venetian-blind shadows. It is also frequently associated with certain sounds: wise-guy patter and erotic double talk, moody voice-overs and even moodier music – a lone saxophone soaring in the night, for example.

These evocative sounds and images can be said to constitute the imaginary of the genre which, like the Maltese Falcon, is at once real and phantasmatic. Although critics of noir have endlessly debated its origins and essence, it is nonetheless striking, especially given how many people can hum the theme from *Laura* (1944), how little attention has been paid to the sonic or acoustic dimensions of the genre (but see Butler 2002 and Porfirio 1999). In this, the sound of noir is as generic as its look, conjuring up a jazz ambience of the sort featured in *Phantom Lady* (1944), a soundscape composed less of jazz per se than of gin, marijuana and cigarette smoke.

While voice-over narration and the hard-boiled language of the genre have been the subject of critical commentary, sound in noir is a function not only of these conventional semantic elements but of sound effects, both diegetic and non-diegetic music, and, of course, silence. Accordingly, in what follows I will endeavour to talk about a number of canonical, neo-modernist films from 1967 to 1976 (see Spicer 2002: 130) from this integrated perspective as well as, as much as possible, in conjunction with the image and narrative tracks.

New Wave noir: *Point Blank*

If *Point Blank* (1967), which appeared almost a decade after Orson Welles' *Touch of Evil* (1958), can be interpreted as one man's fantasy of revenge as he lies dying alone in a cell in Alcatraz, the irony is that John Boorman's film – the

Incarceration: *Point Blank*

'first truly post-noir noir' (Hirsch 1999: 17) – also arguably represents the res-
urrection of noir as a genre. This renaissance is reflected in Johnny Mandel's
music, which reflects the influence of modern serialism and is composed in
the minimalist style of Alban Berg, the mentor of the arch-modernist himself,
Theodor Adorno. Indeed, Mandel's score is the architectural equivalent of *Point
Blank*'s bold, Mondrian-like colours and monumental *mise-en-scène*, so much
so that the film's music becomes an acoustic prison in which Walker (Lee Marvin), implacable, traverses the mean streets of the metropolis.

The popular music in *Point Blank* is showcased in the Movie House se-

Boorman's recourse to expressionist sound effects, popular music and period audio technologies also distinguishes his film. The sound – designed by
Frank Artenez, Larry Jost and Franklin Milton – is, first of all, a virtual montage
of special effects, from the sound of Walker's steps resounding as he walks
down what seems like the longest airport corridor in the world to the whirling
racket of a helicopter, the sonic antipode of Alcatraz which, Walker's unreliable
narration aside, is escape-proof and silent as a morgue.

The popular music in *Point Blank* is showcased in the Movie House sequence. In this sequence, set in a discothèque-cum-movie palace complete
with go-go dancers, the early monophonic sound of the Beatles circa 'She
Loves You' is subjected to the distorting filter of the late 1960s. Backed by a
trio playing Archie-Bell-and-the-Drells-style R&B, the EST-like vocal antics of Stu
Gardner on 'Mighty Good Times' mimic Walker's monosyllabic delivery, dully
and drolly foregrounded by the waitress's first question upon seeing him, 'You
still alive?' The multimedia presentation – images of a Botticelli Madonna alternating with black-and-white photos of a blonde model – simulate the bad acid
trip from which Walker cannot, for the life of him, escape. The sequence as
a whole reaches its surreal, absurdist denouement when Walker tries to exit
and is set upon by two of Stegman's (Michael Strong) thugs. (Earlier, Boorman
stages an automotive set-piece, a demolition-derby symphony, when Walker
repeatedly crashes one of Stegman's used cars to get him to talk.) As Walker
fights off the minions of the Organisation, the sound of cascading movie reels

provides a sonic counterpunch to the visual mêlée. A concluding shot of the model's face, frozen in a mask as in Edvard Munch's *Scream*, echoes the opening close-up of the black singer's mouth and precipitates the final shot of the sequence: Walker's face awash, as if with blood, with the multicoloured light of the slide projector.

If the Movie House *tour de force* is all about noise, the equally striking sequence in Brewster's (Carroll O'Connor) house is about the interplay between noise and silence. After a romantic rendezvous at a diner with Chris (Angie Dickinson), Walker has brought her, her romantic illusions momentarily intact, to a house where Brewster holds meetings for the Organisation. After Chris, frustrated by Walker's alternately passive and aggressive behaviour, physically attacks him, he mechanically walks over to a couch, sits down and uses the remote control – new-fangled technology for its time – to turn on the TV, switching channels until he pauses on a black-and-white commercial in which a model blankly intones, 'All I did was cream twice every night with Pond's cold cream'. Walker, however, does not appear to be interested in anything but the $93,000 the Organisation owes him. Suddenly, the house, if not Walker, comes alive as, offscreen, Chris has turned on every gadget on the premises, retaliating this time with light and sound – with, as it were, technology itself.

Walker, who in his own way is as hard-wired as the Terminator (see Hirsch 1999: 165), proceeds to walk through the house, methodically turning off lights and appliances – toaster, blender, electric mixer – until he discovers Chris, drink in hand, dancing to big-band music in the billiards room. Although Walker finally tracks down the strangely up-tempo music to a reel-to-reel player in another room and promptly turns it off, the silence is broken by Chris's mocking voice on the intercom, 'You're a pathetic sight, Walker, from where I'm standing … Why don't you just lie down and die?' The climax occurs when Walker returns to the billiards room and Chris knocks him over the head with a pool cue. This moment – the moment that Walker finally falls, literally as well as figuratively, catching Chris's ankle as he goes – is the cue for one of the most lyrical passages in Mandel's score. The ensuing montage, in which Walker is on top of Chris who metamorphoses into Lynne (Sharon Acker) who changes into Reese (John Vernon) who in turn changes back into Chris, resumes the film's pervasive sense of *déjà vu*, as if Walker is mourning his life even as he is living it.

In this extraordinary sound/image montage, the dream-like sequencing of the images, the kaleidoscopic quality of which is heightened by the non-diegetic status of the score, suggests that Walker's fantasy is something of a nightmare, not least as his downfall can be attributed to the exact moment when Reese first knocked him down at a party and, mounting him, screamed, 'Trust me'. Appropriately, the sequence ends on an audio-punctuated flashback that jolts us back to the very beginning of the film: the sound of a gunshot – the sound, that is, of Walker being shot at point-blank range in a cell in Alcatraz.

'Hooray for Hollywood': *The Long Goodbye*

While it anticipates early 1970s 'rogue cop' and right-wing vigilante films such as *Dirty Harry* (1971), *The French Connection* (1971) and *Death Wish* (1974), as well as later, paranoid-conspiracy films such as *The Parallax View* (1974) and *Three Days of the Condor* (1975), *Point Blank*, perhaps because of its new-wave provenance, is something of an anomaly in 1960s noir. In fact, in their chronology of the period, Alain Silver and Eizabeth Ward list *Harper* (1966) as the first neo-noir (see 1992: 440). However, the film that most radically deconstructs the investigative narrative that subtends the genre is neither *Chandler* (1971) nor even *Mean Streets* (1973) – a Martin Scorsese feature, part neo-noir, part neo-gangster, that takes its title from Raymond Chandler's celebrated essay – but *The Long Goodbye* (1973). Robert Altman's film not only deconstructs the myth of Marlowe, turning him into a kind of 'Rip van Marlowe', but reinvents the audiovisual language of classic noir.

In *The Long Goodbye*, the camera – panning, tracking, zooming, ceaselessly *moving* – is always, to paraphrase the director, in the wrong place. The result, combined with a *mise-en-scène* composed of mirrors, windows and glass doors, is a profusion of focal points that, as in cubism, pulverises classical cinematic space. Equally importantly, *The Long Goodbye* has a new soundtrack – dense, multilayered – 'to match its new look for noir' (Hirsch 1999: 116). The most conspicuous aspect here is Altman's anti-theatrical bias against looping and post-synchronisation. The director's corresponding preference for multiple miking and 'live sound', facilitated by technological developments such as the lavilier microphone (see Beck 2002: 158), flies in the face of traditional Hollywood practice and its penchant for clarity, accuracy and, in the last economic instance, intelligibility; it also arguably subverts the implicit valorisation of language that derives, however residually, from Chandler's text.

The other conspicuous aspect of the soundtrack in Altman's film is the use of John Williams and Johnny Mercer's 'The Long Goodbye'. Altman saw the song as a 'character in itself' (2006: 80) and appearing as it does throughout the film, changing in volume according to context, it becomes something of a hermeneutic code in its own right: 'There's a long goodbye/Can you recognise the theme?' Whether as a song on Marlowe's (Elliott Gould) car radio or muzak in the supermarket that he goes to for Curry Brand Cat Food, a tune that a piano-player is working on for the lounge-time bar crowd or as the chime of the Wades' doorbell, it is simultaneously indigenous *and* obtrusive or, like the man bandaged head to foot in the hospital bed next to Marlowe, visible and invisible.

In fact, the referential play of the hospital scene (Marlowe to 'mummy', 'I seen all your pictures too') partakes of the film's general, parodic mode of intertextuality illustrated by the Malibu Colony gatekeeper's cheesy imitations of movie stars, including Barbara Stanwyck in *Double Indemnity* (1944). Given that it simultaneously invokes and satirises classical Hollywood film music, it is no surprise that *The Long Goodbye* also remembers the origins of sound film itself. So in the sequence set in the since-demolished Los Angeles City Jail in Lincoln Heights, Marlowe, responding to the interrogating police officers who are also watching through a two-way mirror, uses the ink from his fingerprinting to blacken his face, then, after talking about a 'banjo' and flashing some 'jazz hands', breaks into a chorus of 'Sewanee'. This scene, like the score, operates on at least two levels at once. Diegetically, it is Marlowe's way of letting the police know that *he* knows that their questions are stale as a 'vaudeville routine' (Keysaar 1991: 93). From a non-diegetic point of view, Marlowe's minstrel act italicises the performative elements of his character: Gould may be Jewish like Al Jolson, but in 1970s America, he cannot pass as a black jazz singer any more than Altman's Marlowe, notwithstanding the fact that he smokes unfiltered cigarettes, drives a 1948 vintage Lincoln Continental, and wears the same ratty coat day in and day out, can be seamlessly post-synchronised with Chandler's. He is, in fact, as out-of-sync as his renditions, whether hummed, sung or whistled, of the ubiquitous theme song (see Rosenbaum 1975: 95).

In the conclusion to *The Long Goodbye*, in a subversive departure from the original novel, Marlowe blows away his ex-buddy Lennox (Jim Bouton). Cut to a tree-lined road in Mexico that could have been 'made in a Hollywood movie' (Altman 2006: 75) down which Marlowe, his meanness spent, saunters, passing Eileen Wade (Nina van Pallandt) driving by in a yellow jeep on her way – shades of *The Third Man* (1949) – to a romantic rendezvous with a corpse. Wade stops, but Marlowe does not even bother to turn his head; instead, he takes the harmonica the 'mummy' gave him ('the smallest one [he's] seen') and starts playing. Although Marlowe earlier told the 'mummy' he has a 'tin ear', the sprightly tune suggests that he has practised in the meantime. Then he grabs an old woman and does a quick jig with her as Johnny Mercer and Richard A. Whiting's 'Hooray for Hollywood' blares on the soundtrack.

Unlike the earlier reference to *A Star Is Born* (1954), when Roger Wade (Sterling Hayden) commits suicide by wading into the roaring surf outside his Malibu home at night, Altman's use of 'Hooray for Hollywood' at the very end of *The Long Goodbye* momentarily breaks the film's dramatic spell signified on the soundtrack by the final appearance of John Williams' theme sparsely and sombrely scored to drums, strings and acoustic guitar. Anticipating his own 'anti-musical' *Nashville* (1975), the concluding allusion to *Hollywood Hotel* (1938), Busby Berkeley's last feature for Warner Bros., also denotes the text's status as a noir musical, a film whose noir motifs – blood money, sexual betrayal, murder in the first degree – are reflexively sublimated in a musical *deus ex machina* that says 'Only in the movies'. Or, better yet, to cite the closing number from one of the paradigmatic American musicals, *The Band Wagon* (1953), 'That's entertainment!'

Private ear: *Chinatown*

Chinatown (1974) is, to understate the matter, a very different sort of film noir than *The Long Goodbye*. Robert Towne had the 'prototype' of Philip Marlowe, Chandler's 'tarnished knight', squarely in mind when he wrote the script and Roman Polanski, the director, has talked about the film's protagonist, Jake Gittes (Jack Nicholson), as a 'private eye in Marlowe's style' (1999).

The director's 'radically subjective' vision of Gittes also necessitated that, as in Chandler, everything should be 'seen or heard' from the character's point of view or, if you will, point of audition (1999). Ears in this context take on particular significance. Consider, for example, the memorable scene where the 'midget' played by Polanski slashes Gittes' nose. Although the 'man with knife', an allusion to the director as 'cutter', was originally supposed to slit Gittes' ear, no one today, especially given the association of private eyes with nosiness, would gainsay the decision to have 'Polanski' cut Gittes' nose. Still, as Towne's initial intention was no doubt meant to suggest, to be a private eye is also, in some sense, to be a private ear. Thus, Jake's ears prick up when he hears certain 'enigmatic' sounds: a servant wiping down the Mulwrays' car with a chamois cloth, Hollis Mulwray's (Darrel Zwerling) name being scratched off his office door.

In fact, the sound of *Chinatown*, mixed by Larry Jost, edited by Robert Cornett and re-recorded by Bud Grenzbach, is as elaborate as its period-perfect Art Deco design, producing a veritable tapestry of colourful sound effects – in particular, those having to do with water, gunshots and car horns – that embellish the deeply entangled themes of sexuality and political economy. Whether it is the waves, accented by gull cries, crashing at Mulwray's feet as he stands contemplating the nature of things at Point Fermin Park or the tap dripping like a metronome in Ida Sessions' (Diane Ladd) house, the sound of water insinuates that in the often morally arid world of *Chinatown*, water is one, if elusive, piece of the puzzle.

Similarly, the sound of gunshots, which periodically punctuate the soundtrack from the warning shots fired at Jake at the Oak Pass Reservoir to those fired at Evelyn (Faye Dunaway) and him as they escape in her car from the Mar Vista Rest Home, intimate that violence can materialise anywhere, even in the otherwise prototypically sunny orange groves of the San Fernando valley where, hemmed in by irate farmers, Jake is met with a shotgun blast. Finally, among the welter of acoustic effects in *Chinatown* – the Albacore flag snapping in the ocean wind, the incessant chorus of cicadas outside Evelyn's Alameda bungalow, the whirring fan and clacking typewriter in the background of Jake's office – there is the sound of car horns, a sound that in everyday life, at least in a city as car-crazy as Los Angeles in the 1930s, is as common as a palm tree.

Upon first seeing *Chinatown*, a casual 'viewer' might not make much of the moment when Jake is interrogating Evelyn in her parked car and, momentarily distraught, she lets her head fall against the steering wheel, accidentally setting off the horn. Certainly, the random sound of car horns at the beginning of the concluding sequence set on North Broadway in Chinatown are, even for the experienced audio-spectator, relatively inaudible, appearing as so much urban ambient 'colour'. However, coupled with the shots fired by Loach (Dick Bakalyan) and the blood-curdling scream made by Evelyn's sister *and* daughter, Katherine (Belinda Palmer), these horns prefigure the horrifying moment when we realise – like Jake, from an excruciating distance – that Evelyn has been fatally wounded. What we do not know because our ears cannot tell us is that she has been shot, true to the film's Oedipal logic, right through the eye – an image that combines with Noah Cross's (John Huston) blinding of Katherine's vision to mock the very idea of justice.

Given the film's continual metatextual play on the camera eye (see, for example, Jake's own investigative recourse to camera and binoculars), the score might appear to function as a mere supplement to Polanski's vision. But as Michael Eaton notes, before any image there is the sound of a 'solo trumpet played against strings', followed by a 'sepia-tinted monochromatic' Paramount logo that 'evokes early sound cinema' (1997: 12–13). Despite the latter retro flourish, Jerry Goldsmith's score is successful because it 'avoids all the pitfalls of a retrospective soundtrack' (Eaton 1997: 51). In other words, it works precisely because it works against itself, playing a certain avant-grade dissonance off its more conventional melodic and harmonic passages.

The score in fact called for an 'unusual combination of instruments' – harp, strings, trumpet, percussion, prepared piano – and the aforementioned moment when the trumpet enters also effects an elegant segue from 'avant-garde colour' to 1930s, blues-based 'jazz harmonies' (Hickman 2006: 317). As for *leitmotifs*, it is not too reductive to say that if Evelyn from the very first, 'photographic' shot of her in Hollis's office is associated with the harp, then Jake is affiliated with the trumpet (see Darby & Du Bois 1990: 506). Hence the initial contrast in *Chinatown* between strings and trumpet, a contrast that can be read as a musical figure for Jake's initial resistance to romance.

Goldsmith, who would later go on to write the score for *L.A. Confidential* (1997), was the perfect person to 'orchestrate' this theme. Although he studied film composition with Miklós Rózsa, the man who wrote the 'killer' music for *The Killers* (1946) and *Criss Cross* (1948), Goldsmith's scores, especially compared to the high romantic ones of Max Steiner, Erich Korngold and Franz Waxman, tend to exhibit an 'extreme economy of melodic means' (Darby & Du Bois 1990: 518). At the same time, if Goldsmith's orchestral music dramatises the 'changes which accompanied the demise of the studio system' (Darby & Du Bois 1990: 496), the soundtrack of *Chinatown* nevertheless incorporates, like *The Long Goodbye*, source music from the classical Hollywood period. For example, the Paramount vaults were raided for Brian Hooker and Rudolf Friml's 'Some Day' and 'The Vagabond King Waltz' from *The Vagabond King* (1930), while the Bunny Berigan, coronet-studded standard 'I Can't Get Started' from the 'Ziegfeld Follies of 1938' plays under the scene where Jake, employing one of the tricks of his trade, places an Ingersoll watch under Hollis Mulwray's rear left tyre to time his departure.

Still, the most significant source music in *Chinatown* is doubtlessly 'The Way You Look Tonight' from the Astaire and Rogers RKO musical, *Swing Time* (1936). In Polanski's film, Jerome Kern and Dorothy Fields' song appears for the first time as background diegetic piano music at the Brown Derby where Jake has gone to settle accounts with Evelyn. The scene, like the music, is understated, although the sexual tension is palpable, as explicit as Evelyn's rouged, Cupid-Bow's lipstick. 'The Way You Look Tonight' is later reprised in *Chinatown* when Jake returns to the Department of Water and Power and, in order to annoy the secretary and thereby hasten his meeting with Mulwray's successor, Russ Yelburton (John Hillerman), he first hums, then whistles the first few bars of the song.

After a short pause, Jake proceeds to sing a couple of lines under his breath as he studies with increasing wonder the black-and-white photographs of Mulwray and Noah Cross on the walls. The use of 'The Way You Look Tonight' is especially resonant here not simply because Jake performs it but because the lyrics, despite their original serio-comic context, anticipate the tragic circumstances in which Jake will unaccountably find himself at the end of the film:

Some day,
When I'm awfully low
And the world is cold
I will feel a glow just thinking of you
And the way you look tonight.

The chorus of Kern and Fields' song is equally, if not more resonant: 'Lovely, / Never, never change. / Keep that breathless charm / Won't you please arrange it, 'cause I love you.'

This is the paramount Faustian predicament, one that Jake and Evelyn share for one brief, fleeting moment as they bask in the post-coital glow after having made love for the first time. This intimate bedroom scene set, like the preceding bathroom one, in the most private, recessed part of Evelyn's house, opens with a classically fluid panning shot that appears to confirm Jake's status as the kind of guy who always gets the girl and does not care what happens once he has had her. As such, the 'cigarette' shot underscores the phallic connotations of the instrument that is ritually associated with him, the trumpet. And yet, the retrospective point of view of Kern and Fields' song, combined with Jake's defensive, because emotionally naked, pose, does not so much counterpoint as point up the inexorable progress of Polanski's film: paradise is mutable, perishable as an apple, and Jake has always already lost Evelyn.

This intensely lyrical subtext rematerialises with all the force of the return of the repressed in the operatic finale of *Chinatown*. In the long wake of the car horn that signals Evelyn's death, the ethereal sound of a harp shimmers one final, ghostly time as if to mark her passing. Then, as the camera begins to crane upward and the ambulance sirens swell on the soundtrack, the solo trumpet performed by Uan Rasey responds to the harp's call with a brief, bluesy wail. The concluding note of the film, 'a sustained non-tonic C', may be 'ambiguous as to destination' (Darby & Du Bois 1990: 503), but about one thing we can be sure: some destinies cannot be averted, and like Polanski himself after the senseless death of Sharon Tate, itself a traumatic repetition of his mother's death in a concentration camp, Jake Gittes will never be quite the same again.

This ear for hire: *The Conversation*

If the technological pessimism of *The Conversation* (1974) links Francis Ford Coppola's film to the anti-corporate thematics of *Point Blank*, its downbeat conclusion rehearses the tragic ending of *Chinatown*. Although Harry Caul (Gene Hackman) may not be, like Gittes, a private eye in 1930s Los Angeles (the setting, as in *Point Blank*, is contemporary San Francisco), at the end of *The Conversation* he is arguably even more alienated. In fact, Harry is not so much a 'run-of-the-mill hard-boiled detective' (Goodwin & Wise 1989: 144) as a private ear for hire. His *métier*, to redeploy Jake Gittes' *recherché* description of himself in *Chinatown*, is electronic surveillance, a vocation he pursues with a compulsion that borders on the obsessional.

Given these topical concerns, the plot of *The Conversation* is inevitably carried, as the film's sound editor Walter Murch says, 'by the sound' (in Clarke 2003: 58) and can therefore be interpreted as an allegory about the production of film sound or the sound designer as auteur. More generally, Coppola's film constitutes an acoustic inversion of Michaelangelo Antonioni's *Blow-Up* (1966), maximising the conspicuous sound effects that distinguish a film like *Chinatown* and deconstructing, as in the Hollywood musical, the sound/image hierarchy that underwrites classical realist cinema. The result is a claustrophobic, topsy-turvy audio-vision that encapsulates the paranoia and conspiratorial *Stimmung* at the very heart of 1970s neo-noir.

True to this audiovisual aesthetic, the multidimensional narrative of *The Conversation* is designed, as Coppola has admitted, 'like a piece of music' (in Clarke 2003: 58). For example, the score, which was composed by David Shire, who also wrote the music for *Farewell, My Lovely* (1975), provides a running instrumental commentary on the visual action, becoming distinctly more dissonant as the film progresses. Composed for only one instrument, the piano, Shire's *pre*-synchronised music not only bears an inverse relation to *The Godfather* (1972) and *The Godfather: Part II* (1974) that precede and succeed it but is the 'antithesis of the big-budget epic score' (Anderson 1987: 17). Like the conversation that Harry and his cohorts endeavour to decode, it is also rife with electronically synthesised noise and interference.

In addition to Shire's piano score, *The Conversation* boasts, as in *Chinatown*, a number of source songs from the canon of American popular music, including Jay Livingston and Ray Evans' 'To Each His Own' (1946), which plays, tellingly, in the background at the surveillance convention at the Saint Francis Hotel, as well as Duke Ellington's 'Sophisticated Lady' (1933) and Johnny Green and Edward Heyman's 'Out of Nowhere' (1931) which can be heard at the warehouse party where Harry falls for the femme fatale. *The Conversation* begins, in fact, on a musical note. In the opening sequence, the slightly distorted music on the soundtrack is Hughie Cannon's 'Bill Bailey, Won't You Please Come Home' (1902), played Dixieland-style by a rag-tag band of street musicians.

While this diegetic street music is the most audible part of the initial 'audio-zoom' (Beck 2002: 158), a straight cut from Union Square to a long shot of a man perched underneath the neon-lit 'City of Paris' sign followed, in turn, by a swish pan to a shot of a man wedged in a window of an office building across the quad indicates the acoustic parameters of the scene. The subsequent close-up of the second man, who is armed with a shotgun microphone with telescopic sights, introduces, however, a sinister note: caught within the crosshair of his 'rifle' like so many insects are his 'targets', Ann (Cindy Williams) and Mark (Frederic Forrest).

After an establishing shot of Union Square, we are suddenly plunged into the action at street level. Ann and Mark, we soon realise, are not only being surveilled from above but are being trailed on foot by yet another man, Paul (Michael Higgins), who is wearing a hearing aid and carrying a directional microphone concealed as a Christmas present in a shopping bag. A later shot, though fleeting, elucidates the intricate web of relations that the film ravels: a man is playing the saxophone in the foreground, Ann and Mark are in the middle ground, and in the background, on the same side of the screen as the saxophonist, is Harry, balding, bespectacled, wearing (not unlike Marlowe in *The Long Goodbye*) the same clothes he wears every day, a transparent plastic trench coat. It will soon become apparent that Harry's proximity to the saxophone player, in concert with that of the illicit lovers, is not accidental; that it bespeaks a countervailing desire on his part, one signified by the snatch of song that Ann sings right after she and Mark have moved out of Harry's immediate orbit, 'Wake up, wake up, you sleepy head…'.

Harry's dream wish, which goes totally against the grain of his self-proclaimed desire for isolation, achieves its most elaborate musical expression via the signature song of *The Conversation*, 'When the Red, Red Robin Comes Bob, Bob, Bobbin' Along'. As with the bookended use of 'Hooray for Hollywood' in *The Long Goodbye*, the recourse to this Harry Woods standard in *The Conversation* can be said to reiterate the beginning of sound cinema since one of the very first Vitaphone shorts, *A Plantation Act* (1926), features Al Jolson singing 'Red, Red Robin' – as in *The Jazz Singer* (1927) – in blackface.

Not unlike the repetition of 'The Long Goodbye' in Altman's film, the recurrence of Ann's fragmentary recitation of 'Red, Red Robin' throughout the convoluted course of *The Conversation* also engenders a lyrical motif whose contextual variations are as complex as Harry Caul himself. For example, the Harry Woods song is exploited for both lyrical and dramatic effect in the crucial post-convention sequence set at the warehouse where Bernard Moran (Allen Garfield) discloses Harry's traumatic involvement in the 'Welfare Fund' incident. After Harry throws a fit and everyone except Meredith (Elizabeth McRae) leaves, there is a stunning, deep-focus shot of the wide-open space where he was earlier engaged in conversation with her, an intimate conversation that, to his very real dismay, Moran recorded. In the background an industrial lift can be seen and as the group leaves, we can hear someone (Moran?) not only singing, like Ann, the first verse of 'Red, Red Robin' but the second, symptomatic one as well, 'There'll be no more sobbin'...'.

Harry, meanwhile, is forlornly standing inside the cage where he keeps his equipment, replaying 'the conversation'. Concerned, Meredith comes over and tells him to turn it off, but Henry continues to let it play until we hear Ann's voice on the tape – 'Wake up, wake up, you sleepy head...' – sounding, compared

Private ear: *The Conversation*

at least to the street band's raucous rendition of 'Red, Red Robin', naked and fragile. We then watch in long shot as Meredith, fully assuming her femme fatale persona, strips, but despite the lyrical prompting ('There'll be no more sobbin' when he starts throbbin"), Harry remains completely dressed, lying motionless on a cot, as impassive as Swede (Burt Lancaster) at the beginning of *The Killers*, the wire-mesh cage throwing criss-cross shadows on the clean white pillow on which his troubled head rests.

The Conversation does not conclude, however, with 'Red, Red Robin' but on another musical note that dramatically recapitulates the opening sequence of the film and both Ann and Harry's status as performers. After supervising the recording of 'the conversation', Harry returns to his apartment which is as spartan as his philosophy. The camera cuts from Harry sitting on the couch in his living room, kind of blue even though it is his birthday, to a tight close-up of his face as, glasses off, eyes closed in concentration, he blows away on his tenor saxophone along with a song on the record player. (The song, 'Blues for Harry', was composed by Shire, and Hackman's playing was dubbed by Justin Gordon.) While Harry is completely absorbed in this 'B-flat blues' (Anderson 1987: 21), the ensuing close-up of the record player emphasises, even more so than his slightly out-of-sync playing, the disjunction between live and 'live' recorded performance, an audio note reinforced by the audience applause when the record ends and by the wide centred shot of Harry seated in his straight-back chair, his head bowed as if in humble acknowledgement.

The final sequence of *The Conversation* puts a perverse twist on the above performative moment. It begins with a jarring cut from a shot of the Director's (Robert Duvall) body, covered with a blood-smeared sheet of plastic and laid out like a funeral-parlour corpse in the hotel room that Harry bugged earlier, to a classic American shot of Harry, now wearing glasses and playing the saxophone again to the aptly titled 'Love Bug' in the living room of his apartment. Suddenly, the telephone rings. Harry turns down the stereo, but when he picks up the receiver, the line is dead.

In an encore of the fixed-camera set-up that opens the first sequence set at Harry's apartment, the camera stays on the phone as he walks out of frame while, offscreen, the volume of the stereo goes back up and Harry begins playing more authoritatively than before, the sound of his saxophone expanding expressionistically to fill the room. The phone rings again and as the record ends, Harry goes over to answer it. However, in response to Harry's repeated 'hellos', there is only electronic noise and, finally, clear as a bell, the voice of the Director's nefarious assistant, Martin Stett (Harrison Ford): 'We know that you know. For your own sake don't get involved any further. We'll be listening to you.' Then the *coup de grâce*: as Harry stands up, the sound of his saxophone, distorted, diminished, comes back to him over the telephone. The player is played, the recorder recorded, the bugger bugged.

The final passage of *The Conversation* is visually and acoustically startling. In one of the most devastating conclusions in all of neo-noir, Harry, in an effort to locate the bugging device, dismantles his apartment piece by piece, a paranoia-induced act of self-destruction prefigured by the demolition of the building occurring right outside his living-room window. (Could the bug be located in his beloved saxophone?) The last thing we see is the camera as it slowly, mechanically pans from right to left over the debris-strewn space of the apartment then, before resuming its rhyming reverse pan, stops briefly on Harry, who is seated in his straight-back chair against one good wall, the saxophone to his lips, the sound resounding in the empty space as if in an echo chamber. Since there is no record playing, Harry appears to be trying to keep time to some immaculate measure in his head, an ideal tune signified by the 'piano blues progression' (Anderson 1987: 25) on the soundtrack. The screen goes black, but the audio track continues: the last thing a sound, not Shire's piano but the expiration of Harry's saxophone, dwindling note by note into the deep, enveloping silence.

Travis's 'mood music': *Taxi Driver*

Paul Schrader contends that the 'third and final phase' of film noir was a 'period of psychotic action and suicidal impulse' (1996: 106). Although the ostensible subject of his essay is the final cycle of film noir from 1949 to 1953, he might as well have been describing *Taxi Driver* (1976), which he wrote, and its 'end-of-the-line' anti-hero, Travis Bickle (Robert De Niro). In many ways, Bickle is diametrically opposed to *The Conversation*'s Harry Caul: while Harry, when faced with conflict, retreats into himself and his jazz-cocooned world, Travis, wound up inside like a spring and bereft even of the consolations of popular music, eventually releases his sexually-fuelled aggression on the hostile world around him. In fact, in the world according to Scorsese, one that is virtually unimaginable without music, Travis is effectively othered by this discourse.

For example, in the midst of his first date with Betsy (Cybill Shepherd), she tells Travis that he reminds her of a Kris Kristofferson song, 'The Pilgrim, Chapter 33': 'He's a prophet and a pusher, partly truth, partly fiction, a walking contradiction.' Simultaneously fascinated and put off by her analysis, Travis proceeds to purchase a copy of *Silver-Tongued Devil and I* (1971) at a local record store, giving it to Betsy at the beginning of their second date. This gift exchange, however, represents the apex of their relationship. Even before Travis mistakenly takes her to a matinee screening of *The Swedish Marriage Manual* (1969) at a midtown Manhattan movie theatre – on 42nd Street, no less – this disastrous moment has been foreshadowed by their widely differing views about music: while Betsy 'can't live without it', Travis does not 'follow music much' (his record player is broken, or so he says), and the only kind he appears to be acquainted with is what Scorsese calls the 'melody in his head'.

Unlike the characters in *Mean Streets*, whose restlessness appears to be a reflection of the ongoing battle between traditional Italian and rock'n'roll music fought out on the radios and jukeboxes of Little Italy, the orchestral score of *Taxi Driver*, the last one composed by Bernard Herrmann, does not so much articulate Travis's inchoate emotions as subject him to its discursive rules. Although the solo alto saxophone theme performed by Ronnie Lang is only one, albeit crucial, aspect of Herrmann's music for *Taxi Driver*, it is reflexively associated for many people not only with Scorsese's film but with noir itself. Hence Amy Taubin's résumé of *Taxi Driver*'s noir semantics: the 'first person voice-over narration, the expressionist camera angles and movements, and Bernard Herrmann's moody, jazz-inflected score' (2000: 14).

The univocal association of *Taxi Driver* with the 'jazz' motif, though, is less a reliable index of the range of Herrmann's score than a result of what Michel Chion calls a 'retrospective illusion' (in Butler 2002: 156). It is not simply that, unlike Harry Caul, Travis does not play the saxophone since, to recollect *Chinatown*, Jake Gittes does not play the instrument with which he is identified in that film. Rather, it is that the romantic melody in Travis's head is continually, insistently opposed by another, martial strain of music scored for brass, percussion and woodwinds. The musical chiaroscuro that these two competing strains produce remains counterpoised until the fateful moment when Betsy emphatically rejects Travis. As she departs in a taxi, Travis is left standing alone and bewildered on the sidewalk, a pivotal moment prepared for in the film by the appearance of the street musician (Gene De Palma) who plays in the 'syncopated style' of Gene Krupa and whose solo snare-drum rolls undercut the nostalgic, noir-period swing of the saxophone theme.

Although the 'dark, militaristic music' associated with Travis's sexual and aggressive impulses dominates the score from this moment on (Butler 2002: 160), the saxophone melody introduced by a harp and inspired by Travis's first, pristine vision of Betsy eventually returns on the soundtrack, now displaced onto the figure of the prostitute, Iris (Jody Foster), who henceforth comes to bear the burden of Travis's alternately debased and idealised conception of women. A synthesis of the two modes of music – the romantic and the martial – occurs, mediated by the 'pulsating rhythm of cymbal and snare' (Smith 1991: 351), in the bloody wake of the massacre at the apartment building. As the overhead camera slowly tracks in reverse down the hallway, surveying the carnage that Travis has wrought, the romantic jazz melody is quoted, musically integrating the themes of romantic idealisation and sexualised violence.

Two 'musical' scenes prime us for this apocalyptic climax. In the first, Travis, after having shot a black junkie dead in a convenience store, is sitting in his Bressonian room watching *American Bandstand* as Jackson Browne's 'Late for the Sky' (1974) plays on the soundtrack. A passing shot of a racially mixed couple, a young black male and white teenage girl, comments on Travis's isolation and desire for normality as well as the theme of miscegenation – transplanted from *The Searchers* (1956) – that is threaded throughout the film. In the second scenario, the so-called 'Scar' scene, Iris and Sport (Harvey Keitel), who can be seen as a version of *The Searchers*' renegade Indian, Scar, are together in the candle-lit room where she takes her clients and where Sport does his thing, speaking the discourse of mastery disguised as the language of love. Sport puts on a record (he has a record player and knows how to use it), and the diegetic music that issues is the romantic jazz melody, a cue so disorienting as to constitute a form of distantiation. It is as if Travis, whom we last saw sitting outside the apartment building in his cab, gazing up at Iris's window (not unlike the earlier, murderous fare in his taxi, played by Scorsese), is now inside, watching Sport and Iris slow-dancing.

Of course, neither the climactic massacre nor the 'letter' scene set in Travis's empty room effectively concludes *Taxi Driver*. In fact, inasmuch as one of the sources of inspiration for Schrader's screenplay was Harry Chapin's 'Taxi' (1972), Scorsese's film can be said to end, happily or not, with a taxi-driver picking up an ex-girlfriend. In this sequence, the reprise of the romantic saxophone theme seems to signal Travis's suddenly hip, heroic status, a metamorphosis supported by the 'popular urban myth of the jazz musician as outsider' (Butler 2002: 160). Like Sam Spade (Humphrey Bogart) who renounces the femme fatale, Brigid O'Shaughnessy (Mary Astor), at the end of *The Maltese Falcon* (1941), Travis – in a reversal as symmetrical as the triumphant return of 'Betsy's theme' – does not respond to her intimations of romance, dropping her off like any other fare. This time, though, Travis is the one who drives away, leaving her standing all alone on the sidewalk as he shoots back into the belly of the naked night-time city.

REFERENCES

Altman, Robert (2006) *Altman on Altman*, ed. David Thompson. London: Faber and Faber.

Anderson, Carolyn (1987) '*The Conversation*: An Exemplar and Critique of Sound Technology', *Postscript*, 6, 2, 13–30.

Beck, Jay (2002) 'Citing the Sound: *The Conversation*, *Blow Out*, and the Mythological Ontology of the Soundtrack in 70s Film', *Journal of Popular Film and Television*, 29, 4, 156–63.

Butler, David (2002) *Jazz Noir: Listening to Music from Phantom Lady to The Last Seduction*. Westport: Praeger.

Clarke, James (2003) *Coppola*. London: Virgin.

Darby, William and Jack Du Bois (1990) *American Film Music*. Jefferson: McFarland.

Eaton, Michael (1997) *Chinatown*. London: British Film Institute.

Goodwin, Michael and Naomi Wise (1989) *On the Edge: The Life and Times of Francis Coppola*. New York: William Morrow.

Hickman, Roger (2006) *Reel Music: Exploring 100 Years of Film Music*. New York: Norton.

Hirsch, Foster (1999) *Detours and Lost Highways: A Map of Neo-Noirs*. New York: Limelight.

Keysaar, Helene (1991) *Robert Altman's America*. New York: Oxford University Press.

Polanski, Roman (1999) 'Retrospective Interviews', *Chinatown*, DVD, Paramount.

Porfirio, Robert (1999) '"Dark Jazz": Music in the *Film Noir*', in Alain Silver and James Ursini (eds) *Film Noir Reader 2*. New York: Limelight, 177–88.

Rosenbaum, Jonathan (1975) 'Improvisations and Interactions in Altmanville', *Sight & Sound*, 44, 91–5.

Schrader, Paul (1996 [1972]) 'Notes on Film Noir', in R. Barton Palmer (ed.) *Perspectives on Film Noir*. New York: G. K. Hall, 99–109.

Silver, Alain and Elizabeth Ward (eds) (1992) *Film Noir: An Encyclopedic Reference to the American Style*. Woodstock: Overlook Press.

Smith, Steven (1991) *A Heart at Fire's Center: The Life and Music of Bernard Herrmann*. London: UCL Press.

Spicer, Andrew (2002) *Film Noir*. Harlow: Pearson.

Taubin, Amy (2000) *Taxi Driver*. London: British Film Institute.

3

Paranoia and Nostalgia: Sonic Motifs and Songs in Neo-Noir

HELEN HANSON

Much of the drive and activity of neo-noir criticism has been to negotiate the tensions between old and new, tracing narrative, formal and thematic continuities and breaks (for example, Gallafent 1992, Neale 2000, Bould 2005). Such criticism has been motivated by questions about key character types (for example, Gledhill 1978a, Ward 1996) and the spread of new articulations of noir across genres and media (for example, Erickson 1996, Naremore 1998, Williams 2005). Style and meaning has been a predominant concern, but one governed by visual aesthetics (for example, Place & Peterson 1996). The power of specific sound styles has been much less commonly discussed and analysed in criticism of both classic and neo-noir (see Hanson, forthcoming). These sound styles contribute to the prevailing filmic mood of anxiety that forms a continuity across classic and neo-noir – felicitously described by Todd Erickson as 'the core of its existence: the presence or portent of crime' (1996: 308).

This essay focuses on sound styles in two key neo-noir 'moments' to suggest how sound is deployed to explore different modalities of anxiety. It maps the emergence of distinctive uses of sound and music in the 1970s conspiracy thriller, in which sound recording has an important diegetic role in articulating paranoia about surveillance. It then explores the use of old-fashioned songs in 1980s neo-noirs, as part of stylised nostalgic gestures to the past. In doing so, the essay considers how sound contributes to establishing two additional 'moods' in neo-noir: paranoia and nostalgia.

Listening in: paranoia in 1970s neo-noir

If American film noir of the 1940s and 1950s darkly manifested postwar anxieties, alienation and disillusionment,[1] then the key tone of its revival in the early 1970s was paranoia. The crime film was shot through with themes of conspiracy in neo-noir thrillers, such as *The Conversation* (1974), *The Parallax View* (1974), *Night Moves* (1975) and *All the President's Men* (1976), which centred upon the experience of either suspected or real conspiracies and unfolded through suspense narratives in which the main protagonists are increasingly overwhelmed by faceless institutions or corporations.

The revival and reworking of film noir in this period coincides with a cultural soundscape highly attuned to listening. Between the Watergate break-ins in 1972 and the resignation of President Richard Nixon in 1974, the Watergate scandal brought auditory technologies, surveillance, privacy and the power of political institutions to the forefront of public attention.[2] As Jacques Attali suggests in his work on listening devices, 'the technology of listening in on, ordering, transmitting, and recording noise is at the heart of this [recording] apparatus', asking 'Who among us is free of the feeling that this process, taken to an extreme, is turning the modern state into a gigantic, monopolising noise emitter, and at the same time, a generalised eavesdropping device?' (1985: 7).

The 1970s was also a period in which sound technology was radically changing. As Charles Schreger noted:

In 1978, America seems sound obsessed. You can feel the full impact of a symphony or a rock concert in your living room; you can take it with you in your car or in a pocket-sized radio; you can – must– hear it in a dentist's office or an elevator. You can be transported or anaesthetised by it at the local disco; you can hear a mixed-media simulcast, one track on TV, the other on FM. And you can, of course, buy it on records and tapes. (1978: 34)

Schreger heralded the 'second coming of sound' to film, attributing a new 'sound consciousness' to directors such as Francis Ford Coppola (*The Conversation*) and Alan J. Pakula (*Klute* (1971), *The Parallax View* and *All the President's Men*), as well as Michael Cimino, George Lucas, Terrence Malick and Martin Scorsese – directors who deployed new technologies, such as the Dolby stereo optical system (ibid.). The development of Dolby has come to dominate discussions of sound and film form in 1970s American cinema – indeed, Gianluca Sergi classifies the 1970s as 'the Dolby era' (2004: 2).[3] As Rick Altman argues, every sound recording has a 'material heterogeneity', a signature betraying the space and ambience of its recording context (1992: 19). The dominant practice in mainstream narrative cinema, however, is to disguise or eliminate these specific signatures, silencing sound work so that it appears seamless (see Doane 1985: 54–5). Dolby fits well with this dominant practice, eliminating the mediation of recording: in post-production, filmmakers can reduce background noise and exploit greater clarity and density in their sound mixing; in playback, the stereo soundtrack can be channelled through 'directional' speakers in cinema auditoria, creating new experiences of sonic verisimilitude. Thus, Dolby privileges sonic clarity, aiming to deliver discrete sounds directly to the ears of the audience.

However, 'sound consciousness' means something quite different when we consider pre-Dolby conspiracy thrillers, which skilfully utilise sound to explore and dramatise cultural and personal fears of auditory surveillance. Their aesthetic choices carefully build an intense and discomforting mood, in which there is an interaction of theme and form: the mechanics of recording, mixing and manipulating sound are foregrounded, in order to frame the presence and processes of listening apparatuses and their operators. Consequently, a recurring theme resonates across the films – a theme which might be termed the 'unsoundness of sound'. In these ways, the neo-noir conspiracy thrillers depart from the dominant mainstream practice of seamless sound, instead using sonic signatures that foreground the presence of a mediating 'ear'.

Interviews with key sound personnel reveal this departure as integral to the sonic invention that contributes to the array of neo-noir sonography. In the pre-Dolby era, the Nagra tape recorder was the most significant apparatus in facilitating these experimental practices. The Nagra III, which used reel-to-reel magnetic tape and easily synchronised with cameras on-set, had become the industry standard by the early 1960s (see Monaco 2003: 104–5). The Nagra was small, lightweight and flexible and allowed good recording fidelity, whether it was used for location or studio recording. Its combination of mobility and reliability is repeatedly singled out by sound personnel in discussions of their work in the early 1970s. For example, Jack Solomon, sound mixer on *Night Moves*, reports that the Nagra III's portability 'revolutionised the business' (in LoBrutto 1994: 8). Chris Newman, sound recordist on *Klute*, states his preference for using a Nagra to capture 'direct sound' – particularly dialogue performance – on location, a feature of the trend in 'East Coast sound' that was typical of the move away from studio filmmaking by directors in this period (see Newman 1981: 71). And Les Lazarowitz, sound mixer on *Taxi Driver* (1976), describes the Nagra as 'made like a Rolex watch … mechanically and electronically [it] has fail safes, back ups and metering and devices to tell you when things go wrong' (in LoBrutto 1994: 127). Lazarowitz's perspective is telling, as direct sound is the most difficult element to capture on location. The Nagra permitted the greatest control for sound personnel working on the complex set-ups on films such as *Klute*, *The Conversation* and *All the President's Men*, allowing direct sounds to be reintegrated in a soundtrack that expresses the aural ambivalence of the conspiracy thriller. For example, Walter Murch's opening sound-montage for *The Conversation* achieves a remarkable medley of sound perspectives, overlaid by distortion effects, which compete for the audience's ear and create a soundtrack dense with confusion.

The Nagra finds its fictional counterparts in the recording devices of the neo-noir conspiracy thriller. Such devices are key objects, or symbolic props, in these films. Their diegetic visibility is partnered and underlined by the specific acoustic character given to sounds by strategies of sound recording and mixing. For example, the flattening of the sound range in diegetically recorded and replayed voices, the addition of reverberation, or the presence of mechanical distortion all derive from purposeful stylistic decisions to create a mood of paranoia. The acoustic character of the conspiracy thriller is replete with signatures which mark it *as* recorded or mediated by technologies.

The use and abuse of recording media are central to *Klute* and *The Conversation*, but anxieties about the power of auditory devices also recur more widely in thrillers such as *The Parallax View*, *Night Moves* and *All the President's Men*. Neo-noir conspiracy thrillers are full of scenarios where communication media are intercepted or interrupted. In these films, communications networks are integral to plot development. The protagonists are repeatedly discomfited by a sense that the communication of knowledge is open and leaky. The technologies of contemporary office communications – telephone lines, telephone answering machines, tape recorders, teletype machines – are part of the apparatus through which characters intuit and progress investigations into each narrative's enigmatic conspiracy. But these technologies are simultaneously and anxiously open to manipulation putting an intense focus on the activity of listening and interpretation. It is the manipulation of the voice through diegetic recording, and its reception through diegetic replay, that constitutes one of the most powerful ways that the conspiracy thriller constructs and explores aural ambivalence. This suggests a shift in the status, and uses, of the cinematic voice. Classic era noirs, such as *Double Indemnity* (1944), *Gilda* (1946) and *The Postman Always Rings Twice* (1946), deploy male voice-over as a central narrational device. As Karen Hollinger argues, male voice-over can present 'a point of resistance' (1996: 245), articulating noir's perplexing gender dynamics in ways that undermine the security of male subjectivity, or offer confessions which place male characters on the wrong side of the law. While classic era noir has offered critics ways of productively 'reading against the [ideological] grain' (see Kaplan 1978: 2–3; Gledhill 1978a: 9–11), the formal location of anxieties about the voice in 1970s conspiracy thrillers is different. Incorporating vocal ambivalence within the diegesis the 1970s conspiracy thrillers withdraw confidence in non-diegetic narrational positions outside the text to create a soundscape where interpretive difficulties are located in a culture replete with paranoia about auditory technologies. *Klute* provides a valuable opportunity to look at these issues in more detail.

The credits sequence of *Klute* features a small reel-to-reel tape recorder replaying the voice of sex-worker Bree Daniels (Jane Fonda) as she negotiates with a client, setting the terms of their interaction and establishing the commerce of desire. The opening question of *Klute* is, what was the relationship of the missing family man Tom Gruneman (Robert Milli) to Bree? This is the enigma that the investigative protagonist, John Klute (Donald Sutherland), must unravel and, in this sense, the opening plot elements suggest connections with earlier noir films. For example, *Dead Reckoning* (1947) revolves around war veteran

Rip Murdock's (Humphrey Bogart) search into the past of his missing comrade in arms, Johnny (William Drake), a search that leads him to Johnny's girlfriend, nightclub singer 'Dusty' Chandler (Lizabeth Scott). Like Rip, Klute's investigation is personally motivated – neither character is a member of the police force – and, like Rip, Klute becomes romantically entangled with the woman that the film seems to place at the centre of the mystery. But here the echoes end. Christine Gledhill argues that *Klute* invokes both old generic patterns of the thriller (female sexual misconduct as the centre of a male investigated enigma) and a new 'modernity and seriousness of theme, linking prostitution, psychotherapy and the problem of women, [that] places it within a humanist realist tradition of European art cinema' (1978a: 6). The film's treatment of Bree has been a significant reference point in genre debates, specifically as they relate to the representation of gender (see Giddis 1976; Gledhill 1978a and 1978b). Bree's status is complex. As both diegetic character and gendered representative of an emergent feminist critical practice working within the ideological structures of genre, she articulates a set of resonant questions: what is the status of the female voice and gendered narration in the film's discourse? As both Giddis and Gledhill note, the narration of *Klute* is fractured. The audience is offered the process of Klute's investigation, as well as sequences of the film which offer glimpses into Bree's interiority. These glimpses, though, purposefully construct ambivalence. Scenes that offer the audience access to private moments – Bree feeding her cat, attending a modelling audition, at psychotherapy sessions – are mixed with sound sequences acoustically and ominously framed by surveillance.

Stylistic manipulations of sound are central to the awareness that Bree is being watched and listened to. Specific sonic effects and motifs betray the mediating presence of recording apparatus and the intercepting presence of a listener. A scenic shift from Bree talking freely to her psychotherapist, to Bree talking on the telephone to one of her regular clients, illustrates the film's play with themes of public and private through sound. 'It's silly to think that anyone can help anyone else,' says Bree, her dialogue forming a sound bridge from the evenly-lit interior of the psychotherapist's office to the night-time street outside her apartment. Both image and sonic framing underline contrasts in the scene shift. In the office, Bree is framed in medium close-ups and the recording and mixing of her voice is even and transparent. As her dialogue bridges the transition, her voice (the trace from one location) is laid over a new space suggested by low volume urban ambient effects (faint car horns and the generic motif of city space: a low rumble). A long exterior shot of Bree's building shows her outlined by her window space and a tilt down reveals Klute in the basement listening in to her telephone conversation. Reverberation and a flattened dynamic range form the auditory frames signalling the interception of Bree's conversation, partnered by shots establishing Klute's location and his listening apparatus: the slowly revolving reels of a tape recorder.

You never know who's listening: *Klute*

In this way, the editing structures of the sequence and the mixing and styling of the sound put the act of surveillance centrally in the scene. Surveillance is further underlined as Klute follows Bree to an assignation with one of her regular clients, the elderly and sympathetically-sketched Mr Goldfarb (Morris Strassberg). As Bree, resplendent in a sequinned gown and feather boa, weaves a fantasy scenario for Goldfarb of her fictive sexual adventures, the camera pulls back to show Klute hiding in the shadows and looking on. But when Bree returns to her apartment, where Klute is waiting for her, his control of the investigation is bracketed by a framing camera position that reveals the observing presence of a third party, Peter Cable (Charles Cioffi).

The sinister intent of Cable's presence is rendered by Michael Small's extremely distinctive music.[4] The score forms part of a chorus of dissonant auditory effects in the film that include uses, and abuses, of the voice. Small structures the score with spare and disciplined instrumentation, notably keyboards (electric piano and prepared piano) with guitars and strings (violin, viola, cello and bass), and spikes it with unusual percussion and moments that weave in female vocal elements (see Renick 2005: 31–2). *Klute* was Small's first major assignment and, in interviews, he describes his approach: 'I would consider *Klute* as a thriller score that has a psychological overlay because it really depicts the inner workings of a character along with suspense elements of the genre. It's really scoring Bree Daniels' inner life' (in Koppl 1998: 48). Small designed the score to indicate the presence of the murderer, Cable, but also used female vocal elements as part of 'the siren call theme' which suggest what he calls Bree's 'obsession with control and seduction' (ibid.). Pakula similarly describes the theme as expressing Bree's 'sick calling, a thing within herself was pulling her to her own destruction' (ibid.).

This may well be true, but if Bree is susceptible to a 'sick calling' then so is the murderer, Peter Cable, as he attempts to control, capture and manipulate the voices of the call girls with whom he is obsessed. Cable torments Bree with phone calls, at first remaining silent, then in later calls replaying a tape of Bree's conversation with a client to her. Finally he corners Bree at a deserted garment warehouse and forces her to listen to a recording of the awful screams of Arlyn Page's (Dorothy Tristan) murder. This is the climactic moment of the film's sonic motifs as the score combines with the diegetic replay of Cable's recorded violence. While Bree herself is silent, discordant and disjointed piano figures with the increasingly insistent female voice, as the score elements suggest Cable's chaotic mindset and the danger to Bree. The final scene of the film, though, refuses to resolve the ambiguous narration that has been threaded throughout. The audience are offered images of Klute and Bree leaving her emptied apartment while the concomitant soundtrack offers Bree's voice-over, telling her psychotherapist that she is not going away.

The presence of Cable's tiny reel-to-reel tape recorder as a disturbing diegetic element opens up the issue of auditory media manipulation, an issue which echoes across a number of other neo-noir thrillers of the 1970s, most notably *The Conversation*, in which surveillance expert Harry Caul (Gene Hackman) struggles, and fails, to interpret the correct meaning and implications of a conversation between Mark (Frederic Forrest) and Ann (Cindy Williams), two subjects whom he is hired to bug. As David Cook suggests, ' *The Conversation* describes a world where conspiracies appear and disappear like cobwebs and where recording media are inherently duplicitous' (2002: 200).

The duplicity of technologies is also central to *All the President's Men*, 'the centrepiece of the conspiracy subgenre' (ibid.). The film opens with the keys of a typewriter slamming out 'June 1, 1972'. The extreme close-up that focuses the audience's attention on the page is partnered by the sounds of the machine. *All the President's Men* thus puts a focus on the real historical events, and their mediation, in a way that is appropriate to its mixture of noir and semi-documentary style. The film's main narrative focus – the investigation of *Washington Post* reporters Carl Bernstein (Dustin Hoffman) and Bob Woodward (Robert Redford) into the Watergate cover-up and its political implications – spreads its events across contrasting locations. The brightly-lit *Washington Post* offices, frequently framed in low-angle long shots that stress the extent of the space, are set against a range of distant and disparate locations (and informants) that Bernstein and Woodward must try to map in the course of their inquiry. A recurring and central locus in their quest are their office telephones.

Early in the film, a sequence shows Woodward pursuing a police tip-off about the Watergate Hotel break-in. Howard Hunt's name has been found in the address book of one of the burglars. A montage of close-ups of Woodward and the pad that he writes in and doodles on, and an auditory mix of telephone conversation fragments show him establishing a link between Hunt and the White House. The sound mixing puts Woodward's voice to the fore, and adds reverb to the contacts he pursues, while the sonic background is alive with the sounds of the large, busy office – telephones ring, teletype machines and type-

Alone in the web: *The Parallax View*

writers rattle. Art Piantadosi (re-recording mixer on *All the President's Men*) relates that Pakula got his sound crew to work hard on creating the ambience of the busy newsroom dealing with multiple inputs of information. He recalls Pakula saying: 'I don't want it quiet. I want all that action to go on. I want the people talking on the phone, I want the typewriters, I want the teletypes going, I see television sets so I want them running' (in LoBrutto 1994: 19).

The sequence dramatises the investigative process: Woodward's activity as a listener and interpreter of both the content and vocal intonations of his contacts is crucial, what is not said and the burring sound of broken connections when some contacts hang up is key. Jim Webb (production sound mixer on the film) recalls that a directness and tension was obtained in the scene by going to unusual lengths to record exchanges live on the set. Robert Redford and the actors that he talks to in the scene were provided with earphones so each heard and responded to the other's lines, rather than the common technique of recording each side of a filmed conversation and then reuniting them in post-production. This allowed the sound crew to record overlapping dialogue and preserve the immediacy of performance (see LoBrutto 1994: 77–8).

As their investigations progress Woodward and Bernstein themselves come under surveillance. As they plan to break their story they resort to typing messages to each other, seeking a space of visualised communication outside a leaky network of telephones that could be intercepted. Leaky networks also feature in *The Parallax View*, where newspaper reporter Joe Frady (Warren Beatty) finds himself in over his head as he tries to expose the cover-up of the assassination of Senator Carroll (Bill Joyce). He is drawn into an investigation of the Parallax Corporation, which recruits assassins for secret assignments. Frady confides in his editor, Bill Rintels (Hume Cronyn), reporting in to the office answering machine after he foils a plot to blow up a plane. Soon after he has listened to Frady's message, Rintels is poisoned by a Parallax assassin and the tape disappears, erasing the trace of Frady's actions and his ability to marshal credible evidence with which to expose the machinations of the corporation. *The Parallax View* was also scored by Michael Small, and includes a powerful sequence in which Frady tastes Parallax's manipulative methods. Part of the training of would-be assassins is exposure to a montage of images and captions accompanied by what Small calls 'a skewered patriotic anthem' (in Koppl 1998: 46). The musical structure is grandiose, referencing a rousing, anthemic style, while the editing of the image/caption mix speeds up through the sequence, juxtaposing terms like 'love', 'death' and 'mother' to prompt chaotic affect in the susceptible viewing and listening recruit. As Small suggests, 'Perhaps the conspiracy thriller genre has as its feared villain not a single bad guy, a killer lurking in a doorway, but a state of mind. That state of mind could infect anybody, it has such a universally seductive pull' (in Koppl 1998: 48).

The sonic ambivalence of the diegesis in 1970s conspiracy thrillers thus explores the fears about a secure place from which to speak, and listen, in the Watergate era. The conspiracy film reworked generic noir elements, focusing particularly on investigative narratives. As Peter Lev suggests, 'a world of shadows is appropriate to a situation in which assassination by unknown groups for unknown reasons dominates the body politic' (2000: 52). As the cultural landscape shifted into the 1980s, noir continued to prove remarkably adaptable to new contexts. In 1980s neo-noir, sonic motifs, and aesthetic attitudes to the past, were reworked through the nostalgic use of song. This constituted a different approach to sound, and offered audiences different forms of negotiation of filmic audiovisual content.

'That Old Feeling': songs, nostalgia and the replaying of desire in 1980s neo-noir

Stephen Prince argues that debates about film content in the Reagan era were part of a 'symbolic politics' characterised by 'the waging of political conflicts on cultural terrain' (2000: 341). He notes a particular focus on identity politics: the status of the family, gender relations and nation. Films of this period have also been influentially discussed by Noël Carroll and Fredric Jameson as characterised by a self-conscious referentiality to past themes and forms. They both discuss *Body Heat* (1981) as exemplary of this trend. For Carroll, *Body Heat's* generic allusions to older forms mark a moment in cinema in which 'quotations, the memorialisation of past genres, the reworkings of past genres, *homages*, the recreation of "classic" scenes, shots, plot motifs, lines of dialogue, themes, gestures ... [were] crystallised and codified' (1998: 241). In Jameson's conception, that codification is precisely an empty one, situated within signals of the past taken out of history – that is, the kind of pastiche that, for Jameson, typifies the imitative postmodern style.

Richard Dyer's work on pastiche offers a different viewpoint. Dyer argues for the recognition of complex moves, and affects, that can occur in the layering of past styles within contemporary forms. Rather than jettisoning pastiche as ahistorical, he points out that in the remobilisations of referentiality there is the possibility of contemporary forms bearing an affective freight arising from the dual movement across both likeness and difference. In having 'extreme closeness with elements of discrepancy and slight distortion', a pastiche film is 'very like but not quite' the same as its antecedents and can 'set in play our relationship to the past' (2007: 175; 178).

Prince's perspective, and Dyer's work, suggest that, within the multiple and referential allusions that neo-noirs make to past styles and themes, there is more going on, more being expressed, than just a 'fad' for the repackaging of what Geoffrey O'Brien terms 'a particular sheen' (1991: 168). It is the expressive and symbolic gestures that a number of neo-noirs make towards the past, particularly in their placement and use of songs, that I want to focus upon, with a specific focus on gender politics and their relation to nostalgia.

Body Heat inaugurates its central fatal attraction between lawyer Ned Racine (William Hurt) and femme fatale Matty Walker (Kathleen Turner) by introducing her in a moment heavily marked by fantasy. Early in the film, on a night shimmering with heat, Ned walks past a band playing old-time big-band tunes outside to see Matty walking down the aisle. The controlled colour palette of the cinematography makes Matty glow and flicker, a phantasmatic incarnation of feminine fatality, as the diegetic song adds further layers of association. 'That Old Feeling' – a 1938 song, composed by Sammy Fain with lyrics by Irving Kahal – constructs the moment as both narratively contemporaneous and already marked by a feeling of the past: 'I saw you last night and got that old feeling / When you came in sight, I got that old feeling / The moment that you danced by, I felt a thrill / And when you caught my eye, my heart stood still.' This is a feeling 'as old as desire itself, but also specifically a feeling suggested by jazz noir' (Dyer 2007: 122).

In its use of an old-fashioned song to inaugurate the desire between Ned and Matty, *Body Heat* is doing more than simply supplying a generic reference to an older form. 'That Old Feeling' allows a gesture to the past in a way that is crucial to the modalities of desire in neo-noir. A number of films deploy old songs – that is songs written outside the time frame of the narrative setting – in order to capture a specific affective flavour from the past. Films such as *Blue Velvet* (1986), *Someone to Watch Over Me* (1987) and *Sea of Love* (1989) not only include, but also draw their titles from, old songs.[5] In order to explore the nostalgic symbolism of song in neo-noir, I want to focus upon a particular case study, but one that has wider generic resonances: Ridley Scott's *Someone to Watch Over Me*. To grasp the operation of this nostalgic symbolism we need to be alert to the structures and backgrounds of the songs themselves as well as their uses within the films.

The songs in *Someone to Watch Over Me* – George and Ira Gershwin's 'Someone to Watch Over Me' (1926) and Jerome Kern and Otto Harbach's 'Smoke Gets in Your Eyes' (1933) – hail from the tradition of the American standard song and were written during the golden age of Tin Pan Alley, by some of that era's most accomplished composers and lyricists. Robert Furia points out that Broadway's songwriters worked within the strong constraints of 'the standard':

> Almost every song from the golden age is built upon the same musical pattern of a thirty-two bar chorus structured in four eight-bar units, usually in an AABA sequence ... The formula made songs easy to write: think of a pleasant eight-bar melody, repeat it, shift briefly to another melody for the eight-bar B section, or 'release,' then return to the main melody for the final A section. (1990: 130)

To illustrate, the chorus of 'Someone to Watch Over Me' begins with melody A ('There's a somebody I'm longing to see / I hope that she turns out to be / Someone to watch over me'), repeats this melody with different lyrics ('I'm a little lamb who's lost in the wood...'), then shifts to melody B for the release ('Although he may not be the man some girls think of as handsome / To my heart he carries the key'), before repeating melody A one more time ('Won't you tell him please to put on some speed...').[6] The lyricists had to match this melodic structure, usually in fifty to 75 words. The tight patterning of 'standard' songs gives them the characteristic of expressing 'one moment's feeling in a fluid statement' (Sheila Davis, quoted in Furia 1990: 14).

Perhaps it is the standards' qualities of direct expression that sees them enduringly linked with romance. Ian Garwood suggests that this link is based on 'the perception that older songs engage more transparently and expressively with the idea of romance than more modern, and cynical, artistic texts' (2000: 283). In Hollywood cinema, this link is most commonly associated with contemporary romantic comedy. In neo-noir, however, the standard song plays, or replays, modes of feeling, and character and audience invest in them differently. The narrative structures and events of romantic comedy construct certain verisimilar feelings for the duration of the film (love is true, the union of the couple is fated). The love triangles, dangerous and fatally destined desires of neo-noir produce a different mood, but despite neo-noir's image as cynical, I think it would be wrong to term this 'unromantic'. The strategic placement and presence of the standard song can and does produce a strong affect by expressing feelings or longings that it is not possible, nor ideologically permissible, for the narrative events to fulfil.

Someone to Watch Over Me opens with a sequence that uses its title song non-diegetically as a signifier of old-fashioned romance and old-time urban glamour. The opening credit sounds establish location and spatial dimension.

Distant sirens and the city's generic traffic rumble-and-echo are heard over the credits as the first shot visually establishes a New York night-time setting. Its composition centres upon the Chrysler building, one of the city's most potent cine-architectural metonyms for the glamour of a bygone modern era. On the soundtrack 'Someone to Watch Over Me' comes in. The specific version, performed and arranged by Sting, and the use of a contemporary performer to render an old standard is part of neo-noir's rearticulation of older forms. The opening then moves through three leisurely aerial shots that traverse the city from central Manhattan across the Queensboro bridge to Queens, and is timed according to the duration of the song.

The image and the sonic qualities of the song performance and lyric – 'She's the big affair I cannot forget / The only girl I ever think of with regret' – work together to establish a nostalgic romance to the cityscape, as well as distinguishing two contrasting areas of New York, across which the narrative takes place. Manhattan is the home of Claire Gregory (Mimi Rogers), a seductive, 'classy', independently wealthy and cultured socialite who is the material witness in a murder case. Queens is the down-home neighbourhood where working-class detective Mike Keegan (Tom Berenger) lives with his wife, the tough-but-tender Ellie (Lorraine Bracco), and son, Tommy (Harley Cross). The film exploits the contrasting parts of the city to enhance the differences between Claire's and Mike's social and class backgrounds.

After she witnesses the murder of her friend, Win (Mark Moses), by violent and well-connected crime boss Joey Venza (Andreas Katsulas), Claire is forced to accept round-the-clock police protection while Venza is still at large. Mike, newly promoted to the rank of detective, is one of the team assigned to 'watch over' Claire. While Claire is under police protection, a romance develops between her and Mike. Thus the film plays out the familiar scenario of a noirish love triangle. It also exploits the differences in Claire and Mike's social backgrounds and illustrates how the affair endangers the family unit.

Sexual attraction, followed by the attendant dangers and fracturing of romance, are filtered through the use of standard songs which offer a distinct contrast between the simplicity and transparency of connection – 'one moment's feeling' – and the complexity of adulterous desire in the film's narrative events. For example, as Mike accompanies Claire to a reception, their passage through the city is overlaid non-diegetically with a languorous version of Cole Porter's 'Begin the Beguine' (1935). The lyrics playfully foreground the romantic effect of music – 'When they begin the beguine / It brings back the sound of music so tender... / I'm with you once more under the stars' – that is played out a few scenes later. The night before Claire is due to identify Venza in a police line-up, she invites Mike to celebrate the end of her ordeal. As they drink cocktails and trade confidences, a sensuous instrumental version of 'Someone to Watch Over Me' is played live in the bar. The song's repetition, this time with the characters as listeners, endows the song with a special status. Its perform-ance as mood-mediator in the bar permits it to take on an expressive agency for the characters' desires, and as the film's title song it figures for the audience as a signal that 'This is the big affair / [They] could not forget'.

The song is also nostalgic in several ways. At this point in the story it seems that Claire's role as witness will soon be finished, so the song expresses an idea of desire already out of reach. But it is also symbolically nostalgic, that is, the vision of romance evoked in the standard's condensed lyric imagines a fantasy scenario in which the terms of desire are simple. A tough working-class cop enjoying a dalliance with a classy dame is not only the stuff of classic noir, but of a different formation of gender relations. Stuart Tannock suggests that 'nostalgia approaches the past as a stable source of value and meaning' (1995: 455) and that one key index of that past is gender relations: 'a past in which everything is held in its "proper" place, where '"men were men, women were women and re-ality was real"' (1995: 455, quoting Doane & Hodges 1987: 3). The romantic fan-tasy offered by the song cannot be resolved within the film's narrative relations, bound as they are within a noirish (transgressive) love triangle. In the contrast between lyric and narrative, the film registers difference in a fatalistic tone.

This is clear as the narrative moves to its conclusion. Venza escapes cus-tody, and Mike's developing affair with Claire endangers her, his family and his police colleagues as desire blurs his ability to 'watch over' all those close to him, failing to fulfil a normative masculine position. As Mike spends the night with Claire, Ellie and Tommy are threatened by a prowler, and taken care of by officers from Mike's squad. Later in the film, Mike's work partner T. J. (Tony Di Benedetto) stands in for Mike on the protection night shift, while Mike is sup-posed to be resolving his marriage problems. But, unable to stay away from Claire, Mike comes to her apartment and sleeps, while T. J. keeps watch. The dead night hours are marked by a diegetic radio playing 'Smoke Gets in Your Eyes'; the soft, low volume of the song weaves a mood of longing, but the lyr-ics attest to blindness in love, and plot events form a counterpoint as one of Venza's accomplices silently enters the flat and shoots T. J.

The final diegetic instance of the standard in *Someone to Watch Over Me* has a role in the plot's emotional resolutions. Claire sits alone at a function commemorating a music school, founded by her father. As the band plays the opening chords of 'Someone to Watch Over Me', Mike appears. As they dance to the song that articulates their connection, Mike breaks off their doomed af-fair, telling Claire that 'it couldn't have worked'.

The film comes to a symbolic and bloody denouement in Mike's home. Ellie and Tommy are taken hostage by Venza, and Mike and Claire become involved in a shoot-out in which first Tommy, and then Claire, are endangered. The final shots of the film re-establish the family 'proper' as the errant Mike is reconciled with Ellie.

As the film's final credits roll the title song is heard for the last time, in a version performed by Roberta Flack. The re-use of the song partners the opening credits, but having the song delivered by a female performer suggests Claire's loss. In this replaying of the lyric, 'He's the big affair I cannot forget / The only guy I ever think of with regret', the combination of image and sound expresses the desires that the narrative resolution has ideologically resolved. The old-fashioned song suggests desire as always already out of reach, a feeling common to desire in neo-noir as simultaneously invoked but seldom fulfilled.

In the use of old standards to both articulate and foreclose neo-noir desire, we can hear a 'memorialisation' as well as a longing for a mode of expression that only exists as an echo. As Dyer argues, 'Pastiche noir is able to recognise and mobilise the structure of feeling it perceives to have been caught by classic noir. It does also seem to say: they don't make them like this anymore. This may be a source of regret and nostalgia – if only we still did Angst and sexiness like this' (2007: 130). In this way *Someone to Watch Over Me* can exploit the glamour of classic noir even while it aligns itself with its contextual symbolic politics in its resolution.

In conclusion, attention to the specific sonic styles that are deployed in two different moments of neo-noir allows us to acknowledge the role of sound in neo-noir's ongoing replay and reworking of classic noir's themes and concerns. Attention to the complexity and richness of sound as part of neo-noir's styles and meanings permits us to key into neo-noir's affective array, and its shifting and potent articulations of anxiety. One must of course be wary of making generalisations about periodisations. There are, after all, nostalgic neo-noirs in the 1970s, such as *Chinatown* (1974) and *Farewell, My Lovely* (1975), and paranoid ones in the 1980s, such as *Angel Heart* (1987), *No Way Out* (1987) and *Jacob's Ladder* (1990). Similarly, some 1970s neo-noirs make use of standards and other mainstream popular music from earlier in the century, such as *The Long Goodbye* (1973) and *The Conversation*, while as the lip-synched performance of 'In Dreams' by Ben (Dean Stockwell) in *Blue Velvet* suggests the use of such music in the 1980s is not always straightforwardly nostalgic. However, to the extent that the films I have discussed in detail above can be taken as representative, it is possible to propose some general trends across these two decades. In the 1970s, there was a much greater sense of foregrounding new technical possibilities, including sound technologies. Challenging classical filmmaking conventions by fragmenting and creating dissonance between sound and image opened up an array of potential relationships between them and between the audience and the film. This unsoundness and sense of fluid possibility was well-matched to a focus on public life in a decade of political scandal and countercultural activism. In the 1980s, these potentials were closed down as technical possibilities were increasingly integrated into the construction of overwhelming spectacles and other totalised, self-enclosed film experiences.

This tendency was itself matched by a retreat from public politics and a shift of narrative focus on to the personal and domestic, often promoting reactionary utopian visions – such as the supposed 'authenticity' of the blue-collar nuclear family over the dangerous allure of wealth and class aspiration in *Someone to Watch Over Me* – based upon the profoundly ideological unsoundness of an illusionary past.

NOTES

1   Such associations were recognised even at the time: see, for example, Houseman (1947: 161), Borde & Chaumeton (1996: 25) and Schrader (1996: 54).

2   On 17 June 1972 five men were arrested for breaking into the headquarters of the Democratic National Committee at the Watergate Hotel complex in Washington D.C. The subsequent investigation into the break-in exposed illegal activities and fiscal and political corruption at the heart of the Nixon administration, as well as attempts to cover up the Watergate break-in. Investigations by the FBI, Senate Watergate Committee and House Judiciary Committee exposed Nixon and his staff as party to activities such as campaign fraud and illegal wire-tapping. Nixon's resignation followed after the House Judiciary Committee issued a subpoena for tape recordings of conversations in his office which implicated him in the Watergate cover-up.

3   Dolby was developed in 1973 and was first showcased in spectacular genre films, such as Ken Russell's musicals *Tommy* and *Lisztomania* (both 1975) and Lucas's science fiction blockbuster, *Star Wars* (1977). Given *Star Wars'* position as a watershed film for historians tracing the emergence of New Hollywood's blockbuster era, it is easy to lose sight of the fact that it was preceded by, and overlapped with, experiments in film sound exploiting continuities with earlier sound technologies.

4   Small is renowned for his expertise in scoring neo-noir suspense thrillers, also working on *The Parallax View*, *Night Moves*, *The Postman Always Rings Twice* (1981) and *Black Widow* (1986). Small describes his liking for the genre: 'To me "noir" style always has mystery and distance. There is a space provided for an experience that can be quite subtle' (in Koppl 1998: 48). Small's expertise for scoring in ways that explore this space leads Kyle Renick to dub him 'the poet of paranoia' (2005: 30).

5   A further interesting connection which there is not space to discuss fully here are British neo-noirs which centrally feature old songs, such as Neil Jordan's *Mona Lisa* (1986) and Dennis Potter's television series *The Singing Detective* (1986).

6   'Someone to Watch Over Me' is relatively unusual for a standard in retaining a verse before this chorus. While considered the most important part of popular songs in the preceding century, by the 1920s verses were treated merely as introductions (see Starr & Waterman 2006).

REFERENCES

Altman, Rick (1992) 'The material heterogeneity of recorded sound', in Rick Altman (ed.) *Sound Theory Sound Practice*. London: Routledge, 15–31.

Attali, Jacques (1985) *Noise: The Political Economy of Music*. Manchester: Manchester University Press.

Borde, Raymond and Étienne Chaumeton (1996 [1955]) 'Towards a definition of *film noir*', in Alain Silver and James Ursini (eds) *Film Noir Reader*. New York: Limelight Editions, 17–25.

Bould, Mark (2005) *Film Noir: From Berlin to Sin City*. London: Wallflower Press.

Carroll, Noël (1998) *Interpreting the Moving Image*. Cambridge: Cambridge University Press.

Cook, David (2002) *Lost Illusions: American Cinema in the Shadow of Watergate*. London: University of California Press.

Doane, Janice and Devon Hodges (1987) *Nostalgia and Sexual Difference: The Resistence to Contemporary Feminism*. New York: Methuen.

Doane, Mary Ann (1985 [1980]) 'Ideology and the practice of sound editing and mixing', in Elisabeth Weis and John Belton (eds) *Film Sound: Theory and Practice*. New York: Columbia University Press, 54–62.

Dyer, Richard (2007) *Pastiche*. London: Routledge.

Erickson, Todd (1996) 'Kill me again: Movement becomes genre', in Alain Silver and James Ursini (eds) *Film Noir Reader*. New York: Limelight Editions, 307–29.

Furia, Robert (1990) *The Poets of Tin Pan Alley*. New York and Oxford: Oxford University Press.

Gallafent, Ed (1992) 'Echo Park: Film noir in the "Seventies"', in Ian Cameron (ed.) *The Movie Book of Film Noir*. London: Studio Vista, 254–66.

Garwood, Ian (2000) 'Must you remember this?: Orchestrating the "standard" pop song in *Sleepless in Seattle*', *Screen*, 41, 3, 282–98.

Giddis, Diane (1976 [1973]) 'The divided woman: Bree Daniels in *Klute*', in Bill Nichols (ed.) *Movies and Methods: Volume 1: An Anthology*. London: University of California Press, 194–201.

Gledhill, Christine (1978a) '*Klute* 1: A contemporary film noir and feminist criticism', in E. Ann Kaplan (ed.) *Women and Film Noir*. London: British Film Institute, 6–21.

____ (1978b) '*Klute* 2: Feminism and *Klute*', in E. Ann Kaplan (ed.) *Women and Film Noir*. London: British Film Institute, 112–28.

Hanson, Helen (forthcoming]) 'Sounds of the city: The sonic fabric of film noir', in Ian Franklin and Robynn Stilwell (eds) *The Cambridge Companion to Film Music*. Cambridge: Cambridge University Press.

Hollinger, Karen (1996) 'Film Noir, Voice-Over, and the Femme Fatale', in Alain Silver and James Ursini (eds) *Film Noir Reader*. New York: Limelight Editions, 243–59.

Houseman, John (1947) 'Today's hero: A review', *Hollywood Quarterly*, 2, 2, January, 161–3.

Jameson, Fredric (1983) 'Postmodernism and consumer society', in Hal Foster (ed.) *Postmodern Culture*. London: Pluto Press, 111–25.

Kaplan, E. Ann (1978) 'Introduction', in E. Ann Kaplan (ed.) *Women and Film Noir*. London: British Film Institute, 1–5.

Koppl, Rudy (1998) 'Michael Small: Scoring the director's vision', *Music from the Movies*, 21, Autumn, 46–53.

Lev, Peter (2000) *American Films of the 1970s: Conflicting Visions*. Austin: University of Texas Press.

LoBrutto, Vincent (1994) *Sound-on-Film: Interviews with Creators of Film Sound*. New York: Praeger.

Monaco, Paul (2003) *The Sixties: 1960–1969*. London: University of California Press.

Naremore, James (1998) *More Than Night: Film Noir in its Contexts*. London: University of California Press.

Neale, Steve (2000) *Genre and Hollywood*. London: Routledge.

Newman, Chris (1981) 'East Coast sound: An interview with sound recordist Chris Newman', *Wide Angle*, 4, 3, 70–3.

O'Brien, Geoffrey (1991) 'The return of film noir!', *The New York Review of Books*, 14 August, 168.

Place, Janey and Lowell Peterson (1996 [1974]) 'Some Visual Motifs of Film Noir', in Alain Silver and James Ursini (eds) *Film Noir Reader*. New York: Limelight Editions, 65–75.

Prince, Stephen (2000) *A New Pot of Gold: Hollywood Under the Electric Rainbow 1980–1989*. Berkeley and London: University of California Press.

Renick, Kyle (2005) 'The poet of paranoia: An appreciation of the late, great Michael Small', *Film Score Magazine*, September/October, 30–5.

Schrader, Paul (1996 [1972]) 'Notes on film noir', in Alain Silver and James Ursini (eds) *Film Noir Reader*. New York: Limelight Editions, 53–64.

Schreger, Charles (1978) 'The second coming of sound', *Film Comment*, 14, 5, 34–40.

Sergi, Gianluca (2004) *The Dolby Era: Film Sound in Contemporary Hollywood*. Manchester: Manchester University Press.

Starr, Larry and Christopher Waterman (2006) *American Popular Music: From Minstrelsy to MP3*. Second Edition. New York: Oxford University Press.

Tannock, Stuart (1995) 'Nostalgia critique', *Cultural Studies*, 9, 3, 453–64.

Ward, Elizabeth (1996 [1974]) 'The post-*noir* P.I: *The Long Goodbye* and *Hickey and Boggs*', in Alain Silver and James Ursini (eds) *Film Noir Reader*. New York: Limelight Editions, 237–41.

Williams, Linda Ruth (2005) *The Erotic Thriller in Contemporary Cinema*. Edinburgh: Edinburgh University Press.

4

The End of Work:
From *Double Indemnity* to *Body Heat*

CARL FREEDMAN

Billy Wilder's *Double Indemnity* (1944) is among the earliest major instances of film noir, and it has long been among the most popular and successful as well: 'the greatest movie ever made', in Woody Allen's hyperbolic formulation (quoted in Crowe 1999: 338). Though the genre is too varied and complex for any particular film to be completely typical, it would be difficult to name another that comes closer to providing a paradigm for noir. The three major characters, all sharply drawn and all superbly acted, are as integral to noir as any types one could name. There is the insurance salesman Walter Neff (Fred MacMurray), the ordinary and reasonably genial Everyman, who is not intrinsically evil but led by lust, greed, weakness and gullibility to commit an evil act that results in his own destruction. There is the bored housewife Phyllis Dietrichson (Barbara Stanwyck), the dangerous ice-blonde seductress whose sexual irresistibility is counterpointed by her absolute lack of honour, conscience or emotional warmth. And there is the insurance investigator Barton Keyes (Edward G. Robinson), the smart hard-boiled detective who moves with toughness and savvy through an amoral world while maintaining a personal code of honesty and compassion that he tries to camouflage beneath a gruff manner.

The plot is relatively simple. Walter and Phyllis conspire to murder her rich, unsympathetic husband (Tom Powers) so that they can share both the pay-off from a large accident-insurance policy and (as far as Walter is concerned) the pleasures of romance with one another. It superficially seems like the perfect crime – and Walter's inside knowledge of the insurance business is crucial to making it work – but the whole thing soon falls apart, as Walter himself, with his better judgement, has always foreseen it would. After one or two false starts, Keyes begins to solve the crime with remarkable speed; and so the noose starts to tighten around Phyllis and Walter. Meanwhile, Phyllis's cold nature and cynical motives become increasingly apparent to Walter, and the burning passion he briefly felt for her cools. At the end, Phyllis lies dead in her mansion, shot by Walter, while he, shot by her, lies seriously wounded at the insurance company for which he works, waiting for the ambulance to provide the medical care that will allow him to walk unaided into the San Quentin gas chamber.[1] Keyes, who normally takes great pleasure in cracking a case, is left to survey the scene with unspeakable sadness. The fact that Walter's confession provides him with the final few details of the crime that he was unable to deduce for himself hardly compensates Keyes for the loss of the man who has been his best friend as well as his business associate. Throughout the film Walter has been helping to light Keyes' cigars, but now, as the incapacitated Walter lies bleeding on the office floor, Keyes lights a cigarette for him. The film's final lines are almost unbearably poignant:

Neff: Know why you couldn't figure this one, Keyes? I'll tell you. 'Cause the guy you were looking for was too close. Right across the desk from you.
Keyes: Closer than that, Walter.
Neff: I love you, too.

Though Wilder made many romantic comedies (and co-authored all the screenplays), this is, I believe, the only film where the words *I love you* are uttered with full intent by any Wilder character.

My point, however, is not only that Walter's jocular but totally sincere expression of affection for Keyes – uttered here not for the first time in *Double Indemnity* – gives unusually explicit voice to the homoerotic feeling that many critics consider to be characteristic of film noir. To be sure, Wilder's movie precisely fulfils the familiar noir pattern whereby the solid reliability of masculine friendship is contrasted with the dangers and unpredictability of heterosexual dalliance. Indeed, *Double Indemnity* even places considerable stress on the lifelong bachelorhood of the early-middle-aged Walter and the late-middle-aged Keyes; and both are doing just fine until Walter, while always at heart knowing better, allows himself to fall for the delicious but poisonous feminine charms of Phyllis.

At least as important as the homoeroticism itself, however, is the fact that Walter and Keyes are not just men together but *co-workers* and business associates. It is no accident that the movie's final scene, where the mutual affection between the two is most overt, should take place (like the first substantial scene and many scenes thereafter) at the Los Angeles headquarters of the Pacific All Risk Insurance Company: for a shared participation in and loyalty to the firm has always provided not only the institutional context for the personal friendship but a good deal of its affective content as well. If there is something quasi-sexual between the two men, then the equivalent of a proposition or a marriage proposal comes when Keyes suggests that Walter is 'too good' to remain a salesman and should instead become Keyes' own assistant in the claims department (an offer Walter coyly declines). In a sense, indeed, Walter's worst sin is not so much the murder of both Dietrichsons – for the viewer cannot feel very sorry for either – as the betrayal of the company to which he and, even more, Keyes have devoted their lives.

All work and no play: *Double Indemnity*

I do not mean that Wilder himself particularly endorses corporate loyalty as an ethical ideal. The Austrian director is in many ways a late follower of German Expressionism; and, while never positively socialist, he tends to be sceptical of capitalist values. But he also understands the capitalist transformation and exploitation of labour to be a fact of enormous affective as well as economic weight. A recurring shot in Wilder's films is of rows of identical desks in a large corporate building. Variants occur not only at the Pacific All Risk but also at the headquarters of the New York insurance company in *The Apartment* (1960) and at the Berlin headquarters of Coca-Cola in *One Two Three* (1961). In each case, the shot is neo-expressionist in tone (the Berlin setting of *One Two Three* has important political and aesthetic resonances), and suggests the alienating power of capitalism to render the company big and the human beings who work there relatively small. But, as Wilder implicitly insists, such alienation is, after all, the ground of our psychic being as subjects of capitalist society. In all three films, the characters' actions and emotional lives are inseparable from their involvement with the companies that employ them. It is worth noting that, if most of Wilder's romantic comedies have always seemed insufficiently romantic to many tender-minded viewers, it is because Wilder is nearly always honest enough to insist that love is not really separable from labour and money. Perhaps money can't buy you love, but love is most assuredly *not* all you need. Most people also need a job, and everyone needs hard cash. Even in a comparatively minor Wilder film like *The Fortune Cookie* (1966), a man's yearning for the wife who left him cannot be addressed without insurance fraud and the practice of personal-injury law; and here the results of insurance fraud are less catastrophic than in *Double Indemnity*, but not painless or purely comic either.

Wilder also sees, however, that the reification of labour under capitalism does not necessarily preclude a dialectically antithetical utopian dimension. Walter and Keyes are not just employees of the Pacific All Risk, but unusually talented employees, who take great pride and satisfaction in their work. Walter is consistently the firm's top salesman, and, when Keyes tries to bring him into the investigative side of the business, he insists, 'Nobody's too good to be a salesman'. Keyes himself seems to be virtually a legend in his field: 'the best claim man on the Coast' (Cain 1978: 63). The screenplay that Wilder co-authored with Raymond Chandler discards this particular line from James M. Cain's 1936 novel. But it expands Keyes' role and makes clear that the fearlessness, for instance, with which Keyes can show elaborate disrespect for Mr Norton (Richard Gaines), the company's imbecilic young president, is based on his being that rare employee whose superlative talent and value to the firm render him immune to the terrors of the pink slip. The hard-boiled detective fiction that (as the names of Cain and Chandler remind us) is so consequential for so much film noir leaves its greatest impact on *Double Indemnity* in the film's upholding of the ethic and pride of the jobholder. It is significant that the confession which Walter leaves for Keyes on wax recording cylinders is explicitly designated by him an 'office memorandum'. Even the title (inherited from Cain) ratifies the movie's insistent stress on work and enterprise; there are surely not many films that are called by an arcane technical term from the insurance (or any other) business.

To some degree, Lawrence Kasdan might appear an appropriate candidate to have remade *Double Indemnity*. Kasdan, like Wilder before him, is a versatile, commercially proficient screenwriter/director, with a string of hits in various genres. But the comparison is superficial. Wilder, though always commercial in intention and usually in success as well, is also one of the true artistic giants of Hollywood cinema: the maker not only of *Double Indemnity* but of such other masterpieces that followed as *The Lost Weekend* (1945), *Sunset Blvd.* (1950), *Some Like It Hot* (1959) and *The Apartment* – not to mention lesser but still excellent films like *Stalag-17* (1953), *Witness for the Prosecution* (1957) and *One Two Three*, as well as later and to this day much underrated aesthetic (if not popular) triumphs like *The Private Life of Sherlock Holmes* (1970), *Avanti!* (1972) and *The Front Page* (1974).

Kasdan, by contrast, is seldom more than a competent hack with an undeniable flair for box office. He is best known for such shallow 'feel-good' schlock as *The Big Chill* (1983), *The Accidental Tourist* (1988) and *Grand Canyon* (1991). He has a pronounced imitative bent, which has not, in general, served him well artistically. *The Big Chill*, for example (whose very title, connoting death, is a shameless imitation of Chandler's *The Big Sleep* (1939)), is a not-quite-actionable plagiarism of John Sayles' ground-breaking *Return of the Secaucus Seven* (1980); and it manages to eliminate nearly every thoughtful, vital element in Sayles' movie. *Silverado* (1985) is a lifeless confection of western motifs culled from dozens of earlier and mostly better movies; while Kasdan's *Wyatt Earp* (1994), though surely the most ambitious film ever made about that classic American hero, is hopelessly clumsy and dull compared to such much superior precursors as John Ford's *My Darling Clementine* (1946) or John Sturges' *Gunfight at the O.K. Corral* (1957).

All play and no work: *Body Heat*

Yet in *Body Heat* (1981), his first film as a director, Kasdan manages to craft a film that, if hardly the equal of *Double Indemnity*, is nonetheless not unworthy of comparison with its great predecessor. Far from merely copying his betters like Sayles or the great western filmmakers, Kasdan here establishes a genuinely *revisionary* relationship with Wilder in something like the strict Bloomian sense: that is to say, the interest of *Body Heat* lies not only in the ways that Kasdan follows Wilder but, even more, in the ways that he swerves from the earlier director. Since it thus both accepts and radically modifies the patterns established by one of the major noir classics, *Body Heat* may be considered among the most purely and precisely *neo*-noir of all films.

The storyline of *Body Heat*, for instance, follows the basic trajectory of *Double Indemnity* but with certain elements of the earlier film accentuated and others effaced. 'I killed him for money, and for a woman', Walter Neff confesses near the beginning of Wilder's film. 'I didn't get the money, and I didn't get the woman.' Ned Racine (William Hurt), Kasdan's hapless protagonist, could repeat these sentences word for word. Ned, though like Walter not irredeemably evil, is even greedier, weaker, more lustful and more gullible; and he falls even harder for Matty Walker (Kathleen Turner) than Walter falls for Phyllis. Matty herself is even more ravishingly beautiful than her counterpart (or, at least, the collapse of Hollywood's Production Code Administration in the period between 1944 and 1981 allows the viewer to see a great deal more of Turner's beauty than of Stanwyck's), and, amazingly, she manages to be even more cynical and ruthless. Her husband, likewise, is even more repellent than his predecessor. Whereas Tom Powers' Dietrichson is merely grumpy, tight-fisted and self-absorbed, Richard Crenna skilfully plays the smooth, smiling Edmund Walker as having more than a hint of the genuinely evil about him.[2] One difference between the two films is the absence, in Kasdan's, of any character who fully corresponds to Barton Keyes – an important matter to which I will return. Another difference is that *Body Heat*, unlike *Double Indemnity*, does not end in death. Ned winds up in prison – evidently serving a life sentence for the first-degree murder of Edmund – while Matty gets away scot-free with the entirety of Edmund's large estate. In the movie's final scene she is sun-bathing in some unidentified tropical paradise.[3]

In the best known critical contrast between the two films, Fredric Jameson celebrates *Body Heat* as a 'postmodern' artefact in which the sense of temporality or historicity is self-consciously blurred (see 1991: 20–1). *Double Indemnity* represents, in a comparatively straightforward way, the America of the 1930s (for Wilder maintains the prewar setting of Cain's novel, explicitly dating the action in 1938). But, says Jameson, the apparent 1981 'present' of Kasdan's film is compromised not only by the way that *Body Heat* self-consciously evokes its precursor – so that the spirit of the 1930s maintains a ghostly presence in the later film – but also, and more ingeniously, by the ways that Kasdan's script and cameras manage to avoid any reference or image that would date the movie too precisely. This is a shrewd observation, and Jameson might have gone on to note that at some points the chronological signs in *Body Heat* are not just indeterminate but positively confusing. Perhaps the best example is the sequence where Ned and Matty, during their adulterous transports in the Walkers' Florida mansion, must struggle against the brutal summer heat; Kasdan merely ignores the obvious fact that, at any time even vaguely around 1981, no Florida home of remotely comparable affluence would be without air-conditioning.

But Jameson himself ignores the most important aspect of the relative ahistoricity in *Body Heat*: namely, the way that, as we will see, the film's weakened sense of history helps to make possible Kasdan's determined erasure of the whole problematic of labour, business and economic activity that is so important for *Double Indemnity*. In the later film there is nothing at all that corresponds to the Pacific All Risk Insurance Company, which in a certain sense might almost be considered the dominant 'character' of the earlier film. Ned is an attorney, a small-town solo practitioner; and, whereas Walter Neff is an excellent salesman, Ned is a miserably incompetent lawyer – a point established in an early courtroom scene and later ratified by a key plot twist that depends on Ned's proven inability to accomplish so elementary a legal task as writing a valid will. But then, Ned – again emphatically unlike Walter – dislikes his job anyway. In an interesting exchange between Ned and Edmund over an apparently friendly dinner (where, however, the sense of unspoken tension and menace is unmistakable), the film considers the whole matter of work only to dismiss it:

Ned: I don't like it [practicing law] much. [*To Matty.*] Call me Ned, will
         you?
Edmund: What's to like? That's the way of the world. Most people despise
         their jobs.
Ned: Do you?
Edmund: No. No, I love it. But it's not a job.
Ned: What is it exactly?

Edmund replies vaguely, but 'it' turns out to be a large, shady network of financial and real-estate investments in which Edmund, it appears, serves as a front man for organised crime: something that, for Edmund and for the film, is decisively removed from the world of ordinary labour. Again the contrast is sharp with *Double Indemnity*, in which Dietrichson, straightforwardly enough, works (like co-screenwriter Chandler during one period of his life) at a white-collar job in the oil industry.

Kasdan's retreat from the world of labour is perhaps most markedly displayed by the absence from the film of any character truly comparable to Edward G. Robinson's Barton Keyes, in whose personality the importance of work is most emphatically clear. One could argue, however, that the Keyes figure is not exactly eliminated in *Body Heat*, but merely split in two: that is, into the prosecuting attorney Peter Lowenstein (Ted Danson) and the police detective Oscar Grace (J. A. Preston). These men do indeed appear to be Ned's best friends, and the film stresses both the personal bond of friendship and the latter's homoerotic connotations. Lowenstein, for example, likes to prance around, at least when with Ned, in a stereotypically effeminate way, and at one point jokes that, though married, he derives his sexual pleasure mainly from listening to the stories of Ned's own conquests.[4] But, in contrast to Keyes, Lowenstein and Oscar are not Ned's actual colleagues – even though all three are, very broadly speaking, in much the same line of work – and the amount of attention the film devotes to their professional labour is reduced to the absolute minimum needed for plot coherence. The one exception is a brief montage, entirely without dialogue, that shows Oscar going here and there, doing his work of detecting; in this sequence we can glimpse (barely) the ghost of the police procedural that *Body Heat* otherwise so carefully avoids being. Yet even this exception is not really so very exceptional: for Lowenstein informs Ned (and the viewer) that Oscar's unusually strenuous efforts are motivated not so much by the pride or honour of the jobholder as by the more strictly personal desire to find evidence that may exculpate his good friend Ned in the case of Edmund Walker's murder.

The thing that mainly fills the space left vacant in *Body Heat* by the relative absence of work is – logically enough – leisure. Since Ned is an untalented lawyer who dislikes the practice of law, it is unsurprising that he seems to spend as much time as possible doing other things. Kasdan's camera rarely find Ned attending to professional chores, but – even apart from his sexual trysts with Matty – again and again shows him engaged in various leisure-time activities: driving around in his red convertible, having a drink in a bar, listening to a band at an outdoor concert, walking or jogging down the beach, enjoying some food in a restaurant, or enjoying some carnal pleasures with attractive, anonymous young women (anonymous, that is, for the film and, one suspects, for Ned too). It seems clear that he plans to use the fortune he expects to acquire from Edmund's death not in order to help improve his position within the legal profession but in order to abandon work altogether and thereafter to spend all his time, as it were, on vacation. Work is for Ned essentially a nuisance – a nuisance financially necessary but, he hopes, only temporarily so; and this hope, no less than his passion for Matty, drives him to commit murder. Once again the contrast with *Double Indemnity* is clear: for Walter's turn to crime springs partly from impulses that grow out of his *fascination* with his job. He has worked so long and so hard at trying to prevent fraud from being perpetrated against the Pacific All Risk that he eventually comes to wonder whether he could not work the opposite way and perpetrate the perfect fraud himself. In his confession, he makes clear that this rather technical interest in outwitting the system is a longer-standing motive than his desire for Phyllis and the big money.

The relative occlusion of work in *Body Heat* is related to the film's generic composition. Not only quintessentially neo-noir, it also belongs to a genre that, owing to the Production Code, did not and could not exist in commercial Hollywood cinema when Wilder (whose struggles with the Code are legendary) made *Double Indemnity*: namely, the sex film (or 'soft-core porn' film), whose interest lies largely in the opportunity to gaze at beautiful unclothed bodies, especially when engaged in sexual activity. Kasdan's film made Kathleen Turner a star practically overnight, and her stunning face and figure were hardly less important for her stardom than her fine dramatic performance. William Hurt was already something of a star, but *Body Heat* greatly enhanced his stature; and his own amply-displayed physical charms were in no small part responsible. Of course, it might be argued that the generic tendency of the sex film in *Body Heat* is itself thoroughly neo-noirish, in that it merely actualises certain potentialities always present in classic noir but thwarted by Code censorship. After all, sexual themes are prominent in noir from the beginning, and no motif is more common than the gorgeous femme fatale like Phyllis Dietrichson. There is some truth to this idea; but the matter is also more complex.

Whether, if permitted by the censors, Wilder and the other makers of classic noir 'would have' filmed such sumptuous sex scenes as Kasdan offers with Turner and Hurt is finally, like all other counter-historical questions, a moot point. The fact is that such scenes were impossible during the main cycle of noir, and this comparative visual chasteness leaves considerable cinematic space for the concern with work and professional activity that is so particularly strong in *Double Indemnity* but that is also fairly common throughout much other classic noir – from a founding text like John Huston's *The Maltese Falcon* (1941), which hinges on Sam Spade's standards and professional code of honour as a private detective, to such a late instance as Don Siegel's *The Killers* (1964), which treats contract killing as an occupation and career much like any other. When Kasdan combines neo-noir with the sex film, offering up generous visual servings of spectacular lovemaking, the effect is to help repress the noirish concern with work and to introduce the alternative problematic of leisure – the dominance of which makes *Body Heat* contrast so strongly, as we have seen, with its precursor-film. For sex, as Ned Racine would probably agree, might be considered the ultimate leisure-time activity: both in the sense that sex (except when expressly motivated by the will to propagate) typically strives towards no practical goal beyond itself, no *telos* save for pleasure and love, and also in the sense that to savour the sort of expansive, unhurried lovemaking represented in *Body Heat* it greatly helps to have an economic position or routine that allows for a good deal of free time.

The valorisation of leisure is thus virtually built into the sex film. This point can be usefully illustrated by contrasting Kasdan's movie with another major film of the 1980s, that neglected Brechtian masterpiece of American Marxist-feminist cinema, Lizzie Borden's *Working Girls* (1987). In a sense, this film, set in an upscale brothel, is about nothing *but* sex; the actresses (if not the actors) are uniformly attractive; and a considerable amount of bare skin and sexual action is on view. Yet *Working Girls* is by no means a sex film, and its porno-graphic value – its capacity to stimulate erotic desire – is almost nil. The reason is quite simply that here sex is not a leisure activity. Sex here is, precisely, *work*, at least for the prostitutes from whose viewpoint the film is constructed. Probably the most memorable single line of dialogue in *Working Girls* is the (al-most-)parting shot that the protagonist, the Yale-educated lesbian hooker Molly (Louise Smith), delivers to her exploitative madam and boss (Ellen McElduff): 'Lucy, have you ever heard of surplus-value?' Perhaps Lucy has, for she was once a working girl herself; but it is certain that *Body Heat* has never heard of surplus-value. How could it? Just as Ned aspires to be, the film is on vacation nearly the whole time.

This vacation ethos that Kasdan's film shares with its protagonist is insepa-rable from the film's own 'vacation' from history that Jameson identifies. In order to understand more fully the representation of work, leisure and history in *Body Heat*, it is, however, necessary to historicise the film itself, especially *vis-à-vis Double Indemnity*. One might be tempted here to suggest a typically Jamesonian aesthetic periodisation, for instance the 'modernism' of classic noir as against the 'postmodernism' of neo-noir. But a more concrete and useful way of exploring the terrain is to consider the earlier and later films in relation to what remains the defining and bifurcating event of twentieth-century American (and not only American) culture and economy – namely, World War Two – and also with regard to the later vicissitudes of postwar economic development.

As Walter Neff conveniently illustrates, *Double Indemnity* represents a world in which men still wear hats and in which a man might appropriately be dressed in a white shirt and a dark tie even while hurling a bowling ball down a lane. This small point of fashion neatly encapsulates the prewar big-city America of 'real' (masculine) work, a world that today may be nostalgically viewed as more 'authentic' than its postwar successor. It was a world in which the US still enjoyed a predominantly manufacturing economy rather than the predominantly service economy that was to follow, a world where the 'genuineness' of (largely) urban production had not yet yielded, on the balance sheets or in public consciousness, to the suburban and ex-urban preoccupation with consumption. While representing this world, however, Wilder's film also suggests its imminent decline. It is significant (beyond the mere functioning of plot mechanics) that the business where the work ethic of Walter and Keyes features so prominently is not a traditional industrial or manufacturing firm but an *insurance* company, that is, an economic entity whose output is only ambiguously (or, arguably, not at all) productive in the strict Marxist sense. The postwar world in which the manipulation of FIRE (finance, insurance and real estate) increasingly trumps the production of tangible things – the very world through which Edmund Walker moves so expertly – is thus already prefigured.

Furthermore, *Double Indemnity* is concerned, after all, not only with insurance but with insurance *fraud*. Indeed, the film stresses that such fraud is more-or-less routine – and not *only* to be found in such elaborately malevolent conspiracies as Walter and Phyllis's murder plot – by introducing the audience to Barton Keyes in a scene that shows us a much pettier instance of the same thing. The evidently penniless Sam Garlopis (Fortunio Bonanova), whose truck has been destroyed by fire, sits in Keyes' office, angrily demanding that all he wants is his money, i.e., his claim on a fire-insurance policy. Keyes, of course, is way ahead of him, and, having determined that Garlopis set the fire himself, replies that all Garlopis is going to get is the cops. But Keyes, though always tough, is never cruel. Having defeated the hapless policy-holder in the battle of wills, he does not actually call the police, but only insists that Garlopis sign a waiver on his claim before going on his way – after which Keyes rants to Walter for a while about the lunacy of selling insurance to such a man in the first place.

This emphasis on fraud figuratively suggests a certain instability in American capitalism, a surrounding climate of economic anxiety that is psychologically concretised, for instance, by the way that the threat of false claims is always disrupting Keyes' digestion and his sleep. Such anxiety and instability are, of course, precisely what one would expect to find in a film set during the Great Depression, from which the US was just barely emerging when Wilder's movie was made. *Double Indemnity* is, in fact, a Depression film: not in the overwhelming and social-realist way typified by John Ford's earlier *The Grapes of Wrath* (1940), but not quite so subtly that this aspect of the film should have been overlooked to the degree that it has been. True enough, the major characters are largely shielded from the worst ravages of contemporary capitalist upheaval: Walter and Keyes because they happen to hold jobs at which they are brilliantly accomplished and hence of great value to their employer, and the Dietrichsons because they are rich. Yet even the Dietrichsons are not completely insulated from the general economic anarchy. When Walter drives up to their mansion, he is impressed, but guesses that the owner may well be having trouble paying for it; and, sure enough, we learn from Phyllis shortly thereafter that her husband is having serious cash-flow problems (which is why she prefers insurance fraud to simply killing Mr Dietrichson for his estate). Much more typical of the general American lot than the wealthy Dietrichsons are certain of the film's minor characters, who serve to provide some socio-economic background: Sam Garlopis himself, for instance, who looks extremely unprosperous and who must, presumably, be in pretty desperate financial straits to try his hand at arson; or the irritable but relatively honest Nino Zachetti (Byron Barr), whose medical education has evidently been derailed at least in part by his inability to pay for it.

Double Indemnity, then, possesses a fine sense of its own historical moment. Made during World War Two, it represents the world of the 'classic' pre-war manufacture-based capitalism being thrown into such awful turbulence by the Great Depression, while also – in the choice of the insurance business as its own thematic focus – subtly and presciently looking ahead to the FIRE- and service-based capitalism that was to become increasingly important and eventually dominant after the war. Indeed, the keen historical self-awareness that the film displays is surely enabled, in large part, by its chronological location on the temporal cusp, so to speak, that the year 1944 amounts to. Though all times are times of transition, 1944 – the year, it should be remembered, that saw the establishment of the Bretton Woods international monetary system that so crucially helped to stabilise postwar capitalism for a quarter of a century – remains as far-reachingly transitional a date in modern American history as one could easily name.

1981 is a very different historical moment. By the time that *Body Heat* hit the screens, the de-industrialisation of the US is well underway, and the nation's traditional manufacturing base is being increasingly ravaged by domestic undercapitalisation and the concomitant export of manufacturing jobs overseas and south of the border. Indeed, this process is just about to intensify yet further, as the newly-elected Reagan administration prepares a massive reorientation of American tax, fiscal and monetary policy to the greater glory of the bond market and the greater immiseration of labour.[5] The 'long down-turn' in the US domestic economy can, of course, be traced back to the end of the spectacular postwar boom than ran aground by the late 1960s or early 1970s; Richard Nixon's 1971 abrogation of the Bretton Woods agreement is often taken as a convenient temporal marker.[6] But, by the early 1980s, the ominous decline of the domestic American economy (for most Americans other than those in a position to enjoy the profits from FIRE and from certain large, low-waged service industries) had widely penetrated mass consciousness. In much popular imagination it was typified, for example, by the alarming crisis that had struck the US auto industry. During the postwar boom, Detroit had been home to America's signature manufacturing enterprise, a branch of industry in which the global dominance of the US had seemed invulnerable; but now domestic auto-making was in a panic caused largely by efficient competition from Japan. It might be added that, when *Body Heat* appeared, America's terrible economic malaise had recently been aggravated by the political and moral humiliations of the Iranian hostage crisis that began in 1979.

We are now in a position, then, to articulate the *fundamental* contrast between Wilder's film and Kasdan's – and to see that this contrast is a function not so much of the strictly generic shift from classic noir to neo-noir as of the passage from one moment to another in the history of American capitalism. At the moment of *Double Indemnity*, history, despite the ravages of the Depression and the uncertainties of wartime, is still going *with* the United States: so that it is no surprise to find this American film possessing such a keen sense of its own position in the march of time. The American work ethic is alive and well, and work can be amply and properly rewarded. Despite the film's tragic ending for Walter and Phyllis – and, indirectly, for Keyes – there remains an underlying optimism condensed in the fact that the ending is in fact perfectly *happy* for the movie's largest 'character', the Pacific All Risk Insurance Company. Such optimism seems well founded. It is reasonable to suppose that, in the parallel universe where the Pacific All Risk actually exists, the firm went on to grow mightily during the postwar boom and, even after the boom collapsed – by 1981, say – was continuing, as a member of the charmed ring of FIRE, to rake in profits that would have astounded the late Mr Keyes and that even the ineptitude of the ageing Mr Norton could not spoil.

For most Americans, however, history is clearly going *against* their country by 1981; and *Body Heat* responds by turning its back on history. This is the deep logic of the deliberate 'postmodern' fuzziness that the film adopts with relation to its own temporal setting; and, since it is ultimately nothing other than human labour that makes human history, the retreat from history is at one with the larger retreat from work itself. In a society in which the ability to create actual wealth is steeply declining in relation to the manipulation of the paper profits of FIRE, labour becomes an increasingly uncongenial and marginal topic. Edmund Walker is, in a way, perfectly right to say that what he does in order to get money is 'not a job'. Wholly engaged, it seems, on the wilder illegal shores of FIRE, he does not hold a job in any sense that a traditional factory worker – or Sam Garlopis – or even Walter Neff or Barton Keyes – would understand the term.

What mainly distinguishes Matty and Ned from Edmund is that, whereas Edmund's entrepreneurial intelligence appears to be razor-sharp, Matty's only conspicuous talent is for heartless seduction and murderous scheming; and poor Ned does not seem to possess any real talents at all. Both yearn only for leisure. Matty achieves it; the final shot of her on a sun-drenched beach is as pure and emphatic an image of leisure as a director could offer. Ned, less happily, winds up in prison, enduring an existence that amounts to a hideous parody of leisure. Ironically enough, though, it is while behind bars that Ned, evidently for the first time in his life, becomes genuinely engaged in some purposeful work. He suspects that Matty, whom the police believe to have been blown up in an explosion that she herself set, is actually alive and well; and he performs some quite creditable detective work (which even Keyes himself might have admired) to establish that this is true. But so what? It is, of course, too late. As he lies trapped in his tiny cell like an animal in a cage, work – and everything else – have really ended for Ned Racine, the shining all-American anti-hero at the dawn of the Age of Reagan.

NOTES

1   Wilder actually shot the gas-chamber sequence, and later described it as one of the two finest sequences he ever directed. Excluded from the film's final cut, it has evidently been lost (see Sikov 1998: 210 and Naremore 1998: 81–95).

2   It may be no coincidence that Crenna had played Walter Neff in Jack Smight's undistinguished 1973 television movie version of *Double Indemnity*, which attempts, very clumsily, to follow Wilder's original closely; it is (barely) worth watching for Lee J. Cobb's performance as Barton Keyes.

3   The beach scene, with mountains in the background, looks as though it could be in Hawaii; but Matty is presumably shrewd enough to appreciate the wisdom of being farther removed from US law enforcement authorities.

4   Is this the truth of Sam Malone, Danson's Casanova-like character in the popular television sitcom *Cheers* (1982–93), which Danson made almost immediately after *Body Heat*?

5   The term *immiseration* is used here in its precise Marxist sense: i.e., to refer not necessarily to 'misery' in any colloquial or absolute sense but to a widening discrepancy in the standard of consumption between those who produce surplus-value and those who extract it.

6   See Brenner (1998) for the most nearly definitive treatment to date of the global turbulence of postwar capitalism.

REFERENCES

Brenner, Robert (1998) 'Uneven Development and the Long Downturn: The Advanced Capitalist Economies from Boom to Stagnation, 1950–1998', *New Left Review*, 229, 1–265.

Cain, James M (1978) *Double Indemnity*. New York: Random House.

Crowe, Cameron (1999) *Conversations with Wilder*. New York: Knopf.

Jameson, Fredric (1991) *Postmodernism, Or, The Cultural Logic of Late Capitalism*. London: Verso.

Naremore, James (1998) *More than Night: Film Noir in its Contexts*. Berkeley: California University Press.

Sikov, Ed (1998) *On Sunset Boulevard: The Life and Times of Billy Wilder*. New York: Hyperion.

5

Worlds Without Consequence: Two Versions of Film Noir in the 1980s

EDWARD GALLAFENT

How was film noir present in the crime/police thriller of the mid-1980s? I want to consider two films imbued with noir elements, but which do not identify themselves exclusively with it. They articulate for us why they cannot reproduce classical noir; in both cases it is the limitations of the meanings and functions of sexual desire in the films' 1980s worlds that is the issue. The films are *Jagged Edge* and *To Live and Die in L.A.*, which are both set in contemporary California and were released within a short period of each other in the autumn of 1985. Although they deal with subjects that might be appropriate to noir, and foreground one or two characteristic signs of it, they use them in such a way as to proclaim their distance from classical noir. This may be a way of insisting on their modernity, their freedom from the kind of project where we are either asked to return to the past or to reflect on the poverty of the present in comparison to a remembered but lost world.[1]

I will begin with *Jagged Edge*, in which one noir element is very plain. It is the figure of a private investigator, a single man from a generation older than that of the principal characters, one who is good at his job, drinks too much, was fired from his position at the District Attorney's office when unable to stomach a fix, and affects a cynical view of the figures around him, especially the men. He even has a name which sounds as if it is only one jump away from the classic texts: Sam Ransom (Robert Loggia).

Sam is a minor, although not unimportant character in the film's plot. He does the donkey work of investigation and he is present at the denouement. His position in the film marks a shift from the terms of classical noir, the once central figure reduced to a supporting role. But while this is the overt connection, there are other less obvious ways in which *Jagged Edge* depends on elements drawn from noir and to read those we need to consider its action.

I will give a résumé of the main lines of the plot. After a glamorous establishing shot of the Golden Gate bridge, it turns to night and foul weather and to an isolated luxury house on the coast, in which two women are brutally murdered by a figure whose face is concealed by a mask. They are the wife of the rich couple who live here, and her maid. The third occupant of the house is the husband, who has been taken to hospital with head injuries. The film offers us its central conundrum: is it possible that the injuries are self-inflicted and the husband murdered the two women? Or are all three the victim of an unknown psychopath – 'some fucking Charlie Manson' as District Attorney Krasny (Peter Coyote) says? The words remind us that such things do happen, but that these fears can be manipulated, used to provide a cover for the murder of a spouse.

The professionals in the crime business – the District Attorney and his assistants – rapidly come up with a motive and a sketch of a plot. They see a rich wife who is about to divorce her husband, a man who stands to inherit his wife's business empire. When a witness claims to have seen a knife with a jagged edge in the husband's locker, they charge him with the murders. The man's lawyers want to send for a top defender from New York, but he tells them he wants someone local. As this conversation ends, we cut to the first shot of the top-billed star of the film, Teddy Barnes (Glenn Close). Responding to the offer of a partnership in the law firm, she agrees to meet the man accused, Jack Forrester (Jeff Bridges).

After various pieces of business that I will return to, she agrees to take the case. As the investigation proceeds, so does a seduction, which results in Teddy and Jack sleeping together for the first time on the night preceding the beginning of the trial – as if their being lovers were for one or both of them a necessary preliminary to it.

When it is revealed in court that Jack had an affair which he concealed from Teddy, she briefly loses part of her confidence in him, but continues with the case, accepting the reasonable fact that lying about an affair does not show that he murdered his wife. She now has what appear to be two lucky breaks, one the discrediting of the witness who claimed to have seen the knife, and one which is the product of a series of anonymous letters. This involves the film's version of a Manson, a figure who may possibly be guilty of an earlier assault on another woman and of murdering Jack's wife. She is able to sketch a plausible, alternative plot explaining the murders to the jury, who duly bring in a not guilty verdict.

There seems to be a hesitation on her part, but she overcomes it – after all, a jury has found this man not guilty, so he is not guilty – and she returns to his home, and his bed. When she wakes, after a long sleep, she stumbles across a piece of incontrovertible evidence of his guilt: the typewriter on which the anonymous letters were produced. She flees to her home, in due course letting him know that she has found the typewriter. The film now seems to reprise its opening moments, with the masked figure bearing the knife making his way through a house to find a woman in bed. Only this woman shoots him dead and the mask is pulled off to confirm that this is Jack, guilty all along.

Forms of explanation

In the opening part of the film we will have asked two questions (or needed two explanations) and these are related to questions that Teddy is asked, and asks of herself. One is, why does she agree to take the case? And the other, dependent, of course, on the first, is why does she want to sleep with this man? Or, why is she unable to prevent herself from doing so, given what he may have done? *Jagged Edge* supplies two forms of answers to these questions: a literal piece of plotting which has nothing to do with the terms of film noir; and a narrative of desire which does have noir origins.

The first is a slightly over-elaborate piece of plot to do with moral guilt and redemption. We learn that when she worked in the D.A.'s office Teddy assisted Krasny in the prosecution of Stiles, a career criminal who was convicted despite evidence that would have cleared him, which was withheld by Krasny with Teddy's at least implicit consent. Stiles has committed suicide in prison and Teddy, facing his mother (Phyllis Applegate) at the funeral, recognises her guilt in the eyes of another mother. So to defend Jack is to take another individual accused by Krasny and to invite history to repeat itself (which it obligingly does – Krasny withholds evidence again) but this time to opposite effect, to expose the corruption of the D.A.'s office and to free an innocent man. It seems that this logic has been followed through, as the verdict is followed by a public statement from Teddy linking Krasny's behaviour in the two cases and exculpating Stiles, again under the gaze of the mother. (The fact that Stiles was black underlines the thought that this is being offered as a relatively straightforward narrative of guilt and redemption, that Stiles was an obvious victim of the white, ruthless D.A.).

I want to argue that the Stiles plot is the merest cover for Teddy's behaviour. Even though she might claim it as her motivation in defending Jack, it is less important than the other drives that the film exposes.

Desire and the homme fatal

The issue here of course is Teddy's desire for Jack and this can be understood easily if we notice that *Jagged Edge* reproduces many elements of the structure of relationships of classic film noir, while reversing the gendering of the roles.[2] So Teddy – the ambiguously gendered name is a hint for us – is in the position of the noir hero, posed between two figures of the opposite sex. They are Matthew (Guy Boyd), her ex-husband, whose entirely benign role makes sense once we associate it with the noir role of the good/domestic woman. On the other hand she is fatally attracted to a beautiful body that combines the power of seduction with deadliness. Only here the body is male: the structural position of the femme fatale has been taken by Jack. Again, the name is presumably a hint for an audience who, even in 1985, would have heard the echo of the name of a glamorous American president linked to notorious tales of seduction. And Jack begins the film in a familiar position, analogous to that of the femme fatale contained by a marriage in which the nature of the sexual relationship is cloudy but where the power is based on the retention of financial control by the spouse – Elsa Bannister (Rita Hayworth) in *The Lady from Shanghai* (1947), for example. Once we have recognised this structure, we can analyse Teddy's behaviour in terms of the perverse elements typical of noir, in which the hero, lured by the homme fatal, becomes a victim of her own desires.

The background to this is a familiar story of domesticity and its relation to sexual satisfaction. We learn that Teddy is divorced, with two small children who live with her, and that she is on friendly terms with her ex-husband. He clearly shows interest in reviving their sexual relationship: after leaving his sleeping children at the close of a visit, he attempts to kiss Teddy. Two elements of the moment are interesting – one that it takes place in the children's room, and the other that Teddy is wearing a garment that contrasts with most of her costumes: a bright red housecoat. This garment appears in another, later sequence in Teddy's bedroom, when she discusses boys with her daughter, who goes on to tell Teddy how much she misses her father. So the film offers the domestic/family world as a space in which desire can be variously explicitly and implicitly expressed, but is linked to a feeling of anxiety, or aversion, as if this isn't (or isn't any more) the right location for it. Even on the single occasion on which Teddy asks Jack into her home, their embrace in the living room is ruined by the appearance of her son on the stairs. We could sum this up by saying that while Teddy is constructed as a loving mother, she is not a domestic woman (the children confirm that she cannot cook).

Away from the domestic world Teddy is a very different figure. Let us turn again to her first appearance in the film, in which she is being persuaded to defend Jack. Her appearance – her carefully-dressed blonde hair, and the expensive look of her clothes (a charcoal grey woollen cardigan, light grey skirt) speak to her confidence, her knowledge of her own value and attractiveness. As we see her in public in successive costumes, the cumulative effect is that she is smartly, elegantly, casually dressed – too beautiful, or too independent, to need to conform completely to the dress codes of a law office, or the demands of a family.

Her desire for Jack turns on his being the opposite of the domestic male. He is not a parent, and he too cannot cook – their one meal together is ordered in. He presents himself as an elegant, rich cowboy, as is stressed in small ele-

Dressed to kill: *Jagged Edge*

ments of the set design of the house (the mounted horns), in his clothes and in his associations with wide open space (his horses, and the beach). As the romance takes off, it is constructed visually through Jack and Teddy's carefully harmonised clothes, as if they want to speak to each other sartorially about their suitability. The key colour here is light grey. The film moves from harmony at their first meeting (Teddy all in grey wool, Jack in casual khaki shirt and jeans) to a closer rhyming in the sequence on the beach (both in versions of light grey) to the toning clothes (light turquoise and grey) of their racket match, which they remove to make love for the first time. If we are in danger of missing any of this, director Richard Marquand underlines it with the horses which are part of the apparatus of Jack's seduction: another pair of magnificent animals in grey.

An element of the relation between Jack and Teddy which has its roots firmly in noir is the presentation of the seduction not as a gradual process, but as if it were inevitable from the first seconds of their meeting. Let us look at two moments here. The first might seem to contradict my argument, in that Teddy arrives for the initial meeting with Jack with her children, as if she wants to use them to send a message to him about her status. But they are used not to assert her domesticity, but to underline her theatrical shift from that role. We see Teddy slip on her posh shoes, check her hair. When she asks the children, 'How do I look?' their friendly chorus of 'weird!' recognises that their mother is now a thing from another world.

Jack takes Teddy immediately to the stable and the key moment in her fall is encoded, typically for noir, in what the couple are doing with words. She, not overtly quoting, poses a statement about men and horses. Jack's response is the words 'Oliver Wendell Holmes', locating the quotation. But as he delivers the line he does not turn to or look at her; there is no quality of interrogation, or need to search for a correct answer. His averted glance, the ease with which he responds, carries a message: not 'look what I know, my culture and my scholarship', but 'I already know exactly what you know, as if we had always known each other – we are already intimate'. She watches him – she is lost.

So the affair is presented as a form of spell or trance. It is not breakable by the intrusion of literal data from the world, such as the discovery of Jack's former girlfriend. Even the moment when the D.A. offers the (true) explanation of how Jack attacked his first victim as a cover for killing his wife, Teddy brushes aside as a further example of Krasny's deviousness.

Finally the noir hero has, however reluctantly, to wake up to the truth about the fatal partner – which might involve asking some questions about oneself, or choosing not to ask them. The detail that Teddy has enjoyed a sleep of extraordinary length suggests that her awakening might be potentially more than just literal, and the use of the typewriter raises significant questions about the couple's motivations. We might feel that as Teddy chooses to look for bed linen she is unconsciously searching for something else, and as the typewriter is so poorly concealed we could ask why Jack has not destroyed it or taken more pains to hide it. The same is true a few moments later when Teddy has taken the typewriter to her car. The film uses the familiar routine of a car that will not start and there is some enjoyable suspense involving whether Jack will notice the typewriter under the coat that half conceals it.

All of this taken together suggests that Jack and Teddy are inviting discovery by the other. This is reinforced when Teddy, now in her own home, deliberately lets Jack know that she has the typewriter, rather than simply telling the police or Sam. (The typewriter is itself a gesture to noir. It is an object which has come out of the past: not a modern machine but, as Sam spells out, a 1942 Corona, something left over from a classical noir set.)

Noir closure

There is a configuration in classical noir in which the final confrontation between the hero and the fatal lover destroys them both, although it is not quite clear until the last seconds play out how exactly this will happen. We share a sense of doom with these figures, an acceptance that neither of them will survive the narrative. (I am thinking of both *Double Indemnity* (1944) and *Out of the Past* (1947) as examples of this – in both cases it is not obvious exactly how the participants will die.) A way of putting this is that while the hero finally wakes up to what the fatal lover is, he/she is also destroyed, or lets him/herself be destroyed, by the lover.

If we allow that there is no possibility that Jack can survive and go unpunished, there are three possible endings in play at the point of crisis. Jack breaks into the house intent on killing Teddy, with Sam arriving minutes later:

1. Jack could be killed by Sam after he has killed Teddy, a rescue coming just too late.
2. Jack could be killed by Sam just as he is about to kill Teddy, an act of rescue.
3. Jack could be killed by Teddy and Sam could arrive to find his act of rescue unnecessary, the villain already dead.

The film invokes its noir connections by teasing us elaborately with the possibility of the first scenario in which Teddy would accept that her choices have led to her own death. It does this in several ways: by the mood implicit in her final phone call to Sam: 'I just wanted to say thank you … it's all right now'; by showing us Teddy going upstairs to her bedroom *after* she has heard Jack breaking into the house; and by not allowing us to see that she is concealing a gun. But just as it is clear that Jack must die, so Teddy must survive: her passion is not a transgression requiring her to die in a film made in 1985, and she is a mother. A compromise ending that would retain some noir elements would be the second, the point of which would be that Teddy lacks the authority to kill, a role retained by Sam. The film expresses its distance from the noir world by choosing the third scenario, the ending we have, which has its generic roots in a different source, the horror film. In her unhesitating ability to dispatch the masked Jack, Teddy is a version of the 'Final Girl' (see Clover 1992) and her authority for killing him is of course that he is this film's monster. This feels like a gesture to empowering the woman, but it is purchased at a price. What has been lost is the psychological density of noir, the uneasy thought that Teddy, and sexual desire itself, may have a case to answer here.

The unhomely city

My second example is William Friedkin's *To Live and Die in L.A.*, which presents a sharp contrast to *Jagged Edge*. Where Marquand uses established and well-regarded, attractive stars in Close and Bridges, Friedkin presents us with actors who in 1985 were more or less new cinematic faces. Perhaps the most familiar would have been Willem Dafoe, who was not yet a substantial star. This is William Petersen's second film and his first leading role, and other roles are cast from actors much of whose previous work had been in television, such as John Pankow and Darlanne Fluegel.

The films demonstrate the range of the worlds that can carry noir associations. The setting of *Jagged Edge* is an example of family noir, where the particular horror of the murders is that they take place in the home, indeed in the bedroom: the model is, say, *Sorry, Wrong Number* (1948). In Friedkin's case, the model is *Detour* (1945): it can be aligned with what has been described as homeless noir (see Britton 1992 and MacCannell 1993). The film presents a world in which sexual activity takes place but is disconnected from any trace of mutual care or commitment, one in which a child is mentioned once only and

No way out: *To Live and Die in L.A.*

is never present, and the only social occasion that we see is a group of cops drinking in a bar. It is a world where there are deaths but no funerals, as if a gathering together of family and friends is unimaginable.

While *Jagged Edge* is largely conducted in the homes and orderly public spaces of its bourgeois world, as if to remind us of the values which are being attacked and defended there, Friedkin's film has a *mise-en-scène* which successfully articulates an urban hell. The larger frame is simply the establishing shots of LA itself. There is a key shot of daybreak over the city, which begins the film (that is, precedes the pre-credits sequence) and another, very similarly lit, shot which can be seen behind the main title. Here a couple of palm trees and a tangle of power and communications lines are battered by the winds in an atmosphere of lurid deep orange. The image is not so much of light returning to the city as of the threat of unbearable heat, beating down on the damaged remains of the natural and the world of heavy industry, and the junk that it produces.

Friedkin takes us to a number of spaces which address a human need or appetite, but where that need is met in terms that strip it of everything positive. Rather than a home, or even a neighbourhood diner, we are shown the 'food in a basket' eating place in which two cops sit on the salvaged remains of plastic chairs which have been reused to provide a crude seating area. Another such space is the topless bar in which Ruth Lanier (Darlanne Fluegel) works as a cashier. It is indicative of what is made of sexual desire in the film's world, with its almost comic come-on (the signs reading 'Enter' all the way around the building) contrasting with the interior of barriers and screens. Ruth both manipulates these obstacles and is contained by them, in the cage. The scene is lit with the harsh, markedly artificial colours that seem to be designed to divide the interior from the bright, bland exterior: a saturated deep orange and an acrylic green. We have already seen these colours used in the lettering of the film's opening titles.

This use of lurid colour is appropriate to a city in which there are no places in which sustainable privacy is possible. This is the opposite to *Jagged Edge*, which repeatedly invokes the idea of a house, or a bedroom, as a haven (or a violated haven), as in the morning following the couple's first night together, when Jack opens the curtains to expose the spectacular view over the city. In *To Live and Die in L.A.,* there are bedrooms in which sex takes place but barely anything that we are asked to see as a home.

Just as the undamaged natural world is almost entirely absent, so there is almost nothing physical in the LA of Friedkin's film which invokes the past or the idea of tradition. The use of datelines early in the film establishes that these events are taking place over the Christmas season, evidently so that we may observe the total absence of the festive in every other respect. The single exception to this is that one of the cops who is asked to act unethically comes from a family of cops. But we will see that this is where tradition proves useless.

There is arguably one substantial way in which the past is invoked, not through an object, but a piece of behaviour. It is the issue of loyalty to a partner – the topic with which the film begins, thus signalling its connections to noir and also arguably to another classical Hollywood genre, the western. This is laid out in the plot in the following terms:

1. In the pre-credits sequence we see two cops acting as special agents, Richard Chance (William Petersen) and Jim Hart (Michael Greene), engaged in the protection of an American president. The sequence establishes them as partners and they succeed in averting an assassination. This involves some athletics on the part of Hart, who has the emblematic line, 'I'm getting too old for this shit.' It emerges that Hart is retiring in three days' time.
2. Having insisted on going alone to investigate a lead concerning a major forger of banknotes, Rick Masters (Willem Dafoe), Hart is shot dead by Masters and his sidekick Jack (Jack Hoar).
3. Chance is assigned a new partner, John Vukovich (John Pankow), a decision which he questions but is forced by his superiors to accept. He tells Vukovich, 'I'm going to bag Masters and I don't give a shit how I do it.'

At this point it might seem that the film is offering a familiar argument, hinted at in the names that are derived from westerns: that in a hostile world the one reliable value is carried in the idea of the partner and avenging his death. So we might expect a film that will follow the new partners as they take their revenge on Masters, and a recognition that as a result of their successful efforts Chance and Vukovich have themselves formed a bond. This would not particularly suggest film noir – the narrative sounds more like a reprise of elements of *Dirty Harry* (1971). The noir elements in the film are contained in the presentation of its world, one so dangerous and without value that *all* of the male characters are at risk. The noir hero and the noir villain could both die, leaving the less heroic, more respectable male figure to link up with the more domesticated woman, who has been freed for this possibility by the death of the noir hero.

It is perhaps surprising to realise that this latter path is the one that the film follows, viewed purely in terms of narrative trajectory and stereotypical character types (see Walker 1992). Mapping the roles against the gallery of noir characters, it is striking that they can easily be identified: the villainous controlling male in Masters, the femme fatale in his girlfriend Bianca Torres (Debra Feuer), the hero in Chance, the domestic or potentially domestic woman in Chance's girl Ruth, and the respectable, or at least more respectable, man in Vukovich. (It reinforces these connections to note that Ruth is a mother and Vukovich a son and brother.) In these terms the film possesses the skeleton of a recognisable film noir. But these characters are radically different from their antecedents in terms of two matters, professional competence and sexual desires.

Competence and ineptitude

One of the common qualities of the classical noir hero is his competence, both as investigator and as handler of tricky situations, often a matter of his competence with language itself. (Where suggestions of the incompetent or inarticulate do appear is in minor characters, either villains or victims: an example would be Joe Stephanos (Paul Valentine) in *Out of the Past*.) As *To Live and Die in L.A.* begins, it seems to be establishing Chance and Hart as competent professionals, quick to spot something amiss and possessed of the concentration and timing required to bring events to a successful conclusion.

It is again one of the ways in which the pre-credits sequence of the film turns out to be deceptive. When he investigates the warehouse in which Masters has been forging money Hart makes no effort to approach with caution. He dies, an easy target, because he makes the assumption that it is uninhabited, whereas Masters and Jack are both still hiding there. This strikes a note which is to be continually reinforced, that these agents are not as competent as we might expect. The early examples are sometimes trivial, such as Vukovich casually chewing gum as he investigates the trailer in which Masters had previously hidden, and in which for all he knows, someone might still be hiding; the moment at the airport when the two agents are pursuing Carl Cody (John Turturro), one of Masters' money-carriers, and Vukovich has to borrow an eraser from a check-in clerk to test the forged note, costing precious seconds. The point is more declaratively made in the stakeout of the home of Max Waxman (Christopher Allport), one of Masters' associates in crime. Waxman is murdered by Masters while both

Chance and Vukovich have fallen asleep, even though earlier they have watched Bianca enter the building. Finally, Cody's easy gulling of Chance into taking him to a hospital to visit his 'daughter', and his subsequent escape from custody.

These moments form the background to the last part of the film, in which Chance, with the reluctant assistance of Vukovich, attempts a sting operation. It is made clear that Masters is entirely undeceived by the cops' pretended roles as criminals from out of state, just as he was aware earlier that Waxman's house was being watched. In acquiring the money to set up this deal – they steal it from a group they believe to be crooks – Chance and Vukovich bring about the death of an undercover federal agent. Finally they meet Masters to complete the money exchange, but bungle the arrest, and Chance is killed with a shot to the head fired by Jack. This recalls the death of Hart, also shot by Jack. It is not a matter of the cops outwitted by the criminal mastermind, but despatched by the apparently contemptible, slow-moving thug.

The classical noir hero often dies despite his intelligence – these figures die as a direct result of their incompetence. Perhaps the poor reception of the film at the box office reflects the unfamiliarity of this, which may have to do with our being used to these matters but only as comedy: this is the period of *Police Academy* (1984) and *Police Academy 2* (1985). Even in Friedkin's film, there are moments that would seem to acknowledge this mode, as chases and standoffs wobble into the comedic: see the end of the sequence of the capture of Cody in the airport men's room, and the chasing of the pair of petty thieves in the middle of the film.

Sport and the sexual athlete

The contrast with classical noir is reflected in the different terms in which Chance's and Vukovich's relation to the job is constructed – why they are cops. In the case of Chance, the attraction is not the exercise of skill or intelligence, but the pursuit of sensation. Shortly after the credits, we cut to a sequence of what Chance describes as 'base jumping' – launching himself from one of LA's bridges with a line attached to his body. There are a series of subsequent moments in which we see Chance using his physical fitness, the repeated image of his being able to outrun his quarry. At one point he will talk eagerly to Vukovich about his desire for such sensations, how he used to 'jump off garages when I was a kid'. There is evidence from both costume and dialogue, that Chance regards being a cop as a kind of sport, an arena in which he can express his awareness of his own physical prowess. (This connects to the moments in which Petersen seems to be posing for the camera, as if offering the image of this effective body and what he believes is due to it: see for examples the sequence in which Hart is given the fishing rod, and the end of the sequence in which Chance asks Judge Cedillo (Val DeVargas) to sign a writ.)

The invocation of sport is at its most striking after the fiasco of the acquisition of the money with which to sting Masters. Chance arrives at Ruth's house saying that the taking of the money was 'clockwork', but he is also excitedly, and for no obvious reason, praising the prowess of a star ball player. The unconscious connection is to the feeling of being an athlete still high after the end of a successful game.

These matters are connected with Chance's sexual responses to women, an area in which the contrast with classical noir is most significant. Once, sexual desire for both the femme fatale and the domestic woman, and the fantasies accompanying those desires, were central. But here Chance's desire is a matter of narcissism, just another physical exercise of his fit body. After he has made love with Ruth for the first time (that is, the first time in this film), the dialogue is used to indicate that he has no interest in her other than for sex and a source of information. There is an elegant piece of physical business which seems to support this reading. As Chance comes to Ruth in the bedroom, he takes off his t-shirt. Ruth then puts it on, so that as the lovemaking starts, he can take it off again, this time from her body. It is as if there were no difference here in these attractive bodies, other than gender difference.

Chance's relation to Ruth is in some respects that of a pimp, in that she gets her information by having to 'get close to' Masters' associates, implicitly by the granting of sexual favours. Their final lovemaking scene, if it can be called that, is bleaker than the first: Friedkin cuts off the scene as Chance, against her protests, is trying to pin Ruth down on her sofa, his final act of athleticism and physical power.

In the light of this, it is no surprise, but a radical departure from the patterns of classical noir, that there is an almost complete absence of contact between Bianca, the figure who occupies the position of the femme fatale, and Chance. They meet only once, very late in the film, and Bianca's response to Chance is to laugh at him, as if all she sees is a helpless victim of Masters' operations.

This is not, or not only, a commentary on Chance, but a part of a wider view of the status of sexual relations. In the case of Masters and Bianca, sex seems to be a narcissistic, or voyeuristic, activity: Bianca watches videotapes of herself and Masters making love. Physical sexual acts express only relations of convenience between the participants – just another kind of performance art. In one of the closing sequences, Masters' lawyer, Bob Grimes (Dean Stockwell), asks Bianca why she had stayed with Masters. She replies by asking him the same question, and leaves his reply, that it was just business, hanging in the air: sexual relations are not all that different from male/male business relations. Equally the moments of flirtation in the film with same sex relations are not invoked in terms of a hierarchy of value. The point is not to praise or to criticise such possibilities but to argue that on the indifferent plane on which these contacts are conducted, everything is in effect the same.

Vukovich presents only a partial contrast to Chance. John Pankow plays the part as a man without Chance's athleticism or his narcissism, less fashionably costumed and more physically awkward, but not offered as a particularly attractive alternative. Unlike Chance, he is connected to ideas of tradition and the past. His reason for being a cop, and his feeling about how cops should behave, are based in his family. This seems to be his reason for refusing to take the deal offered by Grimes, on the ground that a cop does not betray his partner. But this is less a basis for action as a cause for paralysis, as what he takes to be the conventions for proper behaviour by cops unravel around him.

Vukovich fits the noir stereotype of the respectable male in that he is not an object of desire, nor does he strongly express desire. We do not see him relate in any way to women – for most of the film Ruth does not even know who he is. The only sequence which might have modified this position was cut before release. The passage shows Vukovich, desperate and confused, trying to re-establish contact with his ex-wife Donna (Tracy Swope). The couple argue at the door to her apartment, into which she will not admit him. Again, the possibility of refuge, either a safe space or by contacting the past, is denied.[3] Had this sequence been included in the final cut it would have reinforced Vukovich's position as the male oriented towards familial relations.

Vukovich's relation to family contrasts sharply to that of Chance. His single encounter with a couple is violently antipathetic, when he breaks into the apartment which Cody shares with his girlfriend in order to beat him up. The scene has little obvious narrative point, but the background to it is the business of Cody deceiving Chance over the visit to his 'daughter'. Cody knows that a man so totally disconnected from family is an easy mark for a piece of deception based on family relations, a language Chance does not speak.

This brings me to the matter of language itself. The language in the whole of the script is predominantly crude, utilitarian, scabrous. Again this is a marked contrast to classical noir, which can offer the pleasure of elegance of expression. The swearing, which seems possibly unremarkable now, attracted negative comment in 1985: but it makes another point about the poverty of resources available to these figures. They can no more retreat behind a phrase than to a home.

No exit

The final sequence of *To Live and Die in L.A.* as it is expresses the film's debt to noir, and revises the meaning of the character configuration that it invokes.[4] This configuration is easy to recognise: now that the noir hero is dead, and the villain and femme fatale are dead or departed, one of the closing images of the film is that of a new couple, the respectable male and the domestic woman.

What Friedkin does is to offer a pair who are identifiably this couple while depriving their connection of all but negative significance.

In classical noir, the establishment of the 'good couple' indicates a moment of change, the restoration of a possible world in which a viable relationship could be constructed. This position is potentially available to *To Live and Die in L.A.*. It would have been quite possible for Vukovich, terminally disillusioned by the way Masters had been defeated and by the death of Chance, to offer to flee the city with Ruth and the film could have ended with this new, provisional couple driving off to an uncertain future. (The final credits sequence, scrolling over the view through the windscreen of a car as it is driven out of LA at dusk and ending with the countryside, seems to retain a trace of such an ending.) But as filmed Friedkin offers the image of entrapment and stasis. Ruth, who does wish to leave the city and her old life, is *prevented* from doing so by Vukovich, who has strangely taken over the role and the character previously occupied by Chance.

Thus the negative qualities embodied in Chance are not dissipated even by his death, but simply reincarnated in another body. Vukovich has the same power over Ruth (to revoke her parole) and the details of the performance in the final scene suggest that he is acquiring the same narcissism. So while this specific plot may have played itself out, the conditions that gave rise to it are untouchable. The mood here is drawn not from noir but again from one strain of the horror film, in which the conventional ending (by 1985) was to suggest that even as the monster, or the monstrous, was destroyed, he/she/it would inevitably appear sooner or later in another form. We should not find this surprising, given Friedkin's background in the genre (most famously his direction of *The Exorcist* (1973)), and the use of horror in the 1980s to present the image of an irredeemable world.

The interlocking relationships of classical noir are the subject of choices and commitments involving sexual desire that are of crucial significance. In these two neo-noir films, desire and its choices have no such transformative function. In *Jagged Edge*, the final position is that the heroine's behaviour was simply a mistake, one which leaves no trace once it is corrected. There is no guilt for us, and her, to share in or contemplate, only a dead monster. *To Live and Die in L.A.* plays out its noir plot in a world in which all fantasies of what a sexual connection might mean are reduced to nothing, in which another world cannot quite be imagined, let alone achieved. The different ways in which the horror film is invoked suggests a connection and also the difference between the two films – between the comforting despatch of a single monster in Marquand's film and a world that has become the property of monsters in Friedkin's.

NOTES

1   I have discussed some of those films in my 'Echo Park: Film noir in the "Seventies"' (1992).
2   The section 'Character relationships', in Michael Walker's 'Film noir: Introduction' (1992: 23–25), lays out the character types of noir and their interlocking relations. Walker describes a configuration composed of three sexual triangles, positioning the noir hero between the domestic woman and the femme fatale, the femme fatale between the noir hero and the noir villain, and the domestic woman between the noir hero and the respectable man.
3   The sequence, with some comment by Friedkin regretting its loss, is included as an extra on the Special Edition Region 1 DVD.
4   At the time of the film's post-production and release, there was anxiety on the part of the producers regarding its conclusion. An alternative ending was shot in which Chance is injured but survives and both Chance and Vukovich are sent into exile in Alaska. This ending seems to have been recognised as both incoherent and potentially ludicrous and to have been abandoned after test screenings. It is included as an extra on the Special Edition Region 1 DVD.

REFERENCES

Britton, Andrew (1992) 'Detour', in Ian Cameron (ed.) *The Movie Book of Film Noir*. London: Studio Vista, 174–83.

Clover, Carol J. (1992) *Men, Women and Chain Saws: Gender in the Modern Horror Film*. London: British Film Institute.

Gallafent, Ed (1992) 'Echo Park: Film noir in the "Seventies"', in Ian Cameron (ed.) *The Movie Book of Film Noir*. London: Studio Vista, 254–66.

MacCannell, Dean (1993) 'Democracy's turn: On homeless noir', in Joan Copjec (ed.) *Shades of Noir*. London: Verso, 279–97.

Walker, Michael (1992) 'Film noir: Introduction', in Ian Cameron (ed.) *The Movie Book of Film Noir*. London: Studio Vista, 8–38.

6

From Lonely Streets to Lonely Rooms: Prefiguration, Affective Responses and the *Max Payne* Single-Player

GREG SINGH

Collecting evidence had gotten old a few hundred bullets back. I was already so far past the point-of-no-return I couldn't remember what it had looked like when I had passed it ... Turn around, walk away, blow town. That would've been the smart thing to do. Guess I wasn't that smart.

Max Payne

Max Payne is a highly successful console videogame franchise, enjoying a cult status few others can boast. Third-person shooters premised around the eponymous player-character, a hard-boiled former NYPD cop working undercover for the DEA, the games relish every opportunity to remind the player of their noirishness. The title of the second game in the series, *Max Payne 2 – The Fall of Max Payne: A film noir love story* (2003), makes this connection overt, even though the game is neither a film noir nor a love story – in fact, it is not even a film or a story. But the claim made by the subtitle implicates the player in a prefigurative mode that threatens to expose the grim realities of the single-player format. Simply put, the term prefiguration is used here to emphasise the way that genre games typically proceed according to type (on prefiguration, see Ricoeur 1984 and Gunn 2006: 36–7). This has implications for the procedural strategies that games employ according to the patterns evinced by generic convention. That is, these games and their back-stories adopt certain stylistic, iconographic and thematic concerns and figurations, thus prefiguring film noir. This also has implications in terms of the way the player/viewer's response is anticipated: the games proceed, enabling the player to anticipate by type and thus understand the gameworld and the protocols determining actions and character behaviour within it. Furthermore, they do this while both mystifying and romanticising the (almost inevitably) insular domestic context of single-player console games. The games' overt references to film noir and evocation of familiar generic protocols prefigure the player every bit as much as the single-player format does. This essay is concerned with the ways in which the games anticipate the player's affective response towards its conceits, assumptions and playful knowledge of film noir and neo-noir, and the ways in which these intertextual relations reinforce structural similarities between the games and film noirs. I will begin by outlining the generic prefigurations evident in the games.

In the back-story, thugs high on the designer drug Valkyr break into Payne's family home and kill his wife and unborn child. Instead of becoming a vigilante in the style of *The Big Heat* (1953) or *Death Wish* (1974), Payne infiltrates a drug cartel. His former partner in the NYPD, Alex Balder, is the only person who knows about his undercover mission, but when Balder is killed, Payne is firmly in the frame for his murder (*Mou gaan dou*/*Infernal Affairs* (2002) and its sequels use a similar conceit). On the lam, Payne hunts down Balder's killers, and in the process falls in lust with femme fatale Mona Sax. A familiar figure from noirs ranging from *Gilda* (1946) to *Body Heat* (1981) and *Jism* (2003), her name alludes to moans, sex and the proliferation of saxophones on the sound-tracks of erotic thrillers and other neo-noirs. The punningly-named protagonist provides a further allusion to neo-noir's revision of film noir character types through his remarkable resemblance to neo-noir stalwart Mickey Rourke.[1]

The setting also is typically noirish. While Los Angeles has been central to film noir, the *Max Payne* games follow the example of television cop series such as *Hill Street Blues* (1981–87), *NYPD Blue* (1993–2005) and *The Wire* (2002–08), which have established eastern cities like Chicago, New York and Baltimore in the popular imagination as a certain variety of decaying, post-industrial metropolis. (In the same period, television series like *Hardcastle and McCormick* (1983–86), *L.A. Law* (1986–94) and *Players* (1997–98) refigured LA as a sun-drenched party city, very much the antithesis of noir.) The games' east coast location makes sense in this context, producing an atmosphere suitable for gang warfare, crime syndicates, government corruption, sleazy nightclubs, decrepit warehouses, guns and the criminals who wield them, trench coats and the detectives who wear them. It is always dark and never seems to stop raining in these strangely empty urban environs, and in the first game this is taken to an extreme as New York suffers the worst blizzard in a century – itself a prefiguration of the justice about to be dealt to Payne's enemies by the player-character. It works metaphorically, as a storm to be suffered, endured, and is as relevant to the diegesis as it is to the repetitiveness and instrumentality of the gameplay itself.

The games' gritty, unrelenting dialogue, delivered at breakneck pace, is often reminiscent of the rapid-fire exchanges between *Double Indemnity*'s Walter Neff (Fred MacMurray) and Phyllis Dietrichson (Barbara Stanwyck). In an uncanny juxtaposition, exposing the relation to melodrama of both noir and American daytime TV, endless repeats of cheap soap operas appear on the television sets within the game's architecture (which the player may both interact with and watch). While aspects of the setting, including a soundtrack of footsteps and sirens, point to certain realist antecedents of film noir, the bullet-time effect of the playable sequences draws upon the genre's expressionist depictions of altered psychological states, such as the multiple descents of Marlowe (Dick Powell) into unconsciousness in *Murder, My Sweet* (1944). This representation of altered states is foregrounded in the second game's disorientating opening sequence in which Max has lost a lot of blood and been medicated, resulting in a blurred field of vision and an avatar which does not respond to the controls 'properly'.

In Hollywood films, the purpose of generic protocols is to appeal to as wide an audience as possible by addressing sensibility and familiarity and thus soliciting affective responses of numerous kinds. In the interstitial realm of film and videogame, theorisations of such responses engage with the ways in which pleasurable consumption and generic expectation have been conceptualised, and generally derive from four rather different critical perspectives. The first, the tradition of genre film criticism, will be familiar to most readers. The second, developed in games research for a number of years but only recently taken up in film studies, articulates affective response in terms of empirical laboratory research into physiological and galvanic effects (see Massumi 2002 for a brief overview). It indicates the extent to which somatic sensation is a vital element of media experience.[2] The third perspective, more useful in considering prefiguration and for a critical engagement with affect and media convergence, is concerned with immersive gaming. For example, Eugenie Shinkle (2003) attempts to deconstruct scopic Cartesianism (common notions of perspective and point of view, as well as the mind/body dichotomy) through phenomenological accounts of sensibility and embodiment, while Melanie Swalwell (2003) demythologises the 'either here or there' aspect of media engagement. She engages with the notion that what happens 'there' onscreen in both televised war and wargames, for instance, has consequences for how the audience feels in the 'here' and now. Her dialectical take on the affective potential to put us 'there' in the action at an emotional level, or bring the event to us 'here', illuminates current consensus on reality effects and the relationship of different media in affective experience. These Games Studies approaches in particular relate to a fourth critical perspective, the phenomenology of film (and recently of videogames), to which I shall briefly return later. I will, however, concentrate on the third perspective.

Rather than attempt to outline the growing field of Games Studies, I will here restrict myself to the so-called narratology/ludology 'debate'.[3] While narratology refers to the systematic study of narrative, ludology refers to the study of both pleasure and play, and in the context of digital games is primarily concerned with the mechanics of gaming and playing, as well as the specific playing contexts within which gamers play. Gonzalo Frasca (2003) argues that while the myth of emerging Games Studies being divided by these diametrically opposed approaches helped to lend it credibility as an academic discipline by implying its plurality and vigour, the debate between 'the narratologists' and 'the ludologists' never really took place. One could argue that, in any debate about play with narrative or narrativised play, all Games Studies academics are essentially ludologists, regardless of their position on narrative in games. Michael Mateas coined the term 'narrativists' to refer to a specific narratologically-informed, anti-game, interactive narrative approach, but insisted that this 'does not imply that all narratologists are anti-game or that narratology is intrinsically opposed to game-like interaction' (2002: 34). The important point to draw from this is that the implication of ludological approaches to media can be just as relevant for film as they are for videogames. The very fact that we *play* with the texts we consume suggests that ludology was always a central, if not fully conscious, aspect of the study of film production and consumption. The usefulness of a ludological approach to film studies can be illustrated by briefly turning to *The Usual Suspects* (1995), a neo-noir narrative that is all about the game of building narratives.

The principal narrator, Verbal Kint (Kevin Spacey) creates a story around the information that Dave Kujan (Chazz Palminteri), the US Customs officer who is interviewing him, requires in order to put career crook Dean Keaton (Gabriel Byrne) in the frame for numerous thefts and frauds. A game of limitation and containment is played upon Kujan and the audience as Kint weaves together a narrative from artefacts he sees in the cluttered office in which he is being interrogated. Assumed to be a minor player, Kint is actually criminal mastermind Keyser Söze, both player and games master, riffing on both noir's form (narrative as a structural game of perspective, emplotment and knowledge) and content (conspiracy, blind alleys, second-guesses and double-bluffs). Beyond its *mise-en-scène*, *The Usual Suspects* signifies noirishness as a figural, mimetic factor (in terms of our awareness that we are being played with through our knowledge/lack of knowledge of the plot and the noir form) and as an affective construct (our fatalistic frustration in the knowledge, central to noir, that we are doomed to make wrong choices and repeat mistakes). It is this signification of knowledge and frustration through mimesis and affect that is common to neo-noir film and the single-player game. The lonely, frustrating existence of the noir protagonist is replicated to an extent in the lonely, frustrating (albeit, arguably pleasurable) experience of achieving the single-player game's instrumental objectives.

Andrew Darley argues that in immersive environments narrative continuity is secondary to the simulation: 'It is the mechanics and pleasures involved in this peculiar pretended residency or *vicarious sense of presence* in a fictional world, which is uppermost' (2000: 155; emphasis in original). However, this somewhat ludological approach fails to appreciate the remediation of narrative through prefigurative practice and technological development, and thus cannot take account of the impact that an affective response generated from the player's recognition of and pleasure in allusions to other texts (which *Max Payne* reformulates as precursors of game noir) might have on his or her 'reading' of the game. The gamer's immediate engagement with *Max Payne* is not merely mechanical but also emotional and sensory, and this is far more difficult to unpack, thanks to the influence of filmic antecedents, the patterns written into the game and those found in playing contexts. The game experience is loaded with values that might be described as ideological, but which are influenced by more immediate forces such as vehicular embodiment, generic structure and economic underwriting, and thus even more so than the film experience offers an insight into perhaps the most 'noirish' of affective responses – the sense of 'no way out'.

In the *Max Payne* games, this sense of entrapment is generated in ways that often also demonstrate the manifestations of noir across different media in the global marketplace, emphasising media convergences and the proliferation of commodity-identities across media forms. I will briefly outline three ways in which this happens in the first *Max Payne* game. First, it has a less than straightforward temporality, confused from its opening moments, which start in the 'now' before establishing a present tense at some point in the immediate past. It is in this 'present past' that most of the playable sequences take place, but it is interspersed with flashback sequences presented in graphic novel form. This complex temporal structure of a retrospective 'present' is evident in the flashback structures of film noirs such as *Murder, My Sweet, Detour* (1945), *Out of the Past* (1947) and *Sunset Blvd.* (1950). Typically, the storyteller's monologue is taken on trust[4] – no one ever doubts the veracity of the tale *Double Indemnity*'s Neff dictates or suspects it of being just some spicy story he has concocted as his final flirtation with Barton Keyes (Edward G. Robinson). Despite its use of flashbacks and a gameplaying present set in the recent past, *Max Payne* is clearly structured and one has little reason to doubt the sequence of events. One of the reasons for this is the game's preoccupation with causality: Payne's idealised family life is destroyed. He is left traumatised, thus giving him all the excuse or motivation he needs to be involved in the destruction of so many lives in the game (the player's task throughout is simply to blast non-player characters into oblivion). *Max Payne 2*, however, is different in that gameplay is interspersed with fantasy/drug-induced sequences and ambiguity. We begin to question the reliability of the narrator (Payne himself) and the relationship of what we are seeing to what has actually happened in the plot. Thus, the relation between the player and the choices to be made in gameplay are dislocated in the sense that they do not always equate to logical narrative progression. The similarity between noir protagonists and single-players is remarkable in this respect. For example, Neff knows that Phyllis is trouble, but nevertheless goes to his doom, 'safe' in the ambivalent knowledge that he will pay for her wickedness. For the single-player, anticipation of wave upon wave of unknown assailants, as well as the constant knowledge of possibly impending 'death', produce a very similar affect of resignation.

The second example is the games' use of cut-scenes – unplayable animated sequences that feature the player-character, usually in dialogue, or in a scene that has some significance to the plot. Cut-scenes are commonplace in third-person shooter games, and are often signified by a 'letter-box' widescreen effect, suggesting a mode of representation to the player that is somehow inherently cinematic rather than televisual despite the typically small size of the screen on which it is played. The games' remediation of widescreen not only lends cinematic authenticity to the cut-scenes by evoking the embrace of wider screen formats in the neo-noir era, but also constitute an invitation to the consumer to embrace 'home cinema' (for example, a video projection unit or a plasma screen) for gameplaying. In the cut-scenes, the affective spectacles offered by both cinemas and video arcades are remediated for domestic spaces and private consumption. It seems that such connections between private consumption, single-playing and modern life are typically 'noirish' and irresistibly alienating, a point to which I will return. For now, it will suffice to note that such home entertainment systems seem to embody a discrepancy between the grand scale of sound and image offered by such technology and the context within which these spectacles are consumed. Perhaps this is because they are configured for spectacle within the living room, entailing the privatisation of pleasure, even in cases of multiple participants, rather than mass consumption in the sense of attending the cinema.

The third example concerns the games' use of comic-strip conventions, formally introduced as 'graphic novel sequences', for the flashbacks. There are clear historical continuities between film and comics, both of them sequential narrative forms emerging in the late nineteenth century and intimately tied to the rise of the modern metropolis. Film noir – and the lurid cover art of associated pulp magazine and paperback crime fiction – has had a clear influence on comic books, from Will Eisner's *The Spirit* (1940–52) to the appearance of Frank Miller's original *Sin City* stories in the *Dark Horse Presents* comics (1991–92). This influence has enjoyed continued prominence – the green-screened *Sin City* (2005) adaptation and the rotoscoped into black-and-white *Renaissance* (2006) use cutting edge digital technologies in order to look as much like comic books as possible. It is also worth noting that Max Payne's motivation – the criminal murder of his family – is similar to that of DC's Batman and Marvel's The Punisher, who debuted in 1939 and 1974, respectively. *Max Payne*'s graphic novel sequences are also highly reminiscent of poster art, allusions to which abound in neo-noir and may be traced back at least as far as one of the most famous intertextual moments in European cinema: Jean-Luc Godard's use of Humphrey Bogart posters in his neo-noir prototype, À bout de soufflé/Breathless (1959). Interestingly enough, it is also in this film that we see an early instance of foregrounded self-referentiality in relation to the fatalism of the noir protagonist. Michel (Jean-Paul Belmondo) clearly models himself on Bogart's fatalist onscreen persona: he anticipates his own doom by attempting a futile getaway, and is also very aware of his doomed relationship to his own femme-fatale-who-is-not-one, Patricia (Jean Seberg). When he calls her a salope for ratting him out to the police, we know that he has fulfilled his fatal fantasy.

It is also significant that the graphic novel flashback sequences are drawn in vivid watercolours rather than black-and-white, which sits well with contemporary Hollywood neo-noir film production. For example, Memento (2000) has a skewed temporality that sees the present, forward-moving time frame filmed in black-and-white, and its retrospective sequences, edited in reverse order, shown in full colour (see Thomas in this volume). This inverts the convention in which the present is shown in colour and flashbacks in black-and-white – which not only connotes past-ness (because it dates from before colour became Hollywood's dominant presentational mode), but also veracity. Memento thus not only lends the subversion of narrative temporality in contemporary mainstream filmmaking an 'authenticity-effect' by depicting the here-and-now in black-and-white, but also provides a precedent. Several urban neo-noirs featuring both traumatic experience and the visibility of the editing process have followed, including Irréversible/Irreversible (2002), in which the viewer is constantly reminded of their complicity in the horrific scenes which unfold before the camera's gaze through the conscious act of looking. As mentioned earlier, at the beginning of Max Payne 2, Payne is introduced wandering around a hospital in an altered state, which is signified by blurred vision and the onscreen avatar's failure to respond accurately to the commands that the player is transmitting via the control pad.[5] The voice-over tells us that this condition is the result of blood loss and medication, but this knowledge does not make the experience any less disquieting. The dissonance between the player's commands and the avatar's actions produces a frustration that may be associated with noir, playing subtly with the player and spectator alike, unnerving and unsettling comfortable playing/viewing strategies. In this sense, Max Payne 2 has much in common with Irréversible, which opens with a disorientating combination of relentless spinning camera movements, paying little heed to laws of gravity or physical relations to proprioceptive state, and the soundtrack's use of a near-inaudible hum, set at the very lowest frequency of human hearing. It gives the sensation of nausea, estrangement and general discomfort – all affective responses that may be attributed (albeit in attenuated form) to the traditions of noir.[6]

The noirish entrapment of the *Max Payne* games is, then, related to the ways in which the games draw upon noir in all its media forms – as a kind of global information capital. The game constructs an environment and experience composed of prefigured generic components that are utterly constraining even as, equally inevitably, it has the capacity to generate an infinite number of permutations as one plays. As a result, the game offers a peculiarly realistic experience for the player. Fredric Jameson writes:

> Realism is conventionally evoked in terms of passive reflection and copying, subordinate to some external reality, and fully as much a grim duty as a pleasure of any kind. Pleasure is, however, generally in aesthetic experience an exercise of praxis, and even the various aesthetics of play are easily adjusted to forms of production, by way of a notion of freedom as control over one's own destiny. (1992: 162)

Here, we get a sense of the ways in which playing according to type is pleasurable and displeasurable in equal measures. The 'grim duty' of playing to type feels like freedom, when it is, in fact, a highly controlled set of choices that enable the player to entertain freedom as a notional option. This is highlighted in the games' complex interplay between real-world referentiality and generic verisimilitude. For example, the sound of footsteps corresponds directly to the footfalls of the Payne avatar, adhering not only to real-world rules but also those of film noir: it is not just the sound of footsteps, but the sound of a smartly adorned foot falling on wet asphalt, echoing in an empty street or stairwell, the sound of countless gumshoes and private dicks walking alone down those very lonely streets. Certainly, in *Max Payne*, noir manifests itself most significantly in the environment in which most of the plot/play takes place: warehouses, dockyards, back entrances to empty buildings, often in a state of dereliction, abandoned sites of burnt-out enterprise. Sirens echo in the distance, reminding the player of Payne's own outlaw status as he seeks to wipe out the drug gangs. However, the social realist setting within which noir seems to thrive is as much to do with recognising it as a noir-ish environment, in the gritty, uncannily too-close-for-comfort sense, as it has to do with any claim to social commentary. The fact that the iconography has been remediated in a form commonly regarded as trivial (a game) seems to amplify this effect in the sense that the pleasurable recognition of such intertextual references appear to be the point of *Max Payne*. Both form and content here arguably prefigure a kind of narrative one might identify with the aestheticisation of the political and, as such, engage an alienated interaction between player and game. It is with some irony that one freely plays the constrained activities of a player-character such as Payne.

Player-agency in the single-player game is felt as embodied and immediate. The player responds to the game, and most of the time the game responds to the player (although it does sometimes ignore commands because of the demands of the plot). More significantly, the game only allows a certain set of actions to sustain play. Thus, player-agency is as much grim duty as it is pleasure, in that, as Max Payne, the player's actions are curtailed by plot, mission and the aims of the noir protagonist. Other games contain subsidiary missions and diegetic games which rarely emphasise the same instrumental focus (goal-oriented accumulation) as the main narrative elements and therefore allow a sense of freedom of choice. For example, in *GTA: San Andreas* (2004), subsidiary gym and gambling games provide avenues of accumulation which enable the player to progress in the main game, but the arcade game in the bar exists merely to be played. That is, their function within the main game's goal-orientation is ambiguous, approaching the possibility of 'pure game' and thus allowing a sense of affective freedom. Within the *Max Payne* series, however, there is very little in the way of subplot to give the excuse to design subsidiary tasks, making its curtailment of agency even more apparent. And just as the noir protagonist goes knowingly to his doom, so too does the single-player,[7] enamoured of the pleasures afforded by late capitalism and deriving a feeling of agency through a consumer's playful, knowing mastery over the game, even as the game negates mastery through its containment of knowledge, movement and response.

In thinking about prefiguration as a process that operates according to type, we might say that 'noirishness' may be signified as both a figural, mimetic factor and as an affective construct – a tone and a mood. This signification through the mimesis and affect of knowledge and frustration is perhaps the recursive element most easily identifiable as prefigured in both neo-noir films and in single-player games. Paul Ricoeur (1984) argues that we need to consider narrative and its presentation through its relationship with time, and the way in which the function of narrative becomes clear to the reader specifically through the retelling. In terms of ludology, this is remarkably useful, as games tend to be habitually replayed. Certain sections of the game appear to be more difficult than others, some require different sets of skills, or demand of the player a more challenging motor or cognitive task, depending on the occasion. Of course, where Ricoeur considers the implications of interpretation and re-iteration upon the reading, telling and retelling of history, we need to think more concretely about the effect of endless repetition of instrumental tasks necessary to the progress of the narrative in replaying particularly difficult passages of the game. Indeed, one must consider the repetition of history in the case of replaying the game in its entirety – a pastime not uncommon in games with multiple endings such as the *Silent Hill* series (1999–present). One needs to regard these prefigurative entanglements as being remediated through the generic conventions of the third-person shooter game. The game, the films and other related texts from which it liberally borrows and the conventions of adaptational strategy (from film to game, from game to film) impact upon one another in various ways to express and exploit the generic conventions and types available to the consumer. By playing with conventional generic type, a strategy upon which the game industry has thrived in recent years, production houses are able to tap into audiences who are familiar with and favour certain game and film genres. This, rather inevitably, leads us to a bottom-line motive for cultural production – the economic.

But the expression of the economic in such cultural production manifests itself in a number of aesthetically interesting ways. First, the third-person shooter genre is one that is both highly popular and flexible in its format, although this flexibility is entirely contained within patterns which are immediately recognisable as belonging to type. It is also usually a single-player game.[8] Second, advances in CGI technology have meant that the viewpoint of the player is very flexible. The default position of the 'camera', which follows the character around the virtual environment, is about six virtual feet behind the avatar. Although increased flexibility allows for greater control of the virtual camera through the game controller-pad (such as 360-degree tilting and tracking), the camera almost always returns to this default position in the heat of play. In this sense it is prefigured, and this prefiguration has the inevitable character of remediation, as this is not only a convention of the third-person shooter, but is also reminiscent of those of film and television. As Geoff King and Tanya Krzywinska point out, 'Games remediate aspects of cinema (including forms of plotting of point-of-view structures), while cinema, in return, remediates aspects of games (especially in the use of digital graphics in special effects)' (2002: 4). This structural play and aesthetic are, of course, driven by available computer technology, but also significantly act as a driver for the development of technology to deliver the kind of impact aesthetics that have become conventional. This is, in effect, a replaying of a familiar technological/cultural determinist reciprocation that tends to characterise the evolution of image technologies.[9] It finds its immediately recognisable expression in such contemporary franchises as the *Doom* first-person shooter series (1992–2004), and the film version, *Doom* (2005), in which an entire action sequence is devoted to the simulation of the gaming experience. It is, significantly, a game-like film experience and the pleasurable recognition aroused in the filmgoer of such a state is palpable.

However, it is not just the technological and the aesthetic that are affected by this evolution/involution. Returning to affective response in the criticism of the interface between gaming and visual culture in general, it is the kinaesthetic that emerges as the important factor here, the embodied relation between player and avatar, through which one interacts with the text physically. As we have seen, however, this physical relation is characterised by a curtailment of knowledge and action, typical of the noir and neo-noir protagonist, but embodied by the grim duty of the single-player in particular. In a sense, then, what is at stake is the very notion of 'interactivity' as a materialisation of agency in both the narrative and kinaesthetic sense. Through ludological analysis, this question becomes more a matter of retrospection: if player-agency in game noir is characterised primarily by curtailed knowledge and action, then perhaps this is a mere reflection of the ways that the more general relationship between spectatorship and film noir was always characterised. In the light of this, one might say that in noir, it is not just the streets that are lonely but also the rooms.

NOTES

1   Rourke's neo-noirs include *Year of the Dragon* (1985), *Nine ½ Weeks* (1986), *Angel Heart* (1987), *Johnny Handsome* (1989), *Desperate Hours* (1990), *Sin City* (2005) and *Killshot* (2007). The casting of Sam Lake as *Max Payne* had less to do with his resemblance to Rourke than with financial constraints. The writer and programmer of the original game, Lake modelled for the character when a suitable actor could not be found within the budget. It may have been a happy accident, but the self-conscious casting of television actor Timothy Gibbs, who also resembles Rourke, in the presumably bigger-budgeted second game, anticipates the resemblance, and therefore is prefigurative.

2   See Grodal (1997) for an introduction to cognitivist film analysis, Frome (2006) for an approach to spectatorship that engages with physiological and cognitive processes, and Hills (2005) for a critique of cognitivist approaches to (horror) film fandom.

3   For an overview of the field, see www.gamestudies.org.

4   Although, for some exceptions see Britton (1992) on *Detour* and Bould (2005: 78–80) on *Lady in the Lake* (1947).

5   This disorientation strategy is fairly common in third-person games. For example, when the player-character drinks too much in *Fable* (2004), the avatar responds sluggishly to the controller and eventually in reverse.

6   Likewise, the first time I saw *Dark City* (1998) I was physically sick, I surmise as a result of the curiously organic and sickening sensation of the sight of a city visibly transformed while its denizens are utterly unaware of their exploitation – a disquietingly realistic representation of contemporary alienation. This demonstrates not only the usefulness of affective response in engaging with film and media form, but also, its elusiveness, both thanks to its materialisation and experience through embodiment rather than the linguistic.

7   I am not, of course, saying that the game ends with no winners – that it does have winners marks out *Max Payne* as decidedly un-noirish – but that the gameplay itself is characterised by the suppression of narrative.

8   While this means that the player-character may usually only be controlled by one player at a time, Games Studies has recently begun to consider the implications of playing context, and in particular, the 'non-player-player' who might be in the same room as the player and giving instructions. Often, there may be a room full of people

all playing the game, but, again, with a single player in control. Although very little has been published on this to date (there have been important interventions at various academic conferences, such as *Playful Subjects* (University of the West of England, May 2005) and *Aesthetics of Play* (University of Bergen, October 2005)), it is a significant phenomenon because it inevitably affects the feel and mood of the game and has implications for the ability of the critic to 'read' viewing contexts effectively.

9   Michael Allen notes that in a sense 'digital imaging technologies and techniques are striving to replicate what already exists: the photographic representation of reality' (2004: 110) and yet, in the case of seminal CGI films such as *Jurassic Park* (1993) and *Titanic* (1997), part of the motivation behind the lingering establishing shots of CGI dinosaurs or ghost ships is to stun the audience through spectacular imagery. It matters little whether or not the audience is 'duped' into thinking that these images are realistic – as long as they are spectacular enough they will signify production expense, if not an original referent object's image recorded on film.

REFERENCES

Allen, Michael (2004) 'The impact of digital technologies on film aesthetics', in Dan Harries (ed.) *The New Media Book*. London: British Film Institute, 109–18.

Bould, Mark (2005) *Film Noir: From Berlin to Sin City*. London: Wallflower Press.

Britton, Andrew (1992) 'Detour', in Ian Cameron (ed.) *The Movie Book of Film Noir*. London: Studio Vista, 174–83.

Darley, Andrew (2000) *Visual Digital Culture: Surface Play and Spectacle in New Media Genres*. London: Routledge.

Frasca, Gonzalo (2003) 'Ludologists love stories, too: Notes from a debate that never took place'. Available at: http://ludology.org/articles/Frasca_LevelUp2003.pdf. Accessed 10 October 2008.

Frome, Jonathan (2006) 'Representation, reality, and emotions across media', *Film Studies*, 8, 12–25.

Grodal, Torben (1997) *Moving Pictures: A New Theory of Film Genres, Feelings and Cognition*. Oxford: Clarendon.

Gunn, Simon (2006) *History and Cultural Theory*. London: Pearson.

Hills, Matt (2005) *The Pleasures of Horror*. London: Continuum.

Jameson, Fredric (1992) *Signatures of the Visible*. London: Routledge.

King, Geoff and Tanya Krzywinska (2002) *Screenplay: Cinema/Videogames/Interfaces*. London: Wallflower Press.

Massumi, Brian (2002) *Parables of the Virtual: Movement, Affect, Sensation*. London: Duke University Press.

Mateas, Michael (2002) *Interactive Drama, Art and Artificial Intelligence*. Unpublished PhD thesis, Carnegie Mellon University. Available at: http://reports-archive.adm.cs.cmu.edu/anon/2002/CMU-CS-02-206.pdf. Accessed 10 October 2008.

Ricoeur, Paul (1984) *Time and Narrative: Volume 1*, trans. Kathleen McLaughlin and David Pellauer. Chicago: University of Chicago Press.

Shinkle, Eugenie (2003) 'Gardens, games and the anamorphic subject: Tracing the body in a virtual landscape', *Fine Art Forum*, 17, 8, unpaginated.

Swalwell, Melanie (2003) '"This isn't a computer game you know": Revisiting the computer games/televised war analogy', *Fine Art Forum*, 17, 8, unpaginated.

7

The New Lower Depths: Paris in French Neo-Noir Cinema

GINETTE VINCENDEAU

Film noir may be a French expression, as well as – initially – a French critical concept; yet its application to French cinema has traditionally been controversial (see O'Brien 1996; Vincendeau 2007) and the dominant understanding of the term is largely linked to American cinema. The same applies to neo-noir. For Phil Powrie, while 'French noir since the 1970s is very different from Hollywood "neo-noir" ... the post-1968 *polar* is no less indebted to Hollywood than its post-1945 predecessor' (2007: 55). The transatlantic dialectic Powrie is referring to is indeed central to the generic cluster that can be examined under the labels of 'noir' and 'neo-noir' in French cinema, primarily the *policier* (or *polar* in slang, meaning any French thriller, police or crime film, whether the police feature in it nor not), but also the urban drama. My project here, however, is not to examine this transnational dialectic, even though the relationship to America informs any discussion of French noir and neo-noir. Rather, I wish to explore how French neo-noir cinema engages with the social world through its representation of crime and the city – primarily Paris.

My focus will be a number of striking crime films and urban dramas of the last 15 years, book-ended by Bertrand Tavernier's *L.627* (1992) and Jacques Audiard's *De battre mon coeur s'est arrêté/The Beat that My Heart Skipped* (2005), and including in between: *J'ai pas sommeil/I Can't Sleep* (1994), *Regarde les hommes tomber/See How They Fall* (1994), *Assassin(s)* (1997), *Place Vendôme* (1998), *Baise-moi* (2000), *Chaos* (2001),[1] *Sur mes lèvres/Read My Lips* (2001), *Irréversible/Irreversible* (2002), *36 Quai des Orfèvres/Department 36* (2004), *Feux rouges/Red Lights* (2004) and *Le Petit lieutenant/The Young Lieutenant* (2005). Through these films, I explore the way neo-noir cinema inscribes the increasingly multi-ethnic nature of French society narratively and spatially within the metropolis, constructing new topographies for criminals, policemen and victims. I am particularly interested in how French neo-noir films revisit the classic representations of the Parisian 'lower depths', understood as the 'underbelly' of the urban population, the socially and culturally subaltern, living in the poorest quarters of the city. However, as we will see, whereas these traditionally appeared as populist microcosms of the French community in films of the 1930s, such as *Dans les rues/Song of the Streets* (1933), *Les Bas-fonds/The Lower Depths* (1936) and *Le Quai des brumes/Port of Shadows* (1938), or in the colonial context of the Algerian Casbah in *Pépé le Moko* (1937), in contemporary neo-noir films, the place and status of the lower depths has considerably altered.

What is French neo-noir cinema?

I must start by making two detours. The first is French neo-noir literature and the second the film *Série noire* (1979), in many ways the ancestor of French neo-noir cinema.

Classic French noir cinema was predicated on the abundant production of crime literature both before and after the war, in particular the novels of Georges Simenon and those published by the Série noire at Gallimard. While some contemporary films still feed on this heritage (*Feux rouges* is based on Simenon), neo-noir cinema is informed – though less directly – by new trends in crime literature that arose after May 1968, with writers such as Jean-Patrick Manchette, Didier Daeninckx and Thierry Jonquet. The 'new' *roman noir* is characterised by an explicit concern for social and political issues, by increased violence, and by a pervasive dark outlook (see Gorrara 2003). A few of Manchette and Daeninckx's novels have been adapted for film, but on the whole their left-wing political commitment has rarely translated to the screen.[2]

Alain Corneau's film *Série noire* anticipates most clearly contemporary neo-noir cinema. Corneau took his inspiration from an American novel (Jim Thompson's *A Hell of a Woman* (1954)) and transposed it to a grim Paris suburb that seems to contain nothing but squalid, small houses and high-rise blocks. The film opens in a no-man's-land where the hero Franck Poupart (Patrick Dewaere), a sad travelling salesman, incongruously dances to jazz music around his car, in the rain. Characters are either pathetic (Poupart; Mona (Marie Trintignant), an exploited young woman he falls in love with; Poupart's wife) or sinister (his boss, Mona's aunt, a group of Hell's Angels). This is a desperate film where noir is synonymous with *anomie* – *Série noire* only manages not to alienate the spectator because of the mesmerising performance by Dewaere (on *Série noire* see Forbes 1992 and Powrie 2007). Shot in gritty black-and-white, the emblematically named *Série noire*, falling between Jean-Pierre Melville's beautifully stylised classic policiers and the more political and/or naturalistic thrillers of the 1970s, marked a turning point in French noir. Stylistically, it prefigured the more recent neo-noir cinema in several ways: in its hopeless and desolate tone, in its self-consciousness with regards to its own generic past, and in its visual style, in particular the choice of locations and low-key, 'grungy' photography.

As in American cinema, French neo-noir can be understood both as simply coming after classic noir and as a reconfiguration or critique of it (on US neo-noir see Gallafent 1992). While French neo-noir could thus simply designate any noir film made after *Série noire*, the term refers also to a set of reconfigurations of the classic *policier*, during an era when the latter gradually lost the mainstream appeal it had enjoyed since the 1950s.[3] The first wave of neo-noir rewriting in the 1980s was performed by the *cinéma du look*, with films such as *Diva* (1981) and *Subway* (1985) (see Powrie 2007). Another concurrent wave was achieved through the remoulding of the *policier* by auteurs such as Jean-Luc Godard (*Détective* (1985)), Maurice Pialat (*Police* (1985)) and Patrice Leconte (*Monsieur Hire* (1989)). The 1990s saw a different kind of revival with a return to social issues by established filmmakers (*L.627*), as well as under the banner of the *jeune cinéma français* (see Beugnet 2000; Prédal 2005). This is a cinema interested in 'marginality', alienation and social problems, out of which emerged films such as *La Haine/Hate* (1995) and *La Vie rêvée des anges/The Dream Life of Angels* (1998), as well as *Assassin(s)*, *Sur mes lèvres* and *De battre mon coeur s'est arrêté*. Yet another wave came with the films of the 'New French Extremism' which, with their emphasis on extreme sex, dystopia and violence, also produced work that occasionally comes under the neo-noir label, with titles such as *Seul contre tous/I Stand Alone* (1998), *Sombre* (1998), *Irréversible* and *Baise-moi*. Finally, the turn of the twenty-first century has seen a revival of the classic *policier* with *Feux rouges*, *36 Quai des Orfèvres* and *Le Petit lieutenant*.

Classic French noir can be divided into two main trends: on the one hand, the *policiers* which were *visually* noir (with archetypal low-key lighting) but on the whole narratively upbeat and, on the other hand, 'social noir' represented by urban dramas like *Manèges/The Cheat* (1949) or *Voici le temps des assassins…/Deadlier Than the Male* (1956) which, despite not belonging to the crime film genre, were truly noir in narrative, 'mood' and visual style (see Vincendeau 2007). The neo-noir films evidence a blurring of the two trends, the social dimension seeping into the *policier* genre films, while violent crime invades the social films – indeed, in this respect, neo-noir cinema is part of a wider trend in French cinema of the last ten to 15 years, in which genre blurring has become more widespread and, in particular, auteur films have tended to mix social commentary and crime. The narrative tone and visual register of the films is dark and downbeat. Music is low key, bleak or absent (as in *Le Petit lieutenant*). With a few notable exceptions (*Série noire* and *La Haine*), the majority of them are in colour, but they favour either grungy, naturalistic colour (*L.627*) or a cold, grey-blue palette (*36 Quai des Orfèvres*) that can be traced back to Melville's late 'black-and-white films in colour' (*Le Samouraï* (1967), *Le Cercle rouge/The Red*

Circle (1969), *Un Flic/A Cop* (1972)).[4] Indeed the crucial importance of Melville as a model is signalled in overt or covert references, illustrating also the high self-consciousness that informs neo-noir cinema. For instance, *J'ai vu tuer Ben Barka/I Saw Ben Barka Killed* (2005) and *36 Quai des Orfèvres* include Melvillian references in their cool colour scheme, while *36 Quai des Orfèvres* pushes the tribute further with an informer called Silien (Jean-Paul Belmondo's character in Melville's *Le Doulos/Doulos: The Finger Man* (1962)). Some neo-noir films also signal their cinephilic credentials in more explicit ways, for instance in the abundance of film posters in policemen's offices.

French neo-noir films thus show a marked stylistic evolution from their classic antecedents, especially the *policier* – with a darkening narrative tone in tune with a downbeat visual register and extreme self-consciousness, not only towards their American counterparts (as the classic films did) but also towards their indigenous antecedents. We can now turn to their representation of crime and society within the Parisian context.

New crime, new fears, new ethnicities

Classic French noir displayed the nostalgic vision of an ordered criminal world, imbued with a code of honour among gangsters (*Touchez pas au grisbi/Honour Among Thieves* (1954), *Du rififi chez les hommes/Rififi* (1955), *Bob le flambeur/ Bob The Gambler* (1956), *Le Deuxième souffle/Second Breath* (1966)). Crime was characterised by the nobility of craft: elegantly dressed gangsters spent time breaking into safes or robbing casinos and jewellers. The 1970s politicised crime and located it at the heart of state institutions (the legal system, the police, the government: *L'Attentat/Plot* (1972), *Un condé/Blood on My Hands* (1970), *Nada* (1974)). That decade also marked the beginning of a move towards more overt and more prominent representations of drugs and prostitution, which hitherto had been either hinted at or allegorised. Narratives shifted towards the world of petty drug dealing, primarily within immigrant milieux (*Police*, *La Balance/The Nark* (1982), *L.627*) and 'senseless', anomic personal crime (*Série noire*, *L'Appât/The Bait* (1995), *Assassin(s)*). A further shift brought to the screen a new breed of organised crime. Previous portrayals of the mafia, whether Sicilian (*Le Clan des Siciliens/The Sicilian Clan* (1969)), North African Jewish (*Le Grand pardon/Grand Pardon* (1982)) or from Marseille (*Borsalino* (1970)), had been endowed with a strong code of honour, decorous manners and 'family' values. Instead, films in the 1990s moved to a representation of Eastern European mafias, uniformly represented as vicious and completely unscrupulous (*Chaos*, *Le Petit lieutenant*, *De battre mon coeur s'est arrêté*).

Another aspect of the changing nature of crime in French neo-noir cinema is the complex shifts that occurred in terms of representations of the police. The cosy world of the 1950s and 1960s *policiers*, where hard-working policemen (as in the Maigret films, Henri-Georges Clouzot's *Quai des Orfèvres/Jenny Lamour* (1947) or *Razzia sur la chnouf/Razzia* (1955)) interacted with a basically knowable and controllable criminal world, has definitely vanished – or rather it has moved to television series such as *Navarro* (1989–present), *Julie Lescaut* (1992–present) and *PJ/C.I.D.* (1997–present).[5] Such a reassuring vision was first challenged by depictions of the police as inherently corrupt in the wake of May 1968: now policemen frequently *were* the criminals. Since the 1980s, representations have reverted, again, to more sympathetic portrayals of the police, often because the films, scripted by former policemen, are bent on representing the police 'realistically' but from their own point of view (for a detailed discussion of the representation of the police, see Philippe 1996). As in *L.627*, it is their struggle and hard work, this time against uncontrollable elements, that we follow. As a result, compared to the 1970s, police corruption in neo-noir films – despite the darker aesthetics – no longer denotes an oppressive and bankrupt political system, but tends to boil down to internal rivalries between different squads or petty individual powermongering, as in *36 Quai des Orfèvres*. The opening of this film is in this respect emblematic. Two men wearing helmets can be seen removing a street sign bearing the name 'Quai des Orfèvres'. Chased by policemen, they narrowly escape. It is revealed shortly after that the thieves were two policemen. The street plaque, signed by the whole brigade, is given as a leaving present to one of their colleagues – a brilliant image of the moral confusion between crime and the law, but also of the trivialisation of the notion of police corruption.

When not set among the police, contemporary French neo-noir films explore the world of marginality that is typical of the *jeune cinéma français*. Here, anomie, isolation and lack of social bearings are the rule. René Prédal's characterisation of Jacques Audiard's *Regarde les hommes tomber* as about 'human wrecks in a *polar* without cops' (2005: 99; author's translation) sums up this new chaotic world and could equally apply to *Assassin(s)*. In this film, Mathieu Kassovitz explores the notion of violence passing from one generation of males to the next, represented by helpless individuals drifting through a dreary suburb.[6] In *Sur mes lèvres*, violent crime is embodied by a socially dysfunctional petty hoodlum, Paul (Vincent Cassel), who enters the world of business through his relationship with a lonely secretary, Carla (Emmanuelle Devos), who is deaf and, as a result, the butt of her colleagues' jokes. Similarly, *De battre mon coeur s'est arrêté* features a hero on the margins, poised uneasily – in a very postmodern gesture – between the world of sordid crime and the world of high culture (classical music). As Prédal also says, 'Times have changed: what is interesting today takes place in the peripheral social tranche rather than at the centre of the petite bourgeoisie' (2005: 139: author's translation).

If the social positioning of protagonists has changed from classic noir, gender remains more constant and French neo-noir continues to marginalise female characters. There is no equivalent to the American femme fatale and no female protagonist with the narrative stature and/or star power of a Sharon Stone in *Basic Instinct* (1992) or a Linda Fiorentino in *The Last Seduction* (1994). Change, however, has taken place in the depiction of the male figure. Contrary to the patriarchal heroes of the classic gangster films (who survive in television series such as *Navarro*), male protagonists, as in *Série noire*, are invariably explored in their vulnerable and/or dysfunctional dimensions. *La Haine* focuses on three maladjusted young males. In *Irréversible*, the core of the story is the horrifying rape of a young woman, Alex (Monica Belluci), but the narrative is structured 'backwards' in such a way that it focuses on the trauma of her male partner, Marcus (Vincent Cassel). Virtually all the films explored in this chapter illustrate a male focus, with two exceptions, *Sur mes lèvres* and *Le Petit lieutenant* (the female protagonists share the lead with a man in each case). Another transformation is the emphasis on paternity – the child often replaces the woman as the ultimate focus of the narrative. In *36 Quai des Orfèvres*, the wronged policeman, Léo Vrinks (Daniel Auteuil), loses his wife but is reunited with his daughter when he comes out of jail; in *Le Petit lieutenant*, the tragedy of the heroine, Commandant Caroline Vaudieu (Nathalie Baye), is the earlier loss of a son and, within the film, of a son substitute, the 'little lieutenant', Antoine Derouère (Jalil Lespert).

The only significant challenge to the male focus of French neo-noir comes from the violently sexual *Baise-moi*, in which two (literal) femme fatales wreak havoc among a series of men in a gory rape-revenge narrative, while graphically experiencing sexual pleasure in the process – an unusual scenario clearly linked to the fact that the film is directed by two women (Virginie Despentes and Coralie Trin Thi). However, *Baise-moi* remains an exception, at the crossroads of neo-noir, gore, pornography and women's cinema.

Thus several aspects – such as gender and the types of crime depicted – have changed in the depiction of French society in neo-noir cinema, but none as much as the ethnic composition of that society. Back in the 1950s, Série noire books such as *Touchez pas au grisbi* and *Du rififi chez les hommes* included a strong ethnic and racist dimension, but the films that were adapted from them cleansed this, retaining only traces of otherness under the guise of picturesque exotic elements, such as Corsican mafiosi. From the 1980s onwards, crime on-screen became ethnically and racially 'coloured' (on the representation of ethnicity in French cinema, see Tarr 2005). In *La Balance*, for instance, policemen pursue, humiliate and beat up a North African drug dealer in a courtyard, his racial make-up doubly emphasised by his skin colour (further enhanced by his wearing a white suit) and his accent. This film, as well as *Neige/Snow* (1981), *Les Ripoux/Le Cop* (1984) and *Police* among others, routinely showed drug dealing, theft and prostitution as situated within ethnically marked milieux, principally North African and Black African, in line with the legacy of the French colonial past.

In the 1990s, the *beur*/black criminality theme continued,[7] as illustrated by *L.627* in which we follow a group of harassed white policemen in their daily struggles against drug-related petty criminal activities and prostitution in impoverished areas of Paris. Apart from a white, drug-addicted prostitute, most 'criminals' in the film are black or of North African origin. Two scenes encapsulate this racial divide. In the first one, a black woman, Alimata (Laurentine Milebo), whose daughter works as a prostitute in the same cluttered room behind a curtain, offers her daughter to the two (white) policemen in exchange for a favour. In the second one, a particularly harrowing scene towards the end of the film, the policemen bust a squalid building inhabited by miserably poor black families of squatters. A young black woman on crack howls with distress as her baby is taken from her by the policemen to be handed over to social services. In both cases the policemen are portrayed as justified: Alimata volunteers her daughter's sexual services without the policemen requesting it; the young black woman is incapable of looking after her baby. Tavernier and his scriptwriter, former policeman Michel Alexandre, were at pains to defend these representations on the grounds of verisimilitude (see Tavernier 1993) and they received the vocal support of the Parisian police rank and file. It is also the case that the film does not refrain from showing racism in the police and widespread social devastation. Yet there is a clear bias in the film, in which law and order as well as sympathetic or tragic characters are white, while criminals happen to be black or North African (and the effects of the 'foreign' drugs are graphically shown on the tragic white prostitute); in this respect, *L.627* can be regarded as something of a benchmark of ethnic representation.

Subsequently, a number of neo-noir films began to alter this white/non-white divide, in some cases in explicit response to Tavernier's film. In 1994, Claire Denis' *J'ai pas sommeil* controversially told the story (inspired by a real case) of a black, homosexual, HIV-positive serial killer. The film inserts this potentially 'politically incorrect' story – as the filmmaker was aware – into a complex mosaic of race, sexuality and ethnic diversity and the film, unlike *L.627*, also explores pervasive racism as well as a deep-seated malaise within French society. As Martine Beugnet points out in her illuminating analysis of *J'ai pas sommeil*, here 'French [white] society is represented principally by a cynical, ineffectual and unpleasant police force, individuals with libidinous gazes and attitudes, and lonely old women' (2000: 271; author's translation). A year after *J'ai pas sommeil*, *La Haine* also explicitly aimed to challenge the racial divide illustrated by *L.627*. Kassovitz tells the story from the point of view of ethnic 'minorities' – his three heroes are black, *beur* and white-Jewish – and analysed the causes of their violence, even though racism was not his main agenda; he was more interested in pinpointing police violence (see Vincendeau 2005).

A less well-known, yet remarkable, film is *Chaos*, a comedy in which humour and drama derive from the encounter between the comfortable white bourgeoisie and the lower depths (indeed the film is typical of the contemporary genre blurring alluded to earlier). *Chaos* also usefully illustrates the further shifts in the foreignness of villains that occurred in French neo-noir cinema in the 1990s and at the turn of the twenty-first century. A rich bourgeois couple, Hélène and Paul (Catherine Frot and Vincent Lindon), see their life shattered by an encounter with a *beur* prostitute, Noémie/Malika (Rachida Brakni), who is violently beaten up by pimps on the bonnet of their car. Although male violence against her originates in her Arab family (her father trying to force her into an arranged marriage drives her out into prostitution), her pimps are Eastern Europeans. In *36 Quai des Orfèvres*, similarly, the arch villains are 'Yugoslavs'. *Le Petit lieutenant* is another clear example of this new ethnic mapping. While it explicitly celebrates the integration of a *beur* policeman, Solo (Roschdy Zem), among his white colleagues, the film also designates more serious criminality as originating from Eastern Europe. When Antoine, the rookie white lieutenant, is introduced to Solo, another policeman jokes that he 'has the face of one of our customers although he is not one of them'. Later on, at a dinner among colleagues Solo recalls his colleagues' initially racist attitudes towards him, but declares himself now happily integrated. Yet, while the film casually considers most petty criminals as coming from African backgrounds (one policeman says to Antoine, 'You are paid to throw Arabs and Blacks in jail'), tellingly the criminal gang at the centre of the story is a group of ferocious Russians, one of whom shockingly kills Antoine.

Comparing *L.627* to *Le Petit lieutenant* is instructive of the change in the intervening decade. The former empathised with white policemen trying to control a chaotic criminal underworld of mostly Arab origin; the latter shows a wider and more balanced social spread, including a *beur* policeman with a family. Yet a racially marked hierarchy is still in place in the new criminal world: the ringleaders are white Eastern Europeans, vicious yet endowed with a certain glamour, and the lower depths are occupied by the darker-skinned, most socially destitute groups – a situation also perfectly exemplified by *De battre mon coeur s'est arrêté*. In this film, the hero, Thomas Seyr (Romain Duris) and two friends make a living from shady property deals, which involve brutally expropriating dirt-poor families of dark skin colour who squat in derelict buildings, with such methods as releasing rats in the staircases. In two separate scenes featuring such spaces, extremely mobile camerawork and the night-time setting construct a disorientating, opaque, sordid and dangerous world inhabited by non-white people. On the other hand, when Thomas's father is the victim of a powerful and cruel gang, the ringleader turns out to be the rich and glamorous Russian, Minskov (Anton Yakovlev), whom we encounter in the context of his luxury hotel swimming pool. Clean high living for the Russian, grimy derelict environment for the dark-skinned: the new lower depths' foreignness has shifted, but skin colour hierarchies are still in place.

The new lower depths

The ethnic hierarchies just discussed intersect fascinatingly with recognisable mappings across Paris and its suburbs. Neo-noir films in the 1980s, such as *Neige*, *La Balance* and *Les Ripoux* regularly situated criminality in Barbès and Belleville to the north and north east of the city. These formerly traditional white working-class *quartiers* witnessed from the 1960s the arrival of immigrants from Northern and Sub-Saharan Africa. These areas, which cover the 18th, 19th and 20th *arrondissements* of the city (and are often visually signalled by the recognisable silhouette of the overground *métro aérien*) overlap with the traditional criminal areas of Pigalle and Montmartre as featured in the 1950s and 1960s *policiers*. The relationship between the criminals and the city in the intervening years has, however, dramatically changed. Gone are the days of the cosy familiarity between gangsters such as Max (Jean Gabin) in *Touchez pas au grisbi* and Bob (Roger Duchesne) in *Bob le flambeur* and their territory, which they treated as their village – an emotional bond enhanced by closeness to 'ordinary people': concierges, shopkeepers, neighbours and even local policemen. Going further back, the 1930s Poetic Realist dramas, precursors of French noir, similarly blurred the distinction between criminal and 'ordinary' worker, presenting an idealised, romantic view of the lower depths as deeply embedded in the populist community and within the geography of the city. Now by contrast the territories occupied by racially marked criminals or simply the poorest rungs of the French social ladder are depicted as squalid and chaotic spaces, as in *L.627* or *De battre mon coeur s'est arrêté*. Alternatively, they are bleakly anonymous locations, for instance in *Sur mes lèvres* and *36 Quai des Orfèvres*. Either way, at the level of the microcosm – the building, the *quartier*, the *arrondissement* – the connection between the denizens of the lower depths and the ordinary population has been severed. In this way, the neo-noir films take stock of the *fracture sociale*.[8]

Concurrently, at the macro level, a centrifugal movement pushes criminal or illegal habitats further out of the historic city centre towards the outlying *arrondissements*, the periphery and the suburbs (*banlieue*), a trajectory well illustrated by *Chaos*. In this film, the white bourgeois couple who live in the centre encounter violent crime by accident in a street at night in the 9th *arrondissement*. The violence that surrounds the young *beur* prostitute who thereby enters their lives is revealed to originate in the suburbs. Petty criminal activities occur on the *boulevards extérieurs*, where she and other women work as prostitutes, and the vicious imprisoning and 'taming' of the young women by the Eastern European pimps takes place in some distant location (even though the 'moral' of the story is that the encounter benefits both the bourgeois couple and the *beur* woman, the topography just outlined holds). This centrifugal movement itself can be understood in relation to the specificities of Parisian topography that are particularly clear when it comes to crime films and thus many neo-noir titles.

The Parisian police headquarters are situated on Quai des Orfèvres within a unique set of interconnecting buildings on the Île de la Cité at the epicentre of the city. Combining the police (the Quai des Orfèvres building proper), the law courts (the Palais de Justice) and medieval as well as Revolutionary monuments (the Sainte-Chapelle, the Conciergerie), this ensemble constitutes a prestigious historical landmark (see Colson & Lauroa 1997: 559–60) but also a potent spatial symbol of centralised power and control.[9] Towards the beginning of *Le Petit lieutenant,* we see the young hero Antoine smiling as he surveys Paris from a high vantage point. At his feet, the iconic city centre is spread in all its glory, his elevated position an image of his imaginary control. The next scene shows him entering the police station at ground level, an apt metaphor for the chaotic set of events that will follow. *Le Petit lieutenant* stays within Paris – the Canal Saint-Martin area – but the more we progress through the criminal investigation the further we go towards the city limits, as in *L.627.* If Paris is increasingly presented as an ethnic mosaic (see Binh with Garbarz 2005: 205–6), the movement out of the centre towards the city limits in neo-noir duplicates the racial and social hierarchies of Paris.

In a city historically built through the accretion of a series of concentric walls, it is as if the films try to push crime outwards. The double ring of boulevards encircling the city (the *boulevards extérieurs* and the *boulevard périphérique*) becomes a symbolic barrier separating the centre of relative order and power from the more chaotic spaces beyond – in 1997, Bertrand Tavernier and his son Nils made a documentary about the *banlieue* entitled *De l'autre côté du périph*/*On the Other Side of the Périphérique.* The sharply circumscribed centre becomes increasingly the preserve of the white middle class, while the poor working class and immigrants are relegated to the *banlieue* which, with the building of high-rise blocks under Général de Gaulle in the postcolonial period, has come to signify social and racial exclusion.[10]

At the time of *Série noire,* director Alain Corneau said, 'What interests me in the *banlieue* is that it is a devastated space where anything can happen, something very violent. It is the urban space where alienation is at its strongest … It has no historical connotations' (in Guérif 1981: 158; author's translation). If Corneau's view of the *banlieue* lacks nuance, this is indeed how many films treat the area. Godard's *Deux ou trois choses que je sais d'elle*/*Two or Three Things I Know About Her* in 1967 and *La Haine* in 1995 fixed the meaning of the *banlieue* as a place of architectural brutality and social alienation, always sharply divorced from the historic city. In *36 Quai des Orfèvres,* a climactic scene between the police and a gang of criminals takes place in a derelict building in St Ouen, close to the *périphérique,* and the suburb of Gennevilliers

Unanchored space: *Assassin(s)*

is referred to as 'the arsehole of the *banlieue*'. In this respect, the topography of Paris, together with its social history, contradict the assertion that 'the contrast between centre and periphery is no longer a viable tool for reading the contemporary European cinematic city' (Mazierska & Rascaroli 2003: 238). Unlike many other major European cities where industrial no-man's-lands can be situated within the city centre (King's Cross or the Docklands in London, Ruoholahti in Helsinki), in Paris they are located in the suburbs, for example the isolated nightclub in *Sur mes lèvres*, emphasising the social dislocation and violent crime that take place in such locations. In this film, only one brief iconic (and possibly ironic) shot of the Eiffel Tower from the rooftop of the suburban club anchors the story in space, but also thereby reinforces the centre/suburb division.

Assassin(s) and *36 Quai des Orfèvres* signal another evolution in the representation of the *banlieue* where it is figured as a blank, affect-less space, away from the social anchorage of *La Haine*. Here, as in Corneau's quote, the *banlieue* becomes the 'non-place' identified by Marc Augé (1996: 177),[11] or the 'any-space-whatever' of Gilles Deleuze (1989: 272). *36 Quai des Orfèvres* offers a good illustration of such 'non-place'. The attack on a convoy takes place on an anonymous motorway near La Defense. As Inspector Denis Klein (Gérard Depardieu) remarks, there are only offices in the vicinity and therefore no witnesses. In the same film, a criminal is arrested in an anonymous motel. While retaining the centre/periphery dichotomy, French neo-noir films in this respect seem to gesture towards an increasing 'anonymisation' of space. *Sur mes lèvres* is exemplary in this respect, as the camera details at length dreary, anonymous modern offices and cafeterias bathed in a grey colour scheme. By contrast, in the 1930s films, precise locations were designed to stand as microcosms of the community; in Augé's words, the *quartier* was deployed as the 'metonymic city' (1996: 176). Spaces such as the café, the staircase and the courtyard emphasised the bonding of the community, bridging the gap between the lawful and the lawless, and (despite being recreated in the studio) aimed at verisimilitude, anchoring locations within the city. Neo-noir films instead focus on the disconnection between the lawless and the mainstream social space or the anonymity of the latter. Thus, underpasses frequently feature, in films such as *L.627* and *De battre mon coeur s'est arrêté*, connoting loss of bearings and transience and, in the extreme case of *Irréversible*, total urban horror (car parks are similarly used, as in *Sur mes lèvres* where Carla is almost raped and Paul is beaten up). Dark streets, canal and river banks, usually shown at night and deserted, emphasise an anonymous relationship to the city, rather than its identity as social space. Streets and courtyards are no longer the setting for the exploration of communal feelings, as in *Le Crime de Monsieur Lange/The Crime of Monsieur Lange* (1936), but instead act as places of chaos and danger. Cafés, rather than the surrogate homes they were for the lower depths of the 1930s films, underline family breakdown and loneliness, as indeed do apartments (*Chaos, De battre mon coeur s'est arrêté*).

Paris occupies an ambiguous position in cultural discourses on the city in the cinema. While its history is central to any argument about the modern and modernist 'cinematic city' – Baudelaire, Haussmann, Benjamin, the figure of the *flâneur* are obligatory references (among others, see Sheringham 1996; Shiel & Fitzmaurice 2001; Jousse & Paquot 2005) – its place in postmodernity is more complicated, as it seems to buck several trends that have been identified in relation to cities such as Berlin and Los Angeles. Classic studio-reconstructed Parisian décors, as in poetic realism, are far from the 'undifferentiated city' that Geoffrey Nowell-Smith identifies as typical of studio-bound noir cinema (2001: 101); on the contrary they are rooted in specific *quartiers*. Similarly, the lower depths in classic French films had been typically integrated within the 'normal' working-class environment. As Alastair Phillips says, 'Unlike the case of the dark and dangerous streets of cinematic Berlin ... Parisian crime often became fused with a safer and less confrontational perspective' (2004: 128; see also Andrew 1995 for in-depth discussion of Poetic Realist narratives and design). By contrast, in neo-noir, the lower depths are obscure, marginal spaces hidden away within the centre or, more often, pushed out towards the suburbs. In this movement, which we have observed in a number of recent neo-noir films, Paris also contradicts studies of the postmodern city, which argue for a fragmentation that renders the dichotomy between centre and periphery obsolete.

A few filmmakers, notably Claire Denis in *J'ai pas sommeil* and Michael Haneke in *Code inconnu/Code Unknown* (2000) and *Caché/Hidden* (2005), have aimed at rendering the French postmodern urban experience by bringing the ethnic mosaic right into the city centre. The opening of *Code inconnu* (shot near

The margins in the centre: *Code inconnu/Code Unknown*

the Eiffel Tower, although the tower does not appear) shows this clearly in two magnificent tracking shots in which native French, including a 'migrant' from the countryside, a Balkan immigrant and second-generation black African clash. However, in the neo-noir films examined here, the tendency is still rather different. In *policiers* and urban dramas alike, a relatively clear trajectory of power radiates from the centre (sometimes literally, from Quai des Orfèvres) that is more often than not 'white', trying – however ineffectually – to eradicate or push out a criminality that is almost invariably 'foreign' towards the lower depths at the city limits and beyond, in the *banlieue*. As in the title of two films discussed here, there lie – or so the films wish to believe – 'hatred' and 'chaos'.

NOTES

1   Oddly, this remarkable film was never distributed in the UK, but is now available on DVD.

2   *La Crime/Cover Up* (1983) and *Polar* (1984) are based on novels by Manchette; *Héroines* (1997) and *La Repentie* (2002) are based on novels by Daeninckx.

3   An article in the trade journal *Le film français* (Dacbert 1998) perceptively attributed the relative eclipse of the *policier* in the 1980s and early 1990s to two main sources: the success of American thrillers by filmmakers such as Clint Eastwood, Martin Scorsese, Brian De Palma, the Coen brothers and Quentin Tarantino; and the rise of hugely popular French television crime series (see note 5 below).

4   I am, of course, aware that this visual register is also attributable to the influence of Hollywood, for instance the films of Michael Mann. *Place Vendôme*, for example, pays tribute to Hitchcock in its narrative and use of music.

5   These series are among the most popular programmes on French television; other popular police series include *Nestor Burma* (1991–present) and *Commissaire Moulin* (1976–2006), not to mention the series of *Maigret* telefilms starring Bruno Cremer (1991–2005).

6   Kassovitz had explored the same topic in his short *Assassins ...* (1992), which acted as a pilot for the feature *Assassin(s)*.

7   *Beur* is back slang (*verlan*) for Arab. *Beur* is a widely used, yet controversial term to designate second-generation North African immigrants to France. Embraced by militant anti-racists in the 1980s and by many in and outside of this community, the term is also rejected by others as denying differences among '*beurs*' who, for example, are not all Arabs, and ultimately racist.

8   The *fracture sociale*, meaning 'social divide', is an expression coined by sociologist Emmanuel Todd. It refers to the concern that a section of the population, including a high proportion of immigrants, is disenfranchised from mainstream society, leading to a rupture of the social fabric.

9   Although all the films discussed in this chapter were made before June 2007, it is worth mentioning that at that point President Nicolas Sarkozy announced his intention to move police headquarters out of Quai des Orfèvres into the suburbs, in line with his wide-scale reorganisation of the police force. The iconic status of 36 Quai des Orfèvres, however, can be measured by the chorus of disapproval that met Sarkozy's decision, quoting its importance in relation to crime film and literature; for instance the *Independent* ran an article entitled, 'Paris police close book on Maigret's legendary home' (Lichfield 2007).

10 In the first instance, the high-rise buildings represented social progress, compared to the slums that some of their inhabitants had been living in initially. Gradually, though, immigrant populations were increasingly moved to the new suburbs, in a grimly ironic reversal of the French colonial cities in North Africa where the lower depths were situated in the Casbah in the centre, and the 'modern', French-style, areas on the outskirts.

11 Augé developed the concept of 'non-place' further in his 1992 book, *Non-Places: Introduction to an Anthropology of Supermodernity* (see Augé 1995).

REFERENCES

Andrew, Dudley (1995) *Mists of Regret: Culture and Sensibility in Classic French Film*. Princeton: Princeton University Press.

Augé, Marc (1995) *Non-Places: Introduction to an Anthropology of Supermodernity*, trans. John Howe. London: Verso.

____ (1996) 'Paris and the ethnography of the contemporary world', in Michael Sheringham (ed.) *Parisian Fields*. London: Reaktion Books, 175–9.

Beugnet, Martine (2000) *Marginalité, sexualité, contrôle dans le cinéma français contemporain*. Paris: L'Harmattan.

Binh, N.T. with Franck Garbarz (2005) *Paris au cinéma: La vie rêvée de la capitale de Méliès à Amélie Poulain*. Paris: Parigramme.

Colson, Jean and Marie-Christine Lauroa (1997) *Dictionnaire des Monuments de Paris*. Paris: Hervas.

Dacbert, Sophie (1998) 'Le nouveau polar français sort ses tentacules', *Le film français*, 2741/2, October, 28.

Deleuze, Gilles (1989) *Cinema 2: The Time-Image*, trans. Hugh Tomlinson and Robert Galeta. Minneapolis: University of Minnesota Press.

Forbes, Jill (1992) *The Cinema in France: After the New Wave*. Basingstoke: Macmillan.

Gallafent, Ed (1992) 'Echo Park: Film noir in the "Seventies"', in Ian Cameron (ed.) *The Movie Book of Film Noir*. London: Studio Vista, 254–85.

Gorrara, Claire (2003) *The roman noir in Post-war French Culture: Dark Fictions*. Oxford: Oxford University Press.

Guérif, François (1981) *Le Cinéma policier français*. Paris: Henri Veyrier.

Jousse, Thierry and Thierry Paquot (eds) (2005) *La Ville au cinéma*. Paris: Cahiers du cinéma.

Lichfield, John (2007) 'Paris police close book on Maigret's legendary home', *Independent*, 20 June. Available at: http://www.independent.co.uk/news/europe/paris-police-close-book-on-maigrets-legendary-home-453874.html. Accessed 27 March 2008.

Mazierska, Ewa and Laura Rascaroli (2003) *From Moscow to Madrid: Postmodern Cities, European Cinema*. London: I.B. Tauris.

Nowell-Smith, Geoffrey (2001) 'Cities: Real and Imagined', in Mark Shiel and Tony Fitzmaurice (eds) *Cinema and the City: Film and Urban Societies in a Global Context*. Oxford: Blackwell, 99–108.

O'Brien, Charles (1996) 'Film noir in France: Before the Liberation', *Iris*, 21, Spring, 7–20.

Philippe, Olivier (1996) *Le Film policier français contemporain*. Paris: Editions du Cerf.

Phillips, Alastair (2004) *City of Darkness, City of Light: Émigré Filmmakers in Paris 1929–1939*. Amsterdam: Amsterdam University Press.

Powrie, Phil (2007) 'French neo-noir to hyper-noir', in Andrew Spicer (ed.) *European Film Noir*. Manchester: Manchester University Press, 55–83.

Prédal, René (2005) *Le jeune cinéma français*. Paris: Armand Colin.

Sheringham, Michael (ed.) (1996) *Parisian Fields*. London: Reaktion Books

Shiel, Mark and Tony Fitzmaurice (eds) (2001) *Cinema and the City: Film and Urban Societies in a Global Context*. Oxford: Blackwell.

Tarr, Carrie (2005) *Reframing Difference: Beur and Banlieue Filmmaking in France*. Manchester: Manchester University Press.

Tavernier, Bertrand (1993) 'I wake up dreaming: A journal for 1992', in John Boorman and Walter Donohue (eds) *Projections 2: A Forum for Film-makers*. London: Faber and Faber, 252–378.

Vincendeau, Ginette (2005) *La Haine*. London: I.B. Tauris.

_____ (2007) 'French film noir', in Andrew Spicer (ed.) *European Film Noir*. Manchester: Manchester University Press, 23–54.

8

The Shadow of Outlaws in Asian Noir: Hiroshima, Hong Kong and Seoul

HYANGJIN LEE

Western scholarship on Asian cinema tends to pay little serious attention to gangster or crime thrillers, despite the significance of the genre in the region. Asian gangster noir typically critiques the existing social order and expresses a popular vision of an ideal postcolonial society rooted in traditional Confucian ethics. It has evolved within distinct national cinemas and as a transnational practice, rearticulating the pessimism, nihilism and determinism of the American film noir – typically contextualised by the postwar capitalist social order – through local sensibilities. The traditions of noir have engendered generic evolutions in Japanese, South Korean and Hong Kong cinemas, with the influence of noir's distinctive visual style, themes and characters clearly evident in films such as Akira Kurosawa's *Yoidore tenshi/Drunken Angel* (1948), *Nora inu/Stray Dog* (1949), *Warui yatsu hodo yoku nemuru/The Bad Sleep Well* (1960) and *Tengoku to jigoku/High and Low* (1963), Hyunmok Yu's *Obaltan/The Stray Bullet* (1960) and Kiyoung Kim's *Hanyo/The Housemaid* (1960). Such transnational flows have produced in Asian noir a Confucian hybridisation in which a sense of honour, duty and brotherhood (and other aspects of familial moralities) fuse with the cruelty and loneliness of a dark criminal world. In this, there looms the long shadow of postcolonial history in the region.

In the 1970s, despite the general decline of Japanese cinema, gangster films enjoyed great popularity, with Kinji Fukasaku's *Gendai yakuza: hito-kiri yota/Street Mobster* (1972), *Jingi naki tatakai/Battles without Honour and Humanity* (1973) and *Jingi no hakaba/Graveyard of Honour* (1975) proving a major turning point in the nature of the genre, both stylistically and in terms of popularity. During the 1980s, the advent of Hong Kong gangster films, such as John Woo's *Ying hung boon sik/A Better Tomorrow* (1986) and *Dip huet seung hung/The Killer* (1989), stimulated significant intra-Asian cultural flows. Since the

1990s, Japanese neo-noir has attained an international reputation mostly due to the works of Takeshi Kitano, Takashi Miike and Shinya Tsukamoto. Under the South Korean military dictatorship of the 1970s and 1980s, noirish crime film-making was virtually taboo, a situation from which Hong Kong gangster films profited. However, crime films such as Chan-wook Park's *Boksuneun naui geot/ Sympathy for Mr. Vengeance* (2001), *Oldboy* (2003) and *Chinjeolhan geumjassi/ Sympathy for Lady Vengeance* (2005) played an important role in the revival and international success of Korean film since the late 1990s. In Hong Kong, anxieties about an uncertain future were brought into focus by the 1989 Tiananmen Square protest, with fears of disappearance and shifting identities becoming dominant themes for filmmakers, expressing the ambivalence felt by many about the 1997 handover to China: Woo's *Die xue jie tou/Bullet in the Head* (1990) is a tale of friendship and betrayal between three men dislocated in Vietnam, while the stories of two lonely, heartbroken policemen in Wong Kar-wai's *Chung Hing sam lam/Chungking Express* (1994) convey hope for the future even as they provide a moving diary of a disappearing city. Subsequently, the new gangster noir, exemplified by Wai-keung Lau and Siu Fai Mak's *Mou gaan dou/Infernal Affairs* (2002), conveys the transitional identity of post-handover Hong Kong. This essay will explore the dynamic movement of 'Asian film noir' as a movement of transnational cultural influences in the age of globalisation.

Gangster noir as social criticism

Contemporary Asian noir's aesthetics of extremity and excess blend together horror, psycho-thriller and crime drama, with Kitano, Miike, Tsukamoto, Park and Jiwoon Kim the leading figures of this 'Asian extreme'. Raymond Borde and Étienne Chaumeton described 'the moral ambivalence, the criminality, and the complex contradictions in motives and events' which conspired 'to make the viewer co-experience the anguish and insecurity which are the true emotions of classical film noir' (2003: 25). In Asian noir, victim psychology is a critical element in the production of anguish and insecurity as the complex co-existence of old and new social values lead to the moral hazards of modern society. Materialism and the capitalist class order symbolise foreign inventions adopted into traditional Asian life. Traditional human relationships and group-oriented lifestyles are dismantled in contemporary urban settings which foster a social remoteness, isolation and loneliness more frightening than the overt violence in these films. Confusing characterisations, twisted plots and disturbing images express antagonism to a materialistic society in which there is little concern about the suffering of the weak (see Standish 2005: 330).

While mainstream audiences find little or no redeeming social worth or message in the sadistic representation of violence, sex and criminality, 'Asian extreme' provides genre film fans in the West with pleasurable fantasies of exotic lands. Such films often aim to communicate psychological effects to the audience rather than questioning the social gravity of violence. For instance, domestic violence, corporal punishment, incestuous relationships and sexual abuse between family members are common in Asian extreme, and these are the most sensitive issues from a traditional Confucian perspective. The representation of violence and cruelty in hidden spaces such as homes or schools uses personal trauma to criticise the social negligence of those whose suffering goes unnoticed. However, this focus on the individual and the psychological effects of living in an indifferent, remote society, tends to obscure or ignore inequality and the breakdown of the social. Similarly, in much contemporary Asian film noir, the story of crime and revenge centres on individuals abstracted from social history.

According to Tadao Satō (1987; 1995), the Japanese gangster noir is an expression of sentiments against Western domination. Fukasaku emphasised the point that his gangster noir was a popular vision of postwar Japan under the postwar American administration (1945–52) and the rapid economic growth pursued by the Japanese government in the following decades, and he insisted that the American occupation brought an end to the old violence of Japan by generating a new violence. His cinematic treatment of the sufferings of the underprivileged in the rapidly-developing capitalist society revived populist film culture in the 1970s. In contrast, contemporary Japanese noir films are largely indifferent to the demands of popular film culture, focusing on an audience of fans.

However, popularity is a barometer to evaluate the mobilising power of film as social criticism. The reputation of Takeshi Kitano as a director in Japan and overseas is a good example of this argument (see Mes & Sharp 2005). His standing – in the West – as *the* auteur of contemporary Japanese cinema remains unchallenged (see Gerow 2007). Cultural remoteness helps a Western audience to romanticise the cruelty and strangeness of criminal psychology expressed in his works as a creative sublimation of anxiety and emptiness, which they might assume is experienced by the ordinary citizens in everyday Japanese society. Furthermore, an Orientalist gaze has focused on and articulated his aesthetic of extremity and stillness into that of a world cinema artist (*Hana-bi/Fireworks* (1997), for example, was awarded the Golden Lion at the 54th Venice International Film Festival *and* chosen as the first Japanese film to be screened in Korea after a 52-year prohibition).[1] Japanese audiences, however, are largely indifferent to the ethnic politics of world cinema or the deployment strategies of Western film festivals. Of course, Kitano's international reputation is celebrated by Japanese media and his fans, who are a significant sector of the genre audience, but general audiences do not perceive anything as grave as social criticism in his work. Rather, in Japan, his films tend to be considered as a personal articulation of violence,[2] while the nonsensical images of Kitano as a slapstick television comedian tend to overwhelm his reputation as a talented filmmaker (although the sarcastic turn of both bodies of work may not be that different). In contrast, the popularity enjoyed by Fukasaku, Woo and Park as commercial filmmakers might indicate greater effectiveness in communicating with their national audiences. The noirish crime thrillers of Woo and Park also entertained Asian filmgoers across national borders before appearing in the West. The significance of Asian noir as a popular social critique can, therefore, be accessed and understood differently in the national, regional and global contexts.

Asian film noir has a transnational genealogy. Despite US domination of the global film market, transnational flows of popular film culture in the region have visibly influenced the evolution of national cinemas in relation to each other. The common traits of Asian noir – pessimism, psychological emptiness and moral ambivalence in portraying criminality – combine transnational flows of Asian and Hollywood noir (see Bordwell 2000; Kim & Cheong 2001; Richie 2001) with national attributes, localising the regional and global genre. In order to identify these national and transnational elements, this essay will compare the three national cinemas, taking as its key examples Fukasaku's *Jingi naki tatakai* (1973), Woo's *Ying hung boon sik* and Park's *Oldboy*, each of which, at roughly 15 year intervals, established a new tradition of Asian gangster noir. At the same time, their different styles and thematic concerns underline the significance of national cinema in the age of transnational cinema, highlighting the 'unique' historical experiences of a people and the cultural tradition of a nation (see Higson 2002). This essay will conclude with reflections on the significance of diversity and commonality in Asian gangster noir in a global context.

Outlaw, hero and organised thug: three faces of violence

Yakuza (outlaw), *yīngxióng* (hero) and *jopok* (organised thug) are local terms for criminal types in the gangster noir of Japan, Hong Kong and South Korea, respectively. These images of criminality vary in accordance with the different modernising paths each nation followed. However, Asian gangster noir commonly interrogates the political status quo of the *present*, questioning the ideal relationship between the state and the subject within the context of Confucian traditions. The assumption is that in a capitalist society, the public force monopolised by the state does not embody social justice. In other words, money destroys traditional social norms, and crime, rather than being destructive injustice, can be legitimised as a means of restoring social justice (see Magnan-Park 2007). For instance, when a dysfunctional police force proves incapable of protecting them, ordinary citizens have to question the existing social order. Consequently, the onscreen hero often chooses the criminal world, which provides an alternative form of the family-state amid failing social systems that neglect individuals trying to survive in terrible conditions.

The stereotypical opening for Asian gangster noir is the encounter of the protagonist, who has lost touch with ordinary people though being imprisoned or drafted into the military, with a powerful criminal figure (see Igarashi 2006: 368). This meeting offers a form of social rehabilitation. In Confucian teaching, the father/patriarch and the state are conceived as one body, and the protagonist finds in the head of the underworld a surrogate father. Gradually, though, the protagonist's anachronistic desire for the restoration of traditional ethics, bring him into conflict with both the state and the underworld. The three films I discuss in detail below deploy variations on this protagonist and narrative structure.

The lonely outlaw in *Jingi naki tatakai*

In 1947, at the black market in Hiroshima, a veteran called Hirono (Bunta Suga-wara) encounters American soldiers raping a Japanese woman and saves her with the help of Wakasugi (Tatsuo Umemiya), a member of Doi's (Nawa Hiro-shi) gang. Wandering through the aftermath of the atomic bombing, Hirono is involved in a street fight and ends up murdering an unknown samurai. In prison, he meets Wakasugi. When he gets out, Hirono joins Yamamori's (Nobuo Kaneko) gang, becoming his right-hand man. When they sabotage the election campaign of a candidate supported by Doi's gang, confrontation seems inevi-table. To avoid killing his sworn-brother Hirono, Wakasugi turns his back on Doi and serves Yamamori. Yamamori orders Hirono to kill Doi, but when he fails, Yamamori sends somebody to kill him. Hirono is arrested for attempting to kill Doi while fleeing the assassin and goes back to jail. While Hirono is in jail, Wakasugi avenges Hirono by killing the assassin. Yamamori informs the police of Wakasugi's whereabouts and, eventually, Wakasugi is killed. As soon as Hirono is released, he gets caught in the conflicts between the gangs again. Yamamori asks Hirono to kill Sakai (Hiroki Matsukata), his new deputy, for continually chal-

Bunta Sugawara, at gunpoint: *Jingi naki tatakai/Battles without Honour and Humanity*

lenging his power. Hirono refuses, but promises his loyalty is with Yamamori. The gang war never ends; money, not honour or humanity, is its ultimate objective. When Yamamori deceives Sakai and kills him from behind the scenes, Hirono becomes fed up with Yamamori's treachery and declares a one-man war against the greedy world.

Jingi naki tatakai was a huge box-office success, followed by four sequels (known collectively as the *Jingi* series), which revitalised the popularity of *yakuza eiga* in the 1970s. Rejecting the conventions of traditional *yakuza eiga* (the *ninkyō eiga* or 'chivalry films') in the most radical ways (see Yamane & Yonehara 2005), Fukasaku's unreserved, naturalistic representation of violence and cruelty transformed the genre from a moral melodrama into an anarchistic social statement (see Standish 2005: 317, 330). Set in the prewar period, *ninkyō eiga* celebrated the old values, such as honour, humanity, patience and sense of duty, and glamourised the traditional system based on hierarchical human relationships (see Satō 1995; Yomota 2000). This prompted the US occupation authorities to ban them, along with *jidai-geki* (period films), because of their potential to provoke nostalgia for imperial Japan and loyalty to the old power elite (see Satō 1995: 52–3). Fukasaku's *yakuza* noir refuses to glamourise the outlaw, declaring the demise of the samurai tradition which embodied nostalgic sentimentalism and traditional values of loyalty and honour. For example, when Hirono assists Wakasugi's *seppuku*, these imprisoned *yakuza* transform the ritual suicide traditionally intended to prove the sincerity of a samurai to his master into an act of defiance against the state institutions of discipline and punishment. In a later scene, Hirono tries to make a sincere apology to a major figure in the *yakuza* world, but makes a mess of cutting off his finger. This signifies the emptying of ritual by the demise of traditional values – itself signalled by *oyabun* (boss) Yamamori's dependence on his *kobun* (gang members), begging and crying for mercy from them when he is in a difficult situation, and his merciless rejection of them when they are no longer of use to him. Furthermore, when Hirono shoots up Sakai's funeral altar, which is decorated with flowers sent by the boss and local industrialists, the antipathy towards the capitalist development of society, and regret at the failure of old values and systems to repel foreign intrusion, becomes undeniable. The film's pessimism and nihilism represents a critical denunciation of the vision of a high-growth economy endorsed by the Japanese government.

On the other hand, strong antagonism towards foreign intruders and capitalist social development reveals the xenophobic anxieties of the defeated nation. The opening sequence endorses the heroic images of *yakuza*, whose violence is depicted as a form of resistance to foreign occupation as they come to the rescue of the woman being raped (although crime against innocent people is also a mode of survival under the American occupation forces). While the rape scene directly indicts the US military administration led by General MacArthur, the idealisation of the male bond – over the body of a woman which acts as a metaphor for an emasculated nation – is a stereotypical expression of anti-Western sentiment in postcolonial Asian cinema. Hirono's courage in protecting the local woman from the occupation forces leads to him joining the world of organised crime and becoming sworn brothers with Wakasugi.

In Fukasaku's later film, *Yakuza no hakaba: Kuchinashi no hana/Yakuza Graveyard* (1976), anti-American sentiment is displaced onto the Korean population, who were forced to move to Japan to provide cheap wartime labour and who were not repatriated after the war. This offsets the Japanese sense of psychological inferiority, even as it depicts the Korean residents as scapegoats. Protagonist Kuroiwa (Tetsuya Watari), a police detective without principles, does not believe in the traditional qualities of manhood. He swears brotherhood with Iwata (Seizo Fukumoto), the Korean boss of small local gang Nishida, and falls in love with Keiko (Meiko Kaji), the sister of Nishida's former boss, who is also Korean. His relationship is soon discovered by a rival gang and, after being tortured by them, he betrays Iwata. He is discharged from his job, and is eventually killed on the street. His reckless attitude towards authority and his sympathy towards Koreans suggests the contradictory psychology felt by Japanese regarding the consequences of colonial expansion and defeat.

Fukasaku's new type of rebellious anti-hero transformed the traditional *yakuza* genre into social critique, negotiating the consolidation of Western capitalism and the demise of traditional Japanese values. According to Yoshikuni Igarashi (2006), the great popularity of *yakuza eiga* in the 1970s should be seen in the context of the advance of consumer society in Japan. Hitherto, the majority of Japanese maintained a rural lifestyle and were unfamiliar with urban culture, and so the xenophobia expressed either in or by these films can be seen to convey ordinary citizens' conflicting ideas regarding the radical social changes and political upheavals occurring in those years.

Since the Meiji Restoration in 1868, the state ideology of modern Japan was 'Out of Asia, Into Europe'. Although it is not officially stated by the present government, it is still powerful enough for many Japanese to deny that they are part of Asia. The imperial expansion of Japan and its annexation of other Asian countries dislocated many inhabitants of the region who were drafted into military, labour or sexual slavery, including somewhere between 700,000 and one million Koreans. Many of them were unable or unwilling to be repatriated, being forbidden to take their possessions with them and having lost everything in their home country, which itself became a Cold War battleground. They have become the biggest ethnic minority in contemporary Japan, 450,000 of whom refuse naturalisation and retain Korean nationality. The presence of ethnic minorities – especially one so substantial – undermines the popular notion of *nihonjinron*, the myth of a homogeneous nation. Until recently, Japan insisted that it had no ethnic minorities (see Hicks 2004).

Popular images of *yakuza*-associated businesses being operated by Koreans need to be understood in this historical context of colonialism and social ostracism. Koreans who refuse naturalisation have been discriminated against in education and work, and thus often run businesses which tend to be regarded as hard, dirty and not respectable. Japanese pride in ethnic homogeneity serves to justify the discrimination against Asians and their inferiority complex towards Western society and culture. The *yakuza*, a ritual figure created by Japanese mass culture, functions as a site on which these contradictory views on occidental self-identity and xenophobia can be played out, and signifies the secretive desire and political concerns of the masses regarding the massive social changes occurring in Japan since the 1970s (see Igarashi 2006). The state-led modernisation process exploited traditional family values as the state ideology, but forced the sacrifice of individual family lives which were still underpinned by a traditional agricultural lifestyle. However, the sudden rise of consumer society, especially with the nationwide diffusion of television, shocked this predominantly rural mindset, especially when they were confronted with images of urban political demonstrations. Although the audience for Fukasaku's gangster noirs enjoyed the material benefits of capitalist development outside of cinema, representations of criminal violence seemed to meet other needs arising from the stresses and frustrations of social change. Although the *yakuza* have their origins in Japanese cultural traditions, they are a social force created by foreign intrusions into Japanese society, particularly but not exclusively the US occupation. Therefore, the antagonism expressed through the yakuza stories is not only against capitalist development and the loss of tradition but also against the ethnic minorities who remind Japan of its past aggression and lack of homogeneity.

As with many of Fukasaku's other films, *Jingi naki tatakai* is also an anti-war statement (see Yamane & Yonehara 2005). The opening image of the atomic mushroom cloud is iconic of Japanese anti-war films, but it also represents an explosion of anxieties over the birth of new power in revolt against the old systems and values of Japan. Fukasaku's documentary style of shooting and editing – representative of the so-called *jitsuroku eiga* (true document film, based on real-life stories) – skilfully recreates a Japan devastated by war, highlighting the savagery and cruelty which led to a new kind of violence. The inserted newspaper stills, natural lighting, hand-held camera, omniscient voice-over narration and other techniques give a sense of immediacy and authenticity to his depiction of chaotic postwar Japan. The ensuing stories of gang wars over money in the *Jingi* series are 'an alternative history of postwar Japan, and the street-level truth that is covered up by the boastful records of reconstruction and economic growth' (Mes & Sharp 2005: 57).

The popularity of gangster films, including Fukasaku's, slumped with the demise of the studio system in the late 1970s, and although more than a dozen *yakuza eiga* are produced every year they are now mostly direct-to-video. However, the great popularity of his *Jingi* series is suggestive of the leftist politics pursued by popular film culture in that decade. Young intellectuals ran into cinema after the fierce anti-Vietnam war and anti-America political rallies (see Satō 1995: 135–7). Anxious and frustrated radical intellectuals also shared their pleasure, viewing *pinku eiga* (softcore pornography) and violent *yakuza eiga* with the lonely masses who left their old hometowns to work or study in the newly developed urban areas (Yomota 2000: 189). Fukasaku's films still trigger nostalgia among intellectuals who used to be the secret admirers of *yakuza eiga*, but this older generation is not a significant audience for contemporary *yakuza eiga* produced for the home video market. However, the romantic anti-capitalism and postcolonial critique typical of Fukasaku's work suggest rebellious and politically conscious roots for contemporary Asian gangster noir, even if the contemporary *yakuza eiga* remains 'a great guilty pleasure' for an ever-diminishing fan base composed mostly of single men fantasising about heroism in their small apartments (see Schilling 2003: 35).

Yakuza eiga are no longer a popular genre. While the hierarchical relationship between *oyabun* and *kobun* does not attract the younger generation, the *yakuza* as a ritual figure still occupies a significant place in the contemporary Japanese cinematic imagination, expressing the anxiety of the underprivileged masses, symbolising those whom society fails to embrace. Contemporary filmmakers are often concerned with the downfall of the *yakuza* myth and with existential questioning. For example, in Kitano's *Sonatine* (1993), the boss sends Murakawa (Kitano) and his thugs to Okinawa, under the pretence of helping the Nakamatsu gang, who are in trouble with a rival gang. Murakawa, who was thinking of retiring, reluctantly accepts these orders, but on arriving in Okinawa, he finds that his boss has actually made a deal with Nakamatsu's rival to eliminate both Murakawa and the Nakamatsu gang. In response, Murakawa and his men idle at the peaceful seaside, playing childish games in the sand and preparing for the moment of death.

Kitano's stoic representation of the troublesome, treacherous life of social outcasts and, when they eventually come, of motionless gunfights, challenges the gangster noir conventions pioneered by Fukasaku. His dynamic hand-held camera and rapid editing articulated both the ceaseless uproar of the chaotic Japan of the 1970s and the vital, anarchic resistance to the expansion and consolidation of capital in everyday life. In contrast, the contemplative stillness of Kitano's camera and his long takes impart a resigned pessimism about exploitative relationships and echo the absurdity and the emptiness of everyday life. Not only is his treatment of violence cynical, but he tends to establish emotional distance from the suffering he depicts. His picturesque images of oriental Japan further help to postpone any critique of the social origins of violence.

Hero in *Ying hung boon sik*

The nihilism and loneliness expressed through the emotionless representation of violence and moral detachment in *Sonatine* contrasts sharply with the Hong Kong gangster epics which flourished between the late 1980s and mid-1990s, most notably the 'heroic bloodshed' films of director John Woo and producer Tsui Hark. While the historical victims of Japanese expansion, invasion and co-lonial rule might be sceptical of the Japanese outcry about calamities it brought upon itself (as expressed in Fukasaku's gangster noirs), Japanese cinematic traditions influenced other national cinemas in the region through the crea-tive filtering of local filmmakers (see Cho 1996; Yomota 2001; Lie 2006). Woo himself is a great admirer of Kurosawa and *yakuza eiga*, and his gangster films are as much influenced by neighbouring Asian traditions as by Italian westerns, swordplay[3] and film noir (see Bordwell 2000: 100). In particular, he modelled his heroes on the persona of Japanese actor Takakura Ken, the icon of *ninkyō eiga* in the late 1960s. Although Fukasaku's anarchic style and thematic concerns do not seem to constitute a direct influence on Woo, a similar politicisation of interpersonal relationships is evident in his films.

Mark (Chow Yun-Fat) and Ho (Ti Lung) are good friends, working for a syn-dicate who run a counterfeiting operation. Although the counterfeit deals af-ford him a luxurious life, Ho decides to leave the syndicate for the sake of his younger brother, Kit (Leslie Cheung), who is a police cadet and has no idea of Ho's underworld connections. However, before Ho can leave, he is betrayed and sent to prison in Taiwan. The furious Mark avenges Ho, but is crippled by the rival gang. After three years of imprisonment, Ho realises his father was killed by a rival mobster, while Kit blames Ho for their father's death. Mean-while, Mark is in a living hell, working for Shing (Chi-Hung Lee), the new boss of the syndicate, who treats him like a beast and blackmails Kit to threaten Ho. Ho is torn between his conflicting loyalties towards Mark and Kit: Mark wants to take revenge on Shing and take back their position in the syndicate but Kit will never forgive Ho if he goes back to the syndicate.

Ying hung boon sik was a massive box-office success, establishing a cycle of 'heroes' films which revived Hong Kong popular film culture during the 1980s and 1990s. The Hong Kong film industry was then led by the 'new wave', a generation of directors trained in the West and in television. They did not have strong emotional or cultural ties to mainland traditions, and were more inter-ested in sword-and-sorcery fantasy and gangster films than martial art films or melodrama. They received critical recognition at festivals and exhibitions, but the film industry slumped. Woo, who was not part of the new wave, was more inclined towards commercial filmmaking and his heroic bloodshed films boost-ed the international reputation of Hong Kong cinema as entertainment (see Cho 1996: 61–2; Bordwell 2000: 82).

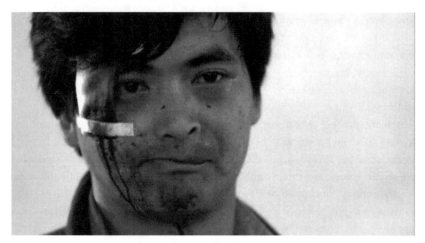

Chow Yun-Fat, beaten but unbowed: *Ying hung boon sik/A Better Tomorrow*

Ying hung boon sik created a significant space for gangster films in the tradition of chivalry action drama. Just as Bruce Lee and Jackie Chan are 'the two dragons of martial art films' (Bordwell 2000: 49), so Chow Yun-Fat became the icon of Asian gangster noir. Woo's subsequent films, including *Dip huet seung hung, Die xue jie tou and Lat sau san taam/Hard-Boiled* (1992), expanded the genre's popularity among Western film fans, who love them, according to Law Kar, 'precisely because such uninhibited wildness is almost impossible to find in Western genre films' (in Teo 1997: 178). Although *Ying hung boon sik* might not be the most aesthetically accomplished hero film, it is still the landmark of Hong Kong gangster noir.

After the handover of Hong Kong to China, Wai-keung Lau and Siu Fai Mak made a new style of gangster noir, *Mou gaan dou*, which recycled the story of two mirror-imaged men and the criminal world with sufficient domestic and international success to prompt Martin Scorsese to remake it as *The Departed* (2006). *Mou gaan dou* and its sequels had bigger budgets than the earlier hero films, and are consequently visually more stylish. However, they do not glamorise the underworld as an alternative form of the present social order: British colonial occupation is over and the new identity of Hong Kong has emerged under the leadership of the Chinese Communist party. However, the moral ambivalence, nihilism or pessimism refuses a clear division between good and bad even in this new society. The emotional male bond and the pursuit of social justice survived to restore Chinese pride, and because nationhood figures the traditional values of friendship and family, when the hero discloses his true identity it is as the servant of his people and nation.

True Colours of a Hero, the original title of *Ying hung boon sik*, suggests, this underworld epic is a national melodrama which confirms the validity of traditional values and social orders. Through the glamorised images of heroes, their robust homosociality leaves no room for a femme fatale or other women – the notion of national identity replaces any questioning of social authority, transforming the anxieties of the citizens of this ex-British colony into pleasurable heroic fantasy. The eternal friendship between the two mirror-imaged male characters, the reformed Ho and the crippled Mark, like the pairs of detectives and heroic gangsters in *Lat sau san taam* and *Mou gaan dou*, highlights the conflicting historical roots of Hong Kong noir: the cultural tradition of mainland China and the postcolonial historicity of the British territory. Colonial Hong Kong made economic profitability the most important social imperative (see Magnan-Park 2007), and this was exacerbated by the Communist takeover of mainland China. But Confucianism remains the moral principle in the Chinese hearts of the people of Hong Kong. In essence, Hong Kong gangster noir is the story of a hero – of chivalric brotherhood and superhuman martial skills – in which the gunfight becomes the contemporary manifestation of swordplay. If Woo's hero met a tragic end because he was the subject of colonial Hong Kong, the hero of *Mou gaan dou* has a different destiny because he serves his nation. He is sent from unified China to fight against the evils of capitalism in postcolonial Hong Kong.

The organised thug in *Oldboy*

Boksuneun naui geot established Park's reputation as a key figure of Asian noir (he prefers to call his films 'hard-boiled', because of his dislike of the genre's clichéd iconography, strongly associated with Woo, of stylish gunfights and men in long coats). Despite becoming a critical favourite among Asian extreme fans, this unsentimental portrayal of crime, violence and sex failed commercially. In contrast, his next feature, *Oldboy*, appealed to a mainstream audience. A compelling story of an unusual kidnapping and consequent cruel revenge, it does not allow the audience emotional distance. O Daesu (Minshik Choi), an ordinary office worker, is held captive in a private prison for 15 years without knowing why. His kidnapper, Yi Woojin (Jitae Yu), tells him that if he finds out why he was released, he will kill himself. He blames Daesu for starting the rumour that drove his sister to commit suicide – that she was pregnant by Woojin. His imprisonment of Daesu was only preparation for his real revenge: Daesu's realisation that his new girlfriend is actually his own daughter, Woojin having hypnotised them to ensure an incestuous relationship is formed.

Oldboy recovered Park's reputation as a popular filmmaker – his *Gongdong gyeongbi guyeok JSA/JSA: Joint Security Area* was the most popular film of 2000 in Korea and one of the representatives leading the *hallyu* (Korean Wave) boom. In addition to *Oldboy*'s box-office success, it was awarded prizes at many international film festivals, including the Grand Prix at Cannes. Minshik Choi became an icon of Asian extreme, along with the monstrous images of him eating a live octopus and fighting his way with a hammer through a long

Minshik Choi, ordinary citizen: *Oldboy*

corridor crowded with gangsters. The simultaneous pursuit of commercial success, aesthetic experiment and social statement, as achieved by *Oldboy*, is the
main gear of the revival of Korean national cinema after decades of suffering
from Hollywood domination (see Lee 2000: 45–56).

Oldboy is replete with film noir conventions: flashbacks and first-person
narration, a twisted plot and shocking reversal, inserted documentary stills and
newsreels and a complexly-characterised femme fatale. Its moral ambivalence
in dealing with its taboo subject matter yields fatalism and pessimism, rendering
the present an unavoidable consequence of the past. Also, as an example of
Asian transnational cinema, its representation of violence, sex and crime discloses certain influences from Japanese gangster noir and popular art traditions. For
example, the visualisation of nature's overwhelming power over human beings
is alien to the traditional aesthetics of South Korean cinematography, which typically pursues harmony between nature and humanity, while the fighting scenes
in the prison corridor are unique in fusing South Korean gangster film action
style within the frame structure of Japanese *manga* (the film is loosely based on
a *manga* of the same name). On the other hand, the thematic concerns of *Oldboy* – as with *Boksuneun naui geot* and Park's later *Chinjeolhan geumjassi* – are
specific to South Korea, particularly the social absurdity of the post-Confucian
society and economic inequity of the capitalist class system (see Lee 2000).

Under the Park Chung Hee military dictatorship (1961–79) South Korea sac-
rificed democratic ideals so as to achieve rapid economic growth (see Choi
1994). In the late 1980s, an alliance between factory workers, student activists
and radical intellectuals supported by progressive religious sectors, put an end
to the military dictatorship. The so-called 386 generation – those who were in
their thirties when democratisation was achieved, went to university during the
1980s and were born in the 1960s (see Robinson 2005: 24) – symbolised the
new forces leading this popular movement. Along with Sangsu Im, Park is a
representative of the 386 generation of directors, concerned with the cultural

and political criticism of the developmental dictatorship and its aftermath. For example, *Boksuneun naui geot* deals with the stories of kidnapping and murder during the late 1990s IMF crisis which resulted from rapid, state-led economic growth without any safeguards from civil society, and which led to huge social problems, including nationwide unemployment, the consequent dislocation of families and a rise in the suicide rate.

Criminality is a medium for Park's questioning of the systemic failure of class society, as in the confrontation between office worker Daesu and the capitalist Woojin in the latter's spectacular penthouse. Woojin's relationship with the organised thugs responsible for transforming Daesu into a beast symbolises the privatisation of power and violence in the class society. The brutality and savagery of the mad Daesu, an ordinary citizen whom the state has failed to protect from the abuse of the strong, is a hyperbolic reaction to privatised violence. The organised thug is the hidden face of capitalism, and state power does not have the authority to punish the capitalist class (the police only appear in the opening scene to hold the drunken Daesu on a charge of street fighting). The image of money as the means of private revenge is a central criticism of post-Confucian society, which is also taken up in the helpless images, in *Boksuneun naui geot* and *Chinjeolhan geumjassi*, of a detective bribed to help an industrialist's private revenge and of another who wrongly charges the heroine with kidnapping and murdering a boy. *Oldboy's* moral ambivalence towards incest radically critiques Confucian patriarchal society, while connecting this critique back to antagonistic capitalist economic classes. The moral dilemmas faced by Woojin and Daesu over their incestuous relationships are resolved in completely opposite ways. Woojin, the rich boy, abetted his sister's suicide and escaped to America, setting up Daesu as a scapegoat to relieve his sense of guilt. However, in sharing the male-centred view of other Asian noir, *Oldboy* undermines its critique of patriarchy in its depiction of Mido (Kang Hyejeong), Daesu's daughter/lover. Unaware of the complex psychological games being played by Woojin and Daesu, she is ultimately nothing more than a poor little pretty girl cruelly exploited by male sexual lust. As with the surrogate father/son relationship and sworn brotherhood in *Jingi naki tatakai*, and the father/son relationship and brotherhood in *Ying hung boon sik*, the patriarchal morality and male-centred familial norm in *Oldboy* attests the irony in using Asian gangster noir as a critique of post-Confucian society: the male-centred view deconstructs the problematics of a patriarchal society.

The social exile: postcolonial history and the Confucian nation

The social criticism manifested by the gangster noir from these three national cinemas discloses opposition towards Western domination and the inferiority complex of a weak nation. In Japanese *yakuza eiga*, the state authority disappeared, replaced by the powerful image of America. In Hong Kong heroic blood-shed, the colonial British government has no authority over the colonised soci-ety: the hero belongs to the criminal underworld and his mirror image is on the side of the colonial power. In their South Korean counterparts, the corrupt crimi-nal world itself is a metaphoric expression of despotic state power serving the capitalist class. Such postcolonial historicity is central to Asian gangster noir's critique of the inequalities of capitalist society, conveying the victim psychology of a people anxious about Western domination. The helpless struggles of the underdog against the merciless and corrupted superior portrayed in Asian noir commonly imply popular discontent with economic development in a postco-lonial society, with depictions of social unrest and economic inequity express-ing popular anguish at systems failure and the demise of traditional values. In this sense, Asian gangster noir clearly reflects the nationalistic sentiments felt by the locals in the era of capital's global consolidation, with the hybridi-sation of indigenous and Hollywood traditions precisely mapping Asian noir's core features: a postcolonial sensibility, anxiety about the demise of traditional social values, fear of Western domination. Hiroshima under the control of GHQ (General Headquarters) in *Jingi naki tatakai* and the tropical island of Okinawa in *Sonatine* convey the complex victim psychology in the combination of the anti-war and postcolonial sentiment.[4] Japan's postcolonial reality, as depicted in these films, is echoed in Hong Kong gangster noir's images of this ex-British territory, with drugs, rape, prostitution and counterfeit dollars as metaphors of the evil of Western capitalism, indicating the territorial intrusion of the outsid-ers. Conversely, the demise of traditionalist values gives moral grounds for the violence of the underdog. His savageness and emptiness expresses nostalgia for traditional group-oriented morality and a sense of being lost in present-day society. Asian noir can, then, be seen to revolve around a questioning of the va-lidity of Confucian traditions in present society. While the films' moral ambigu-ity refuses clear divisions between good and bad, their tragic stories of ruthless dissent stress the unavoidable weight of the human relations their characters accumulate. In Confucian morality, the denial of family relationships is criminal, and when combined with the Buddhist notion of *karma* (i.e., the retribution for the deeds of a former life), the dissolution of such bonds leads everybody into an inferno. This can be considered the root of Asian noir's pessimism.

Postcolonial sensibilities and saturation by Western material culture are of-ten depicted as the triumph of 'foreignness' over traditional values and moral-ity. Various props and actions are used to signify the confrontation between two worlds. For example, the cutting of a finger or *seppuku* (belly cutting) in Japanese *yakuza* films symbolises respect for traditional values and human re-lationships, even if individual films articulate this in complex and contradictory ways. In a similar vein, traditional weapons, such as swords and knives, that appear in Japanese gangster noir signify the demise of traditional social values, while the impromptu use of a hammer as a weapon in *Oldboy* conveys the helpless position of the underprivileged in capitalist class relations. Conversely, Western suits, cars and, most importantly, the possession of a gun, symbolise the superiority of the capitalists.

While the gunfights in Hong Kong gangster films can be seen specifically to express a postcolonial Occidentalism, in South Korean noir the gun symbolises the social status of people beyond state control. In *Oldboy*, Woojin alone possesses this power, the range of the gun enabling him to maintain distance from his victim. The victim's recourse to a hammer for self-defence eradicates the distance between opponents, bringing them face to face with the suffering and fear on both sides. This physical proximity allows the audience to observe their close human interactions and facial expressions, and denies the distance from consequences that the capitalist enjoys. (Woo's numerous dance-like, gunfight sequences likewise reduce the distance between antagonists to that of traditional swordplay: typically, they confront each other up close, holding guns at each other's heads or sat on the floor covered in blood just a couple of feet apart as they shoot each other at close range.)

In conclusion, the examples of neo-noir from the three national cinemas project the different colours of a prism reflecting the criminal world. The memories of colonial power or subjugation, military aggression or occupation, have all had a profound influence on the relation between the state and cinema, but in each national cinema the origins of crime and violence are comparable, signifying a popular reaction against the political abuse of state power and the materialist pursuits of a class society under Western influences. Colonial historicity and moral justification based on Confucian familial ideology are crucial for the emotional identification of the viewer with the criminals. The sense of being lost and helpless expresses the destructiveness of life in modern society. In short, the rise and fall of Asian gangster noir in different years in the three countries offer critical insights into contemporary Asian culture in a globalised context, while the locality and hybridity of Asian gangster noir challenges Eurocentric universalism and Orientalism. At the same time, the different cinematic manifestation of the postcolonial sentiment and Confucianism in each society addresses the specific historical experiences and cultural traditions of the people.

AUTHOR'S NOTE

This study was supported by a Japan Society for the Promotion of Science Postdoctoral Fellowship, entitled '*Hallyu* (Korean Wave) and Transnational Flows of Popular Culture between Japan and Korea'.

NOTES

1   Japan banned Korean-language films for the last ten years of its colonial rule, and only permitted Japanese-language films with pro-Japanese sentiments. The historical trauma of the Japanese invasion and occupation of Korea remains a major obstacle to cinematic co-operation and transnational cultural flows in Asia, not only between these two countries.

2   For example, filmmaker and activist Adachi Masao commented that Kitano fantasises violence without referring to social reality (notes from the director's talk after the screening of *Yūheisha-terorisuto/Prisoner/Terrorist* (2006), the Kitakyushu Biennial, 29 September 2007).

3   A period film based on the chivalric concept of heroism and loyalty and featuring sword-fights.

4   After the postwar occupation, Okinawa remained US military territory until 1972. The setting is so resonant not merely because it questions the continuing US presence in the region but also because of the enduring Japanese prejudice and discrimination towards Okinawa people.

REFERENCES

Borde, Raymond and Étienne Chaumeton (2003 [1955]) 'Towards a Definition of *Film Noir*', trans. Alain Silver, in Alain Silver and James Ursini (eds) *Film Noir Reader*, seventh Edition. New York: Limelight, 17–25.

Bordwell, David (2000) *Planet Hong Kong: Popular Cinema and the Art of Entertainment*. Cambridge: Harvard University Press.

Cho, Jaehong (1996) *Segye Yeonghwa Gihaeng I* [*World Cinema 1*] Seoul: Georeum.

Choi, Changjip (1994) 'Minjunjueuiroeui Ihaenggwa Nodong Undong' ['Transition to Democracy and Labour Movement'], in Eulbyeong Chang (ed.) *Nambukhan Jeongchieui Gujowa Jeonmang* [*The Structures and Prospects of North and South Korean Politics*] Seoul: Hanul Academy, 136–70.

Choi, Hongjae (ed.) (2005) *386eui Kkum, geu Seongchaleui Iyu* [*A Dream of 386, the Reasons of Reflection*]. Seoul: Nanam Publishing.

Gerow, Aaron (2007) *Kitano Takeshi*. London: British Film Institute.

Hicks, George (2004) *Japan's Hidden Apartheid: The Korean Minority and the Japanese*. Aldershot: Ashgate.

Higson, Andrew (2002) 'The Concept of National Cinema', in Alan Williams (ed.) *Film and Nationalism*. New Brunswick and London: Rutgers University Press, 52–67.

Igarashi, Yoshikuni (2006) 'Ninkyō kara jitsuroku e: yakuza hīrō no hensen to 70-nendai no nihon no shakai' ['From Chivalry to "True Documentary": Transfiguration of Yakuza Hero and Japanese Society in the 1970s], *Bunka/hihyō* [*Cultures/critiques*], Winter, 360–86.

Kim, Jongwon and Junghyun Cheong (2001) *Uri Yeonghwa 100 yeon* [*Our Film History: 100 Years*] Seoul: Hyeonamsa.

Lee, Hyangjin (2000) *Contemporary Korean Cinema: Identity, Culture and Politics.* Manchester: Manchester University Press.

Lie, Wenbing (2006) *Chūgoku 10-okunin no nihoneiga netsuaishi-Takakura Ken, Yamaguchi Momoe kara Kimutaku, anime made* [*History of Japanese Film which 100 million Chinese Love: From Takakura Ken and Yamaguchi Momoe to Kimutaku and Anime*]. Tokyo: Shūeisha.

Magnan-Park, Aaron (2007) 'The Heroic Flux in John Woo's trans-Pacific Passage: From Confucian Brotherhood to American Selfhood', in Gina Marchetti and Tan See Kam (eds) *Hong Kong Film, Hollywood and the New Global Cinema: No Film is An Island.* New York: Routledge, 35–49.

Mes, Tom and Jasper Sharp (2005) *The Midnight Eye Guide to New Japanese Film.* Berkeley: Stone Bridge Press.

Richie, Donald (2001) *A Hundred Years of Japanese Film.* Tokyo: Kodansha International.

Robinson Michael (2005) 'Contemporary Cultural Production in South Korea: Vanishing Meta-Narratives of Nation', in Chi-Yun Shin and Julian Stringer (eds) *New Korean Cinema.* Edinburgh: Edinburgh University Press, 15–31.

Satō, Tadao (1987) *Currents in Japanese Cinema.* Tokyo: Kodansha.

____ (1995) *Nihon eigashi 1960–1995*, vol. 3 [*Japanese film history 1960–1995*, vol. 3]. Tokyo: Iwanami Shoten.

Schilling, Mark (2003) *The Yakuza Movie Book: A Guide to Japanese Gangster Films.* Berkeley: Stone Bridge.

Standish, Isolde (2005) *A New History of Japanese Cinema: A Century of Narrative Film.* New York: Continuum.

Teo, Stephen (1997) *Hong Kong Cinema: The Extra Dimensions.* London: British Film Institute.

Yamane, Sadao and Hisashi Yonehara (2005) *Jingi naki tatakai o tsukutta otokotachi: Fukasaku Kinji to Kasahara Kazuo* [*The Men who Made Battle without Honour and Humanity: Fukasaku Kinji and Kasahara Kazuo*]. Tokyo: NHK publishing.

Yomota Inuhiko (2000) *Nihon eigashi 100-nen* [*Japanese Film History: 100 Years*]. Tokyo: Shūeisha.

____ (2001) *Ajia no naka no nihoneiga* [*Japanese Film in Asia*]. Tokyo: Iwanami Shoten.

9

British Neo-Noir and Reification:
Croupier and *Dirty Pretty Things*

MIKE WAYNE

Introduction

There could be no better proof of the power of reification than the marginality of the word itself within the critical discourses of our time. To be able to name something at least indicates a degree of consciousness about it that is a necessary if not sufficient condition for altering that something by combining self-conscious thought with our practices. But without a name for something, we cannot even begin to engage in conscious transformation of our social relations and practices. If the term reification is unfamiliar then the 'something' that it denotes is not. Reification is literally the process of turning human and social relationships into things, the process whereby human and social relationships are subordinated to things. Reification equals 'thingification'. These things are everywhere around us, part of our humdrum lives (or rather, our lives are part of these humdrum things). Their most common manifestation is as commodities and money, but these things in turn dance to the tune of a more powerful master, the *master thing*: capital. Already I have implied a certain discrepancy between something that is pervasive, the reality of reification, and our consciousness of that reality, or at least our consciousness that that reality of thing-dominance is something we should be worried about.

This essay will explore this double question of thing-dominance and the discrepancy between appearance forms of reality and the deeper, concealed relations and forces at work beneath those immediately visible appearances (see Wayne 2003: 189–92). Noir is a genre that has consistently dealt with these issues and contemporary or neo-noir continues to mine this rich ideological seam. I will analyse *Dirty Pretty Things* (2002) (a title that resonates in this context) and *Croupier* (1998) both as texts that can illuminate issues of reification within the broader culture and society and as film commodities. As the latter, *Dirty Pretty Things* and *Croupier* can tell us something about the state of the British film industry and the consequences of its subordination to Hollywood and the American market which Hollywood controls. I read the economic life of these films dialectically, as prefiguring a future that does not include films like them. One of the themes that connects these films, as both cultural texts and film commodities, is the question of *chance*. I shall argue that chance is in fact structurally determined by the concealed forces of capital and commodification; that fortune and *fortunes* are the outcome of the distribution of risk and opportunities by these dominant powers, whether in the form of Hollywood, 'the House' (in *Croupier*) or those who buy and sell body organs (*Dirty Pretty Things*).

Reification and culture

The term reification is associated with the Hungarian Marxist, Georg Lukács, who used it to explore how the effects of living with and under these things, living with and under thingification, effects 'the total outer and inner life of society' (1971: 84). If reification has indeed penetrated into our ways of seeing (and, importantly, *hearing*) the world, then it has presumably penetrated into our visual (and audio) culture as well. Yet, at the same time, a visual and narrative culture could potentially offer us insights into and glimpses of this reified thing-world. One thing culture would have to do in order to offer some critical commentary on reification is to break through the forms of appearance with which it presents itself to us. These forms of appearance are not illusions, mere chimeras (money really does exist) but make up layers of reality that systematically fail to disclose the full range of determinants operating on them. Cultural works then might be thought of as reified commentaries on reification. Part of the question of critical and aesthetic judgement would be to ascertain in cultural works whether the *power of* reification or the *critical commentary on* reification has the upper hand. One place where these debates were fought out in cultural criticism of the twentieth century was modernism, in particular the strand of modernism known as expressionism, which was influential in painting, literature and theatre, as well as film.

As is well known, the first wave of film noir in both America and Britain (see Williams 1999) had, as one of its many influences, German Expressionism imported via German *émigrés* fleeing the rise of Hitler's fascists. In his assessment as to whether expressionism was more reified than commentary on reification, Lukács came to the unshakable conclusion that it was the former. He argued (against fellow but rather more unorthodox Marxist, Ernst Bloch) that in the period of extended crisis out of which expressionism was born (World War One, revolutions, economic crisis), 'the experience of disintegration becomes firmly entrenched over long periods of time in broad sectors of the population which normally experience the various manifestations of capitalism in a very immediate way' (Lukács 1988: 32). As a consequence, all expressionism registered was the 'very immediate' subjective and psychological symptoms of a disintegration which did not penetrate down to the factors that constituted the structural causes and 'unity' of all this perceptual disorder.

Lukács' judgement on expressionism, however, is perhaps a little harsh, because it does not consider whether the work, in its content and form, leaves clues as to the impersonal forces rupturing the world. Kent Minturn's essay on the cross-fertilisation between American Abstract Expressionism and film noir in the 1940s includes an interesting still from the noir film *Scarlet Street* (1945) directed by Austro-German *émigré*, Fritz Lang (see 1999: 270). The still shows a character hawking two paintings. One of them depicts a noirish night-time street scene. Foreground, left and right of the picture are streetlights and under the left lamp stands a woman, in the street, drawn fairly flat. The street, however is made not of tarmac but has the quality of scales, a fact confirmed by the large serpent winding its way down a pillar on the right hand side of the picture. And behind this scene, with its potentially Christian theological readings, lie some precise clues as to what is wrong with this world. We see in the background, on the pavement, a series of shop fronts: café and auto supplies on either side of the picture, but right in the middle of the picture, commanding our gaze, a pawn shop, advertising loans. And above the shops, some advertising hoardings: one for whisky, one for cigarettes, the necessary anaesthetics for a distorted world. So if film can use expressionism in its own making and here deploy it self-consciously as a style of painting that hints at the causal factors responsible for perceptual and experiential crisis, then Lukács' judgement about the style of expressionism wallowing in mere subjective immediacy seems problematic.

Yet if Lukács is too hasty in dismissing expressionism, he is right that relating the experience of fragmentation to more structural causalities does constitute a problem. Fragmentation does constitute an important part of our everyday life, but this fragmentation also conceals the structural and enduring social arrangements that generate the fragmentation in the first place. However, the other side of fragmentation and disintegration is the more positive appearing facet of thing-like life, that of the autonomy of each to do as they please unencumbered, within the rules of law, by consideration of or responsibility towards others. One of the great transmission belts for the promises of this autonomy and access to this autonomy is of course the market place of consumer goods. Here, the surface appearance of life acquires a benign face and one can easily see how expressionist themes and modes of composition (as with the painting in *Scarlet Street*) could be read as intuitive critiques of at least *this aspect* of our reified consciousness.

Covert operations: *Dirty Pretty Things*

Noir was one of the first sustained attempts within the Hollywood film industry to explore the disjuncture between middle-class wealth, affluence, manners, contentment, family life and status, on the one hand, and the repression, discontent and violence lurking beneath the surface of life, on the other. This disjuncture figured prominently in noir's distinctive lighting arrangements which broke with the standardised three-point 'high key' lighting system of the time which had been developed to illuminate high production values and middle-class affluence. Noir by contrast lowered the amount of light suffusing the set ('low key') and experimented with lighting positions in order to produce, literally and figuratively, 'dark worlds' pierced with puddles or shards of light (see Place & Peterson 1976). If neo-noir does not necessarily reproduce this chiaroscuro style, lighting still remains an important signifier in the discrepancy between appearances and realities.

Dirty Pretty Things is in many respects a thriller rather than a noir film, but it does have this discrepancy between commercially constructed appearances and more unpleasant or exploitative realities as a central motif in the film. Indeed it is encapsulated in the film's title, as is clear when Senior Juan (Sergi López), the manager of the Baltic Hotel, tells the film's hero, Okwe (Chiwetel Ejiofor), that strangers 'come to the hotel in the night to do dirty things. And in the morning it is our job to make things look pretty again'. In a world dominated by commercialised messages and environments of all sorts, there is also this processing of reality into a pretty, clean and de*light*ful *thing*. In *Dirty Pretty Things*, Senior Juan's words have a particular resonance because Okwe discovers that the hotel manager is involved in the illegal organ trade, and is indeed using the hotel rooms as the place to carry out the necessary operations on desperate immigrants.

Thus in the public areas of the hotel, such as the lobby and the hallways, the lighting, motivated diegetically from the interior lamps, has a warm yellow/golden glow about it. But the security cameras via which the cleaning staff have to register their identity look at them with a cold blue image, their relationship to their place of work stripped of the cosy associations the hotel constructs for its customers. Meanwhile, in the back of the hotel where Senior Juan has his office, out of sight of the public or the customer, the lighting, again motivated diegetically by interior colour schemes, has a distinctly sick, unhealthy green tinge to it, as befits someone engaged in the ultimate commodification (thingification) of the body.

Let us return to the question of fragmentation raised by Lukács, because it is relevant if we are to consider in what respects *Dirty Pretty Things*, despite being a commentary on reification, is still a reified film. In an interesting critique of the film, Samuel Amago has suggested that the film mobilises a long tradition of European Hispanophobia in its use of Spanish actor Sergi López to play Senior Juan (also called 'Sneaky' in the film). The point is not that the villain of the film happens to be Spanish but that the villain's Spanishness is foregrounded at significant moments (see Amago 2005: 54). This focalisation has the convenient effect of deflecting criticism away from the British national context responsible for the vulnerability of the immigrants and asylum seekers in the context of 'late capitalist globalised society' (2005: 58).

The problem is partly generic, since genres tend precisely to divide the world up into fragmented compartments. While the *political* thriller will focus on agents and representatives of the state but at the expense of the broader social relations which are effected by the state and in turn impact on it, *Dirty Pretty Things* is more of a social thriller, which locates its narrative in everyday social life, but occludes the political and state apparatus, whose actions, in the British context, attracted Stephen Frears to the screenplay in the first place (see Lucia 2003). But perhaps there were other pressures mitigating against addressing the specific context of the British nation-state? A clue as to what those other pressures might be comes in the figure of the displacing mechanism itself. For the Spanish villain is not a particularly recurrent figure in British cinema. However, there is a film market where greedy and untrustworthy Hispanic villains have a long history: namely, the American market. I have argued elsewhere that the subordination and integration of British cinema in terms of production, distribution and exhibition into Hollywood, means effectively that British films, if they want to recover their costs, let alone make a profit, have to take a *cultural detour* through the American market (see Wayne 2006). It is time now to take a look at the question of reification as it pertains to the British film industry.

Reification and the British film industry

As a Marxist, Lukács' critique of reification developed out of the work of Karl Marx. In his early work, the *Economic and Philosophic Manuscripts of 1844*,

Marx wrote that: 'The *devaluation* of the world of men is in direct proportion to the *increasing value* of the world of things' (1981: 63; emphasis in original). Marx calls this devaluation estrangement or alienation. He grounded modern alienation in specific historic conditions, chiefly in the transformation of the worker's power to labour into a commodity that is sold in competition in the market, like any other commodity. Thus, in alienation, 'the object which labour produces – labour's product – confronts it as *something alien*, as a *power independent* of the producer' (ibid.; emphasis in original). Many filmmakers could testify to this experience, where both the conditions under which they sell their labour and the product that is the result of their labour, confronts them as an independent, alien and hostile power.

The British film industry has a double problem in this regard. Not only is it a capitalist industry but also it is a capitalist industry integrated into the biggest, most powerful (most reified) capitalist film industry in the world. For Hollywood, revenues from its overseas markets virtually match domestic box-office revenues for theatrical exhibition (see Miller *et al*. 2005: 10). Figures published by the UK Film Council in their annual statistical report (a document which is a master work of reification, constantly inverting the British film industry's subordinate integration into Hollywood into a success story!) illustrate the extent of the problem. In 2005:

- US (solo produced) films numbered 137 releases in the British market. Together they took £386.2m, which represents a 45.7 per cent share of the box office.
- US and UK co-productions, such as *Harry Potter and the Goblet of Fire* (2005), *Charlie and the Chocolate Factory* (2005), *Wallace & Gromit in The Curse of the Were-Rabbit* (2005), *Batman Begins* (2005), *Pride & Prejudice* (2005) and *Nanny McPhee* (2005), numbered 61 releases and took a further £239.3m and a further 28.3 per cent of the box office.
- US co-productions with non-British companies accounted for 30 releases, £147.2m and a further 17.4 per cent of the box office. (UK Film Council 2006: 11).

This domination of Hollywood films, of films made in the Hollywood mould and of revenues, means that UK films and UK co-productions with other countries are left with 4.7 per cent of the box office, European productions with 1.6 per cent, Indian films with 1.5 per cent and the rest of the world with the close to extinction figure of 0.8 per cent. That is domination on a colossal scale, by any definition. In this context it is hardly surprising that *Dirty Pretty Things*, which had a budget of £5.5 million, did rather poorly in the British market in terms of its overall takings. But, as table A below suggests, this was not a reflection of sovereign consumers simply exercising their choices (a deeply reified concept) but instead was more a reflection of the institutionalised power of the US companies in the market place. The table compares the three-day weekend gross

	Week 1 (3 day gross)	Week 3 (3 day gross)	Week 4 (3 day gross)
Like Mike	£246,169	£158,694	£130,714
Number of sites	279	281	248
Site average	£882	£565	£527
Dirty Pretty Things	£141,865	£76,946	£56,765
Number of sites	50	45	29
Site average	£2,837	£1,710	£1,957

Table A. Source: Screen International (2003a and 2003b)

box-office takings of *Dirty Pretty Things* with the US children's film *Like Mike* (2002), produced by 20th Century-Fox and released in the same weekend as *Dirty Pretty Things* (13–15 December 2002). The key thing to look out for is that *Dirty Pretty Things* is actually doing quite well compared to *Like Mike* given the number of sites (cinemas) it has access to. Across the four weeks, *Dirty Pretty Things* has a gross weekend take that hovers just above, around or just below *half* that of *Like Mike*, and yet the latter film has in weeks three and four more than six and more than eight times as many sites as its competitor. What is clear is that the US film had a market profile out of all proportion to its popularity, but with production and prints and advertising costs of around $55 million (and that makes it a 'low'-budget film in Hollywood terms), it has to be kept on the British screens at the expense of a British film in order to help recover its costs.

It is often said that the British domestic market is too small for British films to recover their costs in it. However true it is that films must circulate on the international market in order to recover their costs, it is also clear that the British market is made rather smaller when it is dominated by US companies and their products. The success of British films internationally and in their own domestic market depends increasingly on the receptiveness of the Hollywood-constructed American market to British films (or judgements about what will succeed in the American market). Yet even success in the American market does not necessarily translate into British films getting decent access to British audiences. As these dynamics become locked into institutional relations and internalised by key social actors (producers, directors, and so forth), so British cinema ends up being a cinema made, first and foremost, for export.

Let us return to *Dirty Pretty Things*, the screenplay for which was written improbably enough by Steven Knight, the man who designed the international hit quiz show, *Who Wants to Be a Millionaire* (1998–present). The film was the first production of Celador Films, owned by Celador Productions, which made *Who Wants to Be a Millionaire*. While the film had some BBC money in it, the key input in terms of the film's likely success came from the US company

Miramax, a subsidiary of Disney. The connection between the companies was forged by the quiz show that had been sold to ABC and ruthlessly exploited by them in the US TV market. ABC is, of course, also owned by Disney. It is perhaps in this context then that we can understand why *Dirty Pretty Things* did not really address the specific political/state construction of UK immigrants and asylum seekers and instead chose to displace and fragment such questions via the figure of the Hispanic villain, which as I have suggested, has a long history in the American film market. If Disney's distribution company was unable to carve out much of a place for *Dirty Pretty Things* in a UK market dominated by Hollywood product or US/UK co-productions dealing in the *ersatz* Britishness of Harry Potter, the film did do well in the enormous American market. Here, after eight weeks, it had access to 493 screens and had grossed $5.7million.

The lack of access that British filmmakers have to British audiences, other than via the American market, is perhaps nowhere better illustrated than in the story of Mike Hodges' film *Croupier*. The film was funded to the tune of £3 million by the Channel Four film arm, Film Four, which had historically adopted a remit closely modelled on Channel Four television's public service aim to provide audiences with material they were not getting on the other channels. This did not always mean stripping *Big Brother* (2000–present) across the schedules. Just as Channel Four's public service remit has been very largely corrupted by the increasing commodification of its airtime and therefore programmes, so Film Four was to undergo a transformation just as *Croupier* came to completion. As one journalist suggested, Film Four 'feared the storyline was too sophisticated for a British audience satiated with gangster capers such as *Snatch* [2000] and *Lock, Stock and Two Smoking Barrels* [1998]' (Bourne 2000: 5). As reviewers later noted, *Croupier* has a distinctly European art film quality to it and this is certainly related to the fact that the other funding sources for the film came from German and French television.

Film Four, however, was evidently becoming increasingly Atlanticist in its commercial orientation. It was relaunched in 1998 as a 'mini studio' with the aim of integrating production, distribution and marketing under one roof. All this was designed to focus their efforts on bigger budget films, more star vehicles and what Film Four called 'international' pictures, a euphemism for films strongly orientated to the American market. With Channel Four increasing Film Four's budget to £30 million a year, a co-production deal with Warner Bros. duly followed, but the returns on films such as *K-PAX* (2001) starring Kevin Spacey, and even more disastrously, the £15 million-budgeted *Charlotte Gray* (2001), starring Cate Blanchett, failed to provide the company with box-office returns. Meanwhile, their *The Full Monty* (1997) wannabe, *Lucky Break* (2001), disappointed at the UK box office. This is the context in which one has to situate Film Four's conclusion that *Croupier* was not the kind of film they wanted to risk further money on with prints, advertising and distribution costs. Accordingly

Croupier looked set to join that stock of British films that never get a theatrical release. It was, however, given a brief outing by the British Film Institute a year later as part of a double feature with Hodges' classic neo-noir/gangster film, *Get Carter* (1971).

What happens next is similar to *Dirty Pretty Things* in that it is paradoxically the American market that comes to the film's rescue. But what has to be remembered is that it is the domination of the British film industry and market by American companies that gives the American market its role as benefactor to British films squeezed out of their own market. The neo-colonial relationship between Hollywood and the British film industry can make the senior decisionmakers in the UK look even more narrow-minded and philistine than their Hollywood counterparts. The colonised other, a mere embarrassment within its own national context, becomes an exotic find in the colonisers' metropolis. *Croupier*'s fortunes turned after a Hodges retrospective at the American Cinematheque in Los Angeles, where the film played to very positive audience responses. A New York distribution company called The Shooting Gallery picked it up as part of a slate of films that the distributors were putting together for a roadshow festival of independent films across the US. *Croupier* did so well that it was then given a separate release where it generated $8 million of box-office revenues, equal to the box-office take of the much more conventional Film Four gangster flick, *Sexy Beast* (2000). Back over in the UK, a somewhat embarrassed Film Four initially resisted moves to re-release the film, later relenting, with the film receiving positive reviews across the board.

The irony that *Croupier* actually did well in the market that Film Four were desperate to break into, is made even more piquant by the terminal fortunes of the film company itself. Faced with losses amounting to a fairly modest £5.4m in the previous year, the new Chief Executive of Channel Four, Mark Thompson, shut Film Four down in 2002 and folded it back into Channel Four, minus its distribution and exhibition arms and with a loss of around 100 jobs. Its annual budget was slashed back to £10m. The *Times* reports Thompson as saying ('through gritted teeth'), 'We are moving away from our recent focus on larger-budget, international projects … and towards the kind of cutting edge British films that have been part of Channel 4's cultural and creative success' (quoted by Nathan 2002: 15).

The story of *Croupier* nicely demonstrates the impossibility of second-guessing audience preferences, upon which the fate of films, careers and jobs depends in a market economy, even when those preferences are subjected to the most controlling institutionalisations of taste (genres, marketing, preview audiences, and so forth). But the game of chance which film producers play with audiences becomes doubly difficult when the producers and the audience belong to different cultures and are separated by the oligopolistic lock that Hollywood has on both its own market and the British market.

Reification and fetishism

Of course, the film's up-and-down fortunes underscored its central motif, that of the roulette wheel and gambling in general as the potent symbol of a society run like a vast series of bets and subject to outcomes that are determined by chances which fluctuate, like the price form itself, within a limited set of parameters structurally determined by the exploitation of labour-power. The sound of the white ball travelling around the rim of the spinning wheel is the first thing we hear in the film's credits sequence and the spinning wheel – with its capricious capacity to make winners, but mostly losers, out of human beings – is the first thing we see. There is a very long history of economic theory, literary fiction and indeed films (such as *Dr Mabuse, der Spieler/Dr Mabuse, the Gambler* (1922) and *Gilda* (1946)) using the metaphor of the casino to think about the nature of capitalist society. Walter Benjamin quotes Marx's son-in-law, Paul Lafargue:

> Modern economic development as a whole tends more and more to transform capitalist society into a giant international gambling house, where the bourgeois wins and loses capital in consequence of events which remain unknown to him ... The 'inexplicable' is enthroned in bourgeois society as in a gambling hall ... Success and failures, thus arising from causes that are unanticipated, generally unintelligible, and seemingly dependent on chance, predispose the bourgeois to the gambler's frame of mind ... The capitalist whose fortune is tied up in stocks and bonds, which are subject to variations in market value and yield for which he does not understand the causes, is a professional gambler. The gambler, however ... is a supremely suspicious being. The habitués of gambling casinos always possess magic formulas to conjure the Fates. (Lafargue in Benjamin 1999: 497)

If the modern capitalist economy more and more resembles a giant international gambling house, then it is not only capitalists who become gamblers, but, indeed, everyone else who is caught up in the web of capitalist relations. Indeed capitalism is precisely about making gamblers of us all, while shifting the risks and losses of gambling away from capital (especially Big Capital) and on to labour. This generalisation of the condition of gambling is particularly true in a society that has been through the Thatcher revolution (continued under New Labour) of privatisation, deregulation, union-emasculation and erosion of public sector provision. As Hodges noted: 'There's an enormous amount of gambling in all our lives now ... everyone's freelance. We're all on our own to a large degree' (in Darke 2001: 2).

We have to probe further this mixture of chance, Fate and magic which Lafargue writes of if we are to fully appreciate the resonance and meaning of the image of gambling which *Croupier* deals with. It was Marx who suggested that capitalism, in so many ways an economy dependent on advanced science and technology and a vast engine for change and innovation, was also an economy that fostered a certain magical, fantastic and primitive attitude towards its own operations. He called this, in a famous section in *Capital*, commodity fetishism (see 1983: 76–7). We have seen that capitalism involves turning social relations into thing-like objects, where human involvement and action in the making of our society has congealed. In their different ways, chance (which reduces outcomes to random probabilities) and Fate (where outcomes are pre-arranged according to mystical suprahuman forces, whether God, astrology, the 'hidden hand' of the market, G. W. F. Hegel's World Spirit or even, in certain versions of vulgar Marxism, the development of the forces of production) are classic forms of fetishising the *object-world* so that it is drained of *collective* human agency and responsibility. What then happens is that this congealed fetishised object-world is dichotomously juxtaposed with an inflated and equally mystified model of subjectivity. In the fetishised universe of capital, human agency returns via equally fetishised objects (or rituals) that the individual can possess, investing in them fantastic and magical qualities which can mediate their relationship to chance and Fate, and indeed thrust responsibility for certain outcomes wholly back on to the individual.

Lafargue argues that success and failure remain largely inexplicable to the capitalist and there is a very good reason for this. For under capitalism, production is organised in competition (and therefore in hierarchically structured separation and isolation) rather than via co-operative co-ordination. Private ownership of the means of production – and the sale of labour-power as private property – means that every action and product produced acquires *the burden of autonomy*. The burden of autonomy means that every action and product of labour acquires sole and full responsibility for success and failure. Capitalist society is thus at one level a profound process of *de-socialisation* since the private act and product occludes the social context (which as we have seen is reduced to chance or some version of 'Fate'). And yet capitalist society is also a society, one that has developed the *socialisation* of production and consumption. Here is the essential contradiction: people and products acquire a burden of autonomy and yet their fortunes are in fact very largely (although not wholly) determined by collective social forces, causes and circumstances. Those forces, causes and circumstances become opaque precisely because our thing-like lives have *contracted* our receptiveness to them – and yet they assert themselves forcibly on our thing-like lives and thing-like products of labour all the time. Like the unconscious. As we have seen, as commodities, *Dirty Pretty Things* and *Croupier* circulate or, rather, failed to circulate in the British film market, under the burden of autonomy. Often people look at the success or failure of films as the outcome of their own characteristics, or at most they may look at 'add-on' characteristics. For example, poor marketing is often blamed for the failure of British films in the British market. What gets concealed and disguised by this fetishism of the film as commodity is the wider economic and institutional relationships, the configurations of power inscribed into them and how these impact on and circumscribe the space within which the 'private' commodity moves.

Chance and Fate are powerful undercurrents in film noir, where unintended meetings and encounters suck characters towards what seems to be inevitable murder and death. In the struggle over the forces of chance and Fate, noir assigns the voice-over a peculiarly powerful role as an *audio-fetish* where the apparent autonomy of masculinity is acted out but also frequently unravelled. Mark Bould has noted how the voice-over of noir characters often invokes a fantasy of control in the act of narration while in the 'intersubjective arena' of the narrative the male characters who control the voice-over show themselves to be rather less omniscient (2005: 58). Christine Gledhill, meanwhile, notes how the voice-over, combined with a flashback structure opens up a 'temporal separation' between the telling of the story and the events retold, allowing the audience to explore the gaps between the two (1998: 28). Both the question of control and perspective are central to the voice-over and flashback narration in *Croupier*.

After the credits sequence, which establishes the centrality of the roulette wheel as a motif, the first scene proper finds Jack Manfred (Clive Owen) in the casino, the camera circling him. Jack's voice-over addresses the implied audience: 'Now he had become the still centre of that spinning wheel of misfortune. The world turned round him leaving him miraculously untouched. The croupier had reached his goal. He no longer heard the sound of the ball.' Unlike most noir voice-overs this one does not begin in a state of distress or in dangerous circumstances which the subsequent flashback will unravel. Quite the contrary – Jack's narrative goal has been accomplished! This underscores

Casino capitalism: *Croupier*

the theme of control that the protagonist believes he has acquired in this/his world. He is at the centre and is untouched by the 'wheel of misfortune' that impacts so disastrously on the customers of the casino. What is peculiar about this voice-over is that Jack speaks of himself in the third person. For Jack is a would-be novelist looking to use his experiences in the casino business as the raw materials of his novel.

By making the character that delivers the voice-over a novelist, *Croupier* elaborates on the noir tradition of foregrounding the process of narration by turning the chief protagonist into a storyteller (see Gledhill 1998: 29). By speaking of himself in the third person, Jack seeks once more the comfort of an Olympian control over events and people that directly impinge on his life. Being a storyteller thus has a structural parallel with being a croupier, as both position Jack in a fetishistic (that is partly fantastic) position of control and masculine autonomy typical of the noir hero voice-over. But being a narrator, like being an employee in a casino, is not quite the Olympian position of control Jack thinks it is. For Jack's storytelling is just one element in a system of narration that is far more omniscient than he is.

The third-person address also has the effect of diminishing the sense of past tense about the narrator's discourse, making it feel much more as if it were a simultaneous commentary on events as they happen, just as the omniscient and invisible narrator would make in a novel. But at the same time the split between Jack the protagonist and Jack the narrator suggests a divided subject and opens up social and psychological disjunctures within Jack and between Jack and his world. Thus in the beginning, Jack's voice-over immediately signals a certain identity crisis when he notes: 'To begin with, he was Jack Manfred.' The voice belongs to Jack but Jack and the voice-over do not seem to coincide entirely. The split is further widened when Jack starts to act more like his emerging fictional character, Jake. Indeed it may be Jack as Jake who is responsible for his girlfriend's mysterious death by a hit-and-run driver. Jack tells us that his girlfriend, Marion Nell (Gina McKee), 'was a romantic and thought he was too'. When he tells Marion that she is all he desires, we have to question whether that is true (he hates cheats – in the casino – but sleeps with Bella (Kate Hardie)). Shortly afterwards, Marion declares her love for Jack, while his voice-over tells us: 'And he half-loved Marion. And she knew that too.'

What Jack desires above all is the work of being a croupier in the casino, whose interior, appropriately enough given noir's German Expressionist roots, was shot in a film studio in Mannheim. *Croupier*'s casino is lined with mirrors that deploy the traditional noir motifs of double identities and narcissism, and because the mirrors are in different segments, they reflect back a fractured and distorted world. The centrality of the casino as Jack's desired object is a significant modification of the traditional noir structure where the object of desire has been the beautiful but dangerous woman or femme fatale. What has to be investigated in *Croupier* is not the sexual desire of the woman but the raw materials of casino life that will become the novel Jack is writing. That is why although Marion closely resembles the figure of the 'nurturing woman' (see Place 1998: 60–3), Jack has no real relationship with a femme fatale. Jack may try to impose a noir filter on Bella (he describes her as 'trouble' and when she is introduced to the film, we can hear in the background of the scene a noir/thriller film on the television, all screeching tyres and gunshots) but he and we soon discover that Bella is forthrightly honest, upfront and transparent. Even Jani de Villiers (Alex Kingston), who persuades him to have a minor role in the casino robbery, does not fit the femme fatale bill, as their relationship is Platonic rather than sexual (in a nice joke, they even sleep – Jack in his pyjamas – in the same bed without 'sleeping' with each other). This shift to the casino as desired object recovers the economic fetishism behind the sexual fetishism of traditional noir. However, arguably the film itself seems to invest in Jack's fetishistic solution to fetishism (including his international success with his novel). Insofar as there is a critique of Jack, it is personal, psychological (Jack's Oedipal issues with his father and mother), moral and subjective (recalling Lukács' reservations about expressionism) and there is little to undercut his final triumphant line that he has acquired 'the power to make you lose'.

Conclusion

This essay has suggested that the structurally determined fluctuations of fortune for British cinema are narrowing down to a range of genres such as adaptations of literary classics, fantasy films, romantic comedies and formulaic gangster films, as British cinema becomes ever more integrated into Hollywood Big Capital and reconfigured for its cultural detour through the American market. What is the future of British neo-noir in this context? Both *Dirty Pretty Things* and *Croupier* did well in the American market and both did less well in the British market. For both, the problems they had in the British market derive from Hollywood's domination. The logic of future development would appear to be clear: British neo-noir, as with every other surviving genre in the repertoire of British cinema, has a future to the extent it can be made for successful export to the American market under guidelines stipulated by Hollywood companies. Just as developing countries find themselves exporting staple foodstuffs to the West instead of providing such goods for their own people, so British cinema will become a cinema designed for export. One important condition for a thriving film culture, its relationship to a concrete place (national context), becomes increasingly hollowed out, leaving a reified shell. There may remain enough differentiation within the system and contradiction to support occasional films like *Dirty Pretty Things* or *Croupier*. But is that enough? If we do not rediscover the critical importance of the concept of reification, we are likely to think that it is.

REFERENCES

Amago, Samuel (2005) 'Why Spaniards make good bad guys: Sergi López and the persistence of the black legend in contemporary European cinema', *Film Criticism*, 30, 1, 41–63.

Benjamin, Walter (1999) *The Arcades Project*, trans. Howard Eiland and Kevin McLaughlin. London: Harvard University Press.

Bould, Mark (2005) *Film Noir: From Berlin to Sin City*. London: Wallflower Press.

Bourne, Brendan (2000) 'British film flop hits US jackpot', *Sunday Times*, 17 September, 5.

Darke, Chris (2001) 'Film: "The only thing I like are the credits"; The first distributor of "Croupier" wasn't impressed', *Independent on Sunday*, 20 May, Features, 2.

Gledhill, Christine (1998 [1978]) '*Klute* 1: Contemporary film noir and feminist criticism', in E. Ann Kaplan (ed.) *Women in Film Noir*. New Edition. London: British Film Institute, 20–34.

Lucia, Cynthia (2003) 'The complexities of cultural change: An interview with Stephen Frears', *Cineaste*, 28, 4, 8–15.

Lukács, Georg (1971) *History and Class Consciousness: Studies in Marxist Dialectics*, trans. Rodney Livingstone. London: Merlin Press.

____ (1988 [1923]) 'Realism in the balance', ed. and trans. Ronald Taylor, in Ernst Bloch, Georg Lukács, Bertolt Brecht, Walter Benjamin and Theodor Adorno, *Aesthetics and Politics*. London: Verso, 28–59.

Marx, Karl (1981) *Economic and Philosophic Manuscripts of 1844*, trans. Martin Milligan and Dirk J. Struik. London: Lawrence & Wishart.

____ (1983) *Capital*, Vol. 1, trans. Samuel Moore and Edward Aveling. London: Lawrence & Wishart.

Miller, Toby, Nitin Govil, John McMurria, Richard Maxwell and Ting Wang (2005) *Global Hollywood 2*. London: British Film Institute.

Minturn, Kent (1999) '*Peinture noire*: Abstract Expressionism and *film noir*', in Alain Silver and James Ursini (eds) *Film Noir Reader 2*. New York: Limelight, 270–309.

Nathan, Ian (2002) 'Blame-spotting', *Times*, 11 July, Features: Times2, 15.

Place, J. A. and L. S. Peterson (1976 [1974]) 'Some visual motifs of *film noir*', in Bill Nichols (ed.) *Movies and Methods: Volume 1: An Anthology*. London: University of California Press, 325–38.

Place, Janey (1998 [1978]) 'Women in film noir', in E. Ann Kaplan (ed.) *Women in Film Noir*. New Edition. London: British Film Institute, 47–68.

Screen International (2003a) 'International box office', *Screen International*, 1386, 6–9 January, 46.

Screen International (2003b) 'International box office', *Screen International*, 1387, 10–16 January, 48 and 50.

UK Film Council (2006) *Statistical Yearbook 2005/6*. London: UK Film Council.

Wayne, Michael (2003) *Marxism and Media Studies: Key Concepts and Contemporary Trends*. London: Pluto.

_____ (2006) 'Working Title Mark II: A critique of the Atlanticist paradigm for British cinema', *International Journal of Media and Cultural Politics*, 2, 1, 59–73.

Williams, Tony (1999) 'British *film noir*', in Alain Silver and James Ursini (eds) *Film Noir Reader 2*. New York: Limelight, 243–69.

10

Laughter in the Dark: Irony, Black Comedy and Noir in the Films of David Lynch, the Coen Brothers and Quentin Tarantino

GREG TUCK

Despite the dynamic and porous nature of film noir and neo-noir, there is of course something very simple and obvious that links, without delimiting, the films concerned. At an aesthetic, thematic or existential level, or indeed a combination of all three, noir is pre-eminently *dark*. While this darkness does not restrict the narrative scope or interpretive richness of these films, it does offer us a form of coherence-in-negation. That is, while we are unable to produce anything other than rather reductive definitions of noir, to say exactly what it is, we know at an experiential level what noir *isn't*; it isn't bright, it isn't lucky and it isn't happy. But, is it funny?

At first, it might seem a stretch to insist on the existence of comedy noir. While thrillers, heist movies and murder mysteries partake of many of the themes found in noir, they seem to preclude themselves from the noir universe precisely when they are too comic. For example, *The Thin Man* (1934), based on the Dashiell Hammett novel, features a story of theft and murder and a very noirish opening, but its screwball aspects seem to place it outside, or beyond, the world of noir. Conversely, many classic film noirs have quick-witted dialogue and moments of comic relief, such as Philip Marlowe's (Humphrey Bogart) comic 'performance' in the bookshop scene in *The Big Sleep* (1946) and the exchange between Walter Neff (Fred MacMurray) and Mrs Dietrichson's maid, Nettie (Betty Farrington), about keys and locked drinks cabinets in *Double Indemnity* (1944). However, as with the humorous asides of westerns and war films, while these lighter moments offer contrast to the central elements of the narrative they do so without reducing the overriding seriousness of the subject matter. Clearly, the difference between the occasional deployment of a mode (the comic) and adherence to an overarching generic purpose (comedy) needs to be accounted for. Yet, there is a sense in which this distinction is itself too easily drawn as the notion of comic purpose is itself a complex one. As Andrew Horton has described it, 'like language and texts in general, the comic is plural, unfinalised, disseminative, dependent on context and the intertextuality of creator, text and contemplator' (1991: 9). Furthermore, any unitary understanding of 'comic purpose' (films designed to entertain and elicit laughter) is always capable of a more complex reversal once one asks what is the 'purpose' of comedy? The laughter elicited by the comic can be light or serious, critical or nonsensical, revolutionary or reactionary, or a strange hybrid of these and other forms. However, if we approach the relationship from the other direction, it is clearly the case that comedy can be dark. We can laugh at war in *M*A*S*H* (1970), death in *Life of Brian* (1979), cannibalism in *Eating Raoul* (1982), disability in *Idioterne/The Idiots* (1998) and serial killers in *American Psycho* (2000) – indeed, there seems little in the way of suffering or death that cannot be presented in a dark comic way. It is in this shared potential for *darkness* that we might be able to identify the interface or crossover between 'black' comedy and film 'noir'.

If, when it comes to representations of violence or death, we care about the individuals concerned, if their fate matters to us in a deep moral or emotional sense, such moments are more usually experienced as tragic or triumphal rather than comic. If we don't, their fate opens up two distinct (but not unrelated or mutually exclusive) black comic possibilities: an ironic comment on their failed aspirations or a black joke at the expense of their embodiment. In other words, dark irony is driven more by a conceptual understanding which diffuses throughout the narrative, often linking moments in a narrative chain, while black comedy is more perceptual, experiential and disruptive. Hence, the irony of Milo Minderbinder (Jon Voight) arranging to bomb his own airfield on behalf of the Germans in *Catch-22* (1970) makes perfect sense, building as it does on his shameless and ruthless pursuit of profit throughout the film. On the other hand, when Russell Franklin (Samuel L. Jackson) is unexpectedly bitten in two in *Deep Blue Sea* (1999), it feels more like a joke, coming as it does directly after he has delivered a heroic speech demonstrating his leadership credentials. While black comedy can employ irony, and irony employ violence, in crude terms, irony is more akin to an experience of the humorous while black comic 'moments' are more structurally akin to jokes. Whereas the diffuse dark humour which often pervades the original cycle's representation of death and violence remains predominantly ironic in tone, I believe the joke form of comedy violence is far more predominant in neo-noir. Of course, many neo-noirs can be as chilling as noir in the randomness or cruelty of their beatings and murders and both noir and neo-noir can take their violence very seriously and/ or ironically, but it is hard to think of much, or indeed any, violence in the original cycle which is overtly comic or jokey. This is not the case with some neo-noirs, as the following examples make clear.

One of the best known moments of neo-noir comedy violence is the accidental shooting in Quentin Tarantino's *Pulp Fiction* (1994). While hit-men, Vincent Vega (John Travolta) and Jules Winnfield (Samuel L. Jackson) are driving a minor villain, Marvin (Phil LaMarr), to an interrogation, Vincent's gun accidentally goes off, blowing the man's head apart, showering both car and occupants in blood, brains and bone. On seeing the film on its release, I can still remember the explosion of laughter from the audience, mine included, that accompanied this moment. While in one sense an ironic demonstration of the unprofessionalism of these supposedly professional killers, the moment is so sudden and unexpected and so hyperbolically violent, it seems to switch the narrative to a more obviously comical mode. Likewise, the kidnap and murders of the Coen brothers' *Fargo* (1996) offer a comic rendition of what are usually represented as much darker acts. It seems both pathetic and absurd when a terrified Jean Lundegaard (Kristin Rudrüd) hides behind the shower curtain from the two kidnappers her husband has sent to abduct her. However, when she attempts to run screaming from the bathroom, she takes the shower curtain with her, accidentally wearing it over her head like a shroud. The image is far too reminiscent of fake comedy ghosts to be taken entirely seriously (particularly as she runs into the wall and knocks herself out) and it is hard not to see the funny side despite, or possibly because of, the cruelty involved. Finally, during the bloody and bungled robbery at the grain store in David Lynch's *Wild at Heart* (1990), one of the storemen has his hand shot off. While the culprit, Bobby Peru (Willem Dafoe), continues his gun battle with the cop outside (eventually falling on his shotgun and blowing his own head clean off), the two storemen search the floor for the hand. No sooner has the less injured man assured his colleague, 'Don't worry. They can sew these things back on', than the film cuts to a shot of a dog, trotting out of the back door with the hand in its mouth.

Quentin Tarantino, the Coen brothers and David Lynch seem particularly keen to present a re-visioning of the darkness of noir in comic ways. This is not to suggest that the laughter or black comedy in their films is of a single type or

Ill-gotten gain: *Wild at Heart*

their violence is always funny, but the conjunction, as in the examples above, is clear to see. However, while black comedy, irony and noir may well have a potentially reinforcing relationship, we must remain alert to the fact that, as with *The Thin Man*, overt comedy can equally work to lighten if not negate a previously dark theme. As Geoff King has suggested, 'In some cases the mixture or merging of comedy with other dimensions can be complex, challenging and unsettling. Elsewhere it seems to have the opposite effect, reducing the potential for the production of disturbing qualities, a factor which helps explain its appeal in many products aimed at a mass audience' (2002: 187–8).

So, scenes such as these seem to raise fundamental questions about moments of comedy violence. First, do they mark a potentially substantive difference between noir and neo-noir? Second, if neo-noir is more overtly comic or joke-like is it consequently less 'noir'? Finally, why is violence (potentially) funny?

In answering the first question, it must be noted that this potential difference is not an either/or matter. The more overtly comic forms employed by these filmmakers have not entirely replaced the ironic elements more common to the main cycle. It is clearly ironic that the hapless robbers, Pumpkin (Tim Roth) and Honey Bunny (Amanda Plummer), of *Pulp Fiction*, choose to hold up the exact diner where the heavily armed, but disguised, Jules and Vincent are having coffee. Similarly, in *Wild at Heart,* there is the irony of Sailor Ripley (Nicolas Cage) asking Perdita Durango (Isabella Rossellini) whether there is a contract out on him without knowing it is she who has been given the contract. Indeed, as Robert Witkin has pointed out, while 'we associate irony easily with humour, we recognise, too, that irony can be bitter and even tragic' (1997), so we must not rush to associate the ironic simply with the humorous. The darkness of noir's irony can frequently render it mirthless, or at least mean that our amusement is often fleeting, if not hollow. For example, when we read 'Man Wanted', towards the beginning of *The Postman Always Rings Twice* (1946), we soon understand the tragic ironic clash between it signifying both employment and erotic need. Likewise, the fate of the murderous couple – Cora Smith (Lana Turner) escapes the gas chamber only to die 'innocently' in a car crash for which her accomplice, Frank Chambers (John Garfield), is ultimately blamed and executed – is ironic, but not in any sense comic. So, while violence or death may accompany these ironic elements, unlike the more shocking and stand-alone black jokes of neo-noir, the violence in the original cycle seems less comedic and more in the service of the irony. For example, in *The Killers* (1964), when – just before shooting her – a bleeding Charlie Strom (Lee Marvin) tells Sheila Farr (Angie Dickinson), 'Lady, I don't have the time', his own death moments later amply demonstrates the other, ironic meaning of this statement.

Such ironic coincidences often have a profoundly determining role within the narrative and the ironic treatment of the violence on display takes us back into the story. Unlike the pure black comic moments of exploding heads, shrouded kidnap victims and handless shop assistants, the violence in the original cycle seems designed to pass judgement on the perpetrator rather than to dwell on the suffering of the victim. Even the shocking moment in *White Heat* (1949) when Cody Jarrett (James Cagney) unloads his gun into the trunk of his car after the hapless occupant, Roy Parker (Paul Guilfoyle), asks for some air, is not without irony. That we see Jarrett murder while casually chewing on a chicken leg is more important than the precise mode of Parker's death, which seems intended to explain Jarrett's depravity rather than be a spectacle in itself. Jules demonstrates an equal degree of callousness when 'collecting' Marvin by casually eating the breakfast of Marvin's accomplices before violently murdering them. However, his manner is far more performative than ironic. Unlike the unseen Parker, the first of Jules' victims dies in shot and the suddenness of the act provides the opportunity for Jules to quip to the now terrified second accomplice, 'I'm sorry, did I spoil your concentration?' The performative element increases as Jules petrifies the young man with theatrical biblical quotes before killing him. Here, it is not enough for Jules, like Jarrett, to demonstrate his capacity for cold violence; his victims must suffer and be seen to suffer. They are not simply the victims of violence, but the butt of jokes.

It could be argued that this difference is simply the result of the main cycle of film noir lacking the gore of films made after the end of the Production Code restrictions and the introduction of squibs and other special effects (see Prince 2000: 6–16). Neo-noir is more spectacular in its representation of death and violence simply because it can be. However, it does not follow that spectacular violence need be funny (even if only darkly so). While the fight that opens *Wild at Heart* or the execution of the eyewitnesses in *Fargo* are equally shocking, they are without comedy so liberalisation alone does not explain the difference. The use of comedy is therefore both novel and a matter of choice, a choice that is not without consequence, particularly with regard to how these representations of violence now differ from the representation of death in classic noir. This brings us to the second question as to the effect of this development: whether black jokes increase or decrease the underlying darkness.

Following John Morreall, Simon Critchley suggests three main explanations of humour – the superiority theory, the relief theory and the incongruity theory – all of which offer possible explanations for the source of our pleasure in these moments of comedy violence (see 2002: 2). As early as Aristotle's *Poetics*, a superiority theory of comedy is identified and defined as 'an imitation of cheaper, more ordinary persons. They are not entirely base, but are embodiments of that part of the ugly which excites laughter' (1942: 8–9). Put simply, our amusement at the fate of the shameful and inferior failures of noir makes us feel better about our own position. The violence is not a thing in itself, but a vivid demonstration of this wider failure. On the other hand, relief theories of comedy, as most famously developed by Sigmund Freud (1976), suggest that violence allows a release of psychic and emotional energy. Rather than enjoying the failure of their plans, dreams and desires in a conscious superior fashion, we unconsciously enjoy the momentary violence unleashed on these people by this failure in itself. Explosive laughter is a pleasurable discharge or reflex caused by the release of feelings that are more usually repressed. It could be argued that our wry response to the ironic violent consequences of noir links it to the superiority theory of comedy while our explosive response to the comic violence of neo-noir links it to relief theories. The darkness on display might therefore seem of a slightly different kind rather than of a different order. However, this does not account for the presence of the third mode of humour, incongruity, which traces our pleasure to the gap between the expected and the actual and which again seems more common to neo-noir than noir. Here, it is the sheer incongruity of heavily pregnant cops (*Fargo*), a hit-man wearing an 'I'm with Stupid' t-shirt (*Pulp Fiction*), psychopaths dancing to 1970s pop music (*Reservoir Dogs* (1992)), or gangsters obsessed with car stopping distances (*Lost Highway* (1997)) that is the source of the comedy. Incompetent violence seems particularly incongruous as it widens the gap between the capacity for and consequence of violence itself. While their unpredictability makes the perpetrators of unintended violence especially dangerous, it equally makes them look stupid. For example, the entire premise of *The Big Lebowski* (1998) rests on the idiocy of the thugs that break into Jeffrey 'The Dude' Lebowski's (Jeff Bridges) apartment mistaking this bathrobed slacker for a millionaire. Far more chilling, however, is the comic violence of the aptly named Joe Messing (Mark Pellegrino) in *Mulholland Dr.* (2001). He begins the scene the epitome of the professional killer by shooting a man while casually talking to him in his office. To make it look like suicide, he wipes his own prints off the gun, places it in his victim's hand, but accidentally pulls the trigger. The bullet goes through the wall and a large woman in the next office starts screaming that she has been bitten. Panicking, and in an effort to silence her, the hit-man wrestles the woman into the same office as his victim, but her cries attract the attention of the janitor who enters the office, vacuum cleaner in hand, just as the hit-man kills the woman. Now he also has to kill the janitor and, out of frustration, he also shoots the vacuum cleaner. Unfortunately, this blows the electrical circuits and sets off the building's alarm system: with three people dead rather than one and the bells loudly ringing, the incompetent hit-man hurriedly leaves. Of course, the incongruous gap between expectation and event is not enough to confer humour on such blackness, yet, as with obvious scenes of comedy violence we can still find humour in such moments. However, in order to decide whether these different modes of dark humour, described in terms of superiority, relief or incongruity, can be mapped on to noir and neo-noir, and whether they are lighter or darker in affect, we need to address our third question: why is violence funny at all?

According to Henri Bergson in his seminal work, *On Laughter*, 'laughter has no greater foe than emotion' (1911: 4) and the comic comes into being or appears 'whenever a group of men [*sic*] concentrate their attention on one of their number, imposing silence on their emotions and calling into play nothing but their intelligence' (1911: 8). Humour and compassion negate each other and for Bergson this is particularly true when subjects are reduced to their bodies. Despite the appeal to intelligence, this can sound like a theory of slapstick, yet it might equally be applied to more ironic moments. For example, it would suggest the 'logical' escalation of Messing's error is the actual source of the comedy. However, this does not explain whether we are laughing at Messing's incompetence or with him in recognition at his frustration – or, more important-ly, *why* in either case we switch off our emotional empathy with the victims. It could simply be a matter of such victims being so underdeveloped and fleeting that they can only be read in a structural or logical way and there is no 'subject' beyond their narrative function with which to identify. However, this begs the question do we laugh because we are distant from these characters or are we distant because we laugh?

Bergson is hardly alone in observing a relationship between a lack of empa-thy and amusement. Indeed, there seems to be a certain emotional coldness at the heart of the superiority, relief and incongruity theories of comedy which makes them seem like articulations of a similar process rather than three dis-tinct tropes. For example, at the end of *Blood Simple* (1984), it is both horrible and hilarious when the hand of murderous private detective Loren Visser (M. Emmet Walsh) is impaled with a knife and stuck to a window frame by his intended victim, Abby (Frances McDormand). His vileness throughout the film allows us to enjoy in a superior fashion not just his pain, but the indignity of his predicament. Likewise, the sudden switch from Abby being potential victim to attacker offers an instant and cathartic sense of relief. Abby, however, has only seen the gloved hand and thinks the assailant is actually her ex-husband Julian Marty (Dan Hedaya). After Visser frees himself and begins to come to the door, but before Abby sees him, she shoots. On hearing him slump to the bathroom floor she declares, 'I'm not afraid of you, Marty', which despite his appalling injuries causes Visser to laugh. He replies to a now very bemused Abby that he will let Marty know when he sees him, a reference to the fact that Visser has already shot (and thinks he has killed) Marty. From a Bergsonian position there is a sense in which Visser's laughter demonstrates his own suspension of emotional engagement with himself and hence he can laugh at the irony of his own fate, encouraging us to do the same. However, any potential pathos such a moment may confer on Visser is denied him as both his attention and ours is drawn to an incongruous point-of-view shot of what he sees as he lies bleeding on the bathroom floor. As he looks up, he sees the underneath of the sink with a particularly odd collection of pipes from which a single drop of water forms and then, just as it falls, the film suddenly ends. Where does our sympathy or empathy lie at this moment? In one sense, Visser has got what he deserves, but one is given little time to 'enjoy' the righteousness of his demise. We do not see him actually die or hear the reassuring sound of sirens or the flash of a blue light. Although Abby ends the narrative with both husband and lover murdered, the film finishes without producing any particular sense of empathy towards her either. She is left knowing she killed the 'right' man in terms of the person who has been trying to kill her, but she is left dumbfounded by killing the 'wrong' man, a stranger whose violent connection to her is a complete mystery. For us, however, the moment makes perfect sense and now that the *logical* possibilities of the narrative's twists and turns have been worked through we do not seem to care about the consequences for either of these characters. Their 'pain' is a source of indifference rather than enjoyed in itself in either a cold or cruel fashion.

The ironic humour of the classic cycle though less explicitly violent seems to be equally unemotional. Despite the (normative) punishment of transgression, it is precisely our sense of ironic distance which means we do not 'feel' for these characters, or not to the degree necessary for their fate to be properly tragic or deserved. This is not the fall of 'great men' through some personal flaw and neither is it the fatal collision of equally justifiable, but incompatible, aims or ideals. Instead, it is the fall of the already low, the punishment of action rather than psychic attribute and the collision of equally unjustifiable aims that drives these narratives. In this shared absence of compassion, noir and neo-noir begin to look more alike, but we must be careful not to confuse this lack of sympathy with a lack of interest. While we do not care about the characters of noir, we still *identify* with them. The drifters, singles, divorced, unemployed and unemployable of the original cycle are not simple clowns to be laughed at. They are too much like ourselves to be dismissed so easily and we recognise their failings and limitations as our own. Yet the darkness seems to warn us off from emotionally investing in them. So the irony and violence of noir is not simply enjoyed via a generalised coldness, as claimed by Bergson. Instead, I would suggest that the pleasure we gain is not limited to a logical or philosophical appreciation of structure, such that we simply suspend emotion, but a recognition of a more active and indeed political critique of emotion itself. What we enjoy is that both the irony and comic violence are deeply *unsentimental*.

At one level this seems obvious. Sentiment does not survive being hard-boiled. Even a noir as emotionally charged as *Mildred Pierce* (1945) proves that money and sex are both considerably thicker than blood and love. Indeed, Nino Frank, the man most often cited as the originator of the term film noir, particularly focused on the sense 'that a younger generation of Hollywood auteurs … had rejected the sentimental humanism' of a previous generation (quoted in Naremore 1998: 16). While this pessimistic rejection of humanism chimed well with the pervasive existentialism of the period, as Naremore states: 'what needs to be emphasised is that existentialism was intertwined with a residual surrealism, and surrealism was crucial for the reception of any art described as "noir"' (1998: 17).

Noir's relationship to surrealism and surrealism's antipathy towards sentiment offers a way to understand our mixture of logical interest and emotional suspicion for the victims and perpetrators of film noir. Raymond Borde and Étienne Chaumeton's highly influential study, *Panorama du film noir américain* (1955) was 'profoundly surrealist in its ideological aims … [and placed] great emphasis on the theme of death, and on "essential" affective qualities, which at one point they list in the form of five adjectives typical of surrealism: "oneiric, bizarre, erotic, ambivalent, and cruel"' (Naremore 1998: 19), adjectives which seem equally applicable to the noir universe. Furthermore, in his 1940 *Anthologie de l'humour noir*, André Breton made surrealism's antipathy towards sentiment clear. While at pains to point out that 'black humour is hemmed in by too many things, including stupidity, sceptical sarcasm, light-hearted jokes' to render the relationship between darkness and comedy either a simple or formal one, Breton specifically claimed that despite its many forms black comedy is pre-eminently 'the mortal enemy of sentimentality' (1997: xix). From Jonathan Swift's 'modest proposal' to eat the children of the poor to the Marquis de Sade's tale of an aristocrat with 'live' furniture made from female slaves, from Franz Kafka's human insects to Leonora Carrington's party-going hyena, the anthology celebrated writers who had employed horrific, surreal and violent imagery to comic effect. Yet, while the use of this violence was often gratuitous it was not mindless, but satirical and critical, marking as it did 'a superior revolt of the mind' (Breton 1997: xvi). It was not just having a laugh but making a point, a point which foregrounds the destructive, the threatening, the brutal and the cruel because it was *true*. The vital point here is that the mad, violent, cruel and surreal world suggested by black comedy was *not* incongruent from reality because it *is* reality, or at least its logical extension. What this world of pain and violence was incongruous with, therefore, was not the real conditions of existence from which these tales emerged, so much as the dominant ideology which both produced and denied it. The reason dark humour was to be celebrated was not simply as a rejection of fine feelings or emotional sympathy or empathy per se, but because the sugar rush of sentimentality was bought at the expense of accepting the real violence and cruelty of contemporary life that was its backdrop. As Deborah Knight has summarised, 'sentimentality desensitises: it transforms the aesthetic into the anaesthetic' (1999: 417). It is this attack on sentimentality and the functional support sentiment offers dominant ideology which prevents both black comedy and surrealism from being little but an expression of psychotic estrangement from reality, misanthropic spleen-venting or simply silliness. Swift's proposal that we should eat the children of the starving poor *is* modest and logical if one accepts the ideology that would condemn them to an inhumane existence in the first place.

There was of course a fundamental difference between the darkness manifested in the elite art practices of French surrealism and the blackness of hard-boiled fiction and the contemporary American crime film. Surrealism employed incongruous tropes and images directly within the text, making things strange in order to make its point; popular cultural products such as crime fiction and film noir were instead responding to the external incongruity between the fundamentally surreal and cruel nature of contemporary society compared to its representation in mainstream films. In film noir, it is the sentimental ideology of happy endings, of suckers getting an even break and of bad girls turning good that is seen as the incongruity or as the truly *sur*-real. As Steve Neale has argued, rather than reflect a unitary reaction to postwar conditions, film noir occupied a dark place at the far end of a spectrum of film production that generally produced far more escapist and ideologically complicit musicals, comedies, romances and war films than dark urban thrillers (see 2000: 155–6). Hence it is happy families, heterosexual romance, masculine loyalty, individual freedom, the rewards of honest labour, the usual fare of Hollywood films that is the pervasive background 'film reality' that comes under noir's critical dark gaze. The noir in film noir, like the blackness in black comedy, expressed both an analysis and an attitude, an acknowledgement of the harsh realities of contemporary life which at least gave respite from the distortions and fabrications of ideological domination even if it did not encourage its revolutionary overthrow. The question is, is this still the case with the black comic violence of neo-noir? Is it unsympathetic or unsentimental? Is it ideologically critical or complicit?

Clearly, ultra-violence can have a surreal quality which can seem unsentimental and the incongruity of much neo-noir violence becomes potentially explicable as purposeful and critical rather than simply humorous when viewed in this light. Undoubtedly, of the three directors, Lynch is the most surreal. Indeed, with his penchant for all five of Borde and Chaumeton's surreal affective qualities linked to noir (oneiric, bizarre, erotic, ambivalent, cruel) he produces films that are not so much neo-noir as hyper-noir, a distillation of darkness in all its forms. What often looks like a moral chiaroscuro, such as the stark comparisons between the worlds exemplified by Jeffrey Beaumont (Kyle MacLachlan) and Frank Booth (Dennis Hopper) in *Blue Velvet* (1986), turns out to be nothing of the sort. Lynch's surrealism makes both these worlds equally chimerical and bizarre and reveals that the darkness dwells in the sunshine. These supposed opposites are in reality two facets of the same ideological mystification or dream, namely the American Dream, and Lynch demonstrates that it is in the nature of this most pernicious of ideological constructs (exemplified by the white picket fences of Lumberton) to deny responsibility for creating its own nightmare other. Lynch's unsentimental attack on ideological double vision is most clearly materialised in his use of doubled persons, such as the guilt-ridden yet knowledgeable Fred Madison (Bill Pullman), who mysteriously morphs into innocent but ignorant Pete Dayton (Balthazar Getty), in *Lost Highway*, or Betty Elms/Diane Selwyn (Naomi Watts) in *Mulholland Dr.*, who demonstrates how the perky and the poisonous can dwell in the same character. Indeed, one only has to see the psychopathic Frank crying at emotional songs such as 'In Dreams' and 'Blue Velvet' to realise that a capacity for extreme violence and banal sentimentality are in no sense antithetical and quite possibly complementary. These films also show how the City of Dreams is also always the City of Nightmares maintaining the tradition that Los Angeles is noir's 'spiritual' home. This is why despite the comic potential of Lynch's violence it is disturbing and provocative and more than just a violent joke. Indeed, while outrageous and extreme there is something believable about it that brings us firmly back to an underlying material reality. Returning to our poor storeman in *Wild at Heart*, it must be remembered that the search for the hand comes after the spectacularly violent death of Bobby Peru. Rather than simply surreal, the sight of Peru's head being blown off, hitting a wall and then landing with a sickening squelch in the dust might be better understood as a form of 'grotesque realism' in Mikhail Bakhtin's precise sense of this term. According to Bakhtin, grotesque realism 'degrades, brings down to earth, turns their subject into flesh. The people's laughter which characterised all the forms of grotesque realism from immemorial times was linked with the bodily lower stratum. Laughter degrades and materialises' (1984: 20).

Unlike Bergson's frigid elitism the laughter here is not simply dark but democratic as Peru's own susceptibility to death is made clear. Hence the degradation on display is conceptually as much as topographically downward, as that mocking destruction of the head, the site of 'reason', makes clear. This is not simply a facing up to the visceral reality of mortality and the fragility of the flesh, but a celebration of it. The storeman might not find his hand, but this does not stop him looking. The fragility of his flesh is exposed by his encounter with Peru, but he is not defeated by it and there is something which seems equally irrepressible about his will to live. Furthermore, in feeding the dog, the lifeless lump of flesh that was his hand returns to the world and will not simply rot as will the remains of Peru. If his fate is to go from 'dust to dust', the storeman's hand goes from 'flesh to flesh'. This is another vital aspect of the grotesque, the fact that it 'is based on the conception of the world as eternally unfinished: a world dying and being born at the same time, possessing as it were two bodies. The dual image combining praise and abuse seeks to grasp the very moment of this change, the transfer from old to new, from death to life' (Bakhtin 1984: 166).

The Coen brothers also seem capable of combining the comedic and the dark through moments of grotesque realism. For example, in *Fargo*, the incompetent kidnapper, Carl Showalter (Steve Buscemi) – a man who never stops talking – is shot in the face, yet he *still* keeps talking, until axed to death by his surly accomplice, the almost silent Gaear Grimsrud (Peter Stormare). The denouement, in which we see Grimsrud trying to dispose of Carl's remains in the wood chipper, with nothing but a foot sticking out of the top and the adjacent snow awash with blood, is an even clearer example. Not only does this attempt to 'hide' the body make it even more visible, sprayed as it is over yards of ground, it reminds us how death in itself is never the end as there is always the body, the material remainder which resists being simply disposed of. For the audience, if not always for the protagonists, the problem of the corpse is more than a practical issue as it stands as the perfect counterpoint to the idealistic wishful thinking of the perpetrator. Murder is easy; getting away with it is another matter and the corpse is often a source of more fear than the living person ever was. The fact that Grimsrud is arrested by a pregnant woman also seems particularly metaphoric of life's refusal in the face of death. While without gore, the arrest of Jean's husband, Jerry (William H. Macy), at the end of *Fargo* is equally a moment of grotesque realism. His attempt to escape out of a motel bathroom window in his underwear and his pointless hysteria once handcuffed appear ridiculous and pathetic. However, any empathy we might feel for Jerry's plight at this moment is blocked by our memory of Jean's abduction: the bathroom location links the original crime with Jerry's punishment, vividly reminding us that it is not just incompetent second-rate criminals but also, and more importantly, morally bankrupt husbands who are the source (but not the masters) of the darkness. In returning us to the extraordinary consequences caused by the bad faith of ordinary people, *Fargo* seems closer to the spirit of noir. At other times, however, the Coens' comedy is far less grotesque.

On dangerous ground: *Fargo*

There is little attempt to capture the dark irony or surreal black violence of noir in *The Big Lebowski*, for example, which has narrative elements one might associate with noir yet (like *The Thin Man*) is not really a product of the noir universe. Indeed, in their own fondness for previous cinematic forms, including but not limited to noir, the Coen brothers demonstrate a degree of sentimental attachment which always risks lightening the darkness.

Finally, we must return to poor Marvin in *Pulp Fiction*. The scene might seem to reflect elements of grotesque realism's concern with the problems of the flesh; however, the problem here is not metaphysical or ideological, but very much practical. As Vivian Sobchack has described it, while the killing is both excessive and hyperbolic, it is actually an excuse for an extended sketch in which the headless corpse becomes little more than a comic prop, a 'technical' problem rather than a moral issue (see 2000: 120–4). The vital point that must not be missed is that this emphasis on the practical is not limited to characters (undoubtedly Grimsrud felt the same way about Carl's remains), but extends out to us, the audience. This truly is Bergsonian laughter and, as with David Thomson's description of the 'managerial pleasure in seeing intricate plans work sweetly' (2000: 92) in the classical 'hits' of gangster films like *The God-father* (1972), it is the amoral pleasures of an objective met, a task performed, a problem solved that are enjoyed here. This seems less contemplation on the darkness of the modern, alienated and surreal world of late capitalism, than the adoption of its ideological insistence on the supremacy of productivity and management by objectives. This administrative pleasure is clearly illustrated by Winston 'The Wolf' Wolfe (Harvey Keitel), the 'cleaner' who conjoins the immorality of the hood with the techniques of a management consultant and eventually solves the 'problem'. Unlike the remains and body parts of our previous victims, all traces of Marvin, physically and metaphysically, disappear. This is anathema to the true spirit of noir where once plans start going wrong they continue going wrong. Consequently, as Sobchack points out, there is something casual rather than causal about both our and the film's response to this horror. Somehow, 'the exaggeration and escalating quantification of violence and gore are a great deal less transgressive than they were – and a great deal more absurd' (2000: 122).

This is not the intellectual double-coded absurdity of surrealism, or of absurdist dramatists like Samuel Beckett. Rather than point back to the metaphysical absurdity of our material existence, it is the absurdity of representational excess that is on display here, with little interest in anchoring violence in the capacities and consequences of the quotidian. The violence becomes truly 'senseless' as it seems to have no purchase on us outside the parameters of the narrative. Rather than grotesque realism, such moments seem more a case of grotesque fantasy as we come to identify and care about the success or failure of the gangsters' plans, the style and manner in which they are achieved, rather than feel encouraged to question them. The darkness and comedy counteract each other and the moment is considerably less transgressive or analytical than the disturbing comic violence of Lynch's and (some) Coen brothers' films, where we are made to feel uneasy about our amusement. Here, we simply laugh. Our lack of concern for Marvin does not suggest either 'a superior revolt of the mind' or that we are 'imposing silence on [our] emotions and calling into play nothing but [our] intelligence', but seems little different to our lack of concern for the victims of slapstick. As Stephen Prince has described it, there is little self-reflection here, because despite all the attention to gory detail 'the ultraviolence in *Pulp Fiction* is played as comedy, with no grounding in suffering or pain' (2000: 33). The violence has no moral *understanding* of its consequences and it is not ironically coded, merely ridiculous and pervasive. In Tarantino's films, there is no 'other' world that escapes the corruption and violence; the darkness is totalised. Yet in the end it doesn't matter, in fact nothing matters as seriousness itself is not taken seriously and modernist irony is itself ironised and hence transformed and negated into cynicism.

However, this is not to suggest that *Pulp Fiction* as a film or Tarantino as a filmmaker escapes sentimentalism. For all of his gore, Tarantino's films are often structured around deeply sentimental attachments. These can be between people – Mr White's (Harvey Keitel) faith in, and caring for, Mr Orange (Tim Roth) in *Reservoir Dogs* or Ordell Robbie's (Samuel L. Jackson) uncharacteristic mourning over the death of his 'hippy chick', Melanie Ralston (Bridget Fonda), in *Jackie Brown* (1997) – or between people and things: Butch Coolidge's (Bruce Willis) attachment to his father's watch in *Pulp Fiction* and Jackie Brown's (Pam Grier) to her old vinyl records. These sentimental attachments, rather than their critique, justify and explain these narratives. So while Tarantino's films have gangsters, double-crosses, fixed fights, femme fatales, and so many of the objects and characters of noir, their underlying sentimentality means they lack a noir sensibility, particularly as it is not limited to the form of the narrative, but extends into the mode of consumption. One only has to consider the importance of pop songs as an object of nostalgic sentimental remembrance to understand how these films make us similar to, rather than critical of, people like Frank Booth. Like Frank, we seem to oscillate between the psychotic enjoyment of violence and the sentimental pleasures of old music. Tarantino's films remain more bland than bleak, a postmodern nostalgic pastiche, in Fredric Jameson's (1991) most critical sense of these terms, no more heir to the darkness of film noir than *Scream* (1996) is to the dark horror of *The Texas Chain Saw Massacre* (1974).

If the purpose of comedy or humour in neo-noir remains true to the underlying darkness of the original cycle, as under Lynch's critical gaze, such films remain in the spirit, if not the precise form, of the original cycle. Rather than attempt to live up to some dubious notion of authenticity, they also help demonstrate the potential for surrealism in this hard-boiled world. They extend, merely than comply with, its previous manifestations and demonstrate that we can still laugh at the dark. Similarly, in films such as *Blood Simple*, *Miller's Crossing* (1990) and *Fargo*, the Coen brothers produce films that maintain strong links to the ironic anti-sentimental underpinnings of noir, although elements of parody are present which risk diluting if not entirely negating it. However, despite being violent and comedic, Tarantino's films are also deeply sentimental and ideologically complicit. Consequently, they are simply not dark; they are not noir. However, this does not mean they are not neo-noir and we must guard against our own nostalgia for the original cycle. Tarantino's amoral, even cynical, formalism is undoubtedly more popular than the cult hits of the Coens or the art-house successes of Lynch and therefore might reflect a more accurate description of the dominant relationship between noir and neo-noir. Maybe we have misled ourselves by applying the term 'neo' to Tarantino in the first place and his films are not 'neo' in the sense that the prefix suggests a continuation, revival, homage or even a remediation. Noir is not regenerated by Tarantino's mode of pastiche, but consumed and negated. What his films offer us, therefore, is a *post*-noir world where we no longer laugh at the dark and nor are we afraid of it. We have simply been anaesthetised against it.

REFERENCES

Aristotle (1942) *Poetics*, trans. Preston H. Epps. Chapel Hill: University of North Carolina Press.

Bakhtin, Mikhail (1984) *Rabelais and His World*, trans. Hélène Iswolsky. Bloomington: Indiana State Press.

Bergson, Henri (1911) *Laughter & An Essay on the Meaning of the Comic*, trans. Cloudsley Brereton and Fred Roth. London: Macmillan.

Breton, André (1997 [1939]) 'Lightning Rod', in *Anthology of Black Humor*, trans. Mark Polizzotti. San Francisco: City Lights Books, xiii–xix.

Critchley, Simon (2002) *On Humour*. London: Routledge.

Freud, Sigmund (1976) *Jokes and Their Relation to the Unconscious*. London: Penguin.

Horton, Andrew (1991) *Comedy/Cinema/Theory*. Berkeley: University of California Press.

Jameson, Fredric (1991) *Postmodernism: or, The Cultural Logic of Late Capitalism*. London: Verso.

King, Geoff (2002) *Film Comedy*. London: Wallflower Press.

Knight, Deborah (1999) 'Why we enjoy condemning sentimentality: A meta-aesthetic perspective', *Journal of Aesthetics and Art Criticism*, 57, 4, Autumn, 411–20.

Naremore, James (1998) *More than Night: Film Noir in its Contexts*. Berkeley: University of California Press.

Neale, Steve (2000) *Genre and Hollywood*. London: Routledge.

Prince, Stephen (2000) 'Graphic violence in the cinema: Origins, aesthetic design and social effects', in Stephen Prince (ed.) *Screening Violence*. London: Athlone, 1–46.

Sobchack, Vivian (2000 [1974]) 'The violent dance: A personal memoir of death in the movies', in Stephen Prince (ed.) *Screening Violence*. London: Athlone Press, 110–24.

Thomson, David (2000 [1993]) 'Death and its details', in Stephen Prince (ed.) *Screening Violence*. London: Athlone, 86–98.

Witkin, Robert (1997) 'Irony and the historical', *Europa*, 1, 4. Available online at: http://www.intellectbooks.com/europa/number4/witkin.htm. Accessed 28 March 2008.

11

A Woman Scorned:
The Neo-Noir Erotic Thriller as Revenge Drama

LINDA RUTH WILLIAMS

This essay discusses the revenging 'scorned woman' heroine of some popular neo-noir films since the 1980s. She is a difficult and contested figure for feminism, received both as its champion and as prime symptom of its failure in an era characterised for some feminists by backlash (against the achievements of the 1960s/1970s second wave of feminism), for others by 'post-feminism'. Jacinda Read (2000) sees 1990s rape-revenge films as partly an engagement with 1970s feminism. However, the contradictions of the post-1980s femme fatale, and responses to her, suggest to me that she is more contemporary than this. In her teen incarnation – Darian Forrester (Alicia Silverstone) in *The Crush* (1993), Vanessa Lutz (Reese Witherspoon) in *Freeway* (1996), Hayley Stark (Ellen Page) in *Hard Candy* (2005) – it might be more appropriate to read her as a figure for the so-called 'girlie'-inflected third wave of feminism which has emerged since the 1980s. Her frequent softcore erotic readiness, alluring to female as well as male audiences, also suggests she stirs up the desires and anxieties of a new feminism which takes a different view of sexual representation and expression to that of the second wave.

I will be looking at the almost Jacobean forms of grand retribution wreaked by neo-noir women, such as Alex Forrest (Glenn Close) in *Fatal Attraction* (1987), Kris Bolin (Lara Flynn Boyle) in *The Temp* (1993) and Melissa Nelson (Molly Ringwald) in *Malicious* (1995), as well as the aforementioned teen femmes, asking which feminism do they speak to or for (if any), and which feminism (if any) speaks to them? Why has this revenging woman become such a prominent figure in recent US film history? And why have female revenge stories, including some alarming 'woman beware woman' incarnations, become so popular in the context of contemporary feminist discourses? How is women's rage differently inflected by genre – is the political impact of female revenge in genres such as the erotic thriller defused or augmented by the display of female sexuality? Is revenge liberatory or reactive? One school of thought argues that revenge binds the revenger into ongoing victim-identification. Wrought by *ressentiment*, the revenger is defined by her violent relationship to her abuser. Yet resentment, argues Pamela Hieronymi, constitutes 'a protest that a moral debt that one is owed is still outstanding' (quoted by Scarre 2004: 102). Perhaps, then, revenge restores balance and banishes resentment: 'Revenge does not alter one's status as victim, but ... he becomes your victim as you have been his' (Scarre 2004: 100). Whether a vigilante desire to 'arrogate the right to impose private justice' upon an original wrongdoer (Scarre 2004: 107) – which we will see played out in a number of films – is understandable, or even laudable, depends therefore on the balance of wrong against that of punishment. Geoffrey Scarre proposes that the word 'revenge' might be best applied to retributive acts out-of-proportion to the original wrong (see 2004: 106), whilst 'vengeance' – the righteous force of a god looking to re-establish order – is seen as punishment balancing out crime. Perhaps it is no accident, in a world still characterised by sexual, employment and generational imbalance, that 'vengeance' is more likely to be associated with male forms of 'getting even' and the action thriller (*Dirty Harry* (1971), *Death Wish* (1974)), whilst 'revenge' is more likely to be associated with female forms of 'getting even' and neo-noir.

The female revenge thread I am looking at here runs through a number of neo-noir formations, though I will concentrate on three resonant thematic and generic routes in this study: family noir, corporate noir and teen noir. As Fred Pfeil (1992) has argued, 'family noir' shows the contemporary family to be destabilised through 'noirisation'. It is a hybrid form (including melodrama, the domestic thriller and horror), which sometimes gains its noirishness from revenge exacted in, on and through marriage and the family.[1] 'Corporate noir' features revenge in, on and through the workplace: often an office-based thriller, it gains its noirishness through women's presence in a location from which they had previously been excluded. Their 'look' is over-illuminated plate glass, rather than dark and deadly, but women's violent action – for change or as an expression of anger – effectively 'noirs' this workplace. 'Teen noir', while related at various junctions to teen horror (for example, *Cherry Falls* (2000)) and comedy (for example, *10 Things I Hate about You* (1999)), features psycho-femmes in teen-focused and teen-marketed scenarios; here, too, murderous revenge functions to 'noir' the high school or the home (whether mansion or trailer park).

My research into this area began with work on the erotic thriller, a new genre which has emerged since the 1980s in the wake of the development of neo-noir (see Williams 2005). As a sexed-up formation of neo-noir, the erotic thriller takes its cue from the sometimes transgressive sexuality of film noir proper and the revenge story has proved a rich resource for these thrillers. The genre also trades on the post-1970s development of softcore cinema, which expanded to fill a market opened up by new exhibition opportunities such as cable, video and DVD. As the most significant spectacle of Western cinema, women figure centrally in the steamy stories the erotic thriller weaves. Exploitation genres play well across the boundary of low- and high-budget production as well as across theatrical release, TV movies and made-for-cable or direct-to-video (DTV) production. For every $14 million *Fatal Attraction*, there is a half million *The Corporate Ladder* (1997); for every *Disclosure* (1994), there is a *Sexual Roulette* (1996); for every *Wild Things* (1998), there is a *Wild Things 3: Diamonds in the Rough* (2005). Well-known and well-budgeted theatrically-released films read alongside low-budget DTV titles allow us to ask interesting questions within a feminist framework about the contemporary genre.

So what is 'neo' about the neo-femme fatale and (how) does revenge aid her reincarnation? One issue to which feminists have continually returned is that of punishment and 'getting away with it'. This is how the argument runs: if noir femme fatales presented positive images only so long as they remained alive (paying the price for their oversexed greed in the final reel), their neo-noir counterparts have spectacularly evaded patriarchal/moral retribution, escaping, sexually satisfied, with their ill-gotten gains. The neo-femme fatale is not (often) punished for her crime. This 'happy ending' underpins why she has become such a celebrated figure amongst viewers and critics. Figures like Catherine Tramell (Sharon Stone) in *Basic Instinct* (1992) or Bridget Gregory (Linda Fiorentino) in *The Last Seduction* (1994) have been read as unalloyed positive representations of sexual liberty and financial reward.[2] We might date the advent of this trend as 1981, the year in which Matty Walker (Kathleen Turner) evaded justice and Ned Racine (William Hurt) took the fall in *Body Heat* (perhaps the first clear example of a contemporary erotic thriller). However, 1981 also saw the remake of *The Postman Always Rings Twice*, a film in which the femme fatale fails even to get away with her life. Post-*Body Heat*, there may be more Dolly Harshaws (Virginia Madsen, *The Hot Spot* (1990)) bowing out with the money *and* a sexually enslaved fall-guy, but there are still some Rebecca Carlsons (Madonna, *Body of Evidence* (1993)), leaving the screen as a corpse. Nevertheless, I consider Rebecca's death to be exceptional. By the 1990s, with Hollywood keener than ever to court the sympathies of female audiences, the femme fatale was far more likely to survive the third act, if only to provide producers with a potential franchise. It is no accident that a number of these titles – *Wild Things*, *A Woman Scorned* (1994), *Cruel Intentions* (1999) – have spawned sequels, even if these do not feature the original film's femme. Even the femme's death is no obstacle to repetition, particularly at the lower end of production: neither *Poison Ivy 2* (1996) nor *Poison Ivy: The New Seduction* (1997) were perturbed by the demise of the original Ivy (Drew Barrymore). In the absence of a sequel, producers released a range of *Fatal Attraction* clones, whilst other films were marketed with Adrian Lyne's film as a key reference point. It is, then, female revenge itself rather than a singular female character (the counterpart of a Batman or a Freddy Krueger) which is sequelled in these films.

E. Ann Kaplan suggests: 'If, as [Frank] Krutnik argues, 40s noirs are about the crisis in masculinity following World War II, neo-noirs explore female scorn and derision for men' (1998: 11). Perhaps, then, the very existence of neo-noir is predicated on its women's changing attitudes. Kaplan rationalises this tendency as 'speaking to [women's] anger and perhaps disappointment at what feminist movements have failed to achieve' (ibid.). Citing cases such as Lorena Bobbitt's emasculation of her husband and Amy Fisher's shooting of her sexual rival, she concludes, 'Women are angrier than ever, partly because of the expectations that feminists of earlier decades promised: they now want explicit fantasies of women overcoming weak, stupid and oppressive men' (ibid.). Revenging neo-noirs may be filling a gap opened up by those promises and – in Kaplan's terms – the subsequent failures of feminism to bear out those promises. This posits neo-noir erotic thrillers as wish-fulfilments: 'The *excessive* wealth neo-noir heroines run off with,' writes Kaplan, 'is a kind of symptomatic exaggeration of what women feel they are owed in a culture that has traditionally subjugated them. Money stands in for power in an obvious transference' (1998: 12).

Of course, scorn is nothing if it is not expressed or acted upon. Scorn is also a two-way street. The femme fatale thus has (at least) two manifestations, scorning and scorned: the get-away-with-it form such as the women of *Bound* (1996) or *Basic Instinct*, and the 'furious' scorned women with a score to settle. I am interested here in looking at texts which provide some modicum of justification for the violence which women wreak, and how this serves to maximise box office by speaking to a sense of both popular feminism and popular justice. Women in recent mainstream US cinema may have the luxury of scorning the manipulable men who fail to satisfy them, but they are arguably more often scorned. Classic noir was often closely allied to the woman's film (see Neale 2000: 164); perhaps the revenge story takes neo-noir closer to the woman's picture. What, then, are the pleasures of these 'getting even' stories for men as well as for women? I want to start answering this by first turning to the scorned woman in family noir.

Woman beware woman: family noir in *Fatal Attraction* and *A Woman Scorned*

'If you ever have an affair, I'll cut your balls off.'
– *Fatal Attraction* viewer to her partner (in Nadelson 1988: 1)

Fatal Attraction is the grandmother of the erotic thriller as revenge tragedy, establishing the template for the femme fatale in contemporary film as well as focusing a crisis about career women and the family which also infected wider popular discourse. That 'bunny boiler' has become synonymous with a certain kind of aggressive female derangement is testament to the cultural cachet of Lyne's film. Like some classical revenge dramas, *Fatal Attraction*'s focus of anxiety is the family. Whereas film noir was characterised by a 'terrible absence of family relations' (Harvey 1998: 45), certain strands of neo-noir have spilled over with excessive family.

Fatal Attraction is the story of lawyer Dan Gallagher (Michael Douglas) who has a brief fling with Alex Forrest whilst his wife Beth (Anne Archer) and daughter Ellen (Ellen Hamilton Latzen) are away. When they return, Dan ends the affair: Alex tries to win him back; when that fails, she attacks his home. Finally she is killed by Beth in an infamous bathroom sequence, followed by an even more notorious final shot, attributed great significance in Reaganite cinema: the camera lingers on a framed photograph of mom, pop and child reunited and guaranteeing the safe survival of the family unit.[3] The film developed and reversed the two film noir icons, the femme fatale and the good girl, into figures of pity and vengefulness, respectively. For Susan Faludi (1992) it was the Ur-text of feminist backlash, effectively silencing women and providing a template for what should happen to their feisty screen surrogates. This has dominated feminist readings, although it fails to account for how complex and invested female audience response was, and for some of the contradictions of the film's female protagonists (see Williams 2005: 48–56). *Fatal Attraction* tells us a lot about popular contemporary audiences' views of the revenging woman (viewers famously chorused 'Kill the bitch' at test-screenings). Glenn Close's performance treads an uneasy line between violator and victim. In the ending which was eventually released in most territories, the attack on Beth is also an act of self-destruction: Alex holds the knife by her side, obliviously slicing away at her own leg as she advances towards Beth spouting vitriol – Alex is as fatal to herself as she is to everyone else.

The changed endings of *Fatal Attraction* only serves to demonstrate how contradictory our attitudes to female power remain. In the third act of James Dearden's original screenplay, *Affairs of the Heart*, revenge against Dan is brought about by the woman's self-violence: she commits suicide, but he is charged with her murder and goes to prison. In the version that was shot – *Fatal Attraction* version 1 – Beth secured Dan's release.[4] But what the (socially and sexually mixed) US preview audiences wanted was visibly exacted revenge, so the ending was changed to feature Beth shooting Alex – *Fatal Attraction* version 2. This version has the effect of briefly endowing Alex with a supernatural strength she lacks for much of the film, as she rises from her drowning in the bath for a second attempt at total domestic destruction. Audiences were clearly demanding the wife's revenge, but perhaps they also want their femme fatales to be truly worth knocking down. It is one of the great paradoxes of the politically confused history of this film that in the generally released version of *Fatal Attraction* Alex has an avenging strength she entirely lacks in the suicide-versions, yet this version has nonetheless given rise to deep feminist objection. The name-change which happens between the original and filmed versions of Dearden's script also inflects the possibilities for reading this charged violence with other politics: in *Affairs of the Heart*, Alex is Eve Rubin. What looks suspiciously like a racial shift from Jew (Rubin) to WASP (Forrest) has the effect of making her a less 'othered' monster for white-bread US culture, rendering the story that of WASP against WASP. The implied 'deracination' of these rewrites is also accompanied by a gender shift, from Eve to Alex: the originally-sinning woman Eve has become someone whose name, as well as whose violence, connotes critical gender ambiguity.

Two kinds of revenge are being played out in *Fatal Attraction*, by two different kinds of women. Popularly, Alex's acts of violence against Dan and his family were seen as the prime locus of the film's aggression. Alex combines the pitiable stereotypes of sexually desperate career woman and lonely spinster, and the dominant reading has given that because she has no place in the nuclear family (which has scorned her) she must destroy it. Yet her words cut strongly against the image of pathos she otherwise presents: 'I won't allow you to treat me like some slut you can just bang a few times then throw in the garbage,' she says.[5] It is testament to the power of point of view in Hollywood narrative (or to the audience's prevailing sexism) that this appeal to natural justice hardly shifts sympathy away from the Gallaghers and towards Alex. However sensible her position is ('You thought that you could just walk into my life and turn it upside-down without a thought for anyone but yourself'), we are so sutured into our allegiance to Dan's perspective that feeling any kind of sympathy for 'the bitch' would be reading very hard against the grain of the film. Set against Alex is Beth, the good wife who finally picks up her gun and dispatches her rival. If Alex is as much masochistic as sadistic, Beth learns to supplement nurturing with vengeance. US preview audiences demanded that it was Beth who slays her rival, imbuing the final sequence with the aura of a catfight.

If film noir is predicated on absent families, the erotic thriller often dramatises their threatened eradication. An emblem for this might come from Melissa's family photograph in *Malicious*, in which all the faces are scrubbed out (a knowing counterpoint, perhaps, to *Fatal Attraction*'s closing photographic image). The neo-noir erotic thriller therefore needs the family as much as it is desperate to escape it. This is even true of *Basic Instinct*, a film whose basic

> mythology is the antithesis of family ideology, though it is near kin to Greek mythology or to Freud's: the family slayer becomes the ideal lover. Catherine has of course lost her entire family in a mysterious accident. Her female lovers have variously misplaced theirs. Nick [Michael Douglas] himself survives in the last scene when he renounces his wish to 'raise rug rats'. (Wood 1993: 50)

For 'lost' and 'misplaced' here of course read 'killed' – this is where the erotic thriller segues into the revenge drama, though the genre's matricidal, fratricidal, patricidal women are given to do it mostly for scorn's sake (Catherine has, of course, also inherited the family fortune). The best Catherine's lover, Nick, can do is take the contraceptive way out and insure that he is not a generator of family. Catherine, argues Wood, has wiped out her parents in order to prove that she is her own generation, 'self-contained and even self-replicating' (ibid.).

Alex Forrest and Catherine Tramell are both contemporary formations of the femme fatale, but they are travelling in opposite directions regarding domesticity. Having revealed that she is pregnant with Dan's child, Alex tells him that the year before she had undergone a bad miscarriage. The femme fatale is therefore already in the business of setting up a single parent family so, although she uses Dan's nuclear family as the most effective lever against him, she is not an entirely domestically excluded or opposed figure. Even her apparently supernatural relentlessness, which enables her to just keep on coming like a nightmare-pursuer, is edged with justification: 'No, it's not gonna stop, it's gonna go on and on until you face up to your responsibilities.' So, one spectacular moment of familial voyeurism, in which Alex peeps in through the windows of the Gallagher's life, can be read in at least two ways. Having witnessed a moment of private intimacy (the handing over of the doomed rabbit), she turns and vomits, magnificently, into the bushes. Is this domestic repulsion or morning sickness? Is vomit a symptom of the family growing inside Alex, or an extravagant rejection of its sickly manifestation?

Clearly, *Fatal Attraction* set some rich cultural and sexual formations in motion. If it provides a pernicious view of the revenging woman for a mass audience, DTV *Fatal Attraction* clones have presented much stronger femme fatales who sometimes get away with it. There is also often a knowingness at play as these cheaper films reference Lyne's text as source fodder. In a noirish scene in *Scorned 2* (1997) – the sequel to *A Woman Scorned* – a young woman rejected

Terminator fatale: *Fatal Attraction*

by her married lover screams, 'I will not be ignored!' before controlling herself again and declaring, 'That was my *Fatal Attraction* impression.' Alex Forrest may be a lonely spinster, but her DTV daughters are not. For example, *Exception to the Rule* (1997) sets femme fatale Carla Rainer (Kim Cattrall) against wronged wife Angela Bayer (Sean Young). Sex, work and power are conflated: 'Don't fuck with me,' says Carla. 'I do the fucking.' Angela recalls Beth Gallagher, given the job of dispatching her sexual rival. Unlike Beth, Angela works (as a sculptor) and is able to turn the tools of her trade against her opponent, first attacking her with a blowtorch then impaling her on her prized artwork, a sculpture entitled 'Blind Justice'.[6]

If Alex is masochistically pathetic as well as psychotically aggressive, widowed Patti Langley (Shannon Tweed), in *A Woman Scorned*, is an infallible avenging angel. Patti's husband, Truman (Daniel McVicar) commits suicide, after Alex Weston (Andrew Stevens) is given the partnership he was due. Patti vows to destroy Alex, 'You and your family one by one.' However, Patti's motivation for revenge is multiple: Truman's death is significant, but so is the fact that he pimped her to his employers. Eclectically referencing not just noir and female gothic antecedents, *A Woman Scorned* also pays homage to three other cycles which developed as sub-genres of the horror-thriller movie in the 1980s and 1990s: the yuppie-in-peril film (which usually features working class male revenge against affluence), the rape-revenge film and the killer nanny film. Like other DTV erotic thrillers that draw on the yuppie-in-peril film, *A Woman Scorned* shifts the terrain of attack from property to family psychology. Unlike more classically noirish erotic thrillers in which a woman will use sex to get cash (*Body Heat*, *Body of Evidence*), it separates the erotic from the economic, preferring to wreak psychological rather than fiscal damage. Given the genre's overwhelmingly aspirational *mise-en-scène*, this is perhaps surprising, particularly since Patti starts and leaves the film with so little. Another DTV housewife whose husband will not let her go out to work (they are legion), Patti finds revenge offers a rewarding career opportunity: once she is on the trail of retribution she gets work, a nice place to live and satisfying sex. In this sense, though paying homage to its noir antecedents (*Double Indemnity* (1944), *Body Heat*), in its sex/crime cocktail *A Woman Scorned* also fulfils the DTV erotic thriller's softcore brief, playing out a 'female sexual quest' storyline. Before Patti is widowed she is mostly seen in the kitchen, frequently in tears, a figure of melodrama. After, she invades every corner of her victim's domestic space, acquiring a form of ownership through self-belief. Her identity make-over is accompanied by a shift in scoring, moving into noirish mode when Patti reinvents herself as a femme fatale: discordant strings precede her visit to a man who had assaulted her and whom she now guns down, and this same brooding score augments each act of violence. As she gets closer to murder the score becomes even more Hermannesque, deploying harsher, jagged strings.

This being an erotic thriller, and Tweed being an ex-*Playboy* centrefold, Patti's first weapon is sex, which she has liberally and with everyone. From *Fatal Attraction* through to the *Wild Things* franchise, female scorn has been expressed (and perhaps neutralised) through female spectacle: getting even has been preceded, and facilitated, by getting naked. Read finds this sexualisation in the rape-revenge film: 'the avenging woman leads her victim (and the male spectator) to believe she is about to make love to him but instead she hangs, castrates or shoots him' (2000: 41). Revenge can then be enacted by the sexualised body, presenting a curious conundrum for the heterosexual male viewer: the 'payment' for an enticing female spectacle is a narrative focused on male punishment.

The woman as dangerous carer is also a key trope, referenced just enough by *A Woman Scorned* to enable its heroine access to all areas of family life. Just as in *Fatal Attraction* Alex kidnaps the child in order to get to the parents, in *A Woman Scorned*, Patti poses as a tutor for Weston's teenage son. Like the killer nanny, Peyton Flanders (Rebecca De Mornay), in *The Hand that Rocks the Cradle* (1992) – one of *A Woman Scorned*'s key theatrically-released sources – Patti is an avenger-carer who exposes the flaws in the biological family. The killer nanny film demonises the mother-substitute at the same time as heaping guilt on those biological mothers who have had the temerity to fob their children off on someone else. It exploits 'backlash' anxieties about women leaving their babies, and about the women left in charge of those babies. Yet whereas in killer nanny narratives it is female strangers (entering the family from the outside) who are prime dangers to *children* (with the parents as secondary victims in their relationship to their offspring), in neo-noirs like *A Woman Scorned* and *Poison Ivy* (1992) the femme fatale takes on the family as a whole package. Within the noirised domestic space targeted by the revenging woman, men are particularly vulnerable, more so even than when they roam noir's lonely streets. It is not just men's inability sexually to resist the invader which weakens them, but their attachment to family, a relatively new element which became increasingly visible in 1980s and 1990s cinema. This revenging femme fatale deploys a number of networks of dependence as channels of attack. Children are ready targets: she attacks children to get to parents, and alienates children by seducing parents. Her Lady Macbeth-like unnaturalness extends to animals: Alex boils the bunny; Patti targets her employer's pet birds; and Melissa, in *Malicious*, hangs the pet cat of the man she is pursuing on his apple-pie girlfriend's door. In *Exception to the Rule*, the Labrador owned by the philandering hero is set up as potential victim and, in *The Temp*, only Kris proves capable of squashing flat a hornet which is terrorising her allergenic male boss. It is a sign of the gross abnormality of *Poison Ivy*'s eponymous heroine that she can finish off a dog with a rock after it has been hit by a car.

As with other motifs and narrative elements, there is a mix-and-match quality here which gives viewers the occasional feeling of déjà vu, with a range of films from across the spectrum of sex-thriller genres picking and choosing diverse elements to fulfil their specific sub-generic brief. For example – like Alex in *Fatal Attraction* – Peyton has suffered a miscarriage, signalling a failed family attempt, and – like Patti – Peyton's revenge is provoked by her husband's suicide (following an allegation against him by the mother of the child Peyton subsequently terrorises).[7] Such back-stories motivate a whole gamut of wayward responses for the revenging femme fatale.

Corporate noir: the working femme in *The Temp, The Corporate Ladder* and *Improper Conduct*

He didn't know revenge was on her résumé.
– Tagline for *Improper Conduct* (1994)

Natasha Walter (1999) has argued that the workplace remains a locus of significant inequality for women and should now constitute the main site of struggle. For Walter, feminism's continued obsession with cultural representation (such as, for instance, the analysis of women in film) is a dangerous distraction from 'real' issues. However, the preoccupations of third wave feminism with sexual expression, popular culture and the image demonstrates that younger feminists consider the cultural battle to be anything but over. But what of texts which represent employment discrimination as a pretext for fantasising revenging responses to public inequality? A cluster of 1990s films show women as either motivated to succeed because of past sufferings (professional success as itself a form of revenge) or as using the workplace for revenge-acts because here they can hit a man hardest. There is a noir precedent for this. Lee Horsley discusses 'the protagonist killer' in noir fiction, who can be read as acting 'to change things through revenge, "cleansing" society or righting a wrong' (2001: 97). Horsley also sees revenge-seekers 'as the most direct critics of a corrupt system' (2001: 106). The feminism which inflects some corporate neo-noirs might be read in this light, though inevitably once again revenge takes a sexual form if women are concerned. Yvonne Tasker (1998) argues that, in 1980s and 1990s cinema, women's work rarely escaped the taint of prostitution. This conflation of work and sex is particularly manifest when women take revenge on the workplace in an already sexually inflected genre.

Perhaps this is what drives a film like the mid-budget corporate noir *The Temp*, which took a revenging-femme persona into the workplace a year before the release of *Disclosure*. Kris Bolin replaces Peter Derns' (Timothy Hutton) male secretary when he goes on paternity leave, then excels at the job before lying, cheating and murdering her way up the executive ladder. The workplace is established early on as a battlefield: 'I take no prisoners and I eat the wounded,' says one of Peter's colleagues as a warning, and he is a *friend*. Kris's

Temp fatale: *The Temp*

sexuality is only useful as an aid to ambition: 'This isn't about sex,' she says to Peter, justifying a relationship with his superior: 'It's about work.' However, as a woman it seems she cannot help but import a domestic/familial metaphor to help her explain her relationship to employment: 'We marry our jobs,' she says, explaining why she had a string of temp posts before settling for a permanent one: 'I want to be sure about the job I marry.' Tantamount to promiscuity, temping is, then, the employment version of playing the field before committing. It is hard to imagine a would-be male executive articulating his career philosophy in such a way. Femme fatales in both noir and neo-noir are characterised by their deployment of sexuality in service of criminality; one distinction between pre-1970s and post-1970s versions of this form is a film's ability to render the sex/crime scene more explicitly (changes in censorship and classification practice also underpin the shift from noir to neo-noir). Women's inexorable sexualisation, even in remarkably asexual situations (in *The Temp*'s case, a cookie-making company), has provided neo-femme fatales with an exploitable tool. Male characters frequently view this as dirty tactics: at least Peter's friend/colleague warned him up-front about not taking prisoners and he, of course, was speaking metaphorically. Kris murders for real, out of sight, using sex (the original dirty weapon), as, she argues, the only route available to her: 'While you were in school studying flow charts I had two jobs and a kid to raise,' she tells Peter; 'Every job I've ever had I've known more about the business than the bosses grabbing my ass. Where did it get me?' In an era of equal opportunities legislative changes, it is hard to read this discourse as psychosis, but equally hard to read the bitch-heroine as unalloyed champion of women's rights.

The Temp might be compared to two later DTV softcore noirish potboilers, *Improper Conduct* and *The Corporate Ladder*, although both were made on far smaller budgets than *The Temp*'s $15 million. *The Corporate Ladder*, conceived and marketed as a kind of unholy hybrid of *Fatal Attraction* and *Disclosure*, takes the working woman further into softcore neo-noir mode. As David Andrews notes, 'Corporate softcore deflects the pornographic implications of its spectacle by embracing socially acceptable ideas, many of which centre on the workplace' (2006: 211). Playboy-produced films in particular, argues Andrews, have presented dramas 'in which heroines overcome professional obstacles, drawing on feel-good, girl-power friendships to conquer villainous female bosses' (2006: 214).[8] For example (although not mentioned by Andrews) *The Corporate Ladder*'s various plots and sub-plots featuring workplace infidelity and harassment provide ample opportunities for silicone-enhanced T&A, whilst the murderous ambition of the anti-heroine Nicole Landon (Kathleen Kinmont) drives the thriller plot, augmented by explicitly noirish moments. As with *The Temp*, a vague sense of feminist vigilante justice animates a narrative which might also be read as a supreme example of backlash. The complication of a liberatory plot-line being funded by the Playboy empire only underlines how contradictory these films can be. Nicole is a family-destroyer (she is at one point referred to as 'a cancer that's invading your family', for which the hero is prescribed one remedy: 'You gotta kill it before it kills you.'). She also tackles, violently and on an individualist basis, workplace inequalities. Indeed, *The Corporate Ladder* presents the original 'wrong' upfront, in a flashback sequence in which her presumed rape (obliquely referred to by a repulsive harassing boss) is punished by the death of the rapist. 'I let an employer take advantage of me once – *once*. And then I fixed it', she asserts. 'Fixing it' means a career-long revenge reinforced by the film's sporadic noirish 'look', which emphasises Nicole's madness as well as her successes (her triumphal moment of workplace accomplishment – directing a commercial featuring a black-clad model descending a *Double Indemnity*-style staircase – is shot through with noirishness). In her boudoir, she is reflected/divided by three mirrors, and she is also shot in shadow, backlit or silhouetted, as well as through the opulent, over-bright lighting strategies typical of the aspirational erotic thriller underpinned by the affluent *mise-en-scène*: at one point Nicole smashes someone's head with a champagne bottle in their swimming pool.

Yet until Nicole's own death, only men die in *The Corporate Ladder*, bearing out the tendency of DTV sex-schlock to manifest a surprising sisterliness (she even advises a female colleague on male sexual harassment). These broad streaks of popular feminism might seem surprising coming from the Playboy stable, but this female-appeal is both a strategy designed to reach 'couples audiences' and a reflection of social shifts, as Andrews points out. Nicole is, however, punished eventually, the red sheets on which she and her boss fuck prefiguring the red blood which oozes from her as she lies underneath him in a death-pose which mimics a post-coital embrace: the couple fall from a considerable height, but Nicole's body lands first, cushioning the blow so that the man survives. Is this nasty ending reflective of the genre, or this title's production philosophy? Both, I would argue: most Playboy heroines survive and prosper, as long as they are on display. *Improper Conduct* offers a more appealing feminist agenda, presenting corporate revenge from the female protagonist's point of view. This may seem surprising considering its primary softcore brief, but the erotic thriller was an interesting site for investigation of women's issues in the 1990s. The first section of the movie focuses on Ashley (Tahnee Welch), advised that she will flourish if she is nice to the boss. Resisting first harassment then rape, she continues to be intimidated by her male bosses, who accuse her of over-sexual behaviour when she takes them to court. *Improper Conduct* swerves into more extraordinary exploitation territory when, some way into the film, Ashley dies (the final stage of her harassment) and her sister Kay (Lee Anne Beaman) succeeds as avenger. As with a number of rape-revenge films, Kay's tactic is to deploy sexuality initially to trap (neatly meeting the requirements of exploitation softcore and the noirish narrative agenda). Making herself over as a sexy secretary figure, Kay is given her sister's old job, taking advantage of her boss's predatory urges. First his wife leaves him, then he is fired, then imprisoned, then he commits suicide. The final scene of *Improper Conduct* features Kay weeping over Ashley's grave, a reminder that this is a film underpinned by sisterliness rather than female rivalry. Female vigilante movies are driven by the same ethic – a surprising number of them made at the cheaper end of production. *Sexual Intent* (1994), part erotic thriller, part retribution fable, features a sleazy serial exploiter of women getting his comeuppance when his victims get together and punish him. Films in which women avenge the rape of a sister or friend might form the template for these corporate revenge films. That it is so hard finally to determine whether these femmes provide escapist feminist wish-fulfilment or bear out a pernicious nightmare of backlash suggests again that neo-noir is indeed a politically slippery space for women.

Teen-noir: the revenging pubescent

The 1990s saw two cinematic trends coalesce. The exponential rise in film products focusing on teen culture was largely dominated by comedies, dramas and horror films (see Shary 2003, 2005; Shary & Siebel 2007). However, teen movies also took heed of the wave of neo-noir and noirishly-inflected genre hybrids to form a select group of titles we might call 'teen noir'. This sub-genre has proved a particularly fertile ground for developing the figure of the adolescent femme fatale, often disempowered either by her status as a minor or her wrong-side-of-the-tracks origins, but prepared to use her underage sexuality on a revenging or avenging mission. She might be a figure of social privilege and power, like Kathryn Merteuil (Sarah Michelle Gellar) in *Cruel Intentions*, or of social exclusion, like Ivy in *Poison Ivy* or Vanessa in *Freeway*. Sometimes youth reinforces psychosis, signalled by going 'too far' (Darian in *The Crush* or Melissa in *Malicious*). As Melissa says to her female rival/victim: 'First we make a list of all the wonderful things that you have that I don't. And then we remove them – surgically. Now Doug said something about you having a kind heart....' Though differently inflected by young female sexuality, teen noir nevertheless follows a narrative template similar to the stories of female revenge explored above. And *sometimes* – in noirs dealing with paedophilia – these girls not only get away with it, but are entirely exonerated.

According to its director, Katt Shea, *Poison Ivy* was explicitly commissioned as a teen *Fatal Attraction* (see Norman 1993: 41). Narratively it also plays out like a high school template for *A Woman Scorned*. Both are revenge stories in which a sexy stranger enters the home and proceeds to destroy it from the inside out – not as building or property, but as an assailable psychological state. Ivy sets out to destroy Sylvie Cooper's (Sara Gilbert) family, partly because it was the family she never had, and partly as an exercise in revealing just how dysfunctional it always was. *The Crush* takes the *Lolita*-element of *Poison Ivy*, but augments it with more explicit anxieties about child abuse. Here, it is the man who invades the family: Nick Eliot (Cary Elwes) rents a cottage in the grounds of 14-year-old Darian's home. Darian develops a crush which becomes an obsession; the much older Nick reciprocates, up to a point. Yet when he finally resists her, she takes revenge on his property, his employment and his girlfriend but makes it look as if *he* has been taking revenge on *her*.[9] Like *Poison Ivy*, *The Crush* cannot decide if its revenging anti-heroine is a child or an adult – she is too womanly to be an innocent minor (her friend confesses that Darian 'knows stuff – stuff that other kids don't know'), but too immature to be a full sexual partner. Her exasperating childishness inflects a budding sexuality as well as the forms of revenge she takes, both effective enough to turn Nick into a haunted noir male.

By contrast, *Hard Candy*, a tougher noirish meditation on a girl-child's revenge against sexual abuse, is surer of its child-sexual politics. *Hard Candy* revisits *Freeway* in that both are explicit 'Little Red Riding Hood' tales, featuring a paedophile as the wolf and – in a twist worthy of Angela Carter – a teenage girl as his nemesis rather than his victim. Both are funny, nasty, exhilarating in their conclusions as well as problematic as vigilante tales – especially for male viewers. The male monsters die, the child-heroines avenge the victims who went before them. There is little of *The Crush*'s sympathy for the devil in the shape of a hero who never quite goes too far. Cinematic paedophilia seems to provoke clearer moral responses than sexism. And yet, *Hard Candy* still manages to play a sly trick on its male viewer, who may have exonerated himself from implication in the thirty-something's desire for a 14-year-old, but who must still viscerally identify with the onscreen male during a theatrical castration sequence. Uneasily, *Freeway* and *Hard Candy* also continue to trade in culturally

Teen fatale: *Hard Candy*

acceptable views of the nubile child's body before exacting punishment on those who take pleasure in it. Hayley and Vanessa are exemplary exploitation heroines, but their position on teenage sexuality is highly contemporary – exploiting as well as protecting the ambiguous power of sexualised girlhood.

Conclusion: Going too far

So what is it to go 'too far' in these noirish texts? Is there a distinction between revenging (reactive, spiteful, often female) and avenging (that god-like redressing of the balance – usually male)? As this essay has suggested, there is a lively space which popular culture keeps open for the display of the wronged woman's inventive acts played out for mainstream entertainment. Numerous instances of real-life spousal revenge provide juicy copy in the popular press, from Lorena Bobbitt cutting off her abusive husband's penis to Lady Sarah Graham-Moon cutting off the arms of each of her philandering husband's suits and Hayley Shaw selling her husband's Lotus on eBay for 50p.[10] Graham-Moon has described the feeling of pouring paint over her husband's car as 'a great surge of relief, like a post-orgasm feeling' (in Bennett 2004: 13). This feeling is transferred vicariously to readers and spectators, particularly others in similar positions (Graham-Moon has been called 'the patron-saint of scorned spouses everywhere' (Hattersley 2006: 3)). However, if popular real-life revenging women are the stuff of comedy, and reconciliation scenarios are, generically speaking, the stuff of melodrama, violent gendered revenge is the stuff of noir and horror.

Still we are left with the issue of female disproportionateness. Whereas these films are careful to show some element of cause ('he asked for it'), it is usually outbalanced by effect, in the adult stories if not the teen fables. Revenge plots present a rather different set of questions for women than for girls in contemporary cinema. Grown women (Patti, Kris, Nicole) revenge scorn (or worse) with castration or death; teen vigilantes (Hayley, Vanessa) fare better in the morality of their tales, avenging paedophilia with death, but the films present this as justifiable. Perhaps they are the Charles Bronsons of teen culture, righting the wrongs which society fails effectively to confront. *Hard Candy*'s Hayley gets away with it, but then Jeff Kohlver (Patrick Wilson) was a child molester; Darian does not because *The Crush* exonerates Nick. Despite Nick's visual enjoyment of Darian's nubile flesh, it is Darian who tips over into psychotic transgression because, in the film's morality, Nick never quite 'goes too far'. Amanda Foley (Tane McClure), in *Scorned 2*, wreaks a complicated revenge on her philandering husband, the student he fucks, her shrink and the couple who wronged her in the previous film, which includes making the crimes look like they were the *husband*'s revenging killings.

Excess swings both ways according to the package of entertainment dished up by these popular movies. Hollywood (and filmmakers at its fringes) might continue to pass conservative judgement on its heroine's actions, balancing the weight of done-to against that of getting even, but it also keeps a sharp eye on what provides the most satisfying spectacle for distinct audiences. The pleasures of the 'unbalanced' woman might now outweigh the need for sexual screen morality – something which noir was never particularly concerned with, and which feminism has been less concerned with of late. Indeed, feminism seems to have *helped* these stories of revenge and explicit sex into the marketplace: a new chapter in the story of women in film noir.

If the third wave can be seen as second-wave feminism with lip gloss (see Munford 2004), feisty femme fatales, in all their sexualised contradictions, may be *this* form of feminism's prime expression, emblematic figures for a movement focused on difference which cannot decide whether overt sexual expression is false consciousness or liberation. Then again, as Sarah Gamble puts it, 'third wave feminists feel at ease with contradiction' (2001: 43). Ariel Levy has called *Sex and the City* (1998–2004) a 'deeply seductive feminist narrative [and] also a deeply problematic one' (2005: 174). Contemporary noir's revenging woman is just as seductive and problematic, seeming to embody a feminism, and a cinema, which looks both new and old at the same time.

NOTES

1   'Based on a true story' television movies, such as *A Woman Scorned: The Betty Broderick Story* (1992) and *Beyond Control: The Amy Fisher Story* (1993), would be interesting to discuss here.

2   See Thomas Austin (2002) on female audiences of *Basic Instinct*.

3 Similarly, in *The Temp*, Kris is framed standing adjacent to a photograph of Peter's wife and son, overlaying their image with her reflection; the discovery that the photo of Kris's husband and daughter is fictitious initiates her downfall.

4 This 'Madam Butterfly' ending version has remained popular in Japan.

5 *Fatal Attraction* clones often feature a version of this line: in *Malicious*, Melissa says, 'Did you think I was just some slut plaything you would do what you want with and throw me away afterwards?'; in *Scorned 2*, the student cast off by her professor/lover makes a similar speech.

6 Faludi notes that Dearden originally conceived Beth as a working woman, 'But by the final version all traces of a career were excised and Beth was transformed into the complete Victorian hearth angel' (1992: 149).

7 In *Basic Instinct*, Nick's wife also committed suicide, after he became trigger-happy.

8 For example, Andrews (2006) discusses *Corporate Fantasy* (1999) and *Staying on Top* (2002); the revenge/female psycho-flick *Mutual Needs* (1997) is also interesting in this context.

9 A cop asks him, 'You rape a little girl and you act like *she's* crazy?'

10 Discussion, jokes and celebrations of Lorena Bobbitt's action are rife on the internet. For information about Shaw and Graham-Moon, see Bennett (2004) and Brown (2005).

REFERENCES

Andrews, David (2006) *Soft in the Middle: The Contemporary Softcore Feature in Its Contexts*. Columbus: Ohio State University Press.

Austin, Thomas (2002) *Hollywood, Hype and Audiences: Selling and Watching Popular Film in the 1990s*. Manchester: Manchester University Press.

Bennett, Oliver (2004) 'What it feels like to: Get revenge', *Independent on Sunday*, 22 August, Features: 13.

Brown, Jonathan (2005) 'Wife sells DJ's Lotus on eBay in revenge for his on-air flirting', *Independent*, 22 June, 15.

Faludi, Susan (1992) *Backlash: The Undeclared War against Women*. London: Vintage.

Gamble, Sarah (2001) 'Postfeminism', in Sarah Gamble (ed.) *The Routledge Companion to Feminism and Postfeminism*. London: Routledge, 36–45.

Harvey, Sylvia (1998 [1978]) 'Woman's place: The absent family of film noir', in E. Ann Kaplan (ed.) *Women in Film Noir*. New Edition. London: British Film Institute, 35–46.

Hattersley, Giles (2006) 'What I've learnt about husbands', *Sunday Times*, 9 July, Features: 3.

Horsley, Lee (2001) *The Noir Thriller*. Basingtoke: Palgrave.

Kaplan, E. Ann (1998) 'Introduction to new edition' in E. Ann Kaplan (ed.) *Women in Film Noir*. New Edition. London: British Film Institute, 1–14.

Levy, Ariel (2005) *Female Chauvinist Pigs: Women and the Rise of Raunch Culture*. New York: Free Press.

Munford, Rebecca (2004) '"Wake up and smell the lip gloss": Gender, generation and the (a)politics of girl power', in Stacy Gillis, Gillian Howie and Rebecca Munford (eds) *Third Wave Feminism: A Critical Exploration*. Basingstoke: Palgrave, 142–53.

Nadelson, Regina (1988) 'Fatally yours', *Guardian*, 7 January, Thursday Women: 1.

Neale, Steve (2000) *Genre and Hollywood*. London: Routledge.

Norman, Neil (1993) 'Katt shows her claws', *Evening Standard*, 11 March, 41.

Pfeil, Fred (1992) 'Revolting yet conserved: Family noir in *Blue Velvet* and *Terminator 2*', *Postmodern Culture*, 2, 3, May. Available at http://www.iath.virginia.edu/pmc/text-only/issue.592/pfeil.592. Accessed 19 October 2008.

Read, Jacinda (2000) *The New Avengers: Feminism, Femininity and the Rape-revenge Cycle*. Manchester: Manchester University Press.

Scarre, Geoffrey (2004) *After Evil: Responding to Wrongdoing*. Aldershot: Ashgate.

Shary, Timothy (2003) *Generation Multiplex: The Image of Youth in Contemporary American Cinema*. Austin: University of Texas Press.

____ (2005) *Teen Movies: American Youth on Screen*. London: Wallflower Press.

Shary, Timothy and Alexandra Siebel (eds) (2007) *Youth Culture in Global Cinema*. Austin: University of Texas Press.

Tasker, Yvonne (1998) *Working Girls: Gender and Sexuality in Popular Cinema*. London: Routledge.

Walter, Natasha (1999) *The New Feminism*. London: Virago.

Williams, Linda Ruth (2005) *The Erotic Thriller in Contemporary Cinema*. Edinburgh: Edinburgh University Press.

Wood, Robert E. (1993) 'Somebody has to die: *Basic Instinct* as white noir', *Post Script*, 12, 3, Summer, 44–51.

12

Neo-Noir's Fatal Woman:
Stardom, Survival and Sharon Stone

REBECCA FEASEY

Film noirs were usually low-budget productions – as are many neo-noirs. Consequently, films ranging from *In a Lonely Place* (1950) to *The Last Seduction* (1994) presented beautiful but relatively unknown performers in the role of the femme fatale. In such cases, the portrayal often paved the way to more mainstream success. However, based on the lasting impression of the deadly female, such performers have often found that their subsequent careers remain inextricably linked with this femme fatale persona. And yet, although it is not uncommon for such performers to continue playing to type, it is extremely unusual for an actress to revisit a specific duplicitous role.

After a decade playing beautiful blondes in a long line of forgettable films, Sharon Stone found international stardom with her role in *Basic Instinct* (1992). Michael Douglas played Nick 'Shooter' Curran, a troubled detective who investigates the murder of a one-time rock star, and the relatively unknown Stone played Catherine Tramell, the alluring and aggressive bisexual murder suspect with whom Nick has a dangerous affair. *Basic Instinct*'s investigative structure, characterisation and visual style situate the text firmly within the contemporary noir revival. Indeed, existing literature tells us that *Basic Instinct* is not only 'one of the definitive films of neo-noir' (Williams 2005: 163) but also one of the 'most commercially successful film noirs ever made' (Naremore 1998: 263). Moreover, while *Basic Instinct* is understood as a crucial text in the neo-noir canon, the character of Catherine is acknowledged as 'Hollywood's favourite femme fatale' (Ebert 1996).

Stone became an overnight success after her performance as the explicitly sexual and graphically naked character of Catherine, and her subsequent star image was based single-handedly on her performance in the neo-noir production. The role proved so popular that, more than a decade later, Stone played

A star is born: *Basic Instinct*

Catherine again in *Basic Instinct 2* (2006) – an unprecedented return of the neo-noir femme fatale.[1] However, although Stone was happy to reprise the role that made her famous, the critical and commercial failure of that film suggests that audiences were not ready, willing or able to embrace the representation of an ageing femme fatale. Therefore, although Catherine may have survived the neo-noir sequel, the poor critical and commercial reception of the deadly spider woman points to the demise of sexual power for the forty-something woman in general and for this ageing sexual predator in particular.

With this in mind, this essay outlines the ways in which a wide range of review media have formed a consensus as they circulate a particular image of the actress, an image based on the blurring of the character of Catherine and Stone offscreen. However, rather than suggest that Stone was somehow a passive victim of such image-making discourses, I go on to illustrate the ways in which the actress made a conscious effort to cement a memorable, sexual and hence marketable persona. The image of Catherine became so ingrained in the Stone star image that the actress later struggled to find either audiences or industry credibility beyond that particular role. However, when Stone returned to the role that made her famous in an attempt to reignite her failing career, her reprisal of the predatory Catherine merely illustrated a wider concern with the depiction of the ageing femme fatale. The scathing reception of this neo-noir sequel can be seen to point to the limitations of sexual power for both the actress and the spider woman; this case study might go some way towards explaining why those deadly women who survive the neo-noir narrative must nevertheless be laid to cinematic rest.

Stardom

Since the emergence of the star system, Hollywood has been keen to blur the distinction between 'real' and 'reel' star images through a range of promotion, publicity and review materials. While promotion and publicity refer to those texts which 'were produced as part of the deliberate creation/manufacture of a particular image or image-context for a particular star' (Dyer 1998: 60–1), the discursive representations that are seen in film reviews and star interviews are also part of the cinematic machine that cues public opinion about particular performers (see Dyer 1998: 60–3). Therefore, when referring to a specific star image it is necessary to consider the ways in which that image is made up of both screen performances and a broader set of media texts that includes film reviews, interviews, fan magazines, public appearances and biographies as they help to construct a particular image of a performer. The point here is that academic star studies is not content to simply outline biographical or truthful 'facts' about a performer or to determine the correct reading of a star, but, rather, to examine the image that comes to mind as it is shaped by Hollywood and its surrounding channels of discourse.

Early fan magazines were happy to obscure the distinction between role and star by insisting that actors were often identical to the roles that they played on the screen. In this way, 'fans could feel secure: they had fallen in love with an image, but that image happened to be very much like the real thing' (Barbas 2001: 11). Today's stars tend to conform to a particular image as a strategic way of competing in the marketplace. If one considers that 'actors are heavily over-supplied in Hollywood, more so than in any other part of the labour force' (King 2002: 151) then it is in a performer's interest to foreground unique qualities that will set them apart. Therefore, the development of a star image has the advantage of belonging to a particular performer and of being repeated for the viewing public; or to put it another way, it is 'a way for stars to turn themselves into profitable commodities with ... individual brand images' (ibid.).

Although many of today's stars are keen to create a particular image and contemporary audiences are often keen to see an actor playing to type, star discourses can be both changeable and contradictory. Hollywood performers can be seen to build and then deliberately break a particular star image over the course of a career (be it Meg Ryan's girl next door, Hugh Grant's bumbling English fop or Jim Carrey's rubber-faced comedian) in order to first find an audience and then to secure credibility for their craft. Richard Dyer makes this point when he tells us of the different ways in which a star image can be used in the construction of a character. We are told that the 'perfect fit' refers to those rare performances where all aspects of a star's image are said to parallel those traits of the character being played; the 'selective fit' is where promotion and publicity materials foreground certain features of the star's image and ignore others in order to blur the boundaries between role and star and the 'problematic fit' points to those instances where the associations with a particular star image are heavily at odds with, and thus problematic for, the construction of a character (see Dyer 1998: 126–30). With this in mind, Stone's portrayal of Catherine offers audiences that rare example of a 'perfect fit' between role and star, owing to the fact that those dangerous, sexual and explicit mannerisms of the character are seen to echo those selfsame characteristics of the star in question. Indeed, the fit here seems so perfect that Stone's subsequent performances are routinely derided by news and magazine media as presenting a 'problematic fit' for the viewing public.

Sharon Stone is Catherine Tramell

Stone was so successful in playing *Basic Instinct*'s Catherine that audiences and critics alike have since 'struggled to differentiate' star and role (Williams 2005: 195): review media show a remarkable consistency in their presentation of Stone as an extension of the character in question. For example, while *Esquire* magazine comments that 'it is difficult to work out where ... Sharon Stone ends and her character Catherine Tramell starts' (Zehme 1995: 47), *Time Out* has to question where 'the tough-talking Sharon Stone ends and the hard-fucking Catherine Tramell begins' (Grant 1992: 20). Likewise, *Premiere* informs its readership that 'the lust-stoked ice-pick happy bisexual that Stone played in *Basic Instinct* got her way by outfoxing every man in sight ... Catherine's canniness is pure Stone' (Schruers 1993: 60). Stone's star image is so inextricably connected with the femme fatale persona of the neo-noir genre that more than a decade after Stone's performance in *Basic Instinct*, *Total Film* informed its readers that Stone 'is one of our famous femme fatales ... she'll always be the femme fatale from *Basic Instinct*' (Abele 2004: 74). If 'the bitch role ... of the femme fatale ... offers women the only option they have to be both powerful and sexy' (Baumgold 1998: 482), then it is significant that news and magazine media have recently been commenting that 'Sharon Stone is a bitch. Or rather, no one plays bitches better than Stone' (Cartwright 2004: 6). While Catherine is presented by review literature as a predatory and dangerous femme fatale, so too, Stone is presented by way of the spider woman's deadly character traits.

Review literature routinely presents Catherine as a novelist-cum-murder-suspect who keeps 'ice-picks and sex toys around the house' (Weinraub 1992: 17). But such media texts exploit these selfsame deadly and sexualised references in their coverage of Stone, offscreen. For example, *Empire* employs the ice-pick-wielding femme fatale as a crucial intertext for Stone's portrayal of May Munro in *The Specialist* (1994). Although one might suggest that the medium-budget noir production and the big-budget summer blockbuster have little in common, with the former privileging the suspense narrative and the latter exploiting elaborate pyrotechnics, Stone's portrayal of May Munro is in fact reminiscent of the role that she played in *Basic Instinct*. While Catherine was presented as an unapproachable murder suspect, May Munro was presented as a chilling female avenger: the murderous motives may be different for the characters in question, but both women are positioned as sexual, manipulative, ice-cool killers. In this way, one might argue that the traits of the two characters accord. However, rather than exploit those personality traits which permeate the roles of these killer women, *Empire* goes on to position the offscreen actress – not the role of the deadly avenger – by way of *Basic Instinct*'s predatory femme fatale. The reporter sent to interview Stone 'exchange[d] pleasantries and sh[ook] hands with the actress' (Dawson 1995: 78), then points out that 'amazingly, lying on the bar within easy reach, is an ice pick' (ibid.). The ice-pick reference has no relevance to the article as a whole, so one can only assume that the magazine makes the comment in order to associate Stone's offscreen persona with that of *Basic Instinct*'s femme fatale. Therefore, even though the article was published more than two years after the release of *Basic Instinct*, *Empire* makes a concerted effort to blur the distinction between Stone's performance as Catherine and Stone's offscreen biographical persona, encouraging the reader to see the character of Catherine as both role and star.

One might argue that *Empire* employs the ice-pick as a crucial reference point in its discussion of the actress because the role of May Munro was reminiscent of the role of Catherine. However, this does not explain why the same intertextual reference is also used in relation to a performance that is far removed from the deadly femme fatale persona. For example, when the *Chicago Sun-Times* employs the ice-pick-wielding femme fatale as an intertext for Stone's portrayal of Sally Eastman in *Intersection* (1994), it is difficult to understand how one might relate neo-noir's deadly spider woman with the emotionally and sexually frigid protagonist of this modern-day melodrama. And yet, Roger Ebert deliberately draws on this reference when he comments that 'somehow I got stuck in my head that *Intersection* was a thriller … if I'd known it was a weeper, I wouldn't have been waiting for an hour for someone to pull out an icepick' (1994). Ebert clearly associates Stone's star image with the thriller genre, so much so in fact that his memory of her performance in *Basic Instinct* has actually affected his expectations of this later production. The reviewer is obviously used to viewing 'star vehicles' that 'provide a character of the type associated with the star; a situation, setting or generic context associated with the star; or opportunities for the star to do her/his thing' (Dyer 1998: 62). However, what is interesting here is that he is awaiting Stone's predatory star turn in an urban neo-noir setting based on a single performance, rather than any sense of typecasting over the duration of a longer career. Even though *Intersection* cast Stone against type, Ebert employs the ice-pick as a significant reference point in discussing the film because he is using this dangerously threatening signifier as an intertextual reference for Stone offscreen, irrespective of genre or the role in question.

It is not only review literature that positions Stone as an extension of the dangerous character that she played in *Basic Instinct*. The same pattern can be found in a much wider range of interview, biographical and memoir material.

Both the film's director, Paul Verhoeven, and scriptwriter, Joe Eszterhas, make it clear that they view Stone and Catherine as one and the same. According to Eszterhas, 'Sharon's knowledge of power was learned in modelling sessions and casting couches in the back rooms of shadowy black-lighted discos ... Sharon was good with an ice-pick ... and a soft tongue ... she usually got what she wanted' (2000: 89).[2] In this instance, Eszterhas positions Stone, rather than Catherine, as the powerful and manipulative predator – yet the sense of Stone's power and control derive from her portrayal of *Basic Instinct*'s ice-pick-wielding Catherine. Therefore, while Catherine uses sex as a weapon onscreen, we are led to believe that Stone uses sex in order to marshal power in real life.

Likewise, Verhoeven is heard commenting that 'Stone knows exactly what she wants and knows exactly how to get it, which is something she had in common with the character of Catherine ... Sharon is Catherine without the killing' (in Van Scheers 1997: 251). With this in mind, it is clear that the director has invested in Stone as a modern-day femme fatale, owing to the fact that his presentation of the actress is wholly reminiscent of those neo-noir femme fatales who are motivated by 'a need to control everything and everyone around [them]' (Dickos 2002: 162). What is interesting here is the way in which the commentary presents Stone as Catherine without the killing, but fails to mention that Stone is Catherine without the sexual gymnastics and powerful seduction associated with that particular role. The director makes a case for Stone being a predatory and powerful femme fatale both on- and offscreen by implying that the actress actually performs the same sexual gymnastics and sexual seductions as the character in question. One might suggest that Verhoeven is keen to blur the boundaries between role and star, not because of the power of review media to circulate a dangerous image of the actress, but rather because the director sees himself as the author of this particular figure. After all, it was Verhoeven who cast Stone as a manipulating sexual predator in both *Total Recall* (1990) and *Basic Instinct*. Alternatively, one might suggest that Verhoeven is keen to exploit Stone's femme fatale persona simply because the figure embodies the male sexual fantasy of a dominatrix who will both pleasure and punish the heterosexual male. Ebert says it best when he informs us that 'a fear of women palpitates in all [Verhoeven's] best work – they'll kill you – but if you're lucky, they'll have sex with you first' (Ebert 1995).

From this estimation then, both Eszterhas and Verhoeven seem to view female power as a manipulation of female sexuality, making it clear that the only way that Stone could possibly take control in her real life is, like the neo-noir femme fatale, through the blatant display and exploitation of her body. Indeed, review literature goes further to suggest that the power of the femme fatale in general, and of Stone in particular, is based entirely on her position as the 'sexual omnivore' (Kempley 1992). In this way, we are invited to view a rather limited notion of female power as sexual power here.

The *National Enquirer* goes further to present Stone as an extension of the predatory femme fatale as it tells us that the actress is a 'man-hungry wild woman … [who has] led an offscreen life packed with men, men, men' (Fitz 1996: 46). Similarly, we learn that 'sultry Sharon secretly began romancing movie executive Bill MacDonald while filming the erotic thriller *Sliver* [1993] – just one month after he married Naomi [Baka], his long time live-in-love. And when the screen siren spun her romantic web, Naomi didn't have a chance' (Coates 1993: 36). The reference to Stone spinning her web deliberately suggests that the actress is as sexually aggressive as *Basic Instinct*'s duplicitous spider woman, drawing attention to the ways in which both role and star exploit their sexuality in order to dominate the heterosexual male. Likewise, in a brief feature dedicated to the much-publicised romantic life of the star, the *National Enquirer* informs us that Stone's attempt to find love is 'littered with road kill because the sexy bombshell chews up good men faster then the US Marine Corps … and loves every minute of it' (Fitz 1998: 9). The magazine deliberately exploits the aggressively sexual traits of the narrative character of Catherine as a significant intertext for Stone's star image. Asserting that Stone's path to love is littered with road kill can be read in one of two ways: either the road kill involved is quite literally dead by the hand of the dangerous woman; or it refers to the emotional pain that the actress inflicted on the men in her life. Either way, be it the deadly killer or the heart-breaking vixen, both figures of woman exploit the dangerous, sexual and graphic characteristics of *Basic Instinct*'s infamous Catherine. The publication is not merely accepting the blurring of role and star, but actively cueing this particular image of the performer.

However, before I go so far as to suggest that Stone is victim to a patriarchal system that demands female strength through sexual performance, or argue that her career has suffered due to the circulation of this sexualised image, it is necessary to look at the ways in which the actress has been seen to position herself in relation to the character that made her famous.

Sharon Stone on Catherine Tramell

During the promotion of the original *Basic Instinct*, Stone informed audiences that 'you cannot immerse yourself in a character and remain unaffected' (in Sheff 1992: 64), before commenting on the sexual acrobatics of the role and her own sexual appetite beyond that particular part. In this way, the actress can be seen to be stabilising her on- and offscreen identity in relation to her explicit role in the neo-noir production. More recently, the actress continues to blur the sexualised boundaries between her on- and offscreen persona. When Stone signed up to play a forty-something divorcée who falls in love with a 27-year-old man in *Cougars*,[3] she commented that her own 'basic instinct is a lust for toyboys' (Maxwell 2004: 3). Indeed, Stone seems happy to announce that she has been dating a string of men aged between 22 and 39 since divorcing her third husband in late 2004 (ibid.). This link to younger men (both on- and offscreen) is clearly being used to signal the ageing actress's sexual appetite and seemingly insatiable desires in opposition to those dominant cultural codes that link physical attractiveness, sexual activity and the femme fatale with youth. Moreover, the image of the forty-something sexual woman with a younger male goes further to blur the boundaries between her own biographical persona and the return of *Basic Instinct*'s predatory femme, owing to the fact that much commentary on *Basic Instinct 2* highlighted the age difference between Stone and her younger male co-star, David Morrissey. Indeed, 'it makes a change to have an older actress rolling around and knocking over table lamps with a younger actor' (Anon. 2006a).

Elsewhere, the actress goes further to cement her femme fatale reputation, commenting that she, in fact, came up with the best lines that *Basic Instinct*'s Catherine never had. For example, Stone gives what review media refer to as 'good quote' as she tells us that 'I do know how to travel with only a change of g-string, a passport, something black and an attitude' (Thompson 1994: 72) and likewise that 'if you have a vagina and an attitude in this town then that's a lethal combination' (Cooney 1992: 60). Such racy sound bites encourage news and magazine media to interpret Stone as an extension of the predatory character of Catherine.

Likewise, in an interview with *Playboy* magazine, Stone talks about *Basic Instinct* and the way in which the character of Catherine has kept the men in her life 'in line' since shooting the neo-noir production. We are told that 'after the movie came out, I did so much publicity in which I was such a wise-ass that people realised that I was and I wasn't Catherine Tramell' (in Sheff 1992: 88). Stone positions herself in relation to Catherine by way of a self-aware and knowing 'wise-ass' persona. She makes it clear that she was playing the joker for the sake of promoting *Basic Instinct*, and one might assume that the actress makes a clear distinction between her own offscreen identity and that of the character. However, the distinction becomes blurred when Stone then announces that people realised that she was and she wasn't Catherine. The actress seems to be suggesting that although she is not Catherine per se, she does in fact share some traits with the character that she played in *Basic Instinct*. Stone's blurring of her own biographical persona and the role that made her famous is reinforced as she informs *Premiere* magazine that 'people who are sophisticated enough to know that I'm not Catherine are sophisticated enough to know that I could be, if I wanted' (Schruers 1993: 65). Stone seems aware of the fact that the star system focuses on uniqueness, individualism and the personal characteristics of performers (over and above acting skill or talent) and, consequently, one might suggest that the actress is keen to cement a predatory image as a way of trying to generate public interest and hence mass market profits.

However, although Stone was successful in blurring the boundaries between role and star, she seemed unable to secure critical acclaim for her performance in *Basic Instinct*. After all, her popularity in the role was seen to be entirely dependent on what Barry King has termed personification, whereby a performer is assumed to be playing themselves onscreen, requiring little or no acting skill (see 1991: 178–80). Indeed, it is perhaps due to these charges of poor acting[4] that Stone went on to negotiate her predatory image and separate herself from the sexually explicit role of Catherine. As far back as 1994, Stone was heard commenting on her desire to put some distance between herself and the femme fatale persona, stating that 'just because I got famous for *Basic Instinct* doesn't mean it's the only trick in my bag ... I am sick of that, sick of Catherine Tramell ... She is in my past ... I want to explore other avenues as an artist' (in Andrews 1994: 81). The actress even went so far as to laugh off the possibility of a *Basic Instinct* sequel, informing audiences that reprising the sexually explicit role 'would be stunt pay ... at my age' (in Dawson 1996: 97). Instead, Stone went on to appear in a range of films far removed from the neo-noir genre, including the western *The Quick and the Dead* (1995), the death-row weepie *Last Dance* (1996), the science fiction film *Sphere* (1998) and the comedy *Beautiful Joe* (2000). However, when these films failed to provide either commercial or critical success, the actress was soon seen to re-evaluate her relationship with the role that made her famous. Or, to put it more bluntly, after a string of failures at the box office Stone used the *Basic Instinct* sequel as a way to recreate her sexual star image and therefore try to revive her floundering career.

Basic Instinct 2

In early 2001, Stone showed interest in reprising the part of Catherine in a *Basic Instinct* sequel, commenting that she was 'ready, willing and able to play the role' in question (in Anon. 2001a). However, although the actress was keen to return to the part that made her famous, by late 2001 it appeared as if *Basic Instinct 2* would not be going into production. Stone's original co-star, Michael Douglas, turned down the offer to star in the film (see Sheridan 2001: 13), MGM struggled to find a leading man to support Stone (ibid.), and the studio failed to find an established director who would agree to take on the controversial production (see Anon. 2001b). Perhaps unsurprisingly, the commentaries regarding the delay in production aim to blur the boundaries between the predatory role of Catherine and Stone offscreen. For example, review media commented that Michael Douglas declined the job because 'his bride, Catherine Zeta-Jones, would not be happy if he tried to get naked with Stone ... again' (ibid.). Likewise, we are told that Pierce Brosnan was approached for the role, but that 'he said he'd rather keep his licence to kill, than be killed by

Stone' (ibid.). The actors in question are confounding the predatory nature of the role with the traits and mannerisms of the star in question. What I mean by this is that Brosnan would not be killed by the actress: his character would be killed by (Stone's portrayal of) Catherine. Likewise, although Douglas would be naked with Stone, any sexual gymnastics would simply be a professionally choreographed performance by the pair.[5]

However, after several years of pre-production, the much-awaited sequel was released. In *Basic Instinct 2*, we see Catherine arrested for the murder of her lover. A criminal psychiatrist, Dr Michael Glass (David Morrissey), is brought in by the police to evaluate the mental state of the suspect. Glass diagnoses Catherine with a potentially fatal 'risk addiction' before embarking on a professional and sexual relationship with her. Review media continue to blur distinctions between role and star, irrespective of the time span and Stone's alternative performances between the two neo-noir texts. For example, we are told that 'on screen and off, Sharon really is the ball-busting diva that we know and love' (Anon. 2004: 7) and that 'Stone is still the perfect femme fatale' (Topel 2006). Likewise, it is Stone not Catherine who is positioned as the predatory figure when we are told that 'Stone returns ... an older femme but as fatale as ever' (Dargis 2006). Moreover, when one reviewer comments that 'there's no denying how good she still is at being really, really bad' it is unclear as to whether we are being told about the traits of the role or star (Loder 2006).

Either way, it is clear that the modern-day femme fatale goes further to exploit her sexual powers than her fatal predecessors. The sexuality of the 1940s femme fatale was relatively 'passive': sexual desire and its promise of pleasure belonged to the male; and the femme fatale was usually more interested in money than sex. Because the postwar period was anxious to maintain the nuclear family unit, repress female sexuality and position women as suburban housewives, mothers and homemakers, these original noir texts sought to punish the predatory spider woman for her social and sexual transgressions. Alternatively, the contemporary period has positively embraced and encouraged female sexual desire, with the 1990s witnessing the femidom female contraceptive, the controversial abortion pill, an increasing display of sex and sexuality in the mass media and the growing home video market for heterosexual 'couples' pornography (see Austin 2002: 50). In order to maintain social meaning and sexual relevance for the contemporary audience, neo-noir productions appear keen to present the aggressive sexual power and pleasure of the femme fatale. Indeed, because these spider women 'keep open the bedroom door which was firmly closed by the production codes surrounding classic noir' they have gained themselves a reputation as 'orgasmic femme fatales' (Straayer 1998: 153).

Rather than critique neo-noir texts or condemn review media for circulating a misogynistic image of female power based on sexual performance, it is

Survival of the fittest: *Basic Instinct 2*

worth noting that some feminist and post-feminist critics have been seen to applaud female sexual performances as empowered images of modern womanhood. For example, we are told that '*Basic Instinct* ... points up women's dominance in the sexual realm' (Camille Paglia cited in Chaudhuri 1993: 22) and that it is actually Catherine's 'tornado-like-sexual desire' that endears her to the women in the audience (Francke 1996: 26).[6] Indeed, recent writing tells us that the femme fatale 'is the hunter ... who takes control ... who makes the first move as sexual predator' (Baumgold 1998: 483) and that it is she who 'demands sexual satisfaction' (Straayer 1998: 153). In this way, Catherine's 'display of power, however depraved and unmotivated' is said to offer 'a new version (albeit warped) of female empowerment' (Rich 1995: 9). With this in mind, one might look to congratulate modern noir texts for allowing the deadly spider woman to survive the film and escape punishment for her potent sexuality. However, one might also suggest that allowing the femme fatale to survive and therefore age is simply an alternative way to punish the femme fatale – as both character and star.

Stone reprised the role of Catherine some 14 years after the release of the original *Basic Instinct* and, obviously, the actress has been seen to age during that time. Because the noir movement has so rarely seen an actress revisit a fatale role, critics and commentators seemed unaccustomed to a forty-something woman depicting the deadly black widow. Indeed, although a small number of publications praised the film for using 'an actress in her forties to play the femme fatale' (Hennigan 2006: 50), much news and magazine media formed a consensus as they critiqued the ageing star in a sexual role, reminding us that 'sexpots age fast in Hollywood' (Glaister 2006). We are told that 'the night lighting makes [Stone] look flawless, although in daylight shots her eyeliner goes all the way to her nose' (Topel 2006) and that 'Stone is too old for the part of sexual magnet' (IMDb user comment 2006). Alternatively, those reviewers who were surprised at Stone's youthful appearance went on to mock her lack of expressiveness in the role as a way of hinting at and deriding plastic surgery. We are told that 'the actress retains the same lucid gaze and whippet-thin body, but in this film her face looks strangely inert' (Dargis 2006) and that she 'returns, at 48, with a performance that lends new meaning to "Stone-faced" ... her work here constitutes an eerie tour de force of muscle control – a weirdly minimalist form of mugging' (Lim 2006). Likewise, another reviewer asks, rather bluntly, 'What's up with her forehead?' before telling us, 'It's like an ice pond now' (Phillips 2006). In short, we are told that 'Stone is too old to play Catherine Tramell' (Geradin 2006) even though this star carries the face, voice and style of the dangerous spider woman in question.

Indeed, even though we are informed that Stone is 'the lifeblood' of the *Basic Instinct* franchise and that the 'sequel has always depended on [her] presence in the role' of Catherine (Williams 2006: 42), it is now clear that although the fantasy of Stone is welcome in the neo-noir genre, the ageing reality is found wanting. Therefore, if we consider that the femme fatale offers women the rare chance to be both seductive and powerful onscreen, and that Stone is now seen to be too old to play the predatory femme, we soon become aware of the limitations of female sexual power for both character and star. As such, the presentation of the ageing femme fatale can be understood as a form of punishment: those who see the true age of the actress appear disappointed with this sexual image; while those that comment on the flawless visage of the woman simply go on to mock the performance of the star.

Conclusion

It is generally held within the field of star studies that cultural icons are accepted by the public in terms of a set of personality traits, associations and mannerisms which permeate all of their film roles (see Harris 1991: 40). However, in the case of Sharon Stone, the actress is only accepted in terms of those personality traits, associations and mannerisms which make up the predatory character of Catherine. Even though the actress has appeared in over forty films, her star image remains single-handedly constructed around her performances in the neo-noir texts. From this estimation, this chapter has outlined the ways in which review media and the actress in question have formed a consensus as they blur the distinctions between role and star, concluding that the ageing femme and the forty-something woman have become all but invisible in contemporary society.

If one considers that the original femme fatales were routinely killed for their transgressions and that those modern spider women who escape without punishment fail to return to the silver screen, then it is clear that these deadly females remain ageless and, therefore, perhaps timeless fantasies for the viewing public. Stone's reprisal of the femme fatale seems to demonstrate not only the limitations of a rigid star image, but also – and perhaps more importantly – the demise of sexual power for the forty-something woman. Ironically, Stone was not unaware of the risk of playing the ageing femme fatale; in fact, the actress was often heard to critique the way in which contemporary society tends 'to erase women after they're 40' (in Glaister 2006). However, even though Stone may be vocal about the fact that older women are 'sexual in a different and alluring way' (ibid.) it becomes clear that she made a fatal mistake in trying to 'portray [the] mature [Catherine] as a sexual being' (Anon. 2006b). The *New York Times* makes this point succinctly when it tells us that, 'the problem is, Catherine didn't die ... as bad as that sounds, nothing compares to the fate that awaited Ms. Stone simply by growing older – older at least in Hollywood years' (Dargis 2006). Indeed, even those feminist and post-feminist critics who applauded the original neo-noir text and Sharon Stone's powerful sexual performance in that film appear somewhat slow to comment on the representation of the ageing femme fatale or on Stone's reprisal of the sexual predator. One might question whether their reading of the deadly spider woman as a powerful sexual agent merely goes further to foreground the unconscious weight of a culture that has made the sexual woman synonymous with timeless, ageless youth and, as such, point to a rather limited form of female power for the woman both on- and offscreen.

NOTES

1 Other neo-noirs have spawned sequels, but they usually involve different characters, as in *Poison Ivy 2* (1996). *The Last Seduction II* (1999) is an exception, but Joan Severance replaced Linda Fiorentino in the role of Bridget Gregory. Shannon Tweed has reprised femme fatale roles in films such as *Indecent Behavior* (1993), *Indecent Behavior II* (1994) and *Indecent Behavior III* (1995) and *No Contest* (1994) and *No Contest II* (1997) but – as the rapid production turnover suggests – these films were direct to video titles (see Williams in this volume). *Basic Instinct 2* is the only 'return of the femme fatale' to receive a cinematic release.

2 This anecdote appears in Eszterhas's *American Rhapsody* – a book primarily concerned with the Clinton sex scandal. Although one may question the relevance of an anecdote about Stone in this context, it is worth considering the way in which referring to Stone sets the tone for the sex scandal theme and reinforces Eszterhas's own reputation as a scandalous screenwriter.

3 Stone's role in *Cougars* was announced in September 2004, with filming due to start in 2005. However, as of August 2009, the Internet Movie Database still lists it as 'in development' (for release in 2011), and the title no longer appears on Stone's filmography.

4 Although Stone was nominated for a Golden Globe award for her role in *Basic Instinct*, she was simultaneously voted the worst new star in the infamous Razzies. She is routinely situated as a poor actress whose only talent is to play herself onscreen (James 1994: 11; Maslin 1995: 1). She is presumed to be not only a bad performer but also one who is defined by her body. When her acting is mentioned, it is referred to as a 'tour de farce' (Margulies & Rebello 1995: 138) and she is often dismissed as incompetent, mannered and overblown. Her success is therefore attributed to her looks and particularly her supposed penchant for parts involving 'lots of sex and acres of bare flesh' (Andrews 1994: 78).

5 The conflation of actor/character is reinforced by Sheridan's uses of the word 'naked' to describe the source of Zeta-Jones' unhappiness. Kenneth Clark suggests that to be naked is simply to be without clothes, whereas the nude is a form of dress (cited in Berger 1990: 53–4). Since Douglas and Stone would be acting, they would be 'nude' – displaying their skin as part of the performance. Stone also makes this distinction herself, telling readers that her nudity-friendly performances are disguised behind the narrative character that she is playing, because although 'anybody with seven bucks can see my ass … it doesn't feel like they've seen it because that butt belongs to fictional characters' (in Zehme 1995: 48).

6 Women made up 44 per cent of *Basic Instinct*'s cinema audience and 43 per cent of the sequel's spectatorship (see Austin 2002: 47; Gray 2006).

REFERENCES

Abele, Robert (2004) 'I only come when I'm called…', *Total Film*, 93, September, 72–5.

Andrews, Steve (1994) 'Wits out for the lads', *Empire*, 59, May, 76–81.

Anon. (2001a) 'Leading men shy away from *Basic Instinct 2*', *Guardian Unlimited*, 5 January. Available at: http://film.guardian.co.uk/News_Story/Exclusive/0,4029,418260,00. html. Accessed 7 April 2008.

____ (2001b) 'Stone's basic instinct: Sue the producers', *Guardian Unlimited*, 7 June. Available at: http://film.guardian.co.uk/News_Story/Exclusive/0,,503097,00.html. Accessed 7 April 2008.

____ (2004) 'Celebrity sex clinic: Splitting the difference', *Sunday Times*, 25 July, 7.

____ (2006a) 'Red carpet: *Basic Instinct 2*', *Total* Film, 16 March 2006. Available at: http://www.totalfilm.com/movie_news/red_carpet_basic_instinct_2. Accessed 7 April 2008.

____ (2006b) 'Warning: Legs crossing', *Empire*, 15 March 2006. Available at: http://www.empireonline.com//News/story.asp?nid=18286. Accessed 30 March 2006.

Austin, Thomas (2002) *Hollywood, Hype and Audiences: Selling and Watching Popular Film in the 1990s*. Manchester: Manchester University Press.

Barbas, Samantha (2001) *Movie Crazy: Fans, Stars and the Cult of Celebrity*. New York: Macmillan.

Baumgold, Julie (1998) 'Fatal attractions', *Vogue* (New York edition), March, 480–3 and 539.

Berger, John (1990) *Ways of Seeing*. London: Penguin.

Cartwright, James (2004) 'The new Stone age', *Evening Standard Metrolife*, 6–12 August, 6.

Chaudhuri, Anita (1993) 'Stone unturned', *Time Out*, 1195, 14 July, 22–3.

Coates, Julia (1993) '*Basic Instinct* sexpot stole my hubby, newlywed charges', *National Enquirer*, 30 March, 36.

Cooney, Jenny (1992) 'Naked Hollywood', *Empire*, 36, June, 54–60.

Dargis, Manohla (2006) 'Sharon Stone returns in *Basic Instinct 2*, an older femme but as fatale as ever', *New York Times*, 31 March. Available at: http://movies2.nytimes.com/2006/03/31/movies/31inst.html. Accessed 7 April 2008.

Dawson, Jeff (1995) 'It's a blast', *Empire*, 64, January, 76–85.

____ (1996) 'The best thing about it is the boobs', *Empire*, 84, June, 94–8.

Dickos, Andrew (2002) *Street With No Name: A History of the Classic American Film Noir*. Lexington: University Press of Kentucky.

Dyer, Richard (1998) *Stars*. Second Edition. London: British Film Institute.

Ebert, Roger (1994) '*Intersection*', *Chicago Sun-Times*, 21 January. Available at: http://rogerebert.suntimes.com/apps/pbcs.dll/article?AID=/19940121/REVIEWS/401210301/1023. Accessed 7 April 2008.

____ (1995) '*Showgirls*', *Chicago Sun-Times*, 22 September. Available at: http://rogerebert.suntimes.com/apps/pbcs.dll/article?AID=/19950922/REVIEWS/509220306/1023. Accessed 7 April 2008.

____ (1996) '*Last Dance*', *Chicago Sun-Times*, 3 May. Available at: http://rogerebert.suntimes.com/apps/pbcs.dll/article?AID=/19960503/REVIEWS/605030306/1023. Accessed 7 April 2008.

Eszterhas, Joe (2000) *American Rhapsody*. New York: Alfred A. Knopf.

Fitz, Reginald (1996) 'How brush with death changed Sharon Stone into man-hungry wild woman & left her scarred for life', *National Enquirer*, 24 September, 46–7.

____ (1998) 'Sharon Stone's route to the altar is littered with road kill', *National Enquirer*, 3 March, 9.

Francke, Lizzie (1996) 'Someone to look at', *Sight & Sound*, 6, 3, March, 26–7.

Geradin, Damien (2006) 'The revenge'. Available at: http://professorgeradin.blogs.com/professor_geradins_weblog/2006/11/index.html. Accessed 7 April 2008.

Glaister, Dan (2006) 'Sharon has been posing since she arrived', *Guardian Unlimited*, 17 March. Available at: http://www.guardian.co.uk/international/story/0,,1732694,00.html. Accessed 7 April 2008.

Grant, Steve (1992) 'Sex crimes', *Time Out*, 22 April, 18–21.

Gray, Brandon (2006) '*Ice Age 2* hot, *Basic Instinct 2* not', *Box Office Mojo*, 3 April 2006. Available at http://www.boxofficemojo.com/news/?id=2041. Accessed 7 April 2008.

Harris, Thomas (1991 [1957]) 'The building of popular images: Grace Kelly and Marilyn Monroe', in Christine Gledhill (ed.) *Stardom: Industry of Desire*. London: Routledge, 40–4.

Hennigan, Adrian (2006) '*Basic Instinct 2*', *Total Film*, 115, June, 50.

IMDb user comment (2006) '*Basic Instinct 2*', Internet Movie Database. Available at http://www.imdb.com/title/tt0430912/usercomments. Accessed 7 April 2008.

James, Caryn (1994) 'A perfect match lights the bombs', *New York Times*, 8 October, Section I, 11.

Kempley, Rita (1992) '*Basic Instinct*', *Washington Post*, 20 March. Available at: http://www.washingtonpost.com/wp-srv/style/longterm/movies/videos/basicinstinctrkempley_a0a2a8.htm. Accessed 7 April 2008.

King, Barry (1991 [1985]) 'Articulating stardom', in Christine Gledhill (ed.) *Stardom: Industry of Desire*. London: Routledge, 167–82.

King, Geoff (2002) *New Hollywood Cinema: An Introduction*. New York: Columbia University Press.

Lim, Dennis (2006) 'Romancing the Stone', *Village Voice*, 28 March. Available at: http://www.villagevoice.com/film/0614,lim,72753,20.html. Accessed 7 April.

Loder, Kurt (2006) '*Basic Instinct 2*: Stoned again', MTV.com, 31 March. Available at: http://www.mtv.com/movies/news/articles/1527446/03302006/story.jhtml. Accessed 7 April 2008.

Margulies, Edward and Stephen Rebello (1995) *Bad Movies We Love*. London: Marion Boyars.

Maslin, Janet (1995) 'Sharon Stone as taciturn gunslinger', *New York Times*, 10 February, Section C, 1.

Maxwell, Martel (2004) 'My basic instinct is a lust for toyboys!', *Sun*, 22 July, 3.

Naremore, James (1998) *More Than Night: Film Noir in Its Contexts*. London: University of California Press.

Phillips, Michael (2006) '*Basic Instinct 2*', *Chicago Tribune*, 31 March. Available at: http://metromix.chicagotribune.com/movies/mmx-060331-movies-review-basic,0,260039.story. Accessed 7 April 2008.

Rich, B. Ruby (1995) 'Dumb lugs and femme fatales', *Sight & Sound*, 5, 11, November, 6–11.

Schruers, Fred (1993) 'Stone free', *Premiere*, 6, 9, May, 58–66.

Sheff, David (1992) '*Playboy* interview Sharon Stone', *Playboy*, December, 63–88.

Sheridan, Peter (2001) 'Leading men follow their instinct and turn down Sharon', *Sunday Express*, 4 February, 13.

Straayer, Chris (1998) 'Femme fatale or lesbian femme: Bound in sexual difference', in E. Ann Kaplan (ed.) *Women in Film Noir*. New Edition. London: British Film Institute, 151–63.

Thompson, Douglas (1994) *Sharon Stone: Basic Ambition*. London: Warner Books.

Topel, Fred (2006) '*Basic Instinct 2*', About.Com, 31 March. Available at: http://actionadventure.about.com/od/moviereviews/a/aa033106c_p.htm. Accessed 24 April 2006.

Van Scheers, Rob (1997) *Paul Verhoeven*, trans. Aletta Stevens. London: Faber and Faber.

Weinraub, Bernard (1992) '*Basic Instinct*: The suspect is attractive, and may be fatal', *New York Times*, 15 March, 17–34.

Williams, Linda Ruth (2005) *The Erotic Thriller in Contemporary Cinema*. Edinburgh: Edinburgh University Press.

____ (2006) 'Cupid and psycho', *Sight & Sound*, 16, 5, May, 42–3.

Zehme, Bill (1995) 'Getting naked with Sharon Stone', *Esquire*, April, 44–8.

13

Fatality Revisited: The Problem of 'Anxiety' in Psychoanalytic-Feminist Approaches to Film Noir

SUZY GORDON

Critical debate has firmly established film noir as an articulation of anxiety. Where there is noir, Kelly Oliver and Benigno Trigo (2003) remind us, there is always anxiety. Anxiety is noir's idiom, its *raison d'être*, whether it is attributed to postwar economic shifts; sexual and racial instabilities and a perceived decline in patriarchal authority; the uncertainties of the human condition, moral decay and fatalism; or the unconscious processes of a phallocratic cinema honed in the art of reproducing male subjects tormented by their desires. Most prominent among noir's cast of anxiety-figures is the femme fatale. A self-serving, narcissistic and sexually provocative woman, she promises pleasures that invoke the ravages of the death-drive. She seduces the male protagonist, bends him to her will: the seduction takes place 'at the expense of his own subjectivity' (Hayward 1996: 119). Noir anxiety thus exposes the inextricable connection between male desire and the collapse of 'men's very existence' as men (Place 1998: 47). This 'perversity' is the femme fatale's terrain: she dramatises for men the eternal pull of self-destructiveness against the narcissistic self-identifications required by patriarchy (Krutnik 1991: 84–5).

Three neo-noirs – *Crush* (1992), *The Last Seduction* (1994) and *In the Cut* (2003) – reposition anxiety in relation to the difficulty of desire and subjectivity *for women*. Part of the aim of this chapter therefore is to determine what form anxiety takes as a consequence of this shift. In what follows, I suggest that the neo-femme fatale invokes and reworks the noir femme fatale in ways that point towards the pivotal position of anxiety at the intersection between public and private violence, historical and psychical worlds. I develop a reading of anxiety as a signal of what it feels like simultaneously to exist in history (the 'real' world) and in the psyche (the universe within). This means seeing anxiety not as a crisis in identity (a danger to be feared and so averted), but as its condition of possibility (something to hope for).

Noir anxiety

Focusing on the anxiety involved with *masculine* subjectivity, and drawing on Freudian-Lacanian psychoanalysis, feminist film theory has largely favoured a 'symptomatic' reading of film noir. In this approach, the femme fatale is read as a symptom of castration anxiety: the coded representative of the precariousness of male subjectivity within a hetero-patriarchy. Patriarchy is understood to *require* the femme fatale – the system needs to countenance, even *enjoy*, the prospect of its own destruction. Mary Ann Doane indicates the focus of the debates:

> The femme fatale is an articulation of fears surrounding the loss of stability and central-
> ity of the self, the 'I', the ego. These anxieties appear quite explicitly in the process of
> her representation as castration anxiety ... The power accorded to the femme fatale is a
> function of fears linked to the notions of uncontrollable drives, the fading of subjectivity,
> and the loss of conscious agency. (1991: 2–3)

'Castration' here refers to 'woman' as signifier within a hetero-patriarchal struc-ture of desire where she stands for the 'lack' the male subject must offset (must acknowledge elsewhere) in order to 'be a man', to sustain the fictions of self as self-determining and autonomous. 'Woman' is therefore also a per-manent reminder of the prospect of man's own 'lack': his 'being' is haunted by the potential for destruction. A compromise formation between the need to express (delight in) the risk of non-identity and also (to some extent) extinguish it, the femme fatale secures the male subject while promising his downfall.

This 'symptomatic' mode of reading the femme fatale has proved extreme-ly persuasive, not least because it makes sense of the ideological work of film noir. Clare Johnston summarises: 'It is in relation to the women in the film ... that the internal contradictions of the patriarchal order ... are ... played out. The "woman" is produced as the signifier of the lack ... the "fault" inherent in patriarchy as an order' (1998: 92). Noir is patriarchy's 'safety-net', Frank Krutnik explains, a means of articulating and managing the 'inherent' problems of phal-lic subjectivity by positioning instability elsewhere (1991: 71). Deborah Thomas agrees: film noir is 'about men with women used as decoys in a strategy of denial' (1992: 64). Janey Place has a different emphasis: 'On a strictly narrative level,' she explains, 'sexually aggressive women ... must be destroyed' (1998: 63). But this 'regressive ideological function' is overwhelmed by noir's 'unique-ly sensual visual texture' in which the femme fatale's 'strength and power' is privileged, 'printed in our memory' (ibid.). Film noir may certainly manage anxi-ety, but may also thereby proliferate it.

Occluded within the 'symptomatic' model, it is this legacy of the noir de-bates – the implicit emphasis on the constitutional necessity of anxiety – that this chapter develops. As an example of that occlusion, I quote here in some detail from Thomas, whose work is instructive in its aim to account for anxiety as a psychological *and* historical phenomenon. Thomas interprets anxiety as a sign of an incompatibility between different repertoires of 'normal' masculinity, 'a kind of male schizophrenia' which the 'war and its conclusion … crystallised … by imposing sudden and extreme shifts in the norms invoked' (1992: 59–60). She provides examples:

> What was normal during the war – such as close male companionship, sanctioned kill-ing, and 'easier' and more casual sexual behaviour, all heightened by the constant pos-sibility of one's own sudden death – became deviant in the context of post-war calm, though … lingered on in the *film noir* world as the focus both of longing and of dread. (1992: 60).

Anxiety is bound up with 'normal' masculinity, the difficulties – the impossi-bility – of ever successfully inhabiting its folds (without loss or 'dread'). But anxiety is also equated with the uncertainties and instabilities 'provoked' by 'the adaptation to war and the subsequent return to normal' (1992: 68). This is anxiety mobilised 'in a response to' historical circumstances interpreted as troubling in light of profound investments in the (fictional) stability of self-hood (1992: 61).

There is a contradiction in the delivery of this argument that goes unno-ticed. Anxiety is situated as pivotal in the constitution of male subjectivity – a condition of 'being' in the world, and the sign of its difficulty. But Thomas recuperates the suggestive insinuation of anxiety as a paradoxical mode of possibility, when the contingencies of wartime and the postwar situation take centre-stage. History comes to 'provoke' anxiety rather than 'crystallise' it. The subtle shift in phrasing reframes anxiety as a psychological response to historical events felt to put at risk an *a priori* stability of psyche and identity for men. Compare Richard Dyer's wording: anxiety is '*over* the existence and definition of masculinity' (as though anxiety responds to the problems posed by cultural demands on gendered subjects and not the means by which the subject comes to live by inhabiting those requirements) (Dyer cited in Krutnik 1991: 85; emphasis added). Similarly, Krutnik suggests that anxiety is aroused in response to the dissonances of 'phallic' subjectivity as they were newly fore-grounded in the postwar US (1991: 85–91). More recently, devoting an entire book to the issue of noir anxiety, Oliver and Trigo reproduce the problem, defin-ing anxiety as a generalised 'state' of unease aroused by postwar uncertainties and change (2003).

In all these cases, anxiety is cast as a fearful response to a danger situation – anxiety is elided with 'fear'. The above-quoted passage from Doane is explicit on this point: the femme fatale articulates '*fears* surrounding the loss of stability … of the self', 'fears linked to the … fading of subjectivity', and so on (1991: 2–3; emphasis added). Intriguingly, anxiety is made interchangeable with fear in virtually every account I have read of the anxiety associated with the femme fatale. Consider James F. Maxfield's *The Fatal Woman: Sources of Male Anxiety in American Film Noir 1941–1991*, in which the anxiety of the title is transposed in the text as 'the threat which a woman … poses to the life, welfare, or psychological well-being of a male protagonist' (1996: 9–10). Or E. Ann Kaplan, who suggests that psychoanalytic-feminist theory reads the femme fatale in terms of a 'male fear of … castration' (1998: 9). Thus while symptomatic readings may allow for persuasive interpretations of film noir's ideological premise – the need to reproduce a stable masculinity out of its ruin (and the difficulty of doing so) – they rely on a restricted conception of anxiety which can tend to suggest that woman *as* woman inescapably does violence to men.

This is because to elide anxiety with fear is to give anxiety an origin. This turns anxiety into a consequence of 'what happens' (of historical events), rather than making it integral to the meaning and experience of 'what happens', to the possibility of anything being experienced in the first place. The effect is to isolate anxiety as a figure belonging to the inner world, interpreted as an emotive or affective response, while particular historical circumstances are imbued with an innate capacity to trouble the certainties of masculinity for men. This has troubling consequences. It means that women's increased access to the public sphere during World War Two, their perceived usurpation of the male workplace and the increased visibility of their sexual activity, may easily be read as posing a threat to masculinity (and to men) *in actuality*, as if the dominant fictions of masculinity were genuinely secure elsewhere than in fantasy (or fiction). Were this the case, women could be said to be dangerous onscreen (in male fantasy) because they are dangerous in real life. From this emerges the axiom that *(increasingly independent) women really do pose a threat to men*. Not only is this problematic (an argument that justifies its own misogyny), it is also imprecise. It ignores the idea that the femme fatale materialises the 'perversity' of the male subject fractured by his own desire (the idea, as we have seen, that is right at the heart of investigations into noir's gendered anxiety). But it also assumes incorrectly that historical realities are untouched by the dramas of psychical life.

Women do not *really* pose a threat to men, to the possibility of men being 'men'. To suggest that they do is at the very least to cancel out the validity of a claim for women's autonomy (just think of the restrictions on their actions that would be involved if independent women actually *were* dangerous). Rather, it is through the psychical operations of *fantasy*, specifically in its institutionalised forms (in cinema, for example) that women's increased sexual and economic independence is *interpreted as a threat*. Elizabeth Cowie puts it succinctly: 'the image of woman as devouring' is a fantasy (an unconscious scenario) that gets attached 'to a little bit of reality' ('women have substituted for men at home and at work') (1998: 123). There is then a pressing political need when considering the femme fatale to refuse to elide anxiety with fear and instead to interrogate more precisely the anxiety she articulates. What is needed is an account of anxiety that puts centre-stage the precise terms of the relationship between history and psyche, that is alert to the experience involved in the simultaneous inhabitation of historical and psychical worlds. The following psychoanalytical discussion of neo-noir addresses this claim, explaining anxiety as the means by which the external world becomes meaningful, inhabitable, liveable. Anxiety, I shall suggest, is what it takes for us to 'be' in the world.

Re-screening anxiety

The Last Seduction, In the Cut and Crush pose precisely this challenge, opening up ideas about gendered anxiety that have not been addressed within existing theoretical paradigms. Each film presents the femme not simply as fatale but knowingly so, as a stylised display of the 'anxiety' that 'phallic' female sexuality entails. Each flaunts openly its familiarity with the Freudian-Lacanian themes appointed by feminist film studies to explain the femme fatale as symptom of anxiety, so that the links between desire and castration, said to underpin noir's gendered representations, are brought vividly into the foreground. 'Castration anxiety' becomes a popular slogan littering these films' reflections on gendered power relations, eroticism and violence: men are overdetermined by gender instabilities, neo-femme fatales by their association with a violence linked to their sexuality. The Last Seduction, for instance, almost drowns in the self-conscious irony of its portrayal of Bridget Gregory (Linda Fiorentino) as castrating or phallic woman. A relatively low-budget production, this neo-noir aligns a dangerously seductive female sexuality with the thrills of an urban landscape in which men are perpetually at risk of 'castration'. Bridget is powerful, sexy and pathological, a woman with no conscience or moral sense, motivated by greed (for money and sex) alone. She masquerades as romantic heroine and 'good girl', manipulating and dispatching the men who get in her way by fooling them with performances of passive femininity. Behind their backs she is slashing their tyres, plotting her revenge or their death, investigating their past, setting them up. This is the castrating woman par excellence: pleasurable 'in form', 'threatening in content' (Mulvey 1988: 62). Her capacities for castration are foregrounded through her speech and the way she has sex: she screams, 'I'm a total fucking bitch,' as she orgasms, astride Mike Swale (Peter Berg) and with her back to him – Linda Ruth Williams calls it a 'double reinforcement of her mastery and his submission' (2005: 210–11).

This is typical of Crush and In the Cut too. Both make the male protagonist's passivity and his perverse pleasure in it an object of repeated attention. But they do so from the perspective of broadly 'feminist' concerns with women's agency in matters of identity and desire. Produced during a relatively prolific period of non-commercial women's filmmaking in New Zealand, *Crush* is a 'feminist psychodrama' that brings into play a multiplicity of generic tropes to develop a layered critique of the sexual politics of Hollywood cinema (see Robson & Zalcock 1997: 8). The American femme fatale, Lane (Marcia Gay Harden), violates the bonds of friendship between women, much like *Crush*'s Hollywood contemporaries *Single White Female*, *The Hand that Rocks the Cradle* and *Poison Ivy* (all 1992), which 'portray ... a destructive female relationship that mocks the possibility of women forming ... bonds of loyalty and affection' (Hollinger 1998: 207). Starting out as a road movie, *Crush* explicitly invokes the 'bonds of loyalty and affection' made famous a year earlier in *Thelma and Louise* (1991). But Lane crashes the car and leaves her friend, Christina (Donogh Rees), for dead. Christina recovers sufficiently by the end of the film to walk the few steps required to thrust Lane off a cliff-edge and to her death, in a sequence that draws explicitly on the conventions of the slasher genre. The death can be read as an act of violence against Hollywood, retribution for its sins against women and their friendships.

In the Cut is equally immersed in an interrogation of the gendered politics of popular genres. Since the success of her 'art' cinema/mainstream crossover *The Piano* (1993), Jane Campion has become synonymous with a middlebrow 'feminist' and 'literary' cinema which addresses questions of female sexuality, power and eroticism. Concerns with *mise-en-scène*, cinematography and the complexity of character and desire announce her films' difference from, yet profound engagement with, the gendered preoccupations of the mainstream. *In The Cut* reproduces this conjunction between 'literary', popular and feminist cinemas. In its invocation of 1990s neo-noir as post-feminist urban thriller, it crosses between popular and 'art' or 'authored' cinema: a literary adaptation employing a romance narrative structure, it also relies on the conventions of the feminist detective story.

It is in the context of this critical intertextuality and generic conjuncture that these two films call attention to the embeddedness of castration anxiety in cinema's gendered pleasures. In *Crush*, Lane seduces the reclusive Colin Iseman (William Zappa) by cutting his hair, the sequence making a stylised centrepiece of the drama of castration. The camera revels in Colin's discomfort and the pleasure it arouses, cutting in to close-ups that mirror the commanding movements of Lane's scissored gaze. Her pouting, red-lipsticked mouth is the centre of an eroticism coded as fatal: Colin is transfixed from the outset – willingly subordinated – by Lane's devouring mouth. Sue Thornham picks up on a comparably self-reflexive moment in *In the Cut*: 'Detective Malloy [Mark Ruffalo], handcuffed to a radiator pipe whilst Frannie Avery [Meg Ryan] straddles him to orgasm, eventually requests his release: "Makes you very nervous being in handcuffs," he says. "I'm starting to fucking feel like a chick here"' (2007: 33).

Seduction-castration: *Crush*

These are knowing presentations of the femme fatale as 'symptom' in a system of sexual difference founded on castration anxiety. There is no coded representative here: the recognition of male anxiety (the link between desire and terror) is in full view. Such awareness of the psychoanalytic lexicon deployed in feminist readings of noir is good enough reason, Jacinda Read protests, to ditch the use of psychoanalysis altogether in analyses of neo-noir: *The Last Seduction* 'contain[s] such knowing references to castration anxiety, the phallic woman and fetishism', she argues, 'that to attempt a serious psychoanalytically informed analysis would be to play straight into the film's hands' (2000: 247). This is because Read wants to refute readings of the neo-femme fatale as a 'backlash' against women's increased access to 'masculine' privileges in a post-feminist world (2000: 174). But her wholesale dismissal of psychoanalytic theory is short-sighted. Just because a film is capable of illuminating the femme fatale as symptom of anxiety does not mean that it is detached from anxiety or freed from its influence. As we shall see, these generic reworkings rearticulate anxiety as an ambivalent drama of subjectivity, a mode of 'being' in which the risk of violence is also a means of survival for women. Only psychoanalysis, I will suggest, can offer us the means to fully apprehend such a proposition.

Alongside these knowing acknowledgements of the sexually-active woman/ perversely-passive man binary, anxiety shifts from its associations with the 'crisis' in male identity to the moment in which claims are made for an autonomy of desire and subjectivity for women. Picking up on the fact that the 'masculine bias' of noir narratives is not definitive, each film exploits the potential to tell a woman's story (see Cowie 1998: 135). Women take charge of the narrative action: Bridget investigates the film's narrative enigma (the threat Mike's marriage to Trish (Serena) poses to his masculinity); Frannie is a 'persistent questioner'

(Thornham 2007: 41), but her investigations point towards the wrong man, thereby sealing her fate as victim; all three female protagonists in *Crush* drive the narrative (but with fatal consequences). *In the Cut* makes explicit the role of anxiety in women's adoption of subject-status by privileging language as the means by which the female protagonist is able to articulate her desire. Frannie becomes preoccupied by the meaning of the word 'disarticulation' which Malloy uses to describe what was done to the murdered woman's body. 'Disarticulation' is a material staging of castration – it can also mean to be undone, refused an identity. But its dangers are now *resolutely for women*, anxiety a condition of their entry into the privileges of subjectivity. Plundering noir for icons of anxiety, these films therefore open up to view the vicissitudes of the death-drive, diverting attention away from the idea of anxiety as a consequence of dangerous circumstances and instead towards the necessary difficulties of subjectivity for women. This puts us in a different register entirely from the anxiety of film noir: to understand the anxiety associated with the neo-femme fatale, we must take seriously women's investment in violence.

Feeling anxiety

Two moments in my own cinema-going experience compound the challenge these films pose to existing theories of noir anxiety, calling for a differently nuanced account of anxiety that is emphatically not conceived as a fearful response to a 'danger situation'. These are moments I shall suggest, in which anxiety emerges as *an affective marker of a temporal disjuncture in which the distinction between inner and outer realities is held in suspense.* The value of rethinking anxiety in this way, as an embodied experience of subjectivity, is that it suggests new means of unravelling the relations between history and psyche mediated by cinema. This has consequences for the ways in which filmic representation and reception can be thought to bear on the lived conditions of gendered subjectivity.

First then, to the cinema, and the possibility that anxiety has more to do with 'being' in the world than with responding to triggers. A packed house, and a sudden synchrony of male voices emits a series of gasps and guttural exhalations. For an instant, the cinema heaves under the pressure of 'the embodied and radically material' presence of this group of viewers, huddled in noisy alliance (Sobchack 2004: 1). Onscreen, Bridget answers Mike's sexual invitation – 'I'm hung like a horse; think about it' – with a brusque, 'Let's see', as she unzips his fly and checks the 'goods' for 'a certain horse-like quality' (we are watching *The Last Seduction*). A few years later and I am in a smaller, emptier cinema, when that same sound of bodies momentarily convulsed by their breath fills the air. We are about thirty minutes into *In the Cut* and Frannie sits silently at a bar as Malloy, a man she has only recently met, propositions her. 'I can be whatever you want me to be. You want me to romance you, take you to a classy restaurant … be your best friend and fuck you … treat you good, lick your pussy … no problem … The only thing I won't do is beat you up.' Unlike Bridget, Frannie says nothing, her body fragmented by shaky close-ups on forearm and exposed knee, all bathed in red light as Malloy's fingers brush against her flesh. The camera pivots on her face as he makes his offer, marking out the risky, ambivalent pleasures of sexual seduction for women. Frannie holds her breath, lips parted, then turns away, defusing the erotic charge and asks, 'Why does your partner carry a water pistol?' It is a shift in power: Frannie forces Malloy to retreat, to reveal (and defend) the details of his partner's history of violence against women. At this point, I turn around and look at the audience caught up in their throaty refrain of snorts and sighs. There is real discomfort in my glance: I have intruded in a moment of intimacy which is not about sexuality or desire, but fundamentally to do with the involuntary seizure of the body in sound and motion. These are bodies captivated in the articulation of filmic affect, cracked open in a moment of energetic release or expulsion.

It may seem obvious to read these 'affective encounters' interpretively: they look like 'effects' – physiological and emotional reactions (inner states) activated by textual (external) stimuli. Surely the male bodies heaving at *The Last Seduction* provide dramatic corroboration of the connection between desire and terror – the anxiety – that for men is mobilised by the sexually aggressive yet seductive femme fatale? Surely the disjunctive sounds and movements in the cinema showing *In the Cut* are indications of discomfort (or arousal) at Frannie's troubled pleasure in her sexual objectification? No doubt such interpretations could prove persuasive. But they rely on an unquestioned assumption that I want to place under scrutiny: that affective states are emotional responses mobilised by external events or situations *and are meaningful to the degree that they respond to these affecting events or situations*. I have already suggested that when such an account (of origins and effects) is used to theorise the anxiety involved with film noir, it serves to negate the entwining of real historical events with the dramas of the inner world, with troubling consequences for the possibility of women's empowerment and independence. So what do we stand to gain if we refuse to interpret film's affective encounters as the activation of inner meaning by outside signals or catalysts? In what other ways might the body caught up in the articulation of filmic affect come to bear on, and help us rethink, the meaning of anxiety?

My object of concern then is not the realm of interpretation and intelligibility but the brute fact of the body activated by, alert to, and expressive of sensation – overcome by or cracked open under the pressure of lived feeling, the discharge of an energetic force.[1] Freud develops an account of affect in which the body is conceived rather precisely in these 'energetic' terms, convulsed by sound and movement, its uncertain boundaries breached with the expulsion of energy (see Freud & Breuer 2004; Freud 1991a; 1991b). For Freud, affects are determined by the 'energy-processes' driving the human organism (see Laplanche & Pontalis 1988: 14). They are energetic excitations representative of the 'drives' – the 'qualitative expression' of the quantity of energy embedded in instinctual psychical impulses (Laplanche & Pontalis 1988: 13). They are not responses to events but are involved instead with 'ideas', the mental material attached to the sensory activity of the body at the point of its encounter with the prohibitions of culture.

In his early work on hysteria, Freud first interprets the affective body as signal of the curiously disjunctive relation between real events and internal worlds (and not in terms of meaning and derivation). He attributes hysterical symptoms – unintelligible disturbances of movement and sensation – to an event which 'has been met with no corresponding and proportionate discharge of affect' (Laplanche & Pontalis 1988: 13). Induced under hypnosis to waken 'the memory of the … event with complete clarity, arousing with it the accompanying affect', the patient's hysterical symptom disappears 'immediately' (Freud & Breuer 2004: 10). The peculiarity of affect in hysteria is that it is not (or not yet) attached to an originating event but rather *intrudes retrospectively into the memory of that event.* Only a retroactive gesture will establish affect as the 'corresponding and proportionate' response to an unpleasant event. If there is an origin to affect, it is *grafted on after the event.* In the case of hysteria then, real events take place only once they are recalled as memories. Affect is the signal of that temporal disjuncture, the enactment on the body of an event that 'happens' once experienced as mental material. Here, affect communicates vividly the peculiar interdependence of history and psyche, the sheer illegibility of the former without the presence of the latter.

This proposition is developed further in Freud's later and wide-ranging discussions of affect in which he attends in more detail to the metapsychology of repression in general (and not just in relation to hysterical illnesses) (1990, 1991a, 1991b, 1991c are all good examples). Here Freud ties affect explicitly to the meaning of anxiety and to the possibility that anxiety is without origin (a prospect I have indicated may prove of use in an analysis of the neo-femme fatale). Crucially, affect transmutes into anxiety under pressure of cultural regulation: the acculturation (or socialisation) of the body expressive of psychical impulses involves anxiety. Put differently, because it violates social and sexual propriety, the satisfaction of an instinctual aim provokes 'unpleasure' and so must be repressed (see Freud 1991a and 1991b). The repression 'liberates' affect (see Freud 1991a: 152). This is because all drives are comprised of an ideational and an affective representative (an 'idea' and a 'quota of affect') which are split apart by the act of repression (see Freud 1991a: 152–3). Detached affects may get channelled into the body ('converted into somatic energy'), form physical symptoms, and get interpreted as disguised expressions of emotion (Laplanche & Pontalis 1988: 200). But this is not always the case. When an affect is 'liberated … by repression' from the 'idea' with which it is associated and is 'not *converted*', it is instead 'set free in the shape of *anxiety*' (Freud 1990: 274; emphasis in original). If repression lets us 'be', then 'being' involves anxiety (to exist as a historical subject is not simply to repress instinctual pleasure but also to experience anxiety). Notably, this is anxiety without object or origin. It is 'uninhibitable', an overwhelming energetic impulse flooded with the intensity of the body's sensory capacities but uprooted, not 'rationalised' (Freud 1991b: 185). It is felt on the body as a condition of the entry into culture – into the specificities of any historical moment – as a viable subject. Anxiety we might say, is the story the body tells about the experience of inhabiting a historical moment. Anxiety is distinguished by this fact, a far cry from those assessments which position it as a response to a perceived threat to the stability of identity.[2]

Kleinian anxiety

If anxiety is to live in 'history', to be riven by anxiety is yet to 'be'. In order to unravel such a proposition in the context of the neo-femme fatale, I turn here to the psychoanalytic theories of Melanie Klein. For Klein, psychic life begins in anxiety. The 'self' originates in anticipation of a violent retribution for an inner destructiveness – instinctual impulses directed against the human organism itself – first projected on to objects in the external world. Anxiety refers to the terror associated with the effects of the death-drive. The death-drive is projected on to an external world and the presence of the 'bad', persecuting object in that world is the first step towards a meaningful relation with it. Only once that external 'threat' is internalised is it felt as anxiety (in defence, the ego splits again into 'good' and 'bad' parts, multiplying 'danger' so as to assuage it and so mobilising anxiety in the act of self-preservation).[3] Thus inner world and external reality are uniquely linked by anxiety, and the peculiar temporal structure of repetition and retrospect anxiety involves. I do not intend here, however, to trace in great detail the development of Klein's theory of anxiety or the various forms anxiety takes (paranoid-schizoid or depressive, for example). Rather, I shall interrogate further anxiety's place at the intersection between psyche and history by telling a brief tale of anxiety's emergence at a time of real, historical unease.

In 1940, at the height of the Blitz, Klein left London for the relative safety of Pitlochry, a small Scottish town. For four months during 1941, she analysed ten-year-old 'Richard', a boy so impeded by anxiety that he was barely able to go outside or attend school, 'afraid that they [other children] would all turn on him' (Klein 1998: 103). In Klein's analytic playroom, Richard gave expression to the anxieties that inhibited him in daily life: that Hitler would invade and occupy Britain, that he or his mother would be poisoned, that Klein may be bombed or else a Nazi, and that other children would attack him. In so doing, he demonstrated a comprehensive knowledge of the personalities and developments of the war, a 'lively interest in every detail of the war situation' (Klein 1998: 100). It is difficult to ignore the mark of the war in the dramas of Richard's unconscious life, *the presence of a terrifying historical reality in his inner world*.

This is perhaps unsurprising given the 'backdrop of a particularly tense period of the war' (the Blitz, the fall of Athens, the invasion of Russia, and 'the bizarre appearance of Hess near Glasgow') during which Richard's brother was called up and his house in London bombed (Grosskurth 1986: 266). But Klein was not interested in history and virtually denied that Richard's 'problems might be linked to anxieties about the war' (Jacobus 1996: 176). Instead, she sought out his unconscious phantasies, those 'infantile anxiety situations' – scenarios of assault, retribution, loss and defence – through which the child experienced the world and his relationship with it.[4] 'German destroyers stood for Mummy's babies, whom he felt he had attacked … and therefore … expected … to be hostile to him' (Klein 1998: 86). Not battleships, but babies – it is the internal war that interests Klein (the real war merely confirms or exacerbates the anxiety already inside Richard's mind). Klein sees anxiety not as the consequence of a dangerous world, but of the destructive instincts projected outwards.

I am not proposing to 'apply' Klein's theories of anxiety to an analysis of the neo-femme fatale. Rather my aim is to ask what might be the value of a psychoanalysis that sees the external world – a social and political world involving hatred, aggression and mass murder – only in terms of its significance in phantasy, in the child's unconscious? My answer is that this apparently short-sighted psychoanalysis in fact reveals a profound connection between what happens in the real world and what goes on in unconscious phantasy. There may be no way of making intelligible 'the events of war (reality)' beyond 'the psychic meanings of war – of what it might mean to have a Hitler inside your head' (Stonebridge 1998a: 143). This has important consequences for our understanding of the inner world as political. When Klein uncovers the realities of aggression within the inner world, she *makes the real enemy inconceivable outside of a recognition of the aggressor within*. This is the legacy of Kleinian anxiety: the *historical reality* of the destructive impulses in the mind. Unmasking the 'historicism' of destructive phantasy is not therefore to deny the reality of Hitler and the atrocities of war, but rather to illuminate our deepest implication in the very acts of cruelty we may ourselves condemn or suffer.

Looking to Klein for an account of wartime anxiety, we find that a wish for violence is the key to the internal experience of a social or historical reality that puts you at risk. As such, the relationship between the self (the internal dimensions of experience and 'being') and the world (the external dimensions of space and time, 'being' in history and culture) is enabled and sustained by anxiety. Anxiety is the glue that holds you together (you are constituted by the same thing that tears you apart). As Stonebridge puts it, the story of anxiety is a story of survival: Klein 'turn[s] anxiety into a form of possibility' (1998b: 200). It is the story of a self that owns its potential for violence and violation, to be aggressive and to experience aggression, as a means of being in the world.

Gendering anxiety

The Last Seduction, Crush and In the Cut gender this new narrative of anxiety. Each uses the femme fatale as the emblem of anxiety and, in this way, as shorthand for a male fantasy of female violence in which women must trade (which they may adopt) in their search for sexual and subjective autonomy. Take The Last Seduction, in which Bridget deploys feminist discourses of male violence against women to ensure the success of her violent actions against men (she masquerades as a rape victim, claims she is a battered wife, and uses a can of mace to suffocate her husband, Clay (Bill Pullman)) (see Read 2000: 164–5). This fantasy of the violence women's sexual and economic independence does to men is re-presented as a 'feminist' empowerment in a world dominated by men's violence against women. In a world that assures women's victimisation and is invested deeply in fantasies of their violence, the femme fatale's potential for aggression articulates one means of survival.

Crush inflects the problem slightly differently, appropriating the commercial viability of images of women's violence to expose the terrible violations to female subjectivity that claims for women's agency may ultimately involve. Angela Iseman (Caitlin Bossley) interprets Lane's seduction of Colin (Angela's father) as a betrayal of the bonds of friendship and coaches Christina to take revenge on Lane. From this perspective, Christina kills Lane as retribution for the power and pleasures of an active, transgressive female sexuality. This neo-femme fatale is punished not because she poses a threat to men, but because she exposes the links between sexuality and violence that unsettle the bonds of friendship between women. In this way, Crush vividly captures the contradictions of anxiety, invoking the power of destructiveness specifically as a means of 'being' and desiring for women.

In the Cut crystallises the mode of anxiety that The Last Seduction and Crush map out. Relying on the conventions of the feminist detective story, the investigation pivots on the issue of women's sexual pleasures amid the prevalence of male violence against women. As a consequence, the more usual narrative functions are contorted and the distinction between activity and passivity for women rendered unstable. Frannie is positioned as investigative agent, potential victim and fatal woman. She is a suspect who asks all the questions; she is stalked and held at knifepoint; and she shoots to kill. In circumstances that cast women as victims of male violence this film asks, how can they become agents of their own sexuality? The answer is that women's desires

Agency and violence: *In the Cut*

and their access to subjective agency are necessarily (constitutionally) bound up with violence – with their relationship to male violence and to patriarchal fantasies of women's violence. Violence for women becomes not a means to power, but a structure through which they are enabled to voice their pleasures and their selves. When Malloy first attempts to seduce Frannie in the bar, the camera maps out the visual vocabulary of her passivity, foregrounding her (awkward) pleasure in it. At the same time, Frannie's question about the water pistol ironically invokes castration anxiety, cutting off Malloy's protestations of phallic sexual authority (I'll 'fuck you' but 'won't ... beat you up'). Together with the nuanced performances, the camera-work combines with this ironic dialogue to illuminate a profound indistinction between activity and passivity for women in matters of desire, focusing on the pleasures involved and the risks posed.

This ambivalence is repeatedly worked through Frannie's use of sexual speech. Like Bridget, she 'flouts the status quo through excess in language ... embrace[s] the explicit and forbidden' (Stables 1998: 175). An English teacher and academic, Frannie is researching a book on language, its 'regionalisms' and 'dialects'. She records words and phrases in a notebook, especially the sexual slang of the male streets. 'Slang is either sexual or violent ... but I think it's ... really witty,' Frannie confesses. 'Virginia' means vagina, 'as in "he penetrated her Virginia with a hammer"', she explains in the opening shot. Women's relationship to sexual speech opens up to question the violence of language and its power to violate. Frannie's silent pleasure in men's use of (violent) sexual slang is placed in full view, shots repeatedly lingering on her quivering mouth as she surrenders to the erotic promise of fantasy violations. At stake here is less the woman's castrating sexual speech, more her articulation of autonomy within the vocabularies of sexual violence and aggression.

In their diverse revisions of the femme fatale, all three films reposition anxiety at the heart of contemporary dilemmas of female subjectivity and desire. Without question, they are ambivalent in their relation to any kind of feminist politics. They invite a subtle rethinking of anxiety that is in contrast to 'symptomatic' interpretations in which male subjectivity takes centre-stage and where anxiety is taken to articulate the power of external dangers to compromise – to terrorise – the viability of any self. Instead of interpreting anxiety as a feeling or psychological state belonging to a particular person (or group) and arising from a perceived threat, we are talking here of anxiety as a mark of the contradictions entailed in 'being' simultaneously in historical and psychical worlds. As gendered articulations of the problem, The Last Seduction, Crush and In The Cut present the neo-femme fatale as a cipher for the specific contradictions involved for women inhabiting a post-feminist moment in which male violence prevails and yet fantasies of female violence (as well as sexual and economic autonomy) abound. What we are seeing, therefore, in these generic reworkings of anxiety is a kind of exposure or elaboration of these complexities, of the conditions under which a historical reality of violence is lived psychically.

My reading of Klein has qualified anxiety in at least one additional way crucial to this gendering. If the dangers of the external world originate on the inside, then as a consequence they are experienced internally not as risk but in terms of a need for violence. The distinction between aggressor and victim is never a fixed thing in the unconscious. This is anxiety's terrain, the perpetual oscillation between owning and fearing the prospect of destruction, and this as the condition of possibility of 'being' at all. Such Kleinian anxiety is at the heart of all three films discussed above: each problematises any easy assumption of an autonomy of identity for women, suggesting instead that anxiety is constitutional for women, the paradoxical risk of destruction (to destroy and yet to be destroyed) that is their condition of possibility. A politicised analysis of noir's new forms which engages psychoanalysis, but is not limited to a 'symptomatic' approach, should be interested in anxiety for this reason alone.

NOTES

1   Vivian Sobchack has similar interests in the 'embodied and radically material' nature of the film experience (2004: 1), but these are driven by a concern with the processes of cinematic identification and meaning-making, 'the sense and sensibility', as she puts it, 'of materiality' (2004: 65).

2   Freud later rejected this theory of anxiety as an effect of the transformation of libido (see Freud 1979). This was largely to realign his work within the framework of the

second topography (see Stonebridge 1998b: 193). Here, however, I retain the earlier sense because of its emphasis on the place of anxiety in the acculturation of unruly bodies, and with the experience of 'being' in both psyche and history, inner and outer worlds.

3   In her pioneering analyses of young children, Klein established the pivotal role of anxiety in both psychotic illness and normal development. My summary of the relations between the death-drive, projection and splitting are at the heart of her intervention. Key short works in which these issues are addressed include: 'Infantile anxiety situations reflected in a work of art and in the creative impulse' (1929), 'Mourning and its relation to manic-depressive states' (1940) and 'Notes on some schizoid mechanisms' (1946).

4   The spelling of phantasy with a *ph* is Klein's and is used mainly to distinguish the properties of *unconscious* phantasy from more generalised understandings of 'fantasy' (for example, as daydreaming).

REFERENCES

Cowie, Elizabeth (1998) '*Film noir* and women', in Joan Copjec (ed.) *Shades of Noir*. New York: Verso, 121–65.

Doane, Mary Ann (1991) *Femmes Fatales: Feminism, Film Theory, Psychoanalysis*. London: Routledge.

Freud, Sigmund (1979 [1925]) 'Inhibitions, symptoms and anxiety', in *On Psychopathology*, trans. James Strachey. Penguin Freud Library Volume 10. Harmondsworth: Penguin, 229–333.

____ (1990 [1909]) 'Analysis of a phobia in a five-year-old boy – "Little Hans"', in *Case Histories I*, trans. Alix Strachey and James Strachey. Penguin Freud Library Volume 8. Harmondsworth: Penguin, 165–305.

____ (1991a [1915]) 'Repression', in *On Metapsychology*, trans. James Strachey. Penguin Freud Library Volume 11. Harmondsworth: Penguin, 139–58.

____ (1991b [1915]) 'The Unconscious', in *On Metapsychology*, trans. James Strachey. Penguin Freud Library Volume 11. Harmondsworth: Penguin, 159–222.

____ (1991c [1899]) *The Interpretation of Dreams*, trans. James Strachey. Penguin Freud Library Volume 4. Harmondsworth: Penguin

Freud, Sigmund and Joseph Breuer (2004) *Studies in Hysteria*, trans. Nicola Luckhurst. London: Penguin.

Grosskurth, Phyllis (1986) *Melanie Klein: Her World and her Work*. London: Jason Aronson.

Hayward, Susan (1996) *Key Concepts in Cinema Studies*. London: Routledge.

Hollinger, Karen (1998) *In the Company of Women: Contemporary Female Friendship Films*. London: University of Minnesota Press.

Jacobus, Mary (1996) *First Things: The Maternal Imaginary in Literature, Art and Psychoa-nalysis*. London: Routledge.

Johnston, Clare (1998 [1978]) '*Double Indemnity*', in E. Ann Kaplan (ed.) *Women in Film Noir*. New Edition. London: British Film Institute, 89–98.

Kaplan, E. Ann (1998) 'Introduction to new edition', in E. Ann Kaplan (ed.) *Women in Film Noir*. New Edition. London: British Film Institute, 1–14.

Klein, Melanie (1986 [1929]) 'Infantile anxiety situations reflected in a work of art and in the creative impulse', in Juliet Mitchell (ed.) *The Selected Melanie Klein*. Harmonds-worth: Penguin, 84–94.

____ (1986 [1940]) 'Mourning and its relation to manic-depressive states', in Juliet Mitch-ell (ed.) *The Selected Melanie Klein*. Harmondsworth: Penguin, 146–74.

____ (1986 [1946]) 'Notes on some schizoid mechanisms', in Juliet Mitchell (ed.) *The Selected Melanie Klein*. Harmondsworth: Penguin, 175–200.

____ (1998) *Narrative of a Child Analysis: The Conduct of the Psycho-analysis of Children as Seen in the Treatment of a Ten-year Old Boy*. London: Vintage.

Krutnik, Frank (1991) *In a Lonely Street: Film Noir, Genre, Masculinity*. London: Routledge.

Laplanche, Jean and Jean-Bertrand Pontalis (1988) *The Language of Psychoanalysis*. Lon-don: Hogarth.

Maxfield, James F. (1996) *The Fatal Woman: Sources of Male Anxiety in American Film Noir 1941–1991*. Madison: Farleigh Dickinson University Press.

Mulvey, Laura (1988 [1975]) 'Visual pleasure and narrative cinema', in Constance Penley (ed.) *Feminism and Film Theory*. London: British Film Institute, 57–68.

Oliver, Kelly and Benigno Trigo (2003) *Noir Anxiety*. Minneapolis: University of Minnesota Press.

Place, Janey (1998 [1978]) 'Women in film noir', in E. Ann Kaplan (ed.) *Women in Film Noir*. New Edition. London: British Film Institute, 47–68.

Read, Jacinda (2000) *The New Avengers: Feminism, Femininity and the Rape-revenge Cycle*. Manchester: Manchester University Press.

Robson, Jocelyn and Beverley Zalcock (1997) *Girls' Own Stories: Australian and New Zealand Women's Films*. London: Scarlet Press.

Sobchack, Vivian (2004) *Carnal Thoughts: Embodiment and Moving Image Culture*. Lon-don: University of California Press.

Stables, Kate (1998) 'The postmodern always rings twice: Constructing the femme fatale in 90s cinema', in E. Ann Kaplan (ed.) *Women in Film Noir*. New Edition. London: Brit-ish Film Institute, 164–82.

Stonebridge, Lyndsey (1998a) *The Destructive Element: British Psychoanalysis and Mod-ernism*. London: Macmillan.

____ (1998b) 'Anxiety in Klein: The missing witch's letter', in Lyndsey Stonebridge and John Phillips (eds) *Reading Melanie Klein*. London: Routledge, 190–202.

Thomas, Deborah (1992) 'How Hollywood deals with the deviant male', in Ian Cameron (ed.) *The Movie Book of Film Noir*. London: Studio Vista, 59–70.

Thornham, Sue (2007) '"Starting to feel like a chick": Re-visioning romance in *In the Cut*', *Feminist Media Studies*, 7, 1, 33–46.

Williams, Linda Ruth (2005) *The Erotic Thriller in Contemporary Cinema*. Edinburgh: Edinburgh University Press.

14

The Thin Men: Anorexic Subjectivity in *Fight Club* and *The Machinist*

SHERRYL VINT AND MARK BOULD

'It all started with a girl', states the Narrator (Edward Norton) of *Fight Club* (1999), immediately positioning us in the world of noir, where men struggle to maintain a sense of integrity against their desires. In this case, however, what starts with a girl is not the usual tale of seduction and crime, but the creation of the eponymous all-male society which eventually becomes the anarchist Project Mayhem. Rallying behind Tyler Durden (Brad Pitt), they reject the 'IKEA nesting instinct' in order to embrace the supposedly real masculinity of living for the moment. Rage and rigid discipline transform the alienation of 'working at jobs we hate so we can buy things we don't need' into violent pranks targeted against corporations and their elites. Trevor Reznik (Christian Bale), the protagonist of *The Machinist* (2004), likewise alienated, exists in a zombie-like insomniac state. Not having slept for a year, he is physically – and socially – wasting away, with no life outside of work other than regular visits to a prostitute, Stevie (Jennifer Jason Leigh), and nocturnal trips to an airport coffee shop. While *Fight Club*'s characters suffer from a profusion of consumer commodities, Trevor's life is limited to bare necessities, which he needs to remind himself to replace. He meticulously, compulsively, bleaches and scrubs his small, rented apartment, while Narrator, after the destruction of his artfully-arranged condo, squats in a rambling derelict townhouse. Living among the detritus of the modern city, both protagonists occupy a noir terrain composed of anxieties about masculine impotence, loss of control and the alienating effects of life under consumer capitalism.

Firmly in the tradition of the noir 'tough' thriller, which reveals 'an obsession with male figures who are both internally divided and alienated from the culturally permissible (or ideal) parameters of masculine identity, desire and achievement' (Krutnik 1991: xiii), each film visualises this division: Narrator finally realises that Tyler, the friend who made his transformation possible, is really his own alter ego; and Trevor, who thinks he is being framed by Ivan (John Sharian), eventually works out that his tormentor is a hallucination generated by his suppressed memories of a hit-and-run accident. These split selves connect *Fight Club* and *The Machinist* to such film noirs as *Stranger on the Third Floor* (1940), *Phantom Lady* (1944) and *Dead Reckoning* (1947), whose plots are driven by ambiguous or mistaken identity and split personalities and which also feature expressionist or surreal dream sequences or other visual effects to represent the subjective and often frightening world in which the protagonist attempts to resolve his confusion about his own or others' identities. Narrator and Trevor can also be described in terms of the 'fragmented' *roman noir* protagonist, who is 'tormented by emasculating landscapes of frustration and paranoia' and whose desire is so bound up with self-destructiveness that he can either 'continue to pursue his desire until he enacts an inevitable self-annihilation, or … embrace the zero degree and trade in self-annihilation for self-erasure' (Metress 1994: 155–6, 182). While film noir's exaggerated *mise-en-scène* lent substance to the protagonist's paranoia and alienation, the development of a neo-noir fantasy tradition (and new special effects technologies) has made the noir world increasingly malleable, as in *Fight Club* and *The Machinist*, allowing the fantastic energies which drive consumer capitalism – and its 'emasculating landscapes' – to take on lively form.[1]

In both of these films, the desire against which the protagonist must maintain his integrity is represented not by dangerous women but by his relationship to his own body. Trevor has become so emaciated that Stevie tells him, 'If you were any thinner, you wouldn't exist.' Throughout *Fight Club*, Tyler, who destroyed all the possessions through which Narrator anchored his sense of self, repeatedly displaces Narrator, taking over his body when he sleeps. In both films, fragmented masculinity is displayed through damaged bodies. Narrator and Tyler often appear with bruises and other injuries, although Tyler also appears shirtless in a number of scenes, emphasising his muscled torso and abdomen and indicating the film's ambivalent relationship to its own critique of consumer culture, condemning it while also indulging in Pitt's commodity-identity. In contrast, *The Machinist*'s lingering views of Trevor's skeletal form achieve several moments of genuine horror. In one scene, turning sideways to the camera, he almost does disappear from view, and in another, shot from above, his ribcage and vertebrae are visible through tissue-thin skin. Although Trevor's weight-loss is not a deliberate project, the visual effect (and knowledge that the six-foot Bale achieved this state, dropping a third of his body weight from 180 to 120 pounds) makes him appear anorexic.[2] This essay contends that while *Fight Club*'s and *The Machinist*'s damaged protagonists are not anorexic per se, they are best understood as anorexic subjects, struggling to express – and survive – alienation through regimes of self-restraint.

Anorexia is a disease of self-starvation commonly associated with discourses about fashion and unreasonable standards for slenderness expected of young *women*. It typically, but not exclusively, afflicts adolescent, middle-class, white women in the West, yet its origins are more complicated and overdetermined than simply the slender ideal of feminine beauty. Susie Orbach (1978), Susan Bordo (1990, 1993) and Caroline Walker Bynum (1988) find in anorexia a protest against the restrictions of traditional feminine roles because self-starvation produces an androgynous body (erasing the traits of secondary feminine sexuality, such as menses and breast development) and often allows the anorexic to avoid, through illness, patriarchal institutions such as marriage. It is a way of exerting control in one part of life so as to compensate for a lack of control in others, a 'preoccupation with the "internal" management of the body (i.e., management of its desires) ... produced by instabilities in the "macro-regulation" of desire within the system of the social body' (Bordo 1990: 96). Thus, anorexia is also typically connected to a struggle between desire and will, the experience of which is often characterised by a split self, with eating 'construed as a bodily desire entirely alien to the mind/self' (Malson 1998: 125).

Given that the vast majority of anorexics are white women and that there is an increased incidence of anorexia among non-white young women as they are assimilated into Western consumer society, Vincenzo DiNicola argues that the disorder is best understood as 'a *culture-bound syndrome* of technologically-developed affluent Western societies' (1990a: 166; emphasis in original).[3] Greta Olson (2000) points out that anorexia is most prevalent in Western industrialised societies in which there is an overabundance of food combined with an ideal of the disciplined body that belies this excess, suggesting that one of the factors producing anorexia is a disavowed cultural anxiety about overconsumption. Bryan S. Turner specifically links this discomfort to issues of control, suggesting that 'the practices of restraint and dietary management' help subjects negotiate the contradictions between mass consumption and an ideal of thinness (1987: 104).[4] Maria Selvini Palazzoli argues that the contradictory demands of consumer culture simultaneously require continual spending *and* self-disciplined subjects who will submit to capital's demands for labour-power, and that this contradiction prescribes 'an inverse relationship between abundance of goods and body weight' (1985: 201). Similarly, Bordo argues anorexia manifests the pressure to balance producer-selves, 'capable of sublimating, delaying, repressing desires for immediate gratification' in favour of a work ethic, and consumer-selves, whose 'boundless capacity to capitulate to desire and indulge in impulse' capitalism equally requires (1990: 96).

Bordo also considers the tension between appetite and control in relation to gender. In Western culture, we are continually inundated with invitations to consume products, including food, but paradoxically the terms 'control' and 'mastery' are frequently posited as features of these products that we should desire, as well as qualities we can gain for ourselves by buying commodities (see 1993: 105). The contradictory relationship to consumption and self-discipline that Palazzoli argues capitalist culture produces in us is continually enacted by advertising. As Bordo notes, women are called to control and master their bodies and their appetites, while advertisements directed at men tend to emphasise control and mastery over others. Even when men are hailed by a discourse of body-management, this address tends to appeal to body-building or similar activities which link such discipline to empowering the body and the social self. The traditional connection of women with embodiment reinforces the gendered nature of anorexia. The incidence of male anorexia, although increasing, remains relatively low, and the gendered discourse of embodiment means that in such instances it is experienced as an emasculating or feminising trajectory. Unlike women, who lose negatively-constructed gender specificity and perhaps escape unwelcome roles in patriarchal culture, male anorexics lose the power and privilege associated with the strong male body. In a sexist context, a move towards androgyny tends to register as a gain for women and a loss for men. Bordo's analysis allows us to see that the entrenchment of anorexia in consumer culture is an indicator of its gender specificity.

Without wishing to detract from the lived experience of individual anorexics and their families, cultural critics suggest that eating disorders should not be understood exclusively as an individual pathology: '"anorexia" is expressive of cultural concerns as well as personal predicaments' (Malson 1998: 99). At the same time, however, it is important to remember that reading anorexia as an expression of cultural pathology does not deny its simultaneous existence as an illness that causes suffering for many individual anorexics and their families. Its overdetermined meanings allow us to see anorexia as a social pathology of control and consumption that afflicts feminised subjects in affluent Western society. Such extreme behaviour needs also to be read as an indictment of the conditions of life that produce a subject whose only option for autonomy seems to be starvation. The tensions and contradictions in trying to simultaneously see anorexia as both an expression of cultural pathology and an illness with individual sufferers is the reality of its material existence as a socially- and culturally-specific disease.

In this essay, we argue that this understanding of anorexia as a cultural pathology provides a useful framework for thinking about the protagonists' struggles with control and desire in *Fight Club* and *The Machinist*. Drawing on Pierre Macherey's theory of the symptomatic reading of a text, we argue that the concept of the anorexic subject is a way to read these protagonists' damaged bodies as indicative of something beyond personal pathology. Macherey suggests that literature itself has an unconscious, that it reveals inconsistencies and sites of social struggle over meaning in the culture from which it emerges.

In its telling of a story within a specific cultural setting, a text unintentionally reveals through its gaps and unresolved moments the symptoms of its culture's social pathologies. Macherey calls these revelations 'what it is *compelled* to say in order to say what it *wants* to say' (1978: 94; emphasis in original). *Fight Club* and *The Machinist* reveal the problems of alienated labour in consumer culture through the symptom of the anorexic subject.

The anorexic's battle to repress desire and maintain control over some aspect of life is, structurally, remarkably similar to the noir protagonist's struggle with threatened masculinity. While Trevor's condition in *The Machinist* can thus be seen as a manifestation of fears of emasculation and loss of control, it can also be connected to the idea of anorexia as a disease of affluent, industrialised societies. Understanding anorexia as a symptom of the contradictions and sociopathology of consumer culture also connects the anorexic 'protest' to *Fight Club*'s rejection of materialism. In a world in which food advertising stresses not nutritional benefits but consumption for entertainment (see Bordo 1993), the anorexic denial of a 'natural' need exemplifies our alienation from the body when 'we no longer consume commodities to satisfy relatively stable and specific needs, but to reconstruct ourselves in terms of the lifestyle associated with the consumption of certain commodities' (Lowe 1995: 47). Both films address the alienation which separates the worker from the product of his or her labour and thus from his or her own body.[5]

Fight Club

At the beginning of *Fight Club*, Narrator struggles to find meaning in life by going to a series of self-help groups for survivors of various illnesses: blood parasites, tuberculosis, lymphoma. In the testicular cancer support group, he finds himself comforted between the huge breasts of Robert Paulson (Meat Loaf Aday), a former bodybuilder whose cancer stemmed from steroid abuse and whose hormone treatment has resulted in mammary enlargement. Scenes of this group demonstrate, with equal hamfistedness, that masculinity is under threat: men cry and hug one another, insist they 'are still men'; one laments his lack of children while describing the birth of his ex-wife's child by her new husband. This threat is made all the more noirish by the appearance of Marla Singer (Helena Bonham Carter). Dressed like a femme fatale and accessorised with the obligatory cigarette and linguistic mastery, she, like Narrator, is 'a tourist', not ill but craving the intense, if utterly banal, emotional experience the self-help groups provide. Narrator demands that she leave the groups because her presence keeps him from getting his fix, only to be cut down to size by her potently dismissive, 'I saw you practicing this.' She argues that she is 'technically' more qualified to attend the testicular cancer meeting as, she mocks, 'You still have your balls.'

Shortly after, Narrator 'meets' Tyler and is educated in the rejection of consumer culture, finding solace through physical violence rather than the vaguely empathetic shedding of tears. Narrator's need for *something* is straightforwardly connected to the alienation of life under capitalism. In a business meeting, a manager explains, 'Efficiency is priority #1 ... because waste is a thief,' pointing to the standard practices of maximising surplus-value (profit) by rationalising and intensifying labour, turning the worker into little more than a machine stripped of his or her own desires, creativity and selfhood. Narrator's job makes brutally clear capital's dehumanising imperative: he calculates the feasibility of recalling fatally defective automobiles, weighing projected recall costs against the anticipated costs of lawsuits. Humans, whether as workers or consumers, are reduced to calculations about profitability. It is, therefore, an absurd extension of this logic, if not exactly revolutionary, for Tyler to steal human fat from a liposuction clinic to make boutique soap, to sell 'rich women their own fat asses back to them'.

One of the main targets of Tyler's rebellion against the given order is advertising, a system he accuses of producing 'an entire generation pumping gas, waiting tables' in order to afford commodities that are merely wanted, not needed, and which are then used as a means of self-definition. Initially, Narrator does not seem to feel alienated from a life in which his identity is generated through the commodities he works to purchase, exemplified in the famous shot which converts his condo into a catalogue page, proudly labelling and pricing all the objects on display. It is soon clear, however, that he does not have the upper hand in his relationship to these commodities, but is instead driven by a compulsive urge to consume, neatly captured when he orders things from the IKEA catalogue while sat on the toilet. Clearly a joke about masturbation, this scene further suggests a confusion of appetites (for food, for commodities). It suggests the inevitable disappointments of social relations under consumer capitalism which encourage us to believe that a commodity can give us love or friendship or self-worth. But in the end commodities are only things, all of which sooner or later turn to shit. Narrator thus epitomises Theodor Adorno and Max Horkheimer's grim conclusion that under capitalism 'the most intimate reactions of human beings have been so thoroughly reified' that 'personality scarcely signifies anything more than shining white teeth and freedom from body odour and emotions' (1997: 167).

Advertising – both for food, which encourages us to eat more and other than is nutritionally sound, and for fashion, which features unrealistically thin models – is often blamed for the prevalence of anorexia. Bordo notes the contradictions of late capitalism evident in advertising which juxtaposes images of 'luscious foods' with 'exercise equipment' (1990: 97). Donald M. Lowe argues that fashion advertising featuring clothes that do not look good on any 'normal' body produces anorexia nervosa as 'much less a psychopathology, than a late-capitalist sociopathology' (1995: 166) and Olson points out that capitalism benefits from the double-bind of diet and indulgence advertising encourages, selling fattening fast food to the poor and expensive diet 'solutions' to the rich (see 2000: 79). A similar pattern of desire, indulgence, constraint and control is expressed by Tyler's frustration with his and other men's economic position. They have not become the 'millionaires and movie gods and rock stars' television led them to believe they would be, but instead are trapped in dead-end jobs, unable to afford many of the commodities they desire. The destruction of Narrator's condo can be seen as a rejection of the logic of accumulation and the reduction of human worth to economics. He recognises the poverty of his former existence, when he felt 'close to being complete' through knowing that 'whatever else happens, I've got that sofa problem handled'. However, this rejection of consumer goods seems less a heroic resistance to capitalism and more the desperate control of the anorexic subject who cannot manage desire and appetite within constraints and thus gives up on consumption altogether. Project Mayhem's supposedly revolutionary rhetoric begins to sound more like the sour grapes of those who have not risen as high within the system as they desired. Their culminating plan to destroy the headquarters of credit card companies, erasing their records so that 'we all go back to zero', suggests that they do not want to replace the system but to restart it with their chances of success restored.[6]

Narrator tells us that they did not invent the anxiety expressed in the fight clubs: 'Tyler and I just made it visible.' This concern with 'making visible' is also invoked in the film itself: as a projectionist, Tyler splices pornographic frames into family films; *Fight Club* does something similar, not only including such a frame in its closing moments, but also inserting flashes of Tyler during early scenes in which Narrator is struggling with insomnia. In part, this technique draws attention to the noir protagonist's subjective construction of reality. The film's critique of commodity culture also connects such fantastical elements to the inherently paranoid experience of life under capitalism (see Bould 2002), a world of commodity fetishism in which 'the commodity reflects the social characteristics of men's own labour as objective characteristics of the products of labour themselves' (Marx 1976: 164–5) and thus objects 'appear as autonomous figures endowed with a life of their own, which enter into relations both with each other and with the human race' (1976: 165). The fantastic mode of *Fight Club*, in which Tyler and Narrator exist as separately embodied people for most of the film, is another 'making visible' – of the divided subjectivities required by capital.

Lowe argues that the relative liveliness of commodities compared to humans in late capitalism has less to do with the uncanny animation of commodities than with the ways that we have been alienated from our bodies and turned into commodities whose desires are manufactured for us: we 'are

Commodity torso: *Fight Club*

accordingly less "alive", since our feelings are instigated by the signs of social, cultural values, and our needs repackaged by changing product characteristics' (1995: 73). Tyler's rage against advertising seems to point towards a similar critique of its alienating effects. Fearing a future of 'Microsoft Galaxy' and 'Planet Starbucks', Tyler's followers rebel against wage-labour drudgery, subverting their roles so as to further Project Mayhem and trying to develop some kind of life in which only 'authentic' needs are indulged, thus revealing the naïveté of their project, which fails to recognise that something as common-sense-seeming as needs are in fact complex, relative, social constructions. Likewise, the film's own ability to enact such a critique is, despite Tyler's rhetoric, limited by its status and circulation as a commodity. It induces desire within its audience, indulging our appetite for performative masculinity through the display of Brad Pitt's ripped abs and for the very commodities it takes such delight in blowing up. Although the protagonists aspire to the control of the anorexic subject, this is undermined by their affective investment in commodities, which is shared by the film itself and its audience. Bordo argues that, while 'a slender body may be attainable through hard work', the true sign of adequacy suggested by many diet food advertisements is 'a "cool" relation to food' (1993: 103). *Fight Club* fails to attain this cool relation to commodities, too often making visible its hunger for them.

The Machinist

For all its failures as a critique of consumer capitalism, *Fight Club* does represent capital's indifference to human life and the sociopathology – and need for solace – it produces, and arguably the film itself is a form of fantastic consolation for its viewers. Moreover, it offers a depiction of criminal, perhaps even 'terrorist', deviance as one of the ways that the dispossessed (albeit straight(ish) middle-class white men) attempt to resist capital's colonisation of their lives. Turner argues that sickness can also function as a deliberate resistance to the demands of the working world and that it is important to 'compare and contrast sickness and crime as two forms of deviance' (1987: 216) because they imply opposite relationships to the concept of responsibility and thus represent less and more direct ways of confronting power. Crime tends to be defined by legal concepts of intention, implying culpability as one understands and chooses one's actions (as in Project Mayhem's vandalism). In contrast,

> the sick role legitimises deviant behaviour by removing responsibility, since within the medical view one does not in fact choose to be sick in the same way that one might choose to commit a crime. However, sickness legitimises withdrawal from everyday expectations only on the assumption that sickness will be a short episode of behaviour under the regulation of a doctor. (Turner 1987: 216)

In *The Machinist*, Trevor's insomnia and emaciation can also be seen as resistance to the alienation of life and labour under late capitalism. The film slowly uncovers the mystery of his guilt and charts his willingness to accept responsibility for his actions as he moves beyond sickness to submit himself to the judicial system in a conclusion that is represented as the achievement of justice.

Narratively and stylistically, *The Machinist* is a more conventionally noir film than *Fight Club*, a thriller about escalating paranoia in which the protagonist eventually realises that the mysterious other he pursues or is pursued by is really an externalised projection of some aspect of his own self.[7] It opens with Trevor apparently dumping a corpse in the sea, only for the rug in which it is wrapped to catch on something and unroll down the concrete slipway. The image is dark and filled with shadows, the music ominous, the camera angles low. The camera cuts to Trevor's distressed – and haggard[8] – face before we can see the body spill out. At the end of the film, we return to this scene and, this time, we see the rug unroll to reveal its emptiness rather than Ivan's corpse. This moment confirms the viewer's suspicion that Ivan, Trevor's tormentor, is a hallucination generated by his suppression of the memory of killing a child.

The Machinist's extraordinarily trite conclusion blights its potentially radical critique, reducing Trevor's paranoid reading of reality to personal pathology and implying that order might be restored by individual recognition of guilt.[9] What is most intriguing about this film is that for most of its duration it appears to be about something quite different, namely, Trevor's struggle with the alienating and physically dangerous environment of late-capitalist manual labour. Trevor is a machinist at National Machine, a plant whose product is never revealed. In the first scene set there, the supervisor, Tucker (Craig Stevenson), berates someone for turning off a machine during maintenance because powering it up again afterwards takes too long: 'Where am I going to make up that seven minutes?' he demands. 'Your pay check?' Trevor intervenes, pointing out that safety regulations mean employees cannot be penalised in this way, prompting

Tucker to put him on his 'shit-list'. The prioritisation of productivity and thus of surplus-value is held only slightly in check by the flimsy mechanisms of union representation and safety regulations, both of which Trevor's superiors characterise as emasculating, while the depiction of the plant stresses the need for the workers to accommodate themselves to the relentless pace at which the machines perform their repetitive tasks. The machines, like the emaciated Trevor, are angular, sharp-edged. Brutally industrial, they contrast with the fleshy vulnerability of workers' bodies.

Film noirs such as *Double Indemnity* (1944), *Force of Evil* (1948) and *Pitfall* (1948) articulate an anxiety concerning the disappearance of independent businesses as corporate capital consolidated, resulting in subordinate rather than autonomous roles for most men within the workforce. Likewise, *The Machinist* highlights labour conditions, albeit blue- rather than white-collar, in the increasingly automated workplace. As Lowe argues, the changed nature of labour, including office labour with computers, has resulted in a 'systematic equivalence between humans and machines [which] has yielded a new science – ergonomics or human factors engineering. Ergonomists design systems which include and take into account the necessarily slower and less reliable human responses within them' (1995: 11). The overall trajectory of this science, however, is to adjust humans to fit the machines, to maximise the extraction of surplus-value, rendering the production process itself a struggle between capital and labour for ownership and control of the worker's body. This struggle is typically asymmetrical, as Trevor's several run-ins with his managers demonstrate, with the isolated worker's relative lack of power analogous to that of a child trying to negotiate with parents who always have the final say, even if their decisions are arbitrary and unjustified. Orbach (1978), Kim Chernin (1985) and Helen Gremillion (2003) read anorexia, a disease which emerges during adolescence, as a form of speech, a protest that young women make against their powerlessness through their bodies.[10] Trevor's starvation can be understood in a similar way.

Through workplace conflicts, *The Machinist* articulates anxieties about white men's growing marginalisation within the context of automation and the deskilling of labour (often accompanied in the real world by their displacement by non-white men and women, who are typically paid less). Over the past thirty years, the erosion of labour conditions so as to increase profitability has become normalised, with the threat of unemployment used to discipline the labour force: 'A Congressional study in 1986 reported that it was not the rise of single-parent households, but unemployment and falling wages that mostly accounted for the seven million increase in the number of poor Americans since 1979' (Lowe 1995: 27). Furthermore, automation increases the danger for human bodies – the workplace is designed for the machines, not the people – and capital is reluctant to adopt costly safety measures that might decrease surplus-value: as early as 1981,

> *Business Week* reported that the speed of automation has led to a radical restructuring
> of work, including the devaluation of current work skills and the creation of new ones
> at an ever-increasing rate, so that 45 per cent of the total labour force has already been
> affected … Hazards and stresses are built into the workplace as part of the labour
> process, but usually are over-looked for the sake of capital accumulation. (Lowe 1995:
> 31, 35)

An automated workplace such as National Machine thus represents two of the anxieties about masculine sufficiency commonly explored by film noir: working men's decreasing autonomy as cybernetic systems reinforce hierarchies and the maximisation of surplus-value, and their increasing vulnerability as they accommodate themselves to a mechanised and bureaucratised workplace.[11]

The Machinist displaces anxieties about bodies and machines on to Trevor's automobile accident, but before the mystery is solved and this 'truth' revealed, tension centres on his workplace. Near the beginning, he is called into the manager's office and asked about his distressed appearance. The query 'anything we can help with?' is not motivated by concern for his well-being but is an act of intimidation in response to his 'troublemaking' insistence on safety regulations and freedom from harassment. When he replies, 'I shouldn't even be in here without a union rep,' Tucker comments to their boss, 'See what I mean?' Following this meeting, Trevor 'meets' Ivan for the first time, and when he returns to the floor to assist Miller (Michael Ironside) to repair a machine, he is distracted by Ivan, who, in the distance and obscured by machines, makes a throat-cutting gesture. Trevor accidentally backs into a switch, the machine starts up and Miller's sleeve is caught in a belt which pulls his arm towards a vertical blade. Trevor tries to free Miller, to stop the machine, to get its power cut, but nothing can be done in time. The pace of the machine is unyielding, relentless. Miller's arm is ripped off at the elbow. Defleshed bones, caught in the machine, spin around and around until someone finally manages to turn it off. Unsurprisingly, management's response is to blame the individuals involved – mainly Trevor but also Miller – rather than to change their systems or better enforce safety regulations. Trevor is again called to his manager's office for a meeting in which he is grilled until he admits responsibility for Miller's mutilation.

Trevor becomes increasingly paranoid, reading the other workers' hostility to him – 'nobody wants you here' – and his supervisor's denial of Ivan's existence as part of a larger conspiracy. A few days later, Trevor himself is almost injured when a machine he is repairing comes to life. When he is freed from its dangerous grip, he turns on the men around him, accusing them of setting him up in revenge for Miller, whom he begins to believe is conspiring with Ivan against him. Such paranoia hides the reality that the world might be 'against' one for structural rather than personal reasons. Trevor's near accident, so soon after Miller's, points to an overall disregard for worker safety rather than a conspiracy organised against him, but it is, paradoxically, more comforting to believe that one's suffering is personally directed rather than face the alienating reality of a world made unhomely by capital. *The Machinist* does eventually offer this comfort, reducing Trevor's condition to a combination of individual guilt, psychic mechanisms of suppression and the hallucinatory consequences of long-term insomnia and starvation. However, if we retain our focus on Trevor's experience at work, an alternative reason for his paranoia emerges.

In volume one of *Capital*, Marx suggests that what makes human being distinctive from animal being is labour – that is, activity which transforms the material world – performed consciously and in a social context. While spiders weave webs and bees construct nests, unlike humans they do so instinctively, without imagination or planning. Human labour, in contrast, is a constant dialectical shuttling between imaginative construction and material construction. In the context of an alienating economic system which so dominates human life, such interactions with material reality can be seen as fundamentally paranoid, as constantly reordering elements of a pre-existing order so as to fantasise a meaningful context for the alienated self (see Bould 2002). Trevor's paranoia separates from and thus draws attention to some of the gaps in the illusion that we commonly take to be reality, particularly in terms of understanding the relation between labour and capital in the 'natural' functioning of the economy. Trevor is right to believe himself the subject of a workplace conspiracy, but is wrong to identify it with individual, vengeful workers. Instead, the 'conspiracy' is against the limitations of human bodies, rendering them expendable when they fail to meet the standards set by machines. Even Stevie, the prostitute Trevor regularly visits, refers to her battered face as an 'occupational hazard' and seems unable to imagine a system in which she would not face such risks.

The neoliberal fantasy of the economy – 'the belief in the self-correcting, equilibrial mechanism of the market, if it were freed from the interference of fiscal policies and government regulations' (Lowe 1995: 38) – might also be understood through our model of anorexic subjectivity. Postulating 'natural' mechanisms of adjustment and refinement construes the economy as organic, as something which will 'naturally' achieve an efficient and 'best' balancing point – like a healthy body whose food intake and energy expenditure are in equilibrium. Trevor's emaciated body, whose input and output are radically out of balance, protests the ideology of natural equilibrium. Despite being so visibly damaged, his is the ideal labouring body capital desires: rarely eating and never sleeping, he is like machines which need never rest or go offline for maintenance. The horrific vision of Trevor's body (and the knowledge that Bale as a worker did this to himself) makes visible capital's reduction of human beings

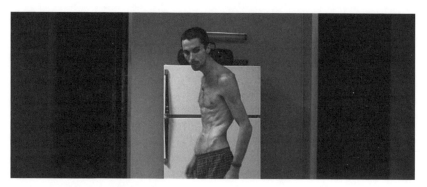

Disciplined apparatus: *The Machinist*

to labour power. It is a body which confronts us with a stark vision of precisely how little is given to labour under capitalism's 'natural equilibrium'.

Shirtless and shot in profile, his abdomen a concave hollow, the spectacle of Bale's body contrasts sharply with Pitt's in *Fight Club*. Both the products of discipline and control, Pitt's seems at one with the alluring weightlessness and apparent immateriality of the film's CGI effects, whereas Bale's is relentlessly material. Just as CGI effects conceal the labour that produces them, so Pitt's fetishised torso disavows the labour of creating and maintaining it. Bale, in contrast, goes too far, tears open the commodity fetish to reveal the suffering, distorted body of labour.

Marx contrasts full human species-being with the alienated existence of life under capitalism, in which relations between people are displaced by relations between things. The disregard National Machine has for its employees is one expression of this alienation which abstracts labour power from the full, sensuous human life. Although this abstraction can never be total, the logic of capital reduces humans in this way to their labour plus the time necessary to reproduce that power through minimal food, rest and recuperation – an ideal Trevor approaches. Under such a system, human subjectivity is distorted so as to treat all our relations through the logic of the commodity form: unable to have a 'relationship to the world [that is] a human one' and thus unable to 'exchange love [only] for love, trust for trust, etc.' (Marx 1977: 111). Trevor struggles with precisely this difficulty. Trapped within the commodity relations of capital, he tells Miller, 'I wish there was some way I could repay you.' Similarly alienated from his own body, Miller jokes, 'Well, for starters you could give me your left arm,' but is clearly relatively content with his financial compensation, effectively selling his arm so as never to have to work again.

Trevor envisions all personal relationships through metaphors of exchange. Indeed, his only affective relationship, with Stevie, is based on financial transactions. Although her earlier expressions of concern for him might be seen as falling within the bounds of their professional relationship – she half-jokingly tells him, 'You're my best client, can't afford to lose you' – she does try to decommodify their relationship: the first time we see her she reminds Trevor, who is dressing to leave, that he still has 'half an hour' and offers to cook him some eggs; later, she offers to let him sleep at her place 'off the meter'. However, Stevie and Trevor are both so damaged by their lives as subjects-for-capital that ultimately they are unable to establish a relationship beyond exchange. When Trevor feels most threatened, she offers comfort as a friend rather than a service provider, and such moments lead to her awkward offer of a 'normal' relationship, asking with both a self-conscious irony and hope, 'Are you going to rescue me from this miserable life or what?' They decide to try to make a life together beyond prostitute-and-client, but it is not to be. Even Stevie's fantasy of escape from a commodified existence is expressed through the clichés of popular culture and incorporates an expectation of disappointment. She plans a future in which she cleans out her apartment, redecorates the kitchen so as to make it 'a white beautiful place' with 'a decent stove' and gets a new job as a menswear salesperson with the luxury of 'paid vacations'. There is something sad about the smallness of her vision of a better life and, as her offscreen voice fades into a murmur, Trevor, examining her photographs, convinces himself that she is part of the conspiracy. Her pathetic dreams are shattered when Trevor confronts her, calling her a whore, returning her to her limited existence as a worker whose body is for sale.

Trevor's relationship with Marie (Aitana Sánchez-Gijón), his waitress in the airport coffee shop he visits every night, is likewise commodified. When they go on a date, she tells him that he does not need to 'buy [her] companionship' by leaving such generous tips. When it is later revealed that this entire relationship is a hallucination based on his desire to compensate the mother whose child he killed, this impulse towards monetary exchange becomes similar to his desire to 'repay' Miller. The film's conclusion insists that the only way Trevor can 'balance' this relationship is by turning himself into the police and allowing 'justice' to take its course. The contrast between this and the Miller plotline reveals the degree to which capitalism disavows the damage it does to the bodies of workers. A sum of money was sufficient compensation for Miller's injury. Indeed, he even, with some irony, calls himself 'lucky' and buys himself an expensive car. In contrast, Trevor must be judged guilty and jailed for the fatal damage his car did to the child – a financial exchange is somehow not enough. The final shot of the movie shows Trevor, in his pure white cell, gratefully drifting off to sleep at last, restored to 'health' by his admission of guilt. Capital, however, never has to admit guilt for the damage done to workers' bodies by its machines and processes.

The denouement, which shifts the focus from the workplace to the accident, reduces Trevor's condition to individual pathology and personal guilt. Having drawn attention to the ways that bodies, machines and responsibility are constructed differently within the workplace, the banal ending abandons the critique of the vulnerability of life under capitalism. While the film offers a closing image of cathartic absolution, it can also be read in terms of the critique this image disavows. Reduced from full human being to a one-dimensional component within the penal system, Trevor's new situation replicates the logic of capital which had reduced him to mere labour-power. His imprisonment can be understood as evidence of the ubiquity of relationships based on the nexus of exchange: he pays for his 'crime' with his body rather than money, handing over his full species-being to a disciplinary apparatus which will further regiment and circumscribe his life. One scene near the end of the film suggests that Trevor has understood something of this logic. As he boxes up his possessions, his landlady admires a glass bowl and asks if he would sell it to her. He refuses, indicating that it has sentimental value, but then tells her that a charity will come by later for his belongings. Trevor refuses exchange here, giving up everything he has and is, in order to surrender to the punitive embrace of a more total exchange.

Conclusion

Both *Fight Club* and *The Machinist* use noir techniques and motifs to represent the anxiety of the masculine subject under late-capitalism. Unfortunately, however, both also retreat into pathologising their individual protagonists rather than condemning the structures which produce such pathologies. In both films, control and discipline of the body represent the male subject's attempt to assert autonomy against an alienating and disempowering system. In the real world, anorexia is often displaced on to the personal or familial pathology of the individual involved, understood as rebellion against an overly controlling mother or a refusal to enter puberty due to a fear of sex. Similarly, these films' inadequate conclusions reduce their protagonists' protest to mere individual complaints: the desire for a better place within the system in *Fight Club* and the need to construct guilt through individual responsibility in *The Machinist*. The limitations of these endings demonstrate the difficulties of understanding the world through the model of the social collective rather than the individual subject, and the very way in which Western culture construes subjectivity may ultimately be the hindrance. The bourgeois model of subjectivity is of an isolated, self-contained, autonomous being. This ideal of subjectivity – called possessive individualism – sees the subject as having ownership of his or her self, a model of full subjectivity that conflicts with capital's need to appropriate labour power, to possess individuals at least part of the time. Gillian Brown connects anorexia to the limitations of this model of the subject, arguing that it reveals 'the paradoxes of self-proprietorship, exaggeratedly measuring how individuals come to matter through their acts, attributes, and accumulations'

(1991: 192). The anorexic continually measures the self, monitoring its extent through obsessive chartings of weight, calorie intake, energy expenditure, and so on. Such activity, combined with the thin ideal to which the anorexic strives, produces anorexia as a model of 'self-possession without acquisition or accumulation' (1991: 196), a subjectivity that thereby 'exposes the territorialism of liberal humanist individualism ... by enacting a more radical ethic of self-mastery ... Anorexia reveals and resists the proprietary imperative in liberal humanism' (1991: 198). Trevor's anorexic body takes this making visible of the problems of capitalist subjectivity one step further, revealing the horror of a body reduced to mere labour power. His skeletal appearance makes visible capital's accumulation by refusing the worker full species-being. While *Fight Club* overtly denounces the consumerism it simultaneously embraces, *The Machinist* materially embodies the damage capital does.

NOTES

1   Two important precursors are the doorman's vision of terrifying buildings in *Der Letzte Mann/The Last Laugh* (1924) and the melting Wall Street of *The Roaring Twenties* (1939). Particularly under the influence of Philip K. Dick, there is a tradition of neo-noir science fiction, including *Alphaville* (1965), *Blade Runner* (1982), *Forbrydelsens element/Element of Crime* (1984), *The Thirteenth Floor* (1999) and *Cypher* (2003), but this essay is primarily interested in neo-noir in which the *mise-en-scène* seems to come alive or in which the fantastic becomes inseparable from the real, including *Videodrome* (1983), *De Vierde Man/The Fourth Man* (1983), *Angel Heart* (1987), *Jacob's Ladder* (1990), *Barton Fink* (1991), *Suture* (1993), *Lost Highway* (1997), *Dark City* (1998), *American Psycho* (2000), *The Gift* (2000), *Ôdishon/Audition* (2000) and *Fear X* (2003). Our understanding of these films, and in particular the two under discussion, is predicated upon the recognition that '"Real" life under capitalism *is a fantasy*' (Miéville 2002: 42; emphasis in original) and that therefore such fantastic elements and involvements are integral to their realism.

2   Bale's commodity-identity, his star persona, is not as clearly-defined or well-established as Pitt's, but with his subsequent bulking-up for *Batman Begins* (2005), there are various indications that it will become focused on his will-to-bodily-transformation. Stories continue to circulate about Bale living on a can of tuna and an apple (or a bottle of whisky and fifty cigarettes) per day in preparation for *The Machinist*; about the producers intervening to stop him dropping another twenty pounds for the role; and about him becoming too massively muscular for Batman and then swiftly dropping down to the required size and shape.

3   For further background on the 'highly specific socio-cultural address' of anorexia, see Turner (1987), DiNicola (1990a and 1990b), Brumberg (1998) and Gremillion (2003);

for a psychoanalytic account, see Chernin (1985). For analysis of how the meanings of food, eating and fasting have changed historically, see Turner (1987), Bynum (1988), Bordo (1990) and Brumberg (1998).

4 Olson describes dieting as 'provid[ing] Americans with something to discipline – bodies and weights – while other forms of consumption, for instance sexual or monetary, are indulged' (2000: 54).

5 Although there are several critical and colloquial uses of the term 'alienation', we intend it here in the specifically Marxist sense, which develops from Marx's *Economic and Philosophic Manuscripts* (1844), in which labouring under capitalism is described as alienating 'nature from man' and 'man from himself, his own active function, his vital activity', and thus from the species, and 'man [from] his own body, nature exterior to him, and his intellectual being, his human essence': an 'immediate consequence of man's alienation from the product of his work, his vital activity and his species-being, is the alienation of man from man' (Marx 1977: 81–3).

6 The temptation of wealth that seems within reach of everyone but the embattled protagonist, who can work with money (as an insurance agent or bank teller) but is denied personal use of it, is a common motif in film noir. See Krutnik (1991: 148) for a discussion of *Double Indemnity* (1944), *Pitfall* (1948) and *The Steel Trap* (1952) in these terms.

7 See also *Angel Heart* and *Jacob's Ladder*. In film noir, the femme fatale often plays this role as the protagonist projects his desires on to the lead female character, as in *Laura* (1944) and *Gilda* (1946).

8 It is impossible to overstate the importance of Bale's skeletal appearance in this film, which is absolutely crucial to its exploration of the damaged body/subject.

9 These disappointing last few minutes conjure a backwards-propagating transformation of everything that was intriguing and different about the film, reducing it to just another – yet another – routine thriller. One cannot help but recall Adorno and Horkheimer's still valid analysis of the culture industry: 'The development of the culture industry has led to the predominance of the effect, the obvious touch, and the technical detail over the work itself – which once expressed an idea, but was liquidated together with the idea … the inferior work has always relied on its similarity with others … The culture industry perpetually cheats its consumers of what it perpetually promises' (1997: 125, 131, 139).

10 Neither we nor these feminist scholars are arguing that anorexia is exclusively a form of speech or protest.

11 See, for example, *Double Indemnity*, *Force of Evil*, *Pitfall* and *The Big Clock* (1948).

REFERENCES

Adorno, Theodor and Max Horkheimer (1997) *Dialectic of Enlightenment*, trans. John Cummings. London: Verso.

Bordo, Susan (1990) 'Reading the slender body', in Mary Jacobus, Evelyn Fox Keller and Sally Shuttleworth (eds) *Body/Politics: Women and the Discourses of Science*. New York: Routledge, 83–112.

_____ (1993) *Unbearable Weight: Feminism, Western Culture, and the Body*. Berkeley: University of California Press.

Bould, Mark (2002) 'The dreadful credibility of absurd things: A tendency in fantasy theory', *Historical Materialism: Research in Critical Marxist Theory*, 10, 4, 51–88.

Brown, Gillian (1991) 'Anorexia, humanism, feminism', *Yale Journal of Criticism*, 5, 1, 189–215.

Brumberg, Joan (1998) *The Body Project: An Intimate History of American Girls*. New York: Vintage Books.

Bynum, Caroline Walker (1988) *Holy Feast and Holy Fast: The Religious Significance of Food to Medieval Women*. Berkeley: University of California Press.

Chernin, Kim (1985) *The Hungry Self: Women, Eating and Identity*. New York: HarperCollins.

DiNicola, Vincenzo (1990a) 'Anorexia multiforme: Self-starvation in historical and cultural context: Part I: Self-starvation as a historical chameleon', *Transcultural Psychiatric Review*, 27, 3, 165–96.

_____ (1990b) 'Anorexia multiforme: Self-starvation in historical and cultural context: Part II: Anorexia nervosa as culture-reaction syndrome', *Transcultural Psychiatric Review*, 27, 4, 245–86.

Gremillion, Helen (2003) *Feeding Anorexia: Gender and Power at a Treatment Center*. Durham, NC: Duke University Press.

Krutnik, Frank (1991) *In a Lonely Street: Film Noir, Genre, Masculinity*. London: Routledge.

Lowe, Donald M. (1995) *The Body in Late-Capitalist USA*. Durham, NC: Duke University Press.

Macherey, Pierre (1978) *A Theory of Literary Production*, trans. Geoffrey Wall. London: Routledge.

Malson, Helen (1998) *The Thin Woman: Feminism, Post-Structuralism and the Social Psychology of Anorexia Nervosa*. New York: Routledge.

Marx, Karl (1976) *Capital: A Critique of Political Economy, Vol. 1*, trans. Ben Fowkes. Harmondsworth: Penguin.

_____ (1977 [1932]) 'Economic and Philosophic Manuscripts', in David McLellan (ed.) *Karl Marx: Selected Writings*. Oxford: Oxford University Press, 75–112.

Metress, Christopher (1994) 'Living degree zero: Masculinity and the threat of desire in the roman noir', in Peter F. Murphy (ed.) *Fictions of Masculinity: Crossing Cultures, Crossing Sexualities*. New York: New York University Press, 154–84.

Miéville, China (2002) 'Editorial introduction', *Historical Materialism: Research in Critical Marxist Theory*, 10, 4, 39–49.

Olson, Greta (2000) *Reading Eating Disorders: Writings on Bulimia and Anorexia as Confessions of American Culture*. Frankfurt: Peter Lang.

Orbach, Susie (1978) *Fat is a Feminist Issue: A Self-Help Guide for Compulsive Eaters.* New York: Berkeley Books.

Palazzoli, Maria Selvini (1985) 'Anorexia nervosa: A syndrome of the affluent society', *Transcontinental Psychiatric Research Review*, 22, 3, 199–204.

Turner, Bryan S. (1987) *Medical Power and Social Knowledge.* New York: Sage.

15

Memento:
Pasting Ourselves Together Through Cinema

DEBORAH THOMAS

For my part, when I enter most intimately into what I call *myself*, I always stumble on some particular perception or other … If any one upon serious and unprejudic'd reflection, thinks he has a different notion of *himself*, I must confess I can reason no longer with him … But setting aside some metaphysicians of this kind, I may venture to affirm of the rest of mankind, that they are nothing but a bundle or collection of different perceptions, which succeed each other with an inconceivable rapidity, and are in a perpetual flux and movement.

— David Hume, *A Treatise of Human Nature* (1984: 300; emphasis in original)

Memento (2000) is a film which can be seen as typically noir in its concern with disordered narrative and with a confused protagonist seeking an orientation within the narrative world, an orientation which can provide him with a plausible, if makeshift, identity. As with the typical protagonist of classic film noir, *Memento*'s Leonard Shelby (Guy Pearce) struggles to rework the past by telling stories, thereby hoping to gain control over a world which is significantly more chaotic than the narrative worlds found in other genres. However, where *Memento* is a specific – if exaggerated – example of this broader generic trend, it also gives us space to explore aspects of film spectatorship, regardless of genre, through its strategy of creating narrative confusion and a constant quest for clarification for its viewers as well. Leonard is an extreme version not only of the film noir protagonist's unstable identity – which, in Leonard's case, has come seriously unstuck – but of our own precarious identity when viewing all kinds of films, temporarily detached from our 'real-life' stories and circumstances as we watch. We will return to this later.

For now, it is enough to note that, in its use of photographs, its concern with unyielding surfaces which resist or confound interpretation and its display of Leonard's body as a text to be read, *Memento* raises questions about the meaning of what we see, which is also a question about the medium of film itself, while its concern with memory and making meaning out of scraps and fragments is equally a concern with narrative and the possibilities of editing it into a comprehensible shape. More specifically, as a result of suffering a head injury when a couple of intruders to his home attacked him and his wife (Jorja Fox), Leonard can no longer make new memories, and his struggle to understand what is going on around him is paralleled, though not fully, by our difficulties in making sense of the film's counter-intuitive temporal structure. On a first viewing of the film, this may feel simply random: paying vigilant attention to detail and cross-referencing amongst scenes are necessary strategies if we wish to reconstruct a convincing train of events, and this requires multiple viewings.

The film has 22 scenes in colour, presented in reverse chronological order, which alternate with 22 black-and-white scenes in sequence. Thus, we have two mathematically precise and intersecting series as follows: Scenes 44, 1, 43, 2, and so on, all the way to Scenes 24, 21, 23, 22 at the end of the film, as the two series approach each other in time, with Scene 22 the meeting point of both series. However, the film's structure is not as mechanical and predictable as this may make it sound, due both to flashbacks interspersed amongst scenes in each series and to the peculiar qualities of Scenes 44 and 22 at either end of the film. In addition, not everything we see is equally 'true', since Leonard's memory plays tricks on him in some of the flashbacks, and there are fantasy moments too. In the end, the quirky subject matter and its realisation offer inventiveness and deadpan humour rather than a mere intellectual puzzle.

However, no matter how fragmented the narrative structure may appear, it is unable to produce in its viewers anything comparable to Leonard's inability to remember fresh events or to register repetitions. Further, the chronology governing his experiences – which provides the impetus behind his investigation and defines its ultimate goal – is derailed for us by our backward movement from effect to cause and explanation. Rather than presenting us with a suspenseful tale focusing on what will happen next, the film offers a more reflective investigation into *why* various actions are performed, by moving us backward to their motivating moments. Finally, the film's tone and the emotions it provokes are necessarily inaccessible to a character who not only does not know he is in a film (and is therefore immune to its tone), but barely knows he is in the world. The extreme attenuation in Leonard's mental life contributes to our sense of his identity as not only fragmented but lacking in emotional depth, with Leonard living on the surface of things as well as in the moment. While his predicament makes him sympathetic, his even inflections and detached manner make it hard to feel any strong emotions on his behalf and allow us, in contrast, to enjoy gentle humour at his expense.

For example, almost halfway through the film, we cut to Leonard running, as he asks himself in voice-over, 'Okay, so what am I doing? Oh, I'm chasing this guy.' The man he thinks he is chasing then blocks his way and aims a gun at him. 'No, he's … chasing me.' The humour of the sudden reversal in his understanding of an important fact about his situation seems to be evoked by the touching innocence about the world which has been thrust upon him by his condition. It is similar to the humour we experience when a young child tries to understand how the world works and gets it seriously wrong. From Leonard's perspective the world's workings are misunderstood because they appear so arbitrary and unconnected, while our laughter, as spectators, results from the perceived discrepancy between his limited understanding and our own. The fact that we smile rather than feel excessively worried may partly be because we have seen the culmination of the film's events from the start and know that Leonard survives, or because his 'innocence' protects him from any anxiety about dangers that fade so quickly from his mind. Or perhaps the separation of Leonard's consciousness from our own and the distinction between the chronology in which he is immersed and the chronology through which we experience the film remind us that this is a cleverly structured film. Our awareness of the filmmakers behind it undoubtedly reassures us and licenses a certain pleasurable collusion between them and us.

Nevertheless, even in 'real-life' cases of people unable to create new memories, sympathetic onlookers may find humour, rather than merely pathos or tragedy, in the way such people transform their confusions into coherent accounts. Neurologist Oliver Sacks describes one such patient: 'He remembered nothing for more than a few seconds. He was continually disoriented. Abysses of amnesia continually opened beneath him, but he would bridge them, nimbly, by fluent confabulations and fictions of all kinds. For him they were not fictions, but how he suddenly saw, or interpreted, the world' (1985: 104). Sacks notes that this patient's improvisations were 'often funny' (ibid.), but, in the initial stages of his disorder, while he 'was still on the boil', he remained 'in an almost frenzied confabulatory delirium … continually creating a world and self, to replace what was continually being forgotten and lost' (1985: 105). The process of storytelling is, Sacks reminds us, the basis for constructing a self in 'normal' persons as well: our life-story and our sense of identity through time are one and the same. However, for those unable to glue together such a self through memory, accuracy is replaced by invention, as they narrate new versions of themselves into existence. For Sack's patient: 'Unable to maintain a genuine narrative or continuity, unable to maintain a genuine inner world, he is driven to the proliferation of pseudo-narratives, in a pseudo-continuity, pseudo-worlds peopled by pseudo-people, phantoms' (1985: 106). A consequence of this sense that one story (and one fabricated life) is as good as another, is that the storyteller is condemned to 'a strange loss of feeling' (1985: 107) and a life without depth: 'What comes out, torrentially, in his ceaseless confabulation, has, finally, a peculiar quality of indifference … as if it didn't really matter what he said, or what anyone else did or said; as if nothing really mattered any more' (ibid.). Fiction and reality appear equally vivid.

Sack's words are suggestive, not just in terms of Leonard's predicament and our positioning as recipients of his stories, but in terms of the process of film narrative and spectatorship more broadly. We should be careful not to reduce film viewers too literally to the condition of amnesiacs, since our deficits as viewers are much less traumatic and, in any case, we settle into our spectatorship voluntarily and for a limited time only. Nevertheless, the process of watching a narrative film and becoming absorbed in its unfolding events requires a suppression of our own identities and memories in the world outside the film for its duration, though we undoubtedly retain our general knowledge of the world in the back of our minds (in what Freud called a 'preconscious' state). Film spectatorship positions us at the interface of film and world (our bodies left in our seats). However, if we are thus 'disembodied', we are also radically 'de-selved', by the temporary loss of the memories which keep ourselves intact throughout our biographical narratives in the world outside the film. Instead, the specific memories which are produced and then later evoked as we navigate our way through the film are neither those of the characters nor of our 'real' selves in the world (what we had for breakfast, say), but memories of the film's events in the manner and order in which they are presented.

The differences between Leonard's grasp of the narrative world and our own are not merely a matter of his peculiar condition nor of *Memento*'s peculiar temporal structure (though the film's strategies raise issues of selfhood and time in an especially salient and dramatic way). Rather, our spectating self will always differ from the selves of onscreen characters. A film's use of close-ups and other rhetorical strategies will necessarily affect the sorts of details we retain as significant, just as a film's music will colour our moods and guide us through stretches of narrative. Watching a film involves forgetting ourselves in order to remake ourselves, though not as characters caught up in events, but rather as spectators caught up in stories and ways of experiencing them.

If films, like the confabulations of those unable to make new memories, proliferate what Oliver Sacks calls 'pseudo-worlds', then opening ourselves up to such narratives, as a way of pasting our spectating selves together as we watch, makes us into 'pseudo-people, phantoms' as well, though our perceptions are genuine enough, even if they cannot always be counted on as good evidence about aspects of the narrative world. Although we may be deceived about the reliability of aspects of the narrative world which we are shown, we are much less likely to be deceived about the reliability of our experience of the *film* and its devices. A character may smile and be a villain, but the smile is really there, regardless of what it signifies. So, the 'life stories' of our phantom selves are co-extensive with the films we experience, and the substance of our identity as we watch is our spectatorship itself in all its detail, including not just the narrative world accessible to the characters, but the perspective provided to us by our unique position as viewers on the rim of that world, rather than fully immersed within it and blind to its rhetoric.

Back to Leonard. Although the scenes in colour make some limited use of Leonard's voice-over, it is above all in the forward-moving black-and-white series of scenes that a coherent ongoing narration is to be found. But first the film's opening scene needs some attention. As the credits begin, an image of a hand holding a Polaroid photograph of a man in blue, with blood splattered on the wall behind him, fades in behind the word 'Memento' on the screen. The hand shakes the photo several times, the image within it becoming increasingly faint with each shake, until it is completely blank. Following a cut to a low-angle shot of the hand holding the photograph, which we now see from behind, the photo is reinserted in the camera, the dead man's picture is taken (or, rather, untaken), and we move up to Leonard's face. By now it is obvious that the scene we are watching is being projected backwards, making it possible for us to get pleasure from various 'magical' effects: blood flows upward, a gun flies up into Leonard's hand, eyeglasses rise up to the murder victim's face as if by themselves, a bullet casing re-enters a gun, a puff of smoke implodes, and a gun is held at the back of the murdered man's head as he half-turns and we get our first view of Teddy Gammell (Joe Pantoliano), still alive, before the image goes black.

The opening scene of *Memento* thus prepares us for the film's thematic interests in time and memory, while simultaneously insisting on its own self-conscious rhetorical strategies, making a sharp and startling break between the narrative world and its unnaturalistic representation by the film, not only

Pictures never lie: *Memento*

through the use of reverse-motion filming, but through the Polaroid photograph appearing to outlast the image it contains within itself. This draining of visual signifiers from the photograph presents a terrifying prospect of the world wiped clean of visible traces.

In his discussion of forgetting (another sort of erasure), Oliver Sacks gives a particularly odd example which combines blindness with amnesia: after a thrombosis in the visual parts of the brain, a patient 'became completely blind – but did not know it', producing what Sacks calls a 'blindness to the blindness': 'He had become, in essence, a non-visual being. His entire lifetime of seeing, of visuality, had, in effect, been stolen. His whole visual life had, indeed, been erased – and erased permanently in the instant of his stroke' (1985: 39). The Polaroid photograph whose image fades to blankness in *Memento* does not just represent the unmaking of time, but the unmaking of the visible world as well: the unmaking of visibility itself.

In contrast to Sack's visual amnesiac who is blind to his blindness, Leonard does not seem to forget his forgetting, frequently telling others about his condition, though there is something strange about this since he forgets so much else subsequent to the traumatic attack. Presumably, his ability to remember both his condition and his ongoing investigation is due to the requirements of the plot, which override the need for strict consistency, since there would not be much of a story without them (at least, from *his* point of view). As it turns out, however, while his memory of his condition is accurate enough, the memory of his unresolved investigation is *not*. What we discover at the end of the film is that he has long since completed the investigation, with Teddy's help, and has already killed his attacker. As the film moves us backward from Leonard's killing of Teddy in the opening scene, we are taken on a wild goose chase ourselves as we appear to discover Leonard's motives and Teddy's identity as the 'John [or Jimmy] G.' who is the object of Leonard's search. We thus believe we are making progress only to realise later that different motives are in operation.

Armed with the truth: *Memento*

The notes and tattoos which Leonard uses to build up an enduring catalogue of facts that will not slip from his grasp, turn out to be profoundly unreliable. First, the captions to some of his photographs are opportunistic and
misleading. For example, after Teddy has told Leonard the truth about his having already killed John G., Leonard writes on his photograph of Teddy, 'Don't
believe his lies,' rather than writing down what Teddy has said. He then writes a
note reminding himself to tattoo a licence plate number (Teddy's) on his thigh,
so that he will track him down and kill him, believing Teddy to be his wife's killer.
'Do I lie to myself to be happy?' he asks in voice-over. 'In your case, Teddy, yes
I will.' Since he cannot remember his murder of the man who took his memory,
he seems doomed to repeat it forever.

Secondly, the tattoo across his chest – 'John G. raped and murdered my
wife' – is also inaccurate, since his wife survived the attack. Like the unreliable note on Teddy's photograph, the unreliable tattoo denies an uncomfortable
truth which Teddy reminds Leonard about in the film's final moments. Indeed,
the fact that Leonard himself was the agent of his wife's death at a later stage
is more than uncomfortable: it is unthinkable. The importance for Leonard of
suppressing the second of the film's climactic revelations is further emphasised by another inscription – 'remember Sammy Jankis' – on Leonard's left
hand, where its prominent position puts it much more insistently in front of his
eyes throughout his waking hours, an over-emphasis that must surely make
us sit up and take notice. However, the stories about Sammy (Stephen Tobo-
lowsky) which this crucial *aide-mémoire* unleashes are riddled with inaccura-
cies, and they function as a screen memory to block out what Leonard *does not*
want to know. Thus, 'remember Sammy Jankis' is another way of saying 'forget
Leonard Shelby'. In this instance, Leonard embraces forgetfulness, rather than
seeing it as a curse.

The black-and-white sequence which runs through the film begins with an
extreme close-up of Leonard's profile as he looks to the right of the screen. In
Scene 6, a shot of Sammy in extreme close-up looking to the right of the screen
establishes a parallel between them, as Leonard explains on the telephone that
he was assigned to look into the genuineness of Sammy's memory loss when
he worked as an insurance claims investigator before the attack. From Scene
4 through Scene 10, Leonard recounts the story of Sammy Jankis, whose wife
(Harriet Sansom Harris) refused to believe that Sammy's inability to make new
memories was outside his control: 'She wasn't a cruel person, she just wanted
her old Sammy back.' In Scene 16, Leonard removes a bandage and uncovers a
recent tattoo ('Never answer the phone'), which stops his conversation in mid-
stream – 'Who is this?' – as he abruptly hangs up, and we cut to a high-angle
shot of a vulnerable Leonard alone and bewildered on the bed. I think we are
once again amused that Leonard has got things wrong, rather than seriously
worried about any awful consequences to follow, since it is hard to imagine

how things could be worse for him than they already are: his personhood is so reduced that, at times, he seems little more than a ghost.

Surprisingly, Leonard manages to narrate Sammy's story both coherently and in sequence: 'She knew beyond a doubt that he loved her. So she found a way to test him.' The terrible climax of the story, which is difficult to watch without a sense of rising horror, is shown in apparent flashback, just as we have been given other such scenes of Sammy and his wife throughout Leonard's narration of their story elsewhere. Sammy's wife reminds him that it is time for her insulin and, as we saw in one of the earlier scenes, he smiles sweetly and gives her the injection. After a short pause, she asks him again, and again he obliges. And again. As Leonard finishes his story of Mrs Jankis's death and Sammy's confinement in an institution – unaware that his wife is dead – he pauses and listens to something that Teddy has said on the other end of the phone, replying uncomprehendingly: 'What drug dealer?'

Clearly Teddy is not unduly moved by Leonard's story and hijacks the conversation for selfish purposes of his own, though his lack of reaction becomes more understandable later when we discover that Sammy had no wife and never killed anyone as Leonard describes: rather, this is how Leonard himself killed his own wife. It is therefore ironic that the brief glimpses we get of Sammy and his wife – which turn out to be fictions – are the most emotionally laden and affecting moments in the film: Leonard's *stories* have far more power to stir our emotions than the actuality of his own truncated sense of self. However, the force of the irony is not felt until Scene 22, when Teddy reveals that Sammy was a faker without a wife, and that Leonard's wife was the one with diabetes, dying at Leonard's hands. Nevertheless, we have had clues to this along the way.

For example, in Scene 21, just before Sammy gives his wife the first of the three insulin injections which will kill her, we cut to a medium close-up of his hands, with the fingers of his left hand flicking against the hypodermic held in his other hand. We may remember a similar shot several minutes earlier which also shows the fingers of a man's left hand tapping against a hypodermic, with an unidentifiable woman wearing a necklace and white shirt visible in the background from the neck down. It follows a point-of-view shot of Leonard's left hand, as he reads the message 'remember Sammy Jankis' written on the side. So it is easy to read the shot of the fingers flicking against the hypodermic as having been elicited by the written message to remember Sammy and thus as an anticipation of the later shot.

However, the fingernails are bitten in the earlier shot, as are Leonard's elsewhere in the film, in contrast to Sammy's well-groomed fingernails in the later shot, and the shirt of the woman in the background is white, whereas Mrs Jankis's shirt will have a leafy pattern (making it match a shirt which Leonard's wife will be seen wearing in a later colour flashback in Scene 22). Furthermore, we will later see the necklace and white shirt from the earlier shot being worn by Leonard's wife in flashback, in the course of Scene 22, as Leonard prepares to give an insulin injection to *her*. So, the earlier shot in colour turns out to be the accurate one: it represents Leonard's uneasily suppressed memory of his wife's diabetes and his own role in administering her insulin, though initially disguised by keeping the faces of his wife and himself offscreen, even if his tell-tale fingernails remain in view.

Leonard's claim that Sammy's wife was testing him has its parallel in the way the shot of Sammy's fingers flicking the hypodermic is a 'test' for us: a test of our memory of the earlier shot and of our perception of the differences. I assume it is a test that most first-time viewers of the film will fail, for we are given no indication that it is important to notice the fingernails, even supposing we had time to do so. Leonard too lacks the ability to distinguish between information which is crucial and that which is more trivial: what things are to be noted and memorialised in some way, and what can be safely ignored? Whose words are to be believed and whose words are lies to be *discounted*? Because of his note to himself not to believe Teddy's lies, Leonard decides not to believe Teddy's advice that Natalie (Carrie-Anne Moss) cannot be trusted, and he crosses out the inscription Teddy got him to write on Natalie's photograph ('Do not trust her'). Right after this, Leonard finds an address Teddy has given him of a place to stay: the aptly-named *Discount* Inn.

The series of scenes in colour are much more difficult to follow than the series in black-and-white. Not only is each scene earlier than the one before, but (with the exception of Scene 44 which opens the film) each scene, though out of order relative to the series as a whole, unfolds chronologically within itself. That is, the end of each colour scene leads chronologically into events at the beginning of the colour scene that precedes it in the series, with some overlapping at these junctures to clarify the temporal progression. Thus, the forward march of the black-and-white scenes is straightforward, though with gaps between them, while the colour scenes continually loop back on themselves. This gives Sammy's story (which is the main concern of the black-and-white series of scenes) much more unity and coherence than Leonard's (which is the focus of the colour scenes). But since Sammy's story (that is, the story *about* him) is, in another sense, Leonard's story (the story Leonard chooses to *tell*), its unity is not to do with the actual details of Sammy's life, since it is full of mistakes. Rather, its apparent coherence is an attempt by Leonard to produce a sustained stretch of narration through time and thus to acquire an illusory self that lasts beyond the series of isolated present moments in which he is trapped. However, Leonard's narration simultaneously serves another purpose in its suppression of memories which *precede* the disabling attack: the memory that Sammy was unmarried and the further memory that it was *Leonard's* wife who had diabetes, not Sammy's. His narration does not merely attempt to bridge over gaps in his memory, but to provide a defensive screen to hide a truth he is physiologically equipped – but psychologically unable – to remember.

By contrast, the scenes in colour are much more disjointed and reflect Leonard's inability to retain any memories of the recent past. However, these difficulties lead in turn to events which intertwine his life with the lives of the other main characters, as if he has wandered into their stories by chance. For example, Teddy is a corrupt cop who deliberately manipulates Leonard into murdering Jimmy (Larry Holden), a drug dealer, by convincing him that Jimmy is his attacker ('Jimmy G.'). However, when Leonard then puts on Jimmy's clothes and takes his Jaguar (in effect, 'putting on' his identity along with his clothes and car), this is not part of Teddy's plan. Leonard's meeting with Natalie is also accidental and comes about when Leonard finds a beer mat from Ferdy's Bar in the pocket of the clothes he took from Jimmy, with a note on the back which he assumes is meant for him: 'Come by after. Natalie.'

What we get in the colour scenes is a shifting landscape of intersecting stories and multiple identities where Teddy is both cop and crook, Natalie pretends to be helping Leonard while using him to get rid of Jimmy's confederate, Dodd (Callum Keith Rennie), and Leonard takes on Jimmy's identity along with his possessions. Since Teddy uses Leonard to kill Jimmy, and Natalie uses him to deal with Dodd, Leonard's actions seem no longer his own, but subject to others' manipulation and control. This loss of agency completes the undermining of his selfhood which his memory loss and emotional lack of depth have previously begun. However, at the end of the film, we discover that Leonard has sabotaged the entire process and stunningly asserted his agency after all, when, after Jimmy's death and Teddy's revelations, he refuses the knowledge that the original 'John (or Jimmy) G.' is already dead and, instead, memorialises Teddy's licence plate number, in the form of a tattoo, as that of his attacker. In this way, Natalie ends up serving his purposes as much as he serves hers when she tracks down Teddy as the owner of the car. Similarly, Leonard turns the tables on Teddy when he kills him in the opening scene of the film (that is, its chronological culmination).

Though there are ironies aplenty, black humour seems more characteristic of *Memento*'s overall tone. The humour we have looked at so far is of this type: it occurs in a narrative world whose bleakness is openly acknowledged, with little hope of it transforming this world for the better. *Memento* invites us to be indulgent towards Leonard without fully forfeiting our awareness of the darkness at the heart of his condition: his loss not only of himself, but of a meaningful world around him, and the utter solitude and bereftness this implies. This is particularly true of the black-and-white sequence, as Leonard narrates Sammy's story into a kind of existential void, addressing his narration first to us and then to a faceless, voiceless person on the telephone whose identity he can never quite pin down. The sequence has something of the feel of a Samuel Beckett play in its evocation of an uncaring and impassive universe into which Leonard pours his endless stream of words. His motel room is a small-scale representation of such a world without meaning, a world to which he is attempting to impart some sort of sense through language: 'So, where are you? You're in some motel room. There's the key. It feels like maybe it's just the first time you've been here, but perhaps you've been here for a week, three months, it's … it's kinda hard to say. I don't know…'. Despite the sense this conveys of someone lost in his own anonymity, Leonard makes a joke in the same even tones as before when he picks up the narration in the next scene in the sequence: 'Nothing in the drawers … Nothing except the Gideon Bible which … which I, of course, read religiously' (here he laughs quietly). The playfulness of language remains, as does Leonard's surprising resilience, even in his straitened, massively attenuated situation where his world is defined by the present moment in a nondescript motel room disconnected from anything else.

If Samuel Beckett's plays are one reference point for *Memento*'s tone, then Alfred Hitchcock's *Psycho* (1960) is another. It is difficult to imagine what it is like to inhabit the conscious mind of Norman Bates (Anthony Perkins) (for an extended discussion of this, see Thomas 1997). The task of sustaining his everyday identity as Norman, given that he spends long periods of time in the guise of his mother, involves confronting inexplicable gaps in his experience, making his life as Norman just as fragmentary and threadbare as Leonard's life in *Memento*. Norman too inhabits a motel around which lurks a dark world of murder and of tainted money in the boot of a car, and he refuses the knowledge that he has killed his mother, just as Leonard forgets his killing of his wife. Both men are pursued and beleaguered by a cop or private investigator whom they end up murdering, and each meets a woman who appears to befriend him while being guilty of a criminal involvement of her own, motivated by her relationship with another man. The narratives of both films involve nightmare repetitions as with *Memento*'s apparently endless supply of 'John (or Jimmy) G.s'. In *Psycho*, Norman is a serial killer (as Leonard is in danger of becoming), and a series of persecutory figures turn up one after the other to seek him out, just as Teddy keeps turning up to confront Leonard in *Memento*, though in this case it is the same man turning up, rather than a series of separate people. Nevertheless, for Leonard, Teddy appears as good as new each time.

I do not know how deliberately *Memento* models aspects of itself on *Psycho*, since they remain very different. Given Norman's propensity for dressing as his mother, however, the moment when Leonard wakes up in bed with Natalie and begins to dress in her shirt may be a playful nod in *Psycho*'s direction, a memory lapse which is more lighthearted than usual. The use of black humour in both films draws out our smiles in the face of our awareness of Norman's and Leonard's devastated inner landscapes, which are so pocketed with shadows and unfathomable gaps. Of course, *Memento* and *Psycho* are by no means the same in tone, despite their shared use of black humour, since each is shaded and enlivened by many further aspects. The much greater use of heart-stopping suspense in *Psycho*, and the shocking and horrific nature of Norman's crimes, make it harder to adopt a relaxed viewing position for Hitchcock's film. *Memento* is far easier to watch, since its mixture of humour and playfulness (as well as its relative lack of suspense) cushions its bleaker implications and encourages us to sympathise with Leonard from a position of detached superiority, rather than to see him as an unsettling reflection of ourselves. Ultimately the darkness at the heart of *Memento* lacks the horror at the heart of *Psycho* and can be left behind us when the movie ends. Though Leonard's situation is desperate, he generally stays calm and unemotional himself and is convincingly differentiated from us as a medical oddity, so we can settle into the film and enjoy its pleasures without much anxiety.

The final scene in the film, where the black-and-white and colour sequences finally meet up, begins with a fade-in on Leonard, who is speaking to Teddy on the telephone. His words – 'I'm as ready as I'll ever be' – suggest an approaching culmination in the imminent killing of Jimmy just as the killing of Teddy at the beginning of the film (but at the chronological conclusion of the plot) suggests another, the two murders book-ending the film as a whole. This doubleness (a double killing, a double culmination) is thematically consistent with doublings – and splittings – elsewhere. For example, Leonard's identity is confused with the identities of both Sammy and Jimmy; he hires a prostitute to double for his wife in his replay of the night of the attack; Teddy speaks of himself in the third person when trying to get Leonard to leave town by telling him that a bad cop is looking for him; the motel clerk rents Leonard a second room when Leonard forgets he is paying for another room already; Leonard goes to the wrong room when tracking Dodd because he mistakes a '9' on the door for a '6'; and both Jimmy and Teddy become surrogates for the original 'John G.' Furthermore, the film's narrative structure overall is based on two alternating sequences of scenes moving in opposite directions, as we have seen, so that the film *doubles back* on itself, in the course of Scene 22.

A series of colour flashbacks of Leonard's wife interrupt the black-and-white section of Scene 22 and continue to appear throughout, intercut with the later colour section of the scene as well: a total of eleven flashbacks. These flashbacks constitute a third set of shots with its own internal coherence (like the black-and-white and colour strands of narrative already considered, which run through the film). They may appear more disconnected and random than these other strands at first, as we begin with various idealised shots of Leonard's wife – walking towards a window, seated against a building, silhouetted in a doorway, turning around in a pink sundress – before a quick cut reveals her covered by a sheet of plastic – perhaps a shower curtain – at the time of the attack (reminiscent of the way Norman Bates wrapped Marion Crane (Janet

Leigh) in a plastic shower curtain, after he killed her), an image we have had versions of earlier.

With this image, the series of flashbacks become increasingly disturbing, as do present-day events, as Leonard strangles Jimmy and takes his photograph, starting to dress in his clothes. As we watch the photograph develop in colour, the narrative world shifts into colour too. The remaining flashbacks are inserted subsequent to Teddy's arrival on the scene, and they illustrate the truth of what he now reveals to Leonard: thus, we see Leonard giving his wife her insulin injection, and we see further shots of her under the plastic sheet, but with her eyes blinking, still alive. However, hints of Leonard's previous self-deception are already present in the earlier idealised shots of his wife: for example, walking towards the window, she wears the same blouse that Sammy's 'wife' was wearing at the time of her 'death' at Sammy's hands, while, in the shot of her seated against the house, she turns her head to meet Leonard's eyeline in the subsequent present-day shot of him in black-and-white, as if in accusation. Similarly, in the shot of her wearing the pink sundress and turning around in her seat to face the camera, her unsmiling face undermines the idealised stream of images so far. In some sense Leonard already knows the truth, and his 'forgetting' in this respect is very different from his inability to make new memories since the attack, which becomes a bit of a red herring.

Ultimately, Leonard turns his back on what Teddy has told him and takes control of the narration: 'I'm not a killer. I'm just someone who wanted to make things right. Can I just let myself forget what you told me?' Of course, 'letting himself forget' takes little effort: it is remembering that involves the vigilant process of note-taking, photographing and captioning. Now he chooses not merely to forget but to *misremember*, further weakening his grasp upon the world while strengthening his own version of events and weaving a (just about) workable version of himself through his confabulations. What Leonard requires is neither truth nor meaningful agency, but merely a believable illusion. In this way, Leonard evokes the film's spectators – and consumers of cinematic fictions more broadly – who willingly forfeit both truth and agency for the sake of a story that will hold our attention over a stretch of time. I have suggested earlier that watching films provides us too with a temporary 'phantom' self so we can hold ourselves together while our 'real' self comes unglued by the suppression of our everyday memories and preoccupations as the film unfolds. Thus, we avoid the fragmentations of a Humean self made up of a chaos of random perceptions. Instead, we achieve a unified and reasonably stable sense of self through the coherence of the films we watch and our experience of watching them. *Memento* ends with a humorous coda appropriate to such concerns. Driving Jimmy's Jaguar, Leonard screeches to a halt outside a tattoo parlour, looking at the note with Teddy's licence plate number on it: 'Now, where was I?' So, at the end of the film (which is also the beginning of Leonard's adventures all over again), *Memento* responds to the bleakness of its narrative world with neither sentimentality nor despair, but embraces the dizzying possibilities of cinema and storytelling instead, allowing us to return to our lives – and our everyday selves – with a smile.

REFERENCES

Hume, David (1984) *A Treatise of Human Nature*. Harmondsworth: Penguin Classics.

Sacks, Oliver (1985) *The Man Who Mistook His Wife for a Hat*. London: Picador.

Thomas, Deborah (1997) 'On being Norman: Performance and inner life in Hitchcock's *Psycho*', *CineAction*, 44, July, 66–72.

Filmography

10 Things I Hate about You (Gil Junger, US, 1999)

36 Quai des Orfèvres/ Department 36 (Olivier Marchal, Fr., 2004)

À bout de souffle/Breathless (Jean-Luc Godard, Fr.,1959)

Accidental Tourist, The (Lawrence Kasdan, US, 1988)

Adorenarin doraibu/Adrenaline Drive (Yaguchi Shinobu, Jap., 1999)

A Kiss Before Dying (Gerd Oswald, US, 1956)

All the President's Men (Alan J. Pakula, US, 1976)

Alphaville (Jean-Luc Godard, Fr./It., 1965)

American Psycho (Mary Harron, US/Can., 2000)

Anderson Tapes, The (Sidney Lumet, US, 1971)

Angel Heart (Alan Parker, US/Can./UK, 1987)

A Plantation Act (no director credited, US, 1926)

Apartment, The (Billy Wilder, US, 1960)

A Star Is Born (George Cukor, US, 1954)

Assassins… (Mathieu Kassovitz, Fr., 1992)

Avanti! (Billy Wilder, US/It., 1972)

A Woman Scorned (Andrew Stevens, US, 1994)

A Woman Scorned: The Betty Broderick Story (Dick Lowry, US, 1992)

Badlands (Terrence Malick, US, 1973)

Baise-moi (Virginie Despentes and Coralie Trin Thi, Fr., 2000)

Band Wagon, The (Vincente Minnelli, US, 1953)

Bande à part (Jean-Luc Godard, Fr., 1964)

Barton Fink (Joel Coen, US/UK, 1991)

Bas-fonds, Les/The Lower Depths (Jean Renoir, Fr., 1936)

Basic Instinct (Paul Verhoeven, US/Fr., 1992)

Basic Instinct 2 (Michael Caton-Jones, Ger./UK/US/Sp., 2006)

Batman Begins (Christopher Nolan, US, 2005)

Beautiful Joe (Stephen Metcalfe, US/UK, 2000)

Beyond Control: The Amy Fisher Story (Andy Tennant, US, 1993)

Big Chill, The (Lawrence Kasdan, US, 1983)

Big Clock, The (John Farrow, US, 1948)

Big Heat, The (Fritz Lang, US, 1953)

Big Lebowski, The (Joel Coen, USA/UK, 1998)

Big Sleep, The (Howard Hawks, US, 1946)

Black Dahlia, The (Brian De Palma, Ger./US, 2006)

Black Rainbow (Mike Hodges, UK, 1989)

Black Widow (Bob Rafelson, US, 1987)

Blade Runner (Ridley Scott, US/Sing., 1982)

Blood Simple (Joel Coen, US, 1984)

Blow-Up (Michelangelo Antonioni, UK/It./US, 1966)

Blue Velvet (David Lynch, US, 1986)

Bob le flambeur/Bob the Gambler (Jean-Pierre Melville, Fr., 1956)

Body Heat (Lawrence Kasdan, US, 1981)

Body of Evidence (Uli Edel, Ger./US, 1993)

Boksuneun naui geot/Sympathy for Mr. Vengeance (Chan-wook Park, S.Kor., 2001)

Bonnie and Clyde (Arthur Penn, US, 1967)

Borsalino (Jacques Deray, Fr./It., 1970)

Bound (Larry and Andy Wachowski, US, 1996)

Caché/Hidden (Michael Haneke, Fr./Austria./Ger./It., 2005)

Catch-22 (Mike Nichols, US, 1970)

Cercle rouge, Le/The Red Circle (Jean-Pierre Melville, Fr./It., 1969)

Chandler (Paul Magwood, US, 1971)

Chaos (Coline Serreau, Fr., 2001)

Charley Varrick (Don Siegel, US, 1973)

Charlie and the Chocolate Factory (Tim Burton, US/UK, 2005)

Charlotte Gray (Gillian Armstrong, UK/Aus./Ger., 2001)

Cherry Falls (Geoffrey Wright, US, 2000)

Chinatown (Roman Polanski, US, 1974)

Chinjeolhan geumjassi/Sympathy for Lady Vengeance (Chan-wook Park, S.Kor., 2005)

Chung Hing sam lam/Chungking Express (Wong Kar-wai, HK, 1994)

Clan des Siciliens, Le/The Sicilian Clan (Henri Verneuil, Fr., 1969)

Code inconnu/Code Unknown (Michael Haneke, Fr./Ger./Rom., 2000)

Conversation, The (Francis Ford Coppola, US, 1974)

Corporate Fantasy (Charles Randazzo, US, 1999)

Corporate Ladder, The (Nick Vallelonga, US, 1997)

Crime, La/Cover Up (Philippe Labro, Fr., 1983)

Crime de Monsieur Lange, Le (Jean Renoir, Fr., 1936)

Criss Cross (Robert Siodmak, US, 1948)

Croupier (Mike Hodges, Fr./UK/Ger./Ire., 1998)

Cruel Intentions (Roger Kumble, US, 1999)

Crush (Alison Maclean, NZ, 1992)

Crush, The (Alan Shapiro, US, 1993)

Cypher (Vincenzo Natali, US, 2003)

Dans les rues/Song of the Streets (Victor Trivas, Fr., 1933)

Dark City (Alex Proyas, US, 1998)

Dead Again (Kenneth Branagh, US, 1991)

Dead Men Don't Wear Plaid (Carl Reiner, US, 1982)

Dead Reckoning (John Cromwell, US, 1947)

Death Wish (Michael Winner, US, 1974)

De battre mon coeur s'est arrêté/The Beat that My Heart Skipped (Jacques Audiard, Fr., 2005)

Deep Blue Sea (Renny Harlin, US/Aus., 1999)

Deep End, The (Scott McGehee, US, 2001)

De l'autre côté du périph'/On the Other Side of the Périphérique (Bertrand Tavernier and Nils Tavernier, Fr., 1997)

Departed, The (Martin Scorsese, US/HK, 2006)

Der Letzte Mann/The Last Laugh (F. W. Murnau, Ger., 1924)

Desperate Hours (Michael Cimino, US, 1990)

Détective (Jean-Luc Godard, Fr./Switz., 1985)

Detour (Edgar G. Ulmer, US, 1945)

Deux ou trois choses que je sais d'elle/Two or Three Things I Know About Her (Jean-Luc Godard, Fr., 1967)

Deuxième souffle, Le/Second Breath (Jean-Pierre Melville, Fr., 1966)

De Vierde Man/The Fourth Man (Paul Verhoeven, Neth., 1983)

Devil in a Blue Dress (Carl Franklin, US, 1995)

Die xue jie tou/Bullet in the Head (John Woo, HK, 1990)

Dip huet seung hung/The Killer (John Woo, HK, 1989)

Dirty Harry (Don Siegel, US, 1971)

Dirty Pretty Things (Stephen Frears, UK, 2002)

Disclosure (Barry Levinson, US, 1994)

Diva (Jean-Jacques Beineix, Fr., 1981)

D.O.A. (Rudolph Maté, US, 1950)

D.O.A. (Rocky Morton and Annabel Jankel, US, 1988)

Dog Day Afternoon (Sidney Lumet, US, 1975)

Doom (Andrzej Bartkowiak, UK/Cz./Ger./US, 2005)

Double Indemnity (Billy Wilder, US, 1944)

Double Indemnity (Jack Smight, US, 1973)

Doulos, Le/Doulos: The Finger Man (Jean-Pierre Melville, Fr./It., 1962)

Dr Mabuse, der Spieler/Dr Mabuse, the Gambler (Fritz Lang, Ger., 1922)

Du rififi chez les hommes/Rififi (Jules Dassin, Fr., 1955)

Eating Raoul (Paul Bartel, US, 1982)

Exception to the Rule (David Winning, Can./Ger./US, 1997)

Exorcist, The (William Friedkin, US, 1973)

Farewell, My Lovely (Dick Richards, US, 1975)

Fargo (Joel Coen, US, 1996)

Fatal Attraction (Adrian Lyne, US, 1987)

Fear X (Nicolas Winding Refn, Den./Can./UK/Braz., 2003)

Femme Fatale (Brian De Palma, Fr., 2002)

Feux rouges/Red Lights (Cédric Kahn, Fr., 2004)

Fight Club (David Fincher, Ger./US, 1999)

Forbrydelsens element/Element of Crime (Lars von Trier, Den., 1984)

Force of Evil (Abraham Polonsky, US, 1948)

Fortune Cookie, The (Billy Wilder, US, 1966)

Freeway (Matthew Bright, US, 1996)

French Connection, The (William Friedkin, US, 1971)

Friday the 13th (Sean S. Cunningham, US, 1980)

Friends of Eddie Coyle, The (Peter Yates, US, 1973)

Front Page, The (Billy Wilder, US, 1974)

Full Monty, The (Peter Cattaneo, UK, 1997)

Fuyajo/Sleepless Town (Chi-Ngai Lee, HK/Jap., 1998)

Gendai yakuza: hito-kiri yota/Street Mobster (Kinji Fukasaku, Jap., 1972)

Get Carter (Mike Hodges, UK, 1971)

Gift, The (Sam Raimi, US, 2000)

Gilda (Charles Vidor, US, 1946)

Godfather, The (Francis Ford Coppola, US, 1972)

Godfather: Part II, The (Francis Ford Coppola, US, 1974)

Gone with the Wind (Victor Fleming, US, 1939)

Gongdong gyeongbi guyeok JSA/JSA: Joint Security Area (Chan-wook Park, S.Kor., 2000)

Grand Canyon (Lawrence Kasdan, US, 1991)

Grand pardon, Le/Grand Pardon (Alexandre Arcady, Fr., 1982)

Grapes of Wrath, The (John Ford, US, 1940)

Grifters, The (Stephen Frears, US, 1990)

Gunfight at the O.K. Corral (John Sturges, US, 1957)

Haine, La/Hate (Mathieu Kassovitz, Fr., 1995)

Halloween (John Carpenter, US, 1978)

Hana-bi/Fireworks (Takeshi Kitano, Jap., 1997)

Hand that Rocks the Cradle, The (Curtis Hanson, US, 1992)

Hanyo/The Housemaid (Kiyoung Kim, S.Kor., 1960)

Hard Candy (David Slade, US, 2005)

Harper (Jack Smight, US, 1966)

Harry Potter and the Goblet of Fire (Mike Newell, UK/US, 2005)

Heat (Michael Mann, US, 1995)

Héroines (Gérard Krawczyk, Fr., 1997)

Hollywood Hotel (Busby Berkeley, US, 1938)

Hot Spot, The (Dennis Hopper, US, 1990)

House of Bamboo (Samuel Fuller, US, 1955)

House on 92nd Street, The (Henry Hathaway, US, 1945)

Hyōryū-gai/City of Lost Souls (Takashi Miike, Jap., 2000)

Hysteric (Takahisa Zeze, Jap., 2000)

I Died a Thousand Times (Stuart Heisler, US, 1955)

Idioterne/The Idiots (Lars von Trier [uncredited], Den./Swed./Fr./Neth./It., 1998)

I'll Sleep When I'm Dead (Mike Hodges, UK/US, 2003)

Improper Conduct (Jag Mundhra, US, 1994)

In a Lonely Place (Nicholas Ray, US, 1950)

In the Cut (Jane Campion, Aus./US/UK, 2003)

Indecent Behavior (Lawrence Lanoff, US, 1993)

Indecent Behavior II (Carlo Gustaff, US, 1994)

Indecent Behavior III (Kelley Cauthen, US, 1995)

Intersection (Mark Rydell, US, 1994)

Irréversible/Irreversible (Gaspar Noé, Fr., 2002)

Italian Job, The (Peter Collinson, UK, 1969)

Italian Job, The (F. Gary Gray, US/Fr./UK, 2003)

J'ai pas sommeil/I Can't Sleep (Claire Denis, Fr./Switz., 1994)

J'ai vu tuer Ben Barka/I Saw Ben Barka Killed (Serge Le Péron and Saïd Smihi, Mor./
  Sp./Fr., 2005)

Jackie Brown (Quentin Tarantino, US, 1997)

Jacob's Ladder (Adrian Lyne, US, 1990)

Jagged Edge (Richard Marquand, US, 1985)

Jazz Singer, The (Alan Crosland, US, 1927)

Jingi naki tatakai/Battles without Honour and Humanity (Kinji Fukasaku, Jap., 1973)

Jingi no hakaba/Graveyard of Honour (Kinji Fukasaku, Jap., 1975)

Jism/Body (Amit Saxena, Ind., 2003)

Johnny Handsome (Walter Hill, US, 1989)

Jurassic Park (Steven Spielberg, US, 1993)

Killers, The (Robert Siodmak, US, 1946)

Killers, The (Don Siegel, US, 1964)

Killshot (John Madden, US, 2007)

Klute (Alan J. Pakula, US, 1971)

K-PAX (Iain Softley, US/Ger., 2001)

La Balance/The Nark (Bob Swaim, Fr., 1982)

L.A. Confidential (Curtis Hanson, US, 1997)

Lady from Shanghai, The (Orson Welles [uncredited], US, 1947)

Lady in the Lake (Robert Montgomery, US, 1947)

L'Appât/The Bait (Bertrand Tavernier, Fr., 1995)

Last Dance (Bruce Beresford, US, 1996)

Last Seduction, The (John Dahl, US, 1994)

Last Seduction II, The (Terry Marcel, UK/US, 1999)

Lat sau san taam/Hard-Boiled (John Woo, HK, 1992)

L'Attentat/Plot (Yves Boisset, Fr./It./W.Ger., 1972)

Laura (Otto Preminger, US, 1944)

Leave Her to Heaven (John M. Stahl, US, 1945)

Life of Brian (Terry Jones, UK, 1979)

Like Mike (John Schultz, US, 2002)

Lisztomania (Ken Russell, UK, 1975)

Lock, Stock and Two Smoking Barrels (Guy Ritchie, UK, 1998)

Long Goodbye, The (Robert Altman, US, 1973)

Lookout, The (Scott Frank, US, 2007)

Lost Highway (David Lynch, Fr./US, 1997)

Lost Weekend, The (Billy Wilder, US, 1945)

L.627 (Bertrand Tavernier, Fr., 1992)

Lucky Break (Peter Cattaneo, UK/Ger., 2001)

Lung fu fong wan/City on Fire (Ringo Lam, HK, 1987)

McCabe & Mrs Miller (Robert Altman, US, 1971)

Machinist, The (Brad Anderson, Spain, 2004)

Madigan (Don Siegel, US, 1968)

Malicious (Ian Corson, US, 1995)

Maltese Falcon, The (John Huston, US, 1941)

Manèges/The Cheat (Yves Allégret, Fr., 1949)

Manhunter (Michael Mann, US, 1986)

Man Who Wasn't There, The (Joel Coen, US, 2001)

Marlowe (Paul Bogart, US, 1969)

M*A*S*H (Robert Altman, US, 1970)

Mean Streets (Martin Scorsese, US, 1973)

Memento (Christopher Nolan, US, 2000)

Mildred Pierce (Michael Curtiz, US, 1945)

Miller's Crossing (Joel Coen, US, 1990)

Mona Lisa (Neil Jordan, UK, 1986)

Monsieur Hire (Patrice Leconte, Fr., 1989)

Mou gaan dou/Infernal Affairs (Wai-keung Lau and Siu Fai Mak, HK, 2002)

Mulholland Dr. (David Lynch, Fr./US, 2001)

Murder, My Sweet (Edward Dmytryk, US, 1944)

Mutual Needs (Robert Angelo, US, 1997)

My Darling Clementine (John Ford, US, 1946)

Nada (Claude Chabrol, Fr./It., 1974)

Nanny McPhee (Kirk Jones, US/UK/Fr., 2005)

Nashville (Robert Altman, US, 1975)

Neige/Snow (Juliet Berto and Jean-Henri Roger, Fr./Bel., 1981)

Niagara (Henry Hathaway, US, 1953)

Night Moves (Arthur Penn, US, 1975)

Nine ½ Weeks (Adrian Lyne, US, 1986)

No Contest (Paul Lynch, Can., 1994)

No Contest II (Paul Lynch, US, 1997)

Nora inu/Stray Dog (Akira Kurosawa, Jap., 1949)

No Way Out (Roger Donaldson, US, 1987)

Obaltan/The Stray Bullet (Hyunmok Yu, S. Kor., 1960)

Ocean's Eleven (Lewis Milestone, US, 1960)

Ocean's Eleven (Steven Soderbergh, US/Aus., 2001)

Ôdishon/Audition (Takashi Miike, Jap./S. Kor, 2000)

Offence, The (Sidney Lumet, UK/US, 1972)

Oldboy (Chan-wook Park, S.Kor., 2003)

One Two Three (Billy Wilder, US, 1961)

Out of the Past (Jacques Tourneur, US, 1947)

Parallax View, The (Alan J. Pakula, US, 1974)

Party Girl (Nicholas Ray, US, 1958)

Payback (Brian Helgeland, US, 1999)

Pépé le Moko (Julien Duvivier, Fr., 1937)

Petit lieutenant, Le/The Young Lieutenant (Xavier Beauvois, Fr., 2005)

Phantom Lady (Robert Siodmak, US, 1944)

Piano, The (Jane Campion, Aus./NZ/Fr., 1993)

Pitfall (Andre de Toth, US, 1948)

Place Vendôme (Nicole Garcia, Fr., 1998)

Point Blank (John Boorman, US, 1967)

Poison Ivy (Katt Shea, US, 1992)

Poison Ivy 2 (Anne Goursaud, US, 1996)

Poison Ivy: The New Seduction (Kurt Voss, US, 1997)

Polar (Jacques Bral, Fr., 1984)

Police (Maurice Pialat, Fr., 1985)

Police Academy (Hugh Wilson, US, 1984)

Police Academy 2: Their First Assignment (Jerry Paris, US, 1985)

Postman Always Rings Twice, The (Tay Garnett, US, 1946)

Postman Always Rings Twice, The (Bob Rafelson, US/W.Ger., 1981)

Pride & Prejudice (Joe Wright, Fr./UK, 2005)

Private Life of Sherlock Holmes, The (Billy Wilder, UK, 1970)

Psycho (Alfred Hitchcock, US, 1960)

Pulp (Mike Hodges, UK, 1972)

Pulp Fiction (Quentin Tarantino, US, 1994)

Quai des brumes, Le/Port of Shadows (Marcel Carné, Fr., 1938)

Quai des Orfèvres/Jenny Lamour (Henri-Georges Clouzot, Fr., 1947)

Quick and the Dead, The (Sam Raimi, US/Jap., 1995)

Razzia sur la chnouf/Razzia (Henri Decoin, Fr., 1955)

Reckless Moment, The (Max Ophüls, US, 1949)

Red Rock West (John Dahl, US, 1992)

Regarde les hommes tomber/See How They Fall (Jacques Audiard, Fr., 1994)

Repentie, La (Laetitia Masson, Fr., 2002)

Reservoir Dogs (Quentin Tarantino, US, 1992)

Return of the Secaucus Seven (John Sayles, US, 1980)

Ripoux, Les/Le Cop (Claude Zidi, Fr., 1984)

Roaring Twenties, The (Raoul Walsh, US, 1939)

Rope (Alfred Hitchcock, US, 1948)

Samouraï, Le (Jean-Pierre Melville, Fr./It., 1967)

Scarlet Street (Fritz Lang, US, 1945)

Scorned 2 (Rodney McDonald, US, 1997)

Scream (Wes Craven, US, 1996)

Sea of Love (Harold Becker, US, 1989)

Searchers, The (John Ford, US, 1956)

Second Chance (Rudolph Maté, US, 1953)

Seconds (John Frankenheimer, US, 1966)

Série noire (Alain Corneau, Fr., 1979)

Serpico (Sidney Lumet, It./US, 1973)

Set Up, The (Strathford Hamilton, US, 1995)

Seul contre tous/I Stand Alone (Gaspar Noé, Fr., 1998)

Se7en (David Fincher, US, 1995)

Sexual Intent (Kurt MacCarley, US, 1994)

Sexual Roulette (Gary Graver, US, 1996)

Sexy Beast (Jonathan Glazer, UK/Sp., 2000)

Shock Corridor (Samuel Fuller, US, 1963)

Silverado (Lawrence Kasdan, US, 1985)

Sin City (Frank Miller and Robert Rodriguez, US, 2005)

Single White Female (Barbet Schroeder, US, 1992)

Slam Dance (Wayne Wang, UK/US, 1987)

Slightly Scarlet (Allan Dwan, US, 1956)

Sliver (Phillip Noyce, US, 1993)

Snatch (Guy Ritchie, UK/US, 2000)

Sombre (Philippe Grandrieux, Fr., 1998)

Some Like It Hot (Billy Wilder, US, 1959)

Someone to Watch Over Me (Ridley Scott, US, 1987)

Sonatine (Takeshi Kitano, Jap., 1993)

Sorry, Wrong Number (Anatole Litvak, US, 1948)

Specialist, The (Luis Llosa, Peru/US, 1994)

Sphere (Barry Levinson, US, 1998)

Stalag-17 (Billy Wilder, US, 1953)

Star Wars (George Lucas, US, 1977)

Staying on Top (John Quinn, US, 2002)

Steel Trap, The (Andrew L. Stone, US, 1952)

Stranger on the Third Floor (Boris Ingster, US, 1940)

Subway (Luc Besson, Fr., 1985)

Sunset Blvd. (Billy Wilder, US, 1950)

Sur mes lèvres/Read My Lips (Jacques Audiard, Fr., 2001)

Suture (Scott McGehee, US, 1993)

Swedish Marriage Manual, The (Torgny Wickman, Swed., 1969)

Sweet Sweetback's Baadasssss Song (Melvin Van Peebles, US, 1971)

Swing Time (George Stevens, US, 1936)

Taking of Pelham One Two Three, The (Joseph Sargent, US, 1974)

Targets (Peter Bogdanovich, US, 1968)

Taxi Driver (Martin Scorsese, US, 1976)

Temp, The (Tom Holland, US, 1993)

Tengoku to jigoku/High and Low (Akira Kurosawa, Jap., 1963)

Terminal Man, The (Mike Hodges, US, 1974)

Texas Chain Saw Massacre, The (Tobe Hooper, US, 1974)

Thelma and Louise (Ridley Scott, US, 1991)

Thieves Like Us (Robert Altman, US, 1973)

Thin Man, The (W. S. Van Dyke, US, 1934)

Third Man, The (Carol Reed, UK, 1949)

Thirteenth Floor, The (Josef Rusniak, Ger./US, 1999)

Three Days of the Condor (Sydney Pollack, US, 1975)

Titanic (James Cameron, US, 1997)

To Live and Die in L.A. (William Friedkin, US, 1985)

Tommy (Ken Russell, UK, 1975)

Total Recall (Paul Verhoeven, US, 1990)

Touch of Evil (Orson Welles, US, 1958)

Touchez pas au grisbi/Honour Among Thieves (Jacques Becker, Fr./It., 1954)

Trap, The (Norman Panama, US, 1959)

Un condé/Blood on My Hands (Yves Boisset, Fr./It., 1970)

Underneath (Steven Soderbergh, US, 1995)

Un Flic/A Cop (Jean-Pierre Melville, Fr./It., 1972)

Usual Suspects, The (Bryan Singer, US/Ger., 1995)

Vagabond King, The (Ludwig Berger, US, 1930)

Vertigo (Alfred Hitchcock, US, 1958)

Videodrome (David Cronenberg, Can./US, 1983)

Vie rêvée des anges, La/The Dream Life of Angels (Erick Zonca, Fr., 1998)

Voici le temps des assassins…/Deadlier Than the Male (Julien Duvivier, Fr., 1956)

Wallace & Gromit in The Curse of the Were-Rabbit (Steve Box and Nick Park, UK, 2005)

Warui yatsu hodo yoku nemuru/The Bad Sleep Well (Akira Kurosawa, Jap., 1960)

White Heat (Raoul Walsh, US, 1949)

Wild at Heart (David Lynch, US, 1990)

Wild Things (John McNaughton, US, 1998)

Wild Things 3: Diamonds in the Rough (Jay Lowi, US, 2005)

Witness for the Prosecution (Billy Wilder, US, 1957)

Wizard of Oz, The (Victor Fleming, US, 1939)

Working Girls (Lizzie Borden, US, 1987)

Wyatt Earp (Lawrence Kasdan, US, 1994)

Yakuza no hakaba: Kuchinashi no hana/Yakuza Graveyard (Kinji Fukasaku, Jap., 1976)

Year of the Dragon (Michael Cimino, US, 1985)

Ying hung boon sik/A Better Tomorrow (John Woo, HK, 1986)

Yoidore tenshi/Drunken Angel (Akira Kurosawa, Jap., 1948)

Yūheisha-terorisuto/Prisoner/Terrorist (Adachi Masao, Jap., 2006)

TELEVISION SERIES

American Bandstand (US, 1952–89)

Big Brother (UK, 2000–present)

'Charmed Noir' (2004), episode of *Charmed* (US, 1998–2006)

Cheers (US, 1982–93)

Commissaire Moulin (Fr., 1976–2006)

Hardcastle and McCormick (US, 1983–86)

Hill Street Blues (US, 1981–87)

Julie Lescaut (Fr., 1992–present)

L.A. Law (US, 1986–94)

Maigret (Fr./Bel./Switz.,1991–2005)

'The Manipulators' (Mike Hodges, 1972), episode of *The Frighteners* (UK, 1972)

Navarro (Fr./Switz.,1989–present)

Nestor Burma (Fr., 1991–present)

NYPD Blue (US, 1993–2005)

PJ/C.I.D. (Fr., 1997–present)

Players (US, 1997–98)

'Rumour' (Mike Hodges, 1970), episode of *Playhouse* (UK, 1967–82)

Sex and the City (US, 1998–2004)

Singing Detective, The (Jon Amiel, Aus./UK, 1986)

Who Wants to Be a Millionaire (UK, 1998–present)

The Wire (US, 2002–2008)

World in Action (UK, 1963–99)

GAMES

Doom series (id software, GT Interactive, US, 1992–2004)

GTA: San Andreas (Rockstar Games, US, 2004)

Max Payne (Remedy Entertainment/3D Realms/Gathering of Developers, Fin./US, 2001)

Max Payne 2 – The Fall of Max Payne: A film noir love story (Remedy Entertainment/3D Realms/Rockstar Games, Fin./US, 2003)

Silent Hill series (Konami, Jap., 1999–present)

Index